Approaching HYSTERIA

Approaching
HYSTERIA
Disease and Its
Interpretations

MARK S. MICALE

PRINCETON UNIVERSITY PRESS

PRINCETON, NEW JERSEY

Library of Congress Cataloging-in-Publication Data

Micale, Mark S., 1957–
Approaching hysteria : disease and its interpretations / Mark S. Micale.
p. cm.
Includes bibliographical references and index.
ISBN 0-691-03717-5 (CL : alk. paper)
1. Hysteria—History. 2. Hysteria—Historiography. I. Title.
[DNLM: 1. Hysteria—history. WM 11.1 M619a 1995]
RC532.M53 1995
616.85'24'009—dc20
DNLM/DLC
for Library of Congress   94-16596 CIP

To Peter Gay

AUTHOR, TEACHER, COLLEAGUE,

FRIEND

The word "hysteria" should be preserved, although its primitive meaning has much changed. It would be very difficult to modify it nowadays, and, truly, it has so grand and so beautiful a history that it would be painful to give it up. However, since every epoch has given to it a different meaning, let us try to find out what meaning it has today.

—Pierre Janet (1894)

CONTENTS

PREFACE

THIS BOOK began several years ago as a set of extended historiographical essays. A portion of the material in the first half of Part
One was initially published in a two-part article that appeared in
1989 under the title "Hysteria and Its Historiography: A Review of Past
and Present Writings" in the journal *History of Science*. The second half
of Part One draws on a succeeding article, "Hysteria and Its Historiography—The Future Perspective," published in 1990 in the first volume
of *History of Psychiatry*.

In gathering these articles into a book, I have reformulated them in a
number of basic conceptual ways. My initial presentation of the topic
took the form of a wide-ranging but rather narrowly conceived and
discipline-bound survey of the scholarly literature for historical specialists. In contrast, in its current form, I have taken as my subject the idea of
the history of hysteria. I have been less concerned with the exhaustive
exposition of books, dissertations, and articles than the consolidation of
these texts into distinct, critical interpretive traditions. I have also used
the history and historiography of hysteria as a means to explore the
larger, complex projects of conceiving and writing the history of psychodiagnostic systems generally and the history of disease as a whole.

A second basic reworking is responsible for the bipartite division of the
book. In my earlier articles, I conceptualized hysteria in strictly medical-
historical terms—that is, as an actual disease entity that over the centuries generated a wealth of theoretical and therapeutic responses from physicians. However, I have since realized that concurrent with the traditions
of commentary issuing from the medical community has been a long,
vibrant, and largely unexamined *cultural* history of hysteria. Accordingly,
I have added a substantial second part to the book, titled "Hysteria as
Metaphor." This section attempts to reconstitute a number of "cultures
of hysteria" in which the disorder appeared figuratively in past social,
political, philosophical, religious, literary, poetic, and visual sources. All
of the material in this second half of the volume is published here for the
first time. I have also added a new introduction and conclusion. Finally,
since the flow of scholarship on the history of hysteria has continued
unabated in recent years, I have modernized the book bibliographically.

In working intermittently on this subject during the past few years, I
have accumulated numerous professional debts that it gives me pleasure
to acknowledge. During 1987–89, my reading was supported by the
Wellcome Foundation through the London Unit of the Wellcome Institute
for the History of Medicine. Bill Bynum, Peter Gay, Godelieve van

Heteren, and Christopher Mace read the manuscript in earlier versions and made valuable and intelligent suggestions. Along the way, I have also profited from detailed conversations or correspondence with Drs. Renate Hauser, Harold Merskey, Giuseppe Roccatagliata, Phillip Slavney, Walter Vandereycken, and Elizabeth Whitcombe. Vivian Nutton and Helen King provided guidance on "hysteria" and ancient Greek gynecology, while Victoria Wilson-Schwartz and Barbara Wallraff supplied indispensable editorial assistance. Peter Brooks and Fernando Vidal kindly read Part Two of the manuscript and made excellent suggestions. I want in addition to acknowledge the assistance of Jacqueline Carroy, Martha Noel Evans, Pierre Morel, and Étienne Trillat in providing me with rare foreign-language materials. I also greatly appreciate the many readers who responded favorably to my earlier articles and contacted me with questions, ideas, and information.

I owe special debts of gratitude to four other individuals who were key in coaxing this project through its various incarnations: to Roy Porter, who graciously accommodated the expansion of my "book review" into a major and rather unwieldy historiographical study; to Sander Gilman and David Joravsky, who encouraged the conversion of my articles into an accessible, broadly conceived, cross-disciplinary volume in cultural studies; and to Elaine Showalter, who indicated in perceptive and constructive detail the ways in which this transformation might proceed. I would also like to express my deep thanks to Robert E. Brown of Princeton University Press for his continuing interest in my work. Finally, for the opportunity to complete the editing of the manuscript in the most exquisite imaginable setting—the Villa Serbelloni in Bellagio, Italy—I thank the Rockefeller Foundation.

Approaching HYSTERIA

INTRODUCTION: THE NEW HYSTERIA STUDIES

THE HISTORY of hysteria—the subject is at once highly important and hopelessly fashionable. It suggests an irresistible blend of science, sexuality, and sensationalism. It conjures up from the historical past a series of colorful and dramatic images: the wandering womb of classical Greek medicine moving mischievously through the female body and causing all manner of physical and behavioral abnormalities; the demonically possessed witch of the Renaissance with her anesthetic *stigmati diaboli*; the "vaporous" salon ladies of eighteenth-century Parisian society swooning from noxious uterine emanations to the heart and head; and of course the celebrated patients of Sigmund Freud in fin-de-siècle Vienna, with their extravagant, erotically charged symptomatologies.

At the same time, hysteria is arguably the oldest and most important category of neurosis in recorded medical history. References to something that may be interpreted as hysteria can be found in the Egyptian papyri of 1900 B.C. and in present-day psychiatric literature. The subject has exercised some of the most powerful minds in the history of medicine, from Hippocrates and Galen, to Thomas Willis and Thomas Sydenham, to Philippe Pinel and Wilhelm Griesinger. Conceptually, the disorder lies at the center of the difficult interchange between the worlds of psyche and soma and for centuries has been key to medical efforts to discriminate meaningfully between organic and functional disorders. Furthermore, hysteria served a century ago as a vehicle for some of the most brilliant psychological theorizing of modern times. In the late nineteenth century, "the heroic period of hysteria," the French neurologist Jean-Martin Charcot was challenged, fascinated, and in a sense defeated by what he called "the great neurosis," on which he published over 120 case studies.[1] At roughly the same time, psychoanalysis—"the child of the hysterical woman,"[2] in the words of one scholar—issued in large part from Freud's intense, decade-long intellectual encounter with the malady. Pierre Janet, one of the founding figures of twentieth-century French psychiatry, derived similar inspiration for his early psychological work from this mysterious, multiform disorder. As the psychiatric historian Henri Ellenberger has written,

---

[1] "La période héroïque de l'hystérie" is Fulgence Raymond's phrase in "Définition et nature de l'hystérie," in *Comptes rendus du Congrès des médecins aliénistes et neurologistes de France et des pays de langue française*, Geneva and Lausanne, August 1–7, 1907, 2 vols. (Paris: Masson, 1907), 2:378.

[2] Carroll Smith-Rosenberg, "The Hysterical Woman: Sex Roles and Role Conflict in Nineteenth-Century America," in *Disorderly Conduct: Visions of Gender in Victorian America* (New York: Knopf, 1985), 197.

with only slight exaggeration, "One could say that the history of modern dynamic psychiatry originated entirely with the study of hysteria."[3]

However, despite this rich historical background, hysteria in our own time—both the medical diagnosis and the pathological entity the diagnosis designates—is believed greatly to have dwindled in frequency. Clinicians working in many different countries and institutional settings and within diverse theoretical systems have reported a sharp and continuing decline in the incidence of the disorder throughout the twentieth century. In particular, the dramatic, polysymptomatic forms of the disease found in Charcot's writings of the 1870s and 1880s and the gross, florid motor and sensory somatizations displayed in the case reports of Freud and Josef Breuer's *Studies on Hysteria* of 1895 are regarded today as extreme rarities. Furthermore, since the mid-twentieth century, in successive editions of *The International Classification of Diseases* and *The Diagnostic and Statistical Manual of Mental Disorders*, the classic hysteria diagnosis has been fragmented, reassigned to a series of alternative clinical categories and replaced by a new, more scientistic vocabulary. As contemporary American and European psychiatry progressively deprivileges the psychodynamic paradigm, hysteria has been replaced by an array of decidedly less poetic appellations, including "factitious illness disorder," "dissociative disorder—conversion type," "histrionic personality type," "psychogenic pain disorder," and "undifferentiated somatoform disorder."[4] Some physicians have called for the wholesale abandonment of the idea and the term.[5] In a monograph about the neurosis published in 1990, a prominent psychiatrist from The Johns Hopkins University Medical School observed, almost nostalgically, that "this could well be the last book with 'hysteria' in its title by a psychiatrist. . . . 'Hysteria,' 'hysteric,' and 'hysterical' are on the verge of becoming anachronisms."[6]

Strikingly, however, the very period that has witnessed the decline of hysteria as medical diagnosis has brought a burst of professional interest in the *history* of the disorder. Until recently, the history of hysteria was by

[3] Henri F. Ellenberger, "La psychiatrie et son histoire inconnue," *L'union médicale du Canada* 90, no. 3 (March 1961): 283.

[4] For accounts of this process within American and European medicine, consult Steven E. Hyler and Robert L. Spitzer, "Hysteria Split Asunder," *American Journal of Psychiatry* 135, no. 12 (December 1978): 1500–1504; and M. Bourgeois, "Le mise en pièces de l'hystérie dans la nosographie contemporaine," *Annales médico-psychologiques* 146, no. 6 (1988): 552–62.

[5] Most importantly and outspokenly, E.T.O. Slater and E. Glithero in "A Follow-Up of Patients Diagnosed as Suffering from 'Hysteria,'" *Journal of Psychosomatic Research* 9 (1965–66): 9–13; and Slater in "Diagnosis of 'Hysteria,'" *British Medical Journal* 1 (1965): 1395–99.

[6] Phillip R. Slavney, *Perspectives on "Hysteria"* (Baltimore: Johns Hopkins University Press, 1990), 190.

any standard a scholarly backwater, the subject of only occasional and specialized antiquarian interest. In contrast, the past twenty-five years, and particularly the past decade, have brought a steady outpouring of publications on one aspect of the subject after another. The final quarter of the twentieth century, it appears, is experiencing an efflorescence of historical interest in hysteria to match the great medical preoccupation with the disease a century ago. This new scholarship originates from many locations in Europe and North America and from a variety of fields of inquiry whose practitioners are not generally familiar with one another's work. These fields include, within the health sciences, neurology, psychiatry, clinical psychology, and psychoanalysis, and within the humanities, intellectual history, medical and science history, legal history, women's studies, psychoanalytic studies, art history, and literary history and criticism. A search of standard bibliographical indexes, printed and computerized, North American and European, reveals a steady stream of books and articles with no sign of slackening. The bibliography appended to this volume records roughly four hundred publications on the topic, all of them historical in nature, a large majority of which appeared during the past ten years.

In the present book, I refer to this corpus of texts as "the new hysteria studies." (I will resist the temptation to call it "the New Hystericism.") The new hysteria studies have appeared during a second fin de siècle and are historical rather than clinical and scientific. In recent years, three full-scale intellectual histories of hysteria have been published, by American, French, and Italian scholars, and a fourth work, by a Belgian scholar, is underway.[7] Three academic conferences, in Britain and the United States, held in 1988, 1990, and 1994, were devoted to the subject.[8] And several key primary texts with substantial historical introductions have been reprinted.[9] A collection of scholarly essays by French and Italian scholars

---

[7] George Randolph Wesley, *A History of Hysteria* (Washington, D.C.: University Press of America, 1979); Étienne Trillat, *Histoire de l'hystérie* (Paris: Seghers, 1986); and Giuseppe Roccatagliata, *Isteria* (Rome: Il Pensiero Scientifico Editore, 1990). A fourth history is being written by Jan Godderis of Leuven, Belgium.

[8] "Representing Hysteria," Trinity College, Hartford, Conn., April 15, 1988; "History of Hysteria," The Wellcome Institute for the History of Medicine, London, April 6, 1990; "Hysteria Today: 100 Years since Freud," the Freud Museum, Hampstead, England, February 5, 1994.

[9] Edward Jorden, *A Briefe Discourse of a Disease Called the Suffocation of the Mother* (1603), repr. in Michael MacDonald, ed., *Witchcraft and Hysteria in Elizabethan London: Edward Jorden and the Mary Glover Case* (London and New York: Tavistock/Routledge, 1991); J.-M. Charcot, *Clinical Lectures on Diseases of the Nervous System*, trans. Thomas Savill (1889), ed. Ruth Harris (London and New York: Tavistock/Routledge, 1991); and Robert Brudenell Carter, *On the Pathology and Treatment of Hysteria* (1853), intro. W. F. Bynum (forthcoming).

appeared in 1980, and a similar volume, featuring a distinguished cast of British and American critics and historians, was published in 1993.[10]

To similar effect, Charcot's clinical work on hysteria, after lying dormant for decades, has now become the subject of intense interest in many quarters as scholars celebrated the centennial of Charcot's death in 1993.[11] And Freud's writings about hysteria, particularly his early case histories, continue to attract passionate and polemical interest from physicians, historians, and critics alike.[12] Moreover, numerous book-length projects are under way by American and British literary critics that investigate the literary history of hysteria[13] while two recent works—one of French origin, the other American—offer first attempts to organize the history of hysteria in our own century.[14] Also, during the past generation, over twenty relevant theses and dissertations, of medical and nonmedical provenance, have appeared.[15] And in 1981, hysteria even provided the

[10] *In materia di amore: Studi sul discorso isterico*, introduced by Armando Verdiglione (Milan: Spirali Edizioni, 1980); Sander L. Gilman, Helen King, Roy Porter, George S. Rousseau, and Elaine Showalter, *Hysteria beyond Freud* (Los Angeles: University of California Press, 1993).

[11] Georges Didi-Huberman, *Invention de l'hystérie: Charcot et l'Iconographie photographique de la Salpêtrière* (Paris: Macula, 1982); *Charcot the Clinician: The Tuesday Lessons*, trans. Christopher G. Goetz (New York: Raven Press, 1987), esp. lesson 5; Mark S. Micale, "Diagnostic Discriminations: Jean-Martin Charcot and the Nineteenth-Century Idea of Masculine Hysterical Neurosis" (Ph.D. diss., Yale University, 1987); Ruth Harris, *Murders and Madness: Medicine, Law, and Society in the Fin de Siècle* (Oxford: Clarendon Press, 1989), chaps. 5 and 6; Mary James, "The Therapeutic Practices of Jean-Martin Charcot (1825–1893) in Their Historical and Social Context" (PhD. diss., University of Essex, 1990); Wanda Bannour, *Jean-Martin Charcot et l'hystérie* (Paris: Éditions Métailié, 1992). For more references on Charcot, see below, 88–97.

[12] To cite only recent book-length studies in English: Max Rosenbaum and Melvin Muroff, eds., *Anna O.: Fourteen Contemporary Reinterpretations* (New York: Free Press, 1984); Charles Bernheimer and Claire Kahane, eds., *In Dora's Case: Freud—Hysteria—Feminism* (New York: Columbia University Press, 1985); William J. McGrath, *Freud's Discovery of Psychoanalysis: The Politics of Hysteria* (Ithaca, N.Y.: Cornell University Press, 1986); Albrecht Hirschmüller, *The Life and Work of Josef Breuer: Physiology and Psychoanalysis* (New York: New York University Press, 1989); Hannah Decker, *Freud, Dora, and Vienna 1900* (New York: Free Press, 1991); Lisa Appignanesi and John Forrester, *Freud's Women: Family, Patients, Followers* (New York: Basic Books, 1992), pt. 2.

[13] Janet Beizer, *Ventriloquized Bodies: Narratives of Hysteria in Nineteenth-Century France* (Ithaca, N.Y.: Cornell University Press, 1994); Elaine Showalter, *Hystories* (work in progress).

[14] Catharine Millot, *Nobodadday: L'hystérie dans le siècle* (Paris: Point hors ligne, 1988); Martha Noel Evans, *Fits and Starts: Theories of Hysteria in Modern France* (Ithaca, N.Y.: Cornell University Press, 1991).

[15] Jean Ann Wharton, "Freud on Feminine Hysteria: A Re-Examination" (Ph.D. diss., University of California, Santa Cruz, 1975); Evelyne Vaysse, "Contribution des études sur l'hystérie à la naissance de la psychanalyse" (Ph.D. diss., University of Paris—Saint-Antoine, 1977); Paul Lechuga, "Introduction à une anatomie de la pensée médicale, à propos de l'hystérie au XIXe siècle" (Ph.D. diss., University of Montpellier, 1978); Ernest

subject for a best-selling work of historical fiction by one of the major novelists of our time.[16] In the latest development, American literary historians and critics since 1990 have fastened their attention on the theme of "hysterical narrativity," which they are exploring as a valuable critical concept in the study of modernist fiction.[17]

Without a doubt, in subject, methodology, and inspiration the largest volume of writing in the new hysteria studies is feminist. Since the middle of the 1970s, virtually dozens of books and articles concerning the history of nervous disease in women, written from a feminist perspective,

---

Hawkins, "The Raging Womb: An Archetypal Study of Hysteria and the Early Psychoanalytic Movement" (Ph.D. diss., University of Dallas, 1978); Georges Haberberg, "De Charcot à Babinski: Étude du rôle de l'hystérie dans la naissance de la neurologie moderne" (Ph.D. diss., Créteil, 1979); Elisabeth Kloë, *Hysterie im Kindesalter: Zur Entwicklung des kindlichen Hysteriebegriffes*, repr. in *Freiburger Forschungen zur Medizingeschichte*, vol. 9 (Freiburg: Hans Ferdinand Schulz, 1979); J. A. Godet, "Lecture de Jean Wier: Réflexions sur l'histoire de la sorcière et de l'hystérique, de leurs maux et de leurs thérapeutes" (Ph.D. diss., University of Paris, 1980); Philippe Miloche, "Un méconnu de l'hystérie: Victor Dumont Pallier (1826–1899)" (Ph.D. diss., University of Caen, 1982); Madeline L. Feingold, "Hysteria as a Modality of Adjustment in *Fin-de-Siècle* Vienna" (Ph.D. diss., California School of Professional Psychology, Berkeley, 1983); Béatrice Auvray-Escalard, "Un méconnu de l'hystérie: Jules Bernard Luys" (Ph.D. diss., University of Caen, 1984); Joelle Cazali, "Histoire de l'hystérie: ses variations sémiologiques et thérapeutiques à travers les siècles" (Ph.D. diss., University of Paris V, 1985); Marie-Elisabeth Chaillou, "Évolution des conceptions étiologiques de l'hystérie" (Ph.D. diss., University of Paris XIII, 1985); Monica Helen Green, "The Transmission of Ancient Theories of Female Physiology and Disease through the Early Middle Ages" (Ph.D. diss., Princeton University, 1985); Helen King, "From Parthenos to Gynē: The Dynamics of Category" (Ph.D. diss., University College London, 1985); Thierry Pioger, "Réflexions sur l'histoire de l'hystérie" (Ph.D. diss., University of Angers, 1985); Frédérique Menzaghi, Annie Millot, and Michèle Pillot, "Évolution de la conception de l'hystérie de 1870 à 1930 dans un service de l'asile de Maréville," 2 vols. (Master's thesis, University of Nancy II, 1987); Christian Mirandol, "Contribution à une étude du concept d'hystérie au 19e siècle" (Ph.D. diss., Aix et Marseille II, 1987); Jann Matlock, "Scenes of Seduction: Prostitution, Hysteria, and Reading Difference in Nineteenth-Century France" (Ph.D. diss., University of California, Berkeley, 1988); Marie E. Addyman, "The Character of Hysteria in Shakespeare's England" (Ph.D. diss., University of York, 1988); Susan Ferry, "Lives Measured in Coffee Spoons? A Study of Hysteria, Class and Women in Nineteenth-Century Britain" (Master's thesis, University of Toronto, 1989); Jacques Gasser, "Jean-Martin Charcot (1825–1893) et le système nerveux: Étude de la motricité, du langage, de la mémoire et de l'hystérie à la fin du XIXième siècle" (Ph.D. diss., École des hautes études en sciences sociales, 1990); Angelika Oberkönig, "Die Hysterie als Frauenkrankheit in den frühen Schriften von Freud und im Vergleich zum Hysteriebegriff heute" (Ph.D. diss., Institute for the History of Medicine, Münster, work in progress).

[16] D. M. Thomas, *The White Hotel* (New York: Simon and Schuster, 1981). In the Author's Note, Thomas describes the "terrain" of his novel as "the landscape of hysteria." More recently, see Peter Michalos, *Psyche: A Novel of the Young Freud* (New York: Doubleday, 1993).

[17] Elaine Showalter provides a good introduction to the concept in "On Hysterical Narrative," *Narrative* 1 (January 1993): 24–35.

have been published, forming by now a veritable sub-literature in its own right.[18] As we will see in the ensuing discussion, the feminist historiography of hysteria is multifaceted. However, the work of historians and critics in this tradition shares the view that hysteria may be read as a kind of metaphor both for women's position in past patriarchal societies and for the image of the feminine in the history of scientific discourses. Among psychologists and psychiatrists, hysteria, in the words of one scholar, has become "a kind of frontier neurosis" in a wide-ranging critical reassessment of the clinical and theoretical status of Freudian theory and in a systematic effort to formulate a feminist-informed psychology and psychiatry in the future.[19]

Equally noteworthy has been the upsurge of interest in hysteria's history within the medical profession. Interestingly, the progressive semantic suppression of hysteria by official psychiatric organizations during the past half century has given rise to a preservationist effort within select medical circles in Britain, Canada, and the United States. Limiting the list again to monographic studies, three substantial works by physicians in each of these countries have appeared since 1980.[20] Important earlier studies have been reissued.[21] And Phillip Slavney's book represents the most comprehensive survey of the English-language medical literature to date.[22] In the United Kingdom, Eliot Slater's cry to abolish hysteria produced an elegant reaffirmation of the concept by some of the most distinguished psychiatric and neurological figures in the country,[23] while other physicians have continued to defend delimited formulations of the concept.[24] A team of Canadian medical researchers has even attempted to

---

[18] See "Feminist Histories of Hysteria" below.

[19] Evans, Fits and Starts, 171.

[20] Harold Merskey, The Analysis of Hysteria (London: Baillière Tindall, 1979); Alec Roy, ed., Hysteria (Chichester: John Wiley and Sons, 1982); Michael I. Weintraub, Hysterical Conversion Reactions: A Clinical Guide to Diagnosis and Treatment (New York: SP Medical and Scientific Books, 1983).

[21] D. Wilfred Abse, Hysteria and Related Mental Disorders, 2d. ed. (Bristol: Wright, 1987).

[22] Slavney, Perspectives on "Hysteria."

[23] Sir Aubrey Lewis, "The Survival of Hysteria," Psychological Medicine 5, no. 1 (February 1975): 9–12; C. D. Marsden, "Hysteria—A Neurologist's View," Psychological Medicine 16, no. 2 (May 1986): 277–88.

[24] Harold Merskey, "The Importance of Hysteria," British Journal of Psychiatry 149 (July 1986): 23–28; idem, "Does Hysteria Still Exist?" Annals of the Royal College of Physicians and Surgeons of Canada 16, no. 1 (January 1983): 25–29; Geoffrey G. Lloyd, "Hysteria: A Case for Conservation?" British Medical Journal 292, no. 6557 (November 15, 1986): 1255–56; Edgar Miller, "Hysteria: Its Nature and Explanation," British Journal of Clinical Psychology 26, part 3 (September 1987): 163–73; Robert E. Kendell, "A New Look at Hysteria," in Roy, Hysteria, 27–36.

synthesize traditional psychodynamic ideas and insights about the neurosis with the new neurosciences.[25]

Pertinently for our purposes, the work of recent "hysterologists" has often been couched in specifically historical terms. The most significant medical initiative in recent years to provide more systematized diagnostic criteria for hysteria under a new and less pejorative label—the St. Louis School's concept of "Briquet's syndrome"—drew its name from a leading nineteenth-century French physician.[26] Two British doctors have provided an intelligent defense of the Charcotian theory of hysteria.[27] And a clinically and theoretically sophisticated defense of Freudian hysterical conversion appeared in the *British Journal of Psychiatry* in 1992.[28] More noteworthy still has been the renaissance of professional interest in Janet's early psychological work, especially his research on hysteria, dissociative states, and traumatic psychopathology. Since 1970, many of Janet's early writings have been republished, older English translations of his books have been reprinted, and international symposia have been held in a major ongoing rediscovery of his work.[29]

Last but by no means least has been the resurgence of hysteria studies in France. This has occurred simultaneously in the French humanities and medical sciences. While to some degree interest in the hysterical neuroses never subsided there, hysteria in the French medical world is again today *en grande vogue*. In *Fits and Starts: A Genealogy of Hysteria in Modern France* (1991), Martha Noel Evans observes that "contemporary French psychiatrists and psychoanalysts have recently initiated a sweeping reassessment of hysteria, its causes, diagnoses, and manifestations. The reevaluation indeed has become one of the central issues through which French psychiatry and psychoanalysis are measuring and redefining themselves."[30] During the 1980s and early 1990s, a raft of works written from

---

[25] P. Flor-Henry, D. Fromm-Auch, M. Tapper, and D. Schopflocher, "A Neuropsychological Study of the Stable Syndrome of Hysteria," *Biological Psychiatry* 16 (1981): 601–26. See also Arnold M. Ludwig, "Hysteria—A Neurobiological Theory," *Archives of General Psychiatry* 27, no. 6 (December 1972): 771–77; and Malcolm Lader, "The Psychophysiology of Hysteria," in Roy, *Hysteria*, 81–87.

[26] P. Briquet, *Traité clinique et thérapeutique de l'hystérie* (Paris: J. B. Baillière, 1859). For more on Briquet, see below, 50–53.

[27] E.M.R. Critchley and H. E. Cantor, "Charcot's Hysteria Renaissant," *British Medical Journal* 289, no. 6460 (December 22–24, 1984): 1785–88.

[28] C. J. Mace, "Hysterical Conversion I: A History," and "Hysterical Conversion II: A Critique," *British Journal of Psychiatry* 159 (1992): 369–77.

[29] For accounts of this development, consult J. C. Nemiah, "Janet Redivivus: The Centenary of *L'automatisme psychologique*," *American Journal of Psychiatry* 146 (1989): 1527–29; and Paul Brown, "Pierre Janet: Alienist Reintegrated," *Current Opinions on Psychiatry* 4 (1991): 389–95.

[30] Evans, *Fits and Starts*, 6.

traditional psychoanalytic, Lacanian, post-Lacanian, and feminist Lacanian perspectives, appeared.[31] Two provocative collections have been published and earlier studies republished.[32] Several French psychiatric journals have devoted special issues to hysteria.[33] The diagnostic concept of "hysterical psychosis" is undergoing a revival.[34] And hysterical pathology was the central theme of the 1988 annual conference of the Association française de psychiatrie.[35] A computerized search of dissertations written during the period 1980–93 at French medical schools reveals no fewer than fifty-five titles dealing centrally with the neurosis.[36] As in the Anglophonic world, contemporary French medical authors are delving deeply into hysteria's past in order to advance their cases about contemporary theory and practice.[37] Furthermore, perhaps because psychoanalysis in France is less medicalized than in the English-speaking world and occupies a more conspicuous position within the university, the continuing French controversy about hysteria and its history has spread beyond the confines of the medical community into many nonmedical academic areas and even into the public domain.[38]

Like the historical object it takes as its subject, then, the new hysteria studies are diverse, protean, and polymorphous. Perhaps most notable is the sheer diversity of disciplinary discourses that are being brought to

[31] Jean-Claude Maleval, *Folies hystériques et psychoses dissociatives* (Paris: Payot, 1981); Gérard Wajeman, *Le maître et l'hystérique* (Paris, Navarin, 1982); Jacques Chazaud, *Hystérie, schizophrénie, paranoïa* (Paris: Privat, 1983); Monique David-Ménard, *L'hystérique entre Freud et Lacan: Corps et langage en psychanalyse* (Paris: Éditions universitaires, 1983; trans. 1989); Charles Melman, *Nouvelles études sur l'hystérie* (Paris: Joseph Clims Denoël, 1984); Jean Guetta, *Un type de couple névrotique: L'hystérique et l'obsessionnel* (Paris: Mémoire pour le CES de psychiatrie, 1985).

[32] *Hystérie et obsession*, in the Bibliothèque des Analytica series (Paris: Navarin, 1986); *Au lieu de l'hystérie I* (Paris: Cartels constituants de l'analyse Freudienne, 1984); Lucien Israël, *L'hystérique, le sexe et le médecin*, 2d ed. (Paris: Masson, 1985).

[33] *Études psychothérapeutiques* 2 (1981); *Revue du praticien* 32, no. 13 (March 1982); *Confrontations psychiatriques* 25 (1985); *Revue française de psychanalyse* 49, no. 2 (January–February 1985); *Psychiatrie française* (May 1988).

[34] For a review of the literature, see Nourradine Bel Bachir, "La psychose hystérique? Revue bibliographique et réflexion personnelle" (Ph.D. diss., University of Paris, 1990).

[35] *Hystérie, cent ans après—résumés* (Abstracts of papers delivered at the seventh annual conference of the Association française de psychiatrie, Paris, January 22–24, 1988).

[36] This tabulation is based on the "Pascal" computer service available today at the Bibliothèque de la Faculté de médecine in Paris.

[37] Monique Schneider, *De l'exorcisme à la psychanalyse: Le féminin expurgé* (Paris: Retz, 1979); Jacques Nassif, *Freud; L'inconscient: Sur les commencements de la psychanalyse* (Paris: Galilée, 1977), part 1; Elisabeth Roudinesco, *La bataille de cent ans: Histoire de la psychanalyse en France* (Paris: Seuil, 1982), part 1; J. D. Nasio, *L'hystérie, ou l'enfant magnifique de la psychanalyse* (Paris: Rivages, 1990).

[38] See, for example, the issue of *Frénésie: Histoire, psychiatrie, psychanalyse* entitled *Hystérus*, no. 4 (Autumn 1987).

bear on the subject today. The history of science and medicine, classical studies, literary history and literary criticism, art history, gender studies, discourse analysis, and cultural studies, British neurology, French Lacanian and post-Lacanian psychiatry, American and French feminist theory, Anglo-American women's studies, and European and American psychoanalytic studies—all have of late converged dramatically on the history of hysteria. Not surprisingly, they have varied enormously in what they have to say.

At the same time, the new hysteria studies as a body of scholarly writing have to date been disparate, fragmented, and uncoordinated. The record indicates unmistakably that, despite its volume, the historical scholarship on hysteria is being pursued concurrently along several very active but almost wholly isolated lines of investigation. Scholars have tended to be closely familiar with the writings of others in their own field; but, with a few exceptions, there has been little familiarity, much less substantive dialogue, across national and disciplinary boundaries. Even specialists often appear unaware of writing on the topic outside their domain. This lack of communication has become particularly acute between scientists and humanists, with both groups evolving easy rationalizations for their intellectual isolationism. Physicians, keen to find historical support for current medical perspectives and with little time to read outside their specific concerns, either remain unfamiliar with the most significant writings of critics and historians or reject this work out of hand as faddish, uninformed, and irrelevant. Conversely, many investigators within the humanities, ignorant of the basic clinical and scientific dimensions of the subject, have been content to cultivate the latest themes and methodologies of their field and to dismiss the work of doctors as uncritical, self-serving, and unsophisticated. In a parallel pattern, other scholars have been absorbed in intense local or national debates while remaining unaware of relevant contemporaneous controversies in other countries.

It is the premise of the present study that the ongoing explosion of interest in the history of hysteria is not simply an event in specialized academic historiography but a development of contemporary cultural significance, a historical phenomenon in its own right. At times, historical commentary on a given topic may become part of the social, cultural, and intellectual history of its time. The new hysteria studies, I want to propose, may usefully be regarded in this manner.[39] This book takes as its

---

[39] For other interpretive historiographies that may be read in broad cultural terms, see Wallace K. Ferguson, *The Renaissance in Historical Thought: Five Centuries of Interpretation* (Boston: Houghton Mifflin, 1948); Pieter Geyl, *Napoleon: For and Against*, trans. Olive Renier (New Haven: Yale University Press, 1949); Edward Bellomy, "Social Darwin-

subject the emergent textual traditions that constitute the new hysteria studies and the many contexts—social, cultural, and political; personal, professional, and ideological—that have contributed to the formation of these traditions. The volume is centrally concerned with the ways in which a range of past authors, inside and outside of medicine, and a still greater diversity of present-day commentators have interpreted a single historical object. When viewed side by side, the major literatures of historical hysteria bear many instructive similarities and differences. A kind of unacknowledged cross-commentary runs between the traditions, a complex of complements and contradictions. Interdisciplinary research in a new area of inquiry, I am aware, entails certain difficulties; but with the subject in question, I believe that the advantages to be gained by pursuing an ambitious interdisciplinary agenda greatly outweigh the dangers. A unique opportunity exists today within hysteria studies for moving beyond a dozen isolated and specialized commentaries to an integrated interdisciplinary discourse. By bringing together in one place ideas, sources, methodologies, and interpretations that have previously remained separate, *Approaching Hysteria* seeks to record, capture, and create that interdisciplinary moment.

I begin below with a brief intellectual history of hysteria. This section is based on a compilation of descriptive materials from the historical scholarship on hysteria that appeared *before* the mid-1970s (i.e., before the appearance of the new hysteria studies) and provides a compact narrative account of medical theories of the disorder from the ancient Greeks to the 1960s. A kind of didactic historical prologue, these pages stand outside the main theoretical body of the work. They are intended solely to educate readers about the basic factual and thematic content of the subject so as better to highlight the critical, interpretive discussions of the new hysteria studies that follow. I have indicated the independence of this section from the central analytical project of the book, and its ironic relation to that project, by citing the term "history" in quotations.

Following this, the body of the book forms a two-tiered analysis. Part One, "Hysteria as Medical Disease," deals with the historical literatures about hysteria viewed as a natural, somatic or psychological malady, that is, as an actual pathological entity. In Part One, chapter 1, titled "The Major Interpretive Traditions," I gather together as wide a range as possible of the past writings on the history of hysteria as a medical disease and consider them in a close and comparative way. Here I review the substance of these writings as evenhandedly as possible with an emphasis on the most recent and important scholarship. I have made an effort to convey to readers a sense of the scope and richness of the work under consideration. In presenting this material, I trace the consolidation of past writings about hysteria into textual sequences and of these sequences into longitudinal interpretive traditions. To this end, I separate the new hysteria studies into five main categories: intellectual histories of hysteria, Freud and the history of hysteria, feminist historical criticism, Charcot and the history of hysteria, and nonfeminist social and political accounts. These groupings are obviously general and approximate with overlaps among them. Moreover, this taxonomy is by no means intended to restrict studies to a single disciplinary identity but rather to coordinate heuristically a large and far-ranging body of commentary. Within the five categories I then reconstruct chronologically the development of the tradition, underscoring the disciplinary, methodological, and ideological factors that have given rise to distinctive readings of hysteria's history. I also highlight the contrasts and clashes among the different schools of interpretation as well as the ways in which the traditions elaborate, revise, and subvert one another.

In chapter 2 of Part One, titled "Theorizing Disease Historiography," the book moves more boldly from description to prescription. In this chapter, I advance a conceptual blueprint for future hysteria studies. The investigative agenda that I set out consists of ten methodological and interpretive guidelines for the prospective study of the history of hysteria in particular and for the historical study of disease generally. This discussion draws on the secondary literature presented in the preceding section and introduces many additional publications. My ten points deal variously with the social, intellectual, theoretical, clinical, therapeutic, and epistemological aspects of hysteria and its past. Several points, such as the one concerning hysteria and social class, draw on established lines of inquiry within historical studies, while others report on the most active areas of research among medical historians today. Still others—for example, my discussions of the role of the neurotic patient in theory production, of hysteria in men, and of the historical cyclicity of psychopathological forms—attempt to break new ground. Necessarily, this portion of the book is more critical and interpretive. However, in those places where I have dealt critically with a given piece of scholarship, I have done so because the work embodies an idea or approach found widely in the literature. Furthermore, by specifying a concrete research program for the future, I by no means seek to exclude other designs.

The second half of *Approaching Hysteria*, "Hysteria as Metaphor," studies the many figurative traditions of commentary on hysteria. Outside of its existence in medical history, hysteria over the centuries has generated exceptionally rich popular and cultural folklores. Indeed, I know of no nonfatal disease that boasts a more extravagant mythopoetic heritage. This part of the book, then, moves beyond the many medico-psychological discourses of hysteria to explore hysteria tropically in a multiplicity of nonmedical media. Throughout this section, I pay particular attention to the historical and conceptual relations between past cultural representations of hysteria and contemporaneous nonmetaphorical, medical-historical traditions of commentary.

While still comparatively small in quantity and very scattered, scholarly writing about the cultural history of hysteria has become one of the most exciting and fastest-growing areas of research within the new hysteria studies. In Part Two, chapter 3, titled "Cultures of Hysteria: Past and Present Traditions," I review straightforwardly the extant scholarship about hysteria's cultural history in different times, countries, and media from the European Renaissance to the early twentieth century. I here emphasize the descriptive figurative uses of hysteria in creative literature (novels, poetry, and drama) and social and political criticism. While in the first half of the book I am at pains to isolate the precise past medical definitions of hysteria, I found in this section that a substantially different reading strategy was necessary. Popular nonmedical usages of the hysteria concept have been so vague and diverse that the historian can at best acquire only a sense of the range of meanings and associations and connotations that the term has carried. In my discussions of fictional texts, I have studied these sources not for their formal, internal literary qualities but as cultural artifacts, for their value as illustrations of—or, perhaps better, symptoms of—larger historical realities. This portion of the book, I believe, may be read as a kind of empirical elaboration of Susan Sontag's well-known essay *Illness as Metaphor* and as a parallel study to Louis Sass's recent ambitious study, *Madness and Modernism: Insanity in the Light of Modern Art, Literature, and Thought.*[40]

In Part Two, chapter 4, "Cultures of Hysteria: Future Orientations," I again move from a critical literature survey to a looser and more interpretive discussion, presenting a number of my own readings of original historical evidence. However, instead of ten short, prescriptive points for the prospective medical-historical study of hysteria, I here offer lengthier, exploratory excursions into three conceptual and methodological issues that are crucial for writing the cultural history of disease. These, to be specific, concern the historical dynamics of cultural influence, past cultural constructions of hysteria and male gender, and the structure of

---

[40] Susan Sontag, *Illness as Metaphor* (New York: Viking, 1978); Louis A. Sass, *Madness and Modernism: Insanity in the Light of Modern Art, Literature, and Thought* (New York: Basic Books, 1992).

historical relations between medical and theological (particularly Catholic) conceptions of hysterical illness. In these three sections, I concentrate overwhelmingly on a single chronological and geographical segment of hysteria's cultural history—namely, France during the second half of the nineteenth century. In part, this focus reflects my personal historical interests and knowledge. Also, the fin-de-siècle era in Europe represents the famous golden age of the neurosis for which the available primary and secondary materials are abundant. In France in particular, hysteria during these decades became part of the general cultural vocabulary, one of the master metaphors of the age. Furthermore, moving in this final quarter of the book from a diachronic to a synchronic historical approach provides an opportunity to explore comparatively the ways in which a nosographical concept has operated as a "cultural signifier" in contemporaneous media within a single culture.

A major theme that I develop in this final chapter is the great intellectual value of abandoning past disciplinary chauvinisms and pursuing creative, cross-disciplinary approaches. On this score, I have attempted to follow two outstanding precedents in writing the cultural history of psychology and psychiatry: *Saturn and Melancholy: Studies in the History of Natural Philosophy, Religion, and Art* (1964), by the trio of Warburg Institute scholars Raymond Klibansky, Erwin Panofsky, and Fritz Saxl, is a richly learned and unprecedentedly interdisciplinary study of the ways in which a psychodiagnostic category was represented in medical, scientific, astrological, philosophical, theological, mythological, poetic, literary, and visual texts from the ancients to Albrecht Dürer.[41] In an altogether different analytical mode are the historical essays of the Genevan literary historian and cultural critic Jean Starobinski; these offer evocative and highly perceptive studies of disease as themes in French poetry, fiction, and philosophy from the seventeenth to the nineteenth centuries.[42]

[41] Raymond Klibansky, Erwin Panofsky, Fritz Saxl, *Saturn and Melancholy: Studies in the History of Natural Philosophy, Religion, and Art* (New York: Basic Books, 1964). See also the 1989 French edition of the work, *Saturne et la mélancolie: Études historiques et philosophiques: Nature, religion, médecine et l'art*, trans. Louis Évrard and Fabienne Durand-Bogaert (Paris: Gallimard, 1989), which includes significant revisions by Klibansky.

[42] From a large offering, see Jean Starobinski, "La nostalgie: Théories médicales et expression littéraire," in *Transactions of the First International Congress on Enlightenment IV, Studies on Voltaire and the Eighteenth Century* 27 (1963): 1505–18; idem, "Sur les fonctions de la parole dans la théorie médicale de l'époque romantique," *Médecine de France* 205 (1969): 9–12; idem, "The Word Reaction: From Physics to Psychiatry," *Diogenes* 93 (1976): 1–27; idem, "Sur la chlorose," *Romantisme: Revue du dix-neuvième siècle* 31 (1981): 113–30; idem, "Brève histoire de la conscience du corps," in Robert Ellrodt, ed., *Genèse de la conscience moderne* (Paris: Presses universitaires de France, 1983), 215–29; idem, *Le remède dans le mal: Critique et légitimation de l'artifice à l'âge des lumières* (Paris: Gallimard, 1989). On Starobinski as a figure in psychiatric historiography, refer to Fernando Vidal, "Jean Starobinski: The History of Psychiatry as the Cultural His-

In the conclusion of the book, I review the different disciplinary perspectives surveyed in the preceding pages. I then close with a series of general queries and speculations: What do hysteria studies need for their future intellectual and disciplinary development? What can we learn from the textual traditions of hysteria about the important and fascinating, but difficult, project of writing the history of a disease? Why in recent years has the history of hysteria in particular carried such resonance for observers and commentators in the sciences and humanities? Why do academic researchers from disparate knowledge systems converge simultaneously on a subject at a particular historical moment? And what is the broad cultural meaning of the new hysteria studies? This is then followed by a detailed bibliography that should further assist scholars in mapping out the field in the future.

Finally, let me address in this introduction, at least preliminarily, a number of methodological and epistemological matters. First, throughout my study I cite liberally from contemporary medical writings about hysteria. However, while I have drawn on and learned from this literature, I have made no attempt to canvass it as comprehensively as I have the historical scholarship. For interested readers, analyses of this medical work are available elsewhere.[43] Similarly, I have made no attempt whatsoever to adjudicate among divergent or conflicting medical models of hysteria today. I have also refrained from trying to formulate a single, uniformly applicable definition of the disorder as well as from attempting to answer the vexed and controversial question of whether hysteria is a "real" disease. To repeat, what interests me in these pages is hysteria and the history of its interpretation; accordingly, I have drawn on the contemporary medical literature only insofar as it illuminates that project.

Second, and on a related point, the need to define one's subject matter accurately, consistently, and rigorously is a challenge to every historian of disease. As I will emphasize below, the obstacles to defining hysteria are especially formidable. Clinically, the disease is highly amorphous and through the centuries has been defined in radically different, if not contradictory, ways. To discuss it at all as a single historical phenomenon may well be largely a heuristic strategy. In his recent excellent study of the

---

tory of Consciousness," in Mark S. Micale and Roy Porter, eds., *Discovering the History of Psychiatry* (New York: Oxford University Press, 1994), chap. 7.

[43] Full and clinically informed accounts of the medical literature in English may be found in Alan Krohn, *Hysteria: The Elusive Neurosis*, monograph 45/46 of *Psychological Issues* 12, nos. 1–2 (New York: International Universities Press, 1978), which discusses the psychoanalytic tradition; Harold Merskey, *The Analysis of Hysteria* (London: Baillière Tindall, 1970), 277–300; and Slavney, *Perspectives on "Hysteria"*. For French sources, see Augustin Jeanneau's monographic "L'hystérie: Unité et diversité," *Revue française de psychanalyse* 49, no. 2, special number (January–February, 1985): 107–326.

British and North American medical literature, Phillip Slavney's solution to this problem is to place the word "hysteria" in quotation marks throughout his book, a procedure that seems to me at once epistemologically correct and visually cumbersome. Therefore, in the ensuing narrative I cite the term without this qualification. However, I adopt this practice only with the important caveat that the present inquiry is, again, historical and historiographical. Therefore, when I use the words "hysteria," "disease," "disorder," "illness," and "pathology," I do so in a neutral, descriptive sense, to denote the human behavioral realities understood as hysteria by doctors in the past and by scholars today.

Third and last, there is the slippery matter of self-placement. In the discussion below, I reflect as a historian and critic on the cumulative body of writing forming the new hysteria studies. In this analysis, I place a good deal of emphasis on the need continually to contextualize historical scholarship, that is, to view the writing of history as itself a historical act that functions within social, intellectual, ideological, and professional contexts of its own. At the same time, *Approaching Hysteria* is, I trust, a part of that very history I am attempting to study. I have no intention of allowing this work, including its introduction, to founder on the shoals of self-referentiality or to digress into an exercise in metahistoriography. Ultimately, my own investments in writing about the history of hysteria will be judged by my readers. Nevertheless, the postmodernist academic sensibility is nothing if not self-aware. Therefore, let me state plainly that my own disciplinary bases for this study are those of intellectual history and the history of science and medicine. In my review of past scholarship in chapters 1 and 3, I do not, insofar as I can determine, have any major ideological axes to grind. Throughout the work, my rather insistent call to interdisciplinarity is most likely part and parcel of the broad goals of the general cultural studies program of the past decade. Furthermore, since the 1970s a quantity of sophisticated scholarship concerning the methodology and epistemology of the history of science has come into being, and there is evidence of late that the histories of psychiatry, psychology, and psychoanalysis specifically are entering a new, more self-reflective phase.[44] This book, I suspect, manifests these developments. In addition, my fascination with the multiple meanings read into a single

---

[44] Arnold I. Davidson, "How to Do the History of Psychoanalysis," in Françoise Meltzer, ed., *The Trial(s) of Psychoanalysis* (Chicago: University of Chicago Press, 1988), 39–64; John E. Toews, "Historicizing Psychoanalysis: Freud in His Time and for Our Time," *Journal of Modern History* 43 (1991): 504–54; Paul Robinson, *Freud and His Critics* (Berkeley: University of California Press, 1993); Roy Porter and Mark S. Micale, "Reflections on Psychiatry and Its Histories" and Elisabeth Young-Bruehl, "A History of Freud Biographies," both in Micale and Porter, eds., *Discovering the History of Psychiatry*, 3–36, 157–73.

pathological phenomenon no doubt reflects a larger preoccupation within the academic humanities today, and of relativist and postrelativist cultures as a whole, with the centrality of interpretation. Lastly, in the conclusion of the book I have speculated on some of the broad cultural forces that may be at work behind the recent heightening of historiographical interest in hysteria; this analysis applies to all of the new hysteria studies, including to the text that readers hold in their hands.

A SHORT "HISTORY" OF HYSTERIA

THE DISEASE entity hysteria has a history as colorful as it is long and venerable. This history incorporates four major paradigms, or models, of the disorder and is less linear than it is cyclical.

The word "hysteria" derives from the Greek word for uterus, *hystera*, which derives in turn from the Sanskrit word for stomach or belly. Inherent in these simple etymological facts is the meaning of the earliest views on the nature and origin of the disease. An Egyptian medical papyrus dating from around 1900 B.C., which is one of the oldest surviving documents known to medical history, records a series of curious behavioral disturbances in adult women. As the ancient Egyptians interpreted it, the cause of these abnormalities was the movement of the uterus, which they believed to be an autonomous, free-floating organism, upward from its normal pelvic position. Such a dislocation, they reasoned, applied pressure on the diaphragm and gave rise to a battery of bizarre physical and mental symptoms. Egyptian doctors developed an array of medications to combat the disease. Foremost among these measures were the placement of aromatic substances on the vulva to entice the womb back down into its correct position and the smelling and swallowing of fetid or foul-tasting substances to repel the uterus away from the upper parts.

These ancient Egyptian beliefs also furnished the basis for classical Greek medical and philosophical theories of hysteria. The Greeks adopted the notion of the migratory uterus and embroidered upon the connections, only implicit in Egyptian texts, between hysteria and an unsatisfactory sexual life. In a famous and colorful passage from the *Timaeus*, Plato wrote: "the womb is an animal which longs to generate children. When it remains barren too long after puberty, it is distressed and sorely disturbed, and straying about in the body and cutting off the passages of the breath, it impedes respiration and brings the sufferer into the extremist anguish and provokes all manner of diseases besides." Various texts of the school of Hippocrates from the fifth century B.C. explain similarly that a mature woman's deprivation of sexual relations causes a restless womb to move upward in search of gratification. As the uterus rampages destructively through the female body cavity, it causes dizziness, motor paralyses, sensory losses, and respiratory distress (including the sensation of a ball lodged in the throat, or *globus hystericus*) as well as extravagant emotional behaviors. Ancient Greek therapies included uterine fumigations, the application of tight abdominal bandages, and, most to the point, immediate marriage.

Ancient Roman physicians wrote about hysteria too. With the growth of anatomical knowledge, the literal hypothesis of the wandering womb became increasingly untenable. However, Roman medical authors, such as Cornelius Celsus, Aretaeus of Cappadocia, Galen of Pergamon, and Soranus of Ephesus, continued to associate hysteria exclusively with the female generative system. The principal causes of hysterical disorders, they believed, were "diseases of the womb" and disruptions in female reproductive biology, including amenorrhea, miscarriages, premature births, and menopause. Accordingly, they identified cases of the condition most often in virgins, widows, and spinsters, and they recommended as treatment a regular regimen of marital *fornicatio*.

The ideas expressed in ancient Egyptian, Greek, and Roman sources represent the historical origins of the medical concept of hysteria in Western civilization. Engraved in the *Corpus Hippocraticum*, the uterine hypothesis formed a medical ideology that remained enormously influential for millennia of medical history. Descriptive and theoretical details evolved, but the basic doctrine of gynecological determinism, the crux of the classical heritage in the history of hysteria, endured. Until the early twentieth century, virtually all medical theorists felt the need to define themselves, positively or negatively, against this classical background.

The coming of Christian civilization in the Latin West initiated the first great paradigm shift in the history of hysteria. From the fifth to the thirteenth centuries, naturalistic pagan construals of the disease were increasingly displaced by supernatural formulations. In the writings of St. Augustine, all human suffering, including organic and mental illnesses, was perceived as a manifestation of innate evil, consequent upon original sin. Hysteria in particular, with its shifting and highly dramatic symptomatology, was viewed as a sign of possession by the devil. The hysterical female was interpreted alternately as a victim of bewitchment to be pitied and the devil's soul mate to be despised. No less powerfully mythopoetic than the classical image of the disease, the demonological model considered the hysterical anesthesias, mutisms, and convulsions of hysteria as *stigmata diaboli*, or marks of the devil.

This sea change in thinking about the meaning and origins of hysteria brought with it changes in treatment modalities. The elaborate pharmacopoeia of earlier times was now replaced by supernatural invocations: prayers, incantations, amulets, and exorcisms. Furthermore, with the demonization of the diagnosis came the widespread persecution of the afflicted. During the late medieval and Renaissance periods, the scene of diagnosis of the hysteric shifted from the hospital to the church and the courtroom, which now became the loci of spectacular interrogations. Official manuals for the detection of witches, often virulently misogynistic, supplied instructions for the detection, torture, and at times execution of the witch/hysteric. The number of such inquisitions remains unknown but is believed to be high.

Happily, the late Renaissance, which witnessed the height of the witchcraft craze in continental Europe, also produced in reaction several substantial efforts to renaturalize the hysteria concept. These efforts, made on scientific and humanitarian grounds, corresponded with the beginnings of the scientific revolution in Britain and western Europe. Paracelsus in Switzerland, Johannes Weyer in the Netherlands, Ambroise Paré in France, and Edward Jorden in England attempted to recapture the disease from the realms of religion and magic by arguing forcefully that hysteria was a medical pathology with naturalistic causes. As such, they urged, it required not religious condemnation or legal punishment but medical ministration.

The seventeenth century was an era of major intellectual innovation in the history of hysteria. Early in the century, the French royal physician Charles Lepois argued importantly that the seat of hysterical pathology was neither the womb nor the soul but the head. Lepois went on to emphasize the passions as causative agents of the disorder. To similar effect, seventeenth-century physicians began to conduct autopsies on hysterical patients, which repeatedly revealed an absence of postmortem uterine pathology. Furthermore, in 1696, the Roman physician Giorgio Baglivi published his general medical treatise, *De praxi medicina*. An acute clinical observer, Baglivi produced the fullest case histories of hysterical patients to date. He followed Lepois in emphasizing the hysterogenic role of "perturbations of the mind." And he stressed the profound influence of the words and actions of the physician on the hysteric as well as the phenomenon of hysterical contagion. The cumulative effect of these ideas was to begin to loosen the age-old association of hysteria with female reproductive anatomy and physiology.

Without a doubt, the most important seventeenth-century development in the history of hysteria was the emergence of a neurological model of the disease. Advances in understanding the structure and function of the human nervous system during this period provided a new paradigm for many previously baffling disorders, including hysteria. As a consequence, the later seventeenth and the eighteenth centuries were characterized by the waning of the gynecological and demonological theories and the appearance of new and imaginative etiological analyses. The new explanations combined ancient humoral ideas with the growing knowledge of neurology and fashionable mechanical and iatrochemical ideas from the physical and chemical sciences. This was particularly true among British physicians, who throughout the seventeenth and eighteenth centuries dominated in the theorization of hysteria.

In his compendious *Affectionum quae dicuntur hystericae et hypo-chondriacae* of 1670, Thomas Willis, the foremost neuroanatomist of his time, proposed that the site of hysteria was the brain and spinal cord. Willis, who coined the words "neuro-logia" and "psyche-logia," expounded a theory according to which an excess of "animal spirits" was released from the brain and carried by the nerves to the spleen and abdomen where it entered the blood stream to circulate through the body. Other English and Scottish physicians questioned Willis's cerebrocentric explanation and concocted schemes of their own. Nathaniel Highmore espoused a cardiac theory that traced the disorder to an engorgement of the heart and pulmonary vessels. Bernard de Mandeville and George Cheyne situated hysteria in the stomach, where they believed it arose from the irregular fermentation of foodstuff. Robert Whytt thought the disorder was caused by a weakness of the nerve fibers, and William Cullen attributed it to a slowing of the nervous fluids through the brain.

The most profound theorist of hysteria in Britain during the early modern era was the great clinician Thomas Sydenham (1624–89). Sydenham is renowned in medical history for his brilliant observational powers, and his comments on hysterical disorders, contained in his *Epistolary Dissertation* of 1681/82 and the posthumously published *Processus Integri* of 1693, live up to the reputation. Sydenham fashioned what may properly be called the first neuropsychological model of the disease. He believed that the condition was produced by an imbalance in the distribution of the animal spirits between body and mind. Such a maldistribution, he hypothesized further, was caused most often by sudden and violent emotions, including anger, fear, love, and grief. Sydenham also judged hysteria to be much more common than was generously supposed. He stressed the extreme clinical fluidity of the disorder as well as its unsurpassed ability to assume the physical form of other diseases. The extraordinary mimetic capacity of hysteria, he pointed out, required the shrewdest diagnostic skills on the part of the physician. Additionally, Sydenham provided memorable clinical descriptions of morbid phenomena that could be hysterical in origin, including intestinal spasm, *clavus hystericus* (feeling as if a nail were being driven into the forehead), and recurrent visceral, muscular, and articular pain. While he maintained that women were constitutionally predisposed to hysteria due to their fragile nervous apparatus, he described a hysteria-like syndrome in males, which he called hypochondriasis.

The period spanning the late eighteenth and early nineteenth centuries brought yet another critical reorientation in the history of hysteria. The most important development during this period was the reintroduction of uterine theories of the disease after their eclipse during the preceding two hundred years. Inspired by the intricate botanical and zoological taxonomies of the naturalists Carolus Linnaeus and the Comte de Buffon, physicians now became preoccupied with the classification of diseases. In new classificatory schemes, they linked hysteria causally to female sexuality. This development, however, represented less a revival than a reversal of Hippocratic teachings. While medical writers in antiquity had connected hysterical symptomatology with female sexual deprivation, eighteenth-century writers blamed it on sexual overindulgence. Thus, in the 1760s Boissier de Sauvages projected seven subforms of hysteria, of which one was *hysteria libidinosa*. Two decades later, William Cullen, who originated the concept of neurosis, endorsed this category, which he likened to the new diagnosis of nymphomania, and which he proposed was caused by a turgescence of blood in the female genitalia. At the turn of the century in Paris, the psychiatric humanitarian Philippe Pinel produced his own vast medical nosography, in which hysteria was classified among the "Genital Neuroses of Women." The reasons for this reeroticization of the disease during the late 1700s and early 1800s are unclear.

In the history of hysteria, the nineteenth century is marked by a great multiplication of texts, theories, and therapies. No single school dominated; rather, half a dozen theoretical currents developed, at times running independent courses and at other times flowing together in the writings of individual physicians. Increasingly, these currents mirrored both the speciality and the nationality of the medical author.

During the first half of the 1800s, a long and largely sterile debate raged among Parisian asylum doctors over the precise anatomical seat of the disease. Again invoking classical authorities, unreconstructed uterinists such as J.-B. Louyer-Villermay (1816), Frédéric Dubois d'Amiens (1833), A. L. Foville (1833), and Hector Landouzy (1846) produced book-length treatises implicating the female reproductive system. Citing the precedents of Willis and Sydenham, contemporaries such as É.-J. Georget (1821), Félix Voisin (1826), and J.-L. Brachet (1847) counterargued that hysteria was a morbid condition of the brain. In the 1840s, the process of ovulation was discovered, and this inspired a new, specifically ovarian theory of hysterical disease that remained popular among gynecologists until the end of the century.

A second strand in the history of hysteria during the nineteenth century derived from mesmerism and so-called animal magnetism. The sensationalistic demonstrations of Franz Anton Mesmer on well-to-do Viennese and Parisian salon ladies during the 1780s are celebrated in the popular historical imagination. Rejected repeatedly as charlatanism by medical academicians, Mesmer's controversial teachings nonetheless initiated a century-long tradition of hypnotic research into unconscious mental processes. The work of the Marquis de Puységur, the Abbé Faria, F. J. Noizet, J.P.F. Deleuze, Alexander Bertrand, and Antoine Despine in

France and John Elliotson, James Braid, and James Esdaile in Scotland extended the Mesmeric heritage. The writings of these figures explored probingly, if unsystematically, a dual model of the mind, the psychogenesis of nervous and mental symptoms, the nature of hysterical anesthesias, and the psychotherapeutic relationship between doctors and hysterical patients.

A third sequence of publications elaborated the idea of the "hysterical constitution" or "hysterical temperament." According to this notion, hysteria was defined less by a physical symptomatology than a set of highly negative character traits. These traits included eccentricity, impulsiveness, emotionality, coquettishness, deceitfulness, and hypersexuality. This conceptualization was first formulated in Germany in Wilhelm Griesinger's *Mental Pathology and Therapeutics* (1845), in Britain in Robert Brudenell Carter's *On the Pathology and Treatment of Hysteria* (1853), and in France during the 1860s in the essays of Jules Falret. Later in the century, it was voiced by the British alienists Henry Maudsley, T. S. Clouston, and George Savage. The idea assumed particularly misogynistic expression in the German-speaking countries around the turn of the century in texts by Paul Möbius (1895, 1905) and Otto Weininger (1905).

The nineteenth century also witnessed many hybrid theories of hysteria that combined components of the approaches above. Most notable was a kind of neuro-uterine model that dominated the thinking of gynecological physicians. According to this view, the pathogenesis of hysteria rested in local diseases of the uterus, vagina, and ovaries and in defective reproductive physiology, especially irregularities of menstruation, parturition, and lactation. The effects of these irregularities, it was believed, were conveyed throughout the female body by means of the plexus of nerves emanating from the uterus. Within this system, therapeutics for the disorder consisted of localized physicalistic procedures, such as douches, dilations, ovarian pressure, intrauterine injections, the cervical and vulvar application of leeches, and clitoral cauterizations. Recalcitrant cases were occasionally subjected to amputative and extirpative gynecological surgery, including bilateral ovariotomies.

Between 1878 and 1893, the most important medical figure in the nineteenth-century history of hysteria accomplished his work. This was the French clinical neurologist Jean-Martin Charcot. Charcot's legendary place in the history of hysteria is as familiar as it is compelling. Working during the 1860s and 1870s at the Salpêtrière, a large and historic hospital on the edge of Paris, Charcot conducted pioneering research on cerebral localization, multiple sclerosis, tabes dorsalis, and amyotrophic lateral sclerosis. For this work, he was awarded during his lifetime with scientific celebrity and in our own century with the title "father of neurology." At the height of his international fame, he turned his attention to "the great neurosis." Charcot was not a theoretician and published no general treatise on hysteria. Rather, he worked out his ideas in a series of formal lectures presented to large medical audiences in the amphitheater of the Salpêtrière and in informal weekly bedside demonstrations to his students, which became known as the *leçons du mardi*. In total, he published over 120 case histories pertaining to the disorder.

In these writings, Charcot formulated a new, comprehensive, neurogenic model of hysteria. He repeatedly and polemically rejected ancient genital etiologies as well as the related image of the sexually voracious hysteric. He insisted that men too were susceptible to the disease, albeit in much lower ratios than women. In his opinion, hysteria was strictly a dysfunction of the central nervous system, akin to epilepsy, syphilis, and other neurological diseases. Like these ailments, hysterical neuropathy was the result of a lesion of an undetermined structural or functional nature that would eventually be discovered through the methodology of pathological anatomy. According to Charcotian theory, such a neurological defect resulted from a combination of hereditary predisposition to nervous degeneration and an environmental agent provocateur, which most often took the form of a physical or emotional shock.

Charcot lavished his attention on the descriptive neurosymptomatology of hysteria. He believed that motor and sensory abnormalities were the most common manifestations, which he referred to as "hysterical stigmata." With his rigorous systematizing intelligence, Charcot divided the generalized hysterical paroxysm into schematized stages: a period of epileptiform agitation, a period of *grands mouvements* (including the famous arched back position), a period of "passional attitudes," and a period of delirious withdrawal. He also believed that the body surface of the hysteric revealed "hysterogenic zones," or points of sensory anesthesia and hyperesthesia, that upon compression could start or stop a hysterical seizure. In the best Sydenhamian tradition, many of Charcot's clinical writings are virtuosic exercises in differential diagnosis.

Charcot's achievements were medico-scientific and not therapeutic. Believing hysteria to be constitutional and degenerative, he held out little hope for its cure. His therapeutics were limited to the alleviation of symptoms. In contrast, his experimental interests in the disease were extensive. In dramatic and widely publicized demonstrations at the Salpêtrière, he deployed hypnosis to demonstrate that a mental mechanism lay behind hysterical symptom formation. However, he refrained from theorizing about the implications of these experiments. Moreover, contemporary critics charged that many of his experiments were staged and his patients abused.

Despite its drama and fame, medical thinking about hysteria had reached an intellectual impasse by the time of Charcot's death in 1893.

The search for the missing lesion of hysteria, and therefore for the hypo-thetical organic basis of the disease, remained fruitless. The degeneration-ist model in medicine was deteriorating, and the therapeutic nihilism in-herent in existing approaches became increasingly unacceptable to private patients. As a consequence, physicians at the turn of the century found themselves open to alternative conceptualizations of the nervous disor-ders. In this context, the final paradigm shift in the history of hysteria—from the gynecological, demonological, and neurological models of past centuries to a psychological theory—took place.

The psychologization of the hysteria concept a century ago was a com-plex process that occurred on many fronts. During the penultimate de-cades of the nineteenth century, Hippolyte Bernheim, an internist from the University of Nancy in Alsace-Lorraine, challenged Charcotian doc-trine directly. Bernheim and the other members of the so-called "Nancy school" interpreted hysteria as an exaggerated psychological reaction that was potentially universal. Under the right circumstances, Bernheim contended, more or less everyone was *hystérisable*. He believed that the role of heightened suggestibility (rather than reproductive anatomy or an innate neuropathic disposition) was the key to its causation. Again unlike his rival in Paris, Bernheim was deeply interested in the psychotherapeu-tics of hysteria. He pioneered a therapy of "desuggestion," including the extensive use of hypnotherapeutics.

Bernheim and his colleagues contributed to the transition to twentieth-century psychological medicine by revealing the errors and excesses of the school of the Salpêtrière. During the same period, other physicians achieved this goal by elaborating on the psychogenic implications of Charcot's work. In his philosophy doctorate, *Psychological Automatisms* (1889), and his medical dissertation, *The Mental State of Hystericals* (1893), Pierre Janet, like Bernheim, championed the idea that hysteria is a mental malady. Janet also shifted the focus of observations away from the physical symptoms and attacks that up until then had captured physi-cians' attention to the unusual altered states of consciousness associated with hysteria: obsessions, amnesias, abulias, fugue states, trances, and multiple personality. Janet proposed that these psychological phenomena were the result of emotional traumas that had weakened the synthesizing abilities of the healthy human psyche. As such, these traumatic memories became "subconsciously fixed"; they existed in a region outside of nor-mal consciousness, and from that region they continued to exert an inju-rious effect on the mental life of the individual. In the therapeutic realm, Janet was skeptical of hypnotherapeutics; he relied heavily instead on the close and careful observation of patients, whose experiences he recorded in unprecedentedly detailed and individualized case histories.

Far and away the most historically significant of the new psychogenic theories of hysteria emerging during the turn of the last century was Freudian psychoanalysis. During the 1880s and 1890s, Sigmund Freud (1856–1939) lived in Vienna, where he worked in the late Victorian mold of the private nerve specialist. Freud's thinking about hysteria developed incrementally. In conversations with a prominent local internist, Josef Breuer, he learned about Breuer's treatment of a particularly complex case of hysteria in 1880–82. This was the case of "Anna O.," probably the single most famous patient in the annals of hysteria. Anna O., who exhibited a welter of idiosyncratic symptoms, was able in a quasi-hypnotic state to trace her individual hysterical symptoms back to specific emotionally disturbing events in her past. Moreover, in reminiscing about these events with Breuer, she was able to bring them into her consciousness, which in turn caused the symptoms to disappear, a procedure that the patient termed "the talking cure" and Freud later christened "the cathartic method."

During the winter months of 1885–86, Freud studied in Paris with Charcot. Freud had been trained in neurological medicine, which, within the German-language medical communities of the time, was strictly somaticist in orientation. However, upon his return from Paris to Vienna, he began an intellectual evolution, extending across the next fifteen years, from a neurological to a psychological construal of nervous illness. No disorder was more important for this historical development of Freud's thinking than hysteria. Psychoanalysis in essence began as a theory of hysteria. Between 1894 and 1901, Freud published a series of essays and books elaborating his evolving ideas about the neurosis. The best-known of these are the *Studies on Hysteria* (1895), written conjointly with Breuer and featuring the cases of Anna O. and four other pseudonymous patients, and *Fragment of an Analysis of a Case of Hysteria* (1901), known colloquially as the "Dora" case.

In these texts, Freud radically reconceptualized medical thinking about hysteria. Like Bernheim and Janet, he reversed the previously projected direction of mind/body causality: hysteria, he claimed, was a psychological disease with quasi-physical symptoms. However, unique among medical investigators, Freud placed the emphasis solidly on the question of the psychological mechanism of hysterical symptom formation. According to his formulation, hysterogenesis rests in the repression of traumatic memories. These memories are usually remote in the emotional past of the individual and invariably libidinal, or sexual, in content. Because these remembrances are painful or unpleasant, they are unable to find conscious psychological expression. Freud postulated further that the negative emotional energy, or "strangulated affect," associated with these memories was then unconsciously converted into the somatic manifestations of hysteria. In the process of hysterical conversion—the core of the

Freudian theory of hysteria—physical functions alter in ways that unconsciously give expression to the repressed instinctual impulses. Moreover, Freud hypothesized that hysterical symptoms are not simply arbitrary and meaningless phenomena but complex symbolizations of repressed psychological experiences.

Beyond this, Freud's conception of conversion changed steadily, again reflecting a movement away from the physiological to the psychological. Initially, Freud put forward a psychophysiological explanation whereby a certain quantity of "psychical affect" was transformed into a "somatic innervation." By 1905, however, he had advanced a purely psychological theory of the etiology of neurotic symptoms. Similarly, he at first conjectured that the repressed pathogenic material consisted of unconscious memories of childhood sexual traumas; however, following the abandonment of the seduction theory in 1897, he asserted that this psychological material was composed of sexual desires and fantasies retained in the unconscious for purposes of self-defense. It should be noted that Freudian psychology in a real sense represents a second resexualization of the hysteria diagnosis; however, this time the sexual appears in the guise of an integrated *psycho*sexuality rather than genital anatomy or reproductive biology.

The psychoanalytic model of the psyche also entailed major changes in method and therapy. Because in Freud's view hysteria was caused by strictly mental entities—ideas, emotions, and desires in the life of the individual—the disorder was now open to psychotherapeutic intervention. Freud believed that by bringing into the conscious mental life of the patient the historical event that had created the hysterical repression, the patient's symptoms disappeared. During the 1880s and 1890s, he moved from medical electricity to hypnosis to the templar pressure technique, and finally to "free association" in an attempt to accomplish this goal. The free-associative technique, which is unique to psychoanalysis, consists of a kind of attentive listening in which the wandering thoughts of the patient reveal unconscious psychic images and structures to the therapist. This mode of observation typically creates an intense and individualized therapeutic relationship between the hysterical patient, or analysand, and the psychoanalyst.

The history of hysteria in the first half of the twentieth century was dominated by psychoanalysis. While Freud's basic ideas remained intact during these decades, several reformulations within the Freudian model occurred. Most significantly, Freud, who had matched neurotic syndromes etiologically to stages of libidinal fixation, associated hysteria with the third stage of psychosexual development, the genital stage. Later psychoanalytic authors, led by W.R.D. Fairbairn, Felix Deutsch, and Karl Abraham, shifted the emphasis from phallic to oral issues and from the

Oedipal father to the pre-Oedipal mother. Numerous nonpsychoanalytic figures also wrote about hysteria, although none of them generated major theoretical structures. Virtually all twentieth-century formulations of the disease have been mentalist in nature.

Ironically, the most consequential development in the history of hysteria during the twentieth century has been the dramatic and mysterious decline in the incidence of the disorder itself. A more or less unbroken textual record of hysteria runs from the ancient Greeks to Freud. Yet in recent generations, a drastic diminution in the rate of occurrence of hysterical neuroses has taken place. Furthermore, those cases that have appeared tend clinically to be much simpler and less flamboyant than their counterparts in centuries past. This development has now been registered in the official rosters of mental diseases, which have deleted the hysteria diagnosis. After twenty centuries of medical history, this extraordinary disease is for all intents and purposes disappearing from sight today. Nobody knows why.

Part ONE

HYSTERIA AS MEDICAL DISEASE

Chapter 1

THE MAJOR INTERPRETIVE TRADITIONS

INTELLECTUAL HISTORIES OF HYSTERIA

A S A RULE, the first tradition of historical commentary about a disease to develop is an intellectual-historical tradition. Before social, political, and cultural analyses, the story of diseases has been presented as a history of the observations and theories of medical practitioners as recorded through the ages in printed texts. The classic example of scholarship in this mold is *The Falling Sickness*, the highly respected and immensely learned study of epilepsy from Greek antiquity to the early twentieth century by Oswei Temkin.[1] Histories of ideas about disease entities are by definition diachronic, or longitudinal, rather than synchronic, or cross-sectional. The evident intellectual appeal of these linear narratives is chronological sweep, whereas the dangers are simplification, overgeneralization, and acontextualism.

Because these histories are concerned primarily with the straightforward exposition of texts in chronological order, their interpretive aspects often appear secondary or insignificant, but this is misleading. Central to the enterprise of writing intellectual histories is the creation of a canon, that is, the retrospective projection of a sequence of texts, figures, and ideas that constitute the main line of theorization about the subject. The selection of figures included and excluded in the canon and the ordering of themes, authors, and books are interpretive acts continually required of the historian of medical ideas. Thus far, the historiographical record suggests that canon construction reflects most importantly the prior theoretical commitments and ideological allegiances of the historian-author. The record indicates further that intellectual histories of disease—perhaps because they are the oldest and most conventional form of writing about the subject, perhaps because of inherent methodological and epistemological weaknesses in the genre—are the tradition that is currently being challenged most seriously by subsequent schools of interpretation.

Four Early Histories

The first attempts to set down in a systematic fashion the intellectual history of hysteria emerged between 1890 and 1910. Four works ap-

[1] Oswei Temkin, *The Falling Sickness: A History of Epilepsy from the Greeks to the Beginnings of Modern Neurology* (Baltimore: Johns Hopkins University Press, 1945).

peared, all of them French. In 1891, Georges Gilles de la Tourette (best known for the convulsive tic syndrome that bears his name today) published volume one of his *Traité clinique et thérapeutique de l'hystérie d'après l'enseignement de la Salpêtrière.*[2] As its title indicates, Gilles de la Tourette's work provides a codification of Charcotian ideas about hysteria by Charcot's most loyal disciple. The thirty-six pages of "Historical Considerations" that preface the trilogy may be read as the official in-house history of hysteria for the school of the Salpêtrière.[3] In this chapter, Gilles de la Tourette presents the history of medical thought about hysteria as the story of two long-running antitheses: between religious and scientific conceptualizations of the disease on the one hand and, within the medical world, between ancient uterine and modern cerebral or neurological theories on the other.

Gilles de la Tourette devotes many pages to ancient, medieval, and modern thinking about hysteria. Yet the genuinely scientific stage of the history of hysteria, according to his presentation, was achieved only in 1862, with the coming of the young Charcot to the Salpêtrière. Furthermore, the author underscores the emergence of a number of beliefs later advanced by Charcot and associated doctrinally with the Salpêtrians, such as the discrediting of gynecological models of the disorder, the championing of hysteria as a subject of serious scientific study, and the rejection of the age-old association between hysteria and sexual lasciviousness. Not the least interesting feature of Gilles de la Tourette's historical review is that it appeared on the eve of the first writings of Janet and Freud. Unlike twentieth-century accounts, his book provides a history of hysteria in which psychological models of the disorder do not figure at all. Whereas Freudian and post-Freudian historiographers have cast hysteria's history as a running confrontation between somatic and psychological models of the mind, nineteenth-century commentators most often conceptualized it as a battle between science and religion, the ancients and the moderns, or uterinists and neurocentrists.

The first full monographic study of the intellectual history of hysteria made its appearance in 1897, six years after Gilles de la Tourette's volume and four years after Charcot's death. This was Glafira Abricossoff's "L'hystérie aux XVIIe et XVIIIe siècles (étude historique)."[4] The first generation of women accepted into French medical schools in the late

---

[2] [Georges] Gilles de la Tourette, *Traité clinique et thérapeutique de l'hystérie d'après l'enseignement de la Salpêtrière,* 3 vols. (Paris: E. Plon, Nourrit et Cie, 1891–95).

[3] Ibid., 1–36. See also Paul Richer, *Études cliniques sur l'hystéro-épilepsie ou grande hystérie* (Paris: Adrien Delahaye et Émile Lecrosnier, 1881), Historical Appendix, 615–726; and J.-M. Charcot and Paul Richer, *Les démoniaques dans l'art* (Paris: Delahaye et Lecrosnier, 1887).

[4] Mme. Glafira Abricossoff, "L'hystérie aux XVIIe et XVIIIe siècles (étude historique)" (Ph.D. diss., University of Paris: G. Steinheil, 1897).

nineteenth century were frequently foreigners, especially of Russian and east European origin. Abricossoff (sometimes cited "Abrikosova") had traveled from Moscow to Paris to receive her professional training, and this study of hysteria served as her medical dissertation. It is surely striking that the first book-length historical study of hysteria in any language was produced not only by a woman but by a member of the first wave of female physicians. As with Gilles de la Tourette, Abricossoff envisioned her subject strictly as a chronology of medical ideas. Her intellectual and institutional allegiances, immediately apparent in the thesis, were also identical to Gilles de la Tourette's. During the early 1890s, Abricossoff had worked as a medical *externe* in the *Service Charcot* at the Salpêtrière. Her dissertation was supervised by Alix Joffroy, Pierre Marie, and Gilles de la Tourette, all Charcot progeny, and a dedication to the thesis reads "à la mémoire de mon illustre maître J.-M. Charcot."

Abricossoff takes as her subject a single chronological segment of the history of hysteria. Bracketed by short chapters on the ancients and the nineteenth century, the body of her thesis reconstructs in impressive detail medical thinking about the neurosis from the Renaissance to the end of the Enlightenment. Abricossoff brings to light ideas and observations of Vesalius, Harvey, Paré, Montaigne, Willis, Sydenham, Highmore, Boerhaave, Cullen, Raulin, Pomme, and a host of lesser-known figures. She highlights the secularization of witchcraft in sixteenth-century medical writings; the work of Lepois in recognizing hysteria in men, children, and elderly people; the regression of European thinking in the post-Sydenhamian era to humoral and uterine models of hysteria; and the resexualization of the diagnosis during the later eighteenth century.[5] Moreover, Abricossoff lards her narrative with extensive and well-chosen quotations from pertinent primary sources. Perhaps because the subject of her analysis was comparatively remote in time, or because as a foreigner she had less invested in the French medical professional system, Abricossoff is the least partisan of the four writers from this period. Nonetheless, she too felt obliged to conclude her story with several paragraphs on nineteenth-century developments in which Charcot's work figures as the crowning accomplishment of a centuries-long history, chronicled now for the first time.[6]

A decade later, the politics of medical history writing shifted markedly with Gaston Amselle's *Conception de l'hystérie: Étude historique et critique* (1907). Like Abricossoff, Amselle wrote in the form of an academic dissertation.[7] However, Amselle's thesis was written at the University of

---

[5] Ibid., 14–16, 21–30, 55–71, 71–76.
[6] Ibid., 118–22.
[7] The thesis was subsequently published as Gaston Amselle, *Conception de l'hystérie: Étude historique et clinique* (Paris: Doin, 1907). See esp. pp. 1–33.

Nancy under Bernheim's tutelage. In the bulk of his work, Amselle relates the same historical episodes as Gilles de la Tourette. Likewise, in Amselle's rendition, the decisive scientization of hysteria comes with Charcot in the 1860s. But at this point Amselle departs from earlier histories. He proceeds to describe Charcot's theories as a mere continuation of the neurological tradition of Sydenham and Willis, suggesting that Charcot's work consisted only in the clinical documentation of other physician's ideas. Moreover, Amselle repeats the influential Nancean critique of the Salpêtrière school by dismissing the Charcotian model of the hysterical fit as a medically enculturated phenomenon that developed only in suggestible female patients at a single hospital. For a signal theoretical contribution to hysteria, Amselle turns, not unpredictably, to his own mentor. Amselle dedicates his thesis to Bernheim, and his version of historical events, which may well have been inspired reactively by Gilles de la Tourette and Abricossoff, ends with an encomium to Bernheim's new "psychodynamic" theory of the disorder.[8]

The last of the four early French histories is Henri Cesbron's *Histoire critique de l'hystérie*.[9] Published in 1909, Cesbron's is the only one of these early texts that devotes a scholarly, book-length study to a comprehensive history of the subject, rather than a chapter in a larger work or an academic dissertation. The longest of the texts and in many ways the most analytically sophisticated, Cesbron's history innovatively discusses hysteria from a thematic rather than a chronological perspective. Cesbron summarizes the major past models of hysteria, and he provides lengthy analyses of the writings of the Salpêtrians and Nanceans. Reflecting the psychologization of the neuroses taking place around him, he examines past medical thinking on topics such as the psychotherapeutics of hysteria, hysteria and hypnosis, hysterical mental states, and the psychogenesis of hysterical symptoms. Unlike Gilles de la Tourette, Abricossoff, and Amselle, Cesbron shows little interest in the conflict between Charcot and Bernheim; however, this is chiefly because his personal, professional, and theoretical allegiances lay elsewhere. As we learn in the preface, Cesbron earlier in his career had studied under Joseph Babinski, another prominent Charcot student and subsequently a distinguished French neurologist. Accordingly, Cesbron's study closes with an enthusiastic endorsement of Babinski's new "pithiatic" theory of hysteria as the culminant scientific product in the history of the disorder:[10] "Après avoir retracé l'histoire des erreurs," Cesbron concludes, "il était légitime de clore la biographie hystérique en exposant une doctrine de vérité. . . . Nous au-

---

[8] Ibid., 30–31.

[9] Henri Cesbron, *Histoire critique de l'hystérie* (Paris: Asselin et Houzeau, 1909).

[10] Cesbron, *Histoire critique de l'hystérie*, 299–313.

rions satisfait à notre ambition si le présent ouvrage contribuait à l'adoption définitive du *pithiatisme moderne.*"[11]

The writings of Gilles de la Tourette, Abricossoff, Amselle, and Cesbron, although read today only very rarely, are in their way impressive preliminary attempts at organizing and conceptualizing disease history. Written as they were in the wake of the Nancy-Salpêtrière controversy, these studies are unavoidably highly partisan. This first generation of writing on the subject failed to free itself from the system of patronal academic politics, then so strongly in force in the French medical world, according to which the educational and professional careers of medical students were presided over by powerful senior patrons. Each of these early works was in effect sponsored by one of the major nineteenth-century theoreticians of hysteria, and each author presented his work as a form of historical validation for their mentor's teachings.

In this light, these histories are also noteworthy for their selective exclusions. Significantly, none of the works cross-reference any of the other three titles. Neither Gilles de la Tourette nor Abricossoff acknowledge, much less discuss fully, Bernheim's work, and neither Amselle nor Cesbron deal at all adequately with Janet. Not coincidentally, Janet had failed, as the French say, to *faire école* and was not a powerful player in the world of Parisian academic politics. Still more conspicuously, if these early French historians of hysteria diverged in the comparative valuation of their medical countrymen, they were of a mind in their attitude toward foreign physicians. The work of British, German, Austro-Hungarian, and North American medical authors (including Breuer and Freud, whose *Studies on Hysteria* had appeared in 1895) are cited only very scantily, if at all.

At the same time, I suspect that these four texts express much more than medical sectarianism and scientific nationalism. It is perhaps significant that these writings appeared not during the height of the intellectual influence of the figures and theories they sought to advance but when these very ideas and theorists were in decline. It may be equally meaningful that this initial cluster of historical writings appeared when the golden French age of hysteria itself was rapidly on the wane and new psychological and psychiatric systems, whether Kraepelinian or Freudian, from the German-speaking countries were increasingly seizing the initiative within European medical psychology. In other words, the production of self-promoting, triumphalist histories of hysteria may well have been a rearguard action to preserve, commemorate, and recapture the glorious "French" phase in the history of hysteria and to secure for posterity a position of centrality for individual figures and theories within the history of that era.

---

[11] Ibid., 320; Cesbron's emphasis.

Ilza Veith and Étienne Trillat

The gradual decline of the hysteria diagnosis during the first half of the twentieth century brought a corresponding diminution of interest in the disease's history. In the half-century following Cesbron, I know of no major piece of historical writing about hysteria. Then, in 1965, the first full-scale critical intellectual history, written in English and based on the investigative and analytical techniques of professional historical scholarship, appeared with Ilza Veith's *Hysteria: The History of a Disease*.[12] No single text in the historiography of hysteria has had a wider readership.

German by birth, Veith attended medical schools in Austria and Switzerland before coming to the United States in the late 1930s. She trained in medical history as a student of Henry Sigerist at The Johns Hopkins University, where in 1947 she received the first doctorate in the history of medicine awarded in the United States. She went on to a teaching career at the University of Chicago and then the University of California, San Francisco. Veith was schooled in the German Sudhoffian medical-historical tradition of scholarship with its emphasis on the close, critical, linguistically-informed explication of historical texts. Taking Temkin's study of epilepsy as her model, she conceived of the history of disease as a scholarly, century-by-century chronicle of texts. As with Abricossoff, Amselle, and Cesbron, she paid relatively little attention to the clinical aspects of the subject and none to social, political, or cultural factors; but, by all accounts, *Hysteria: The History of a Disease* is a thoughtful, well-informed, and intelligent study. Throughout the book, Veith ranges widely though many national cultures, and she proves a splendid explicator of texts. Her book is also exceptionally well written.[13]

Veith's study has several distinguishing interpretive features. Unlike her French predecessors, Veith begins her narrative with the Egyptians of four millennia ago. She proposes that it was not the ancient Greeks but the Egyptians who first described hysterical phenomena. She reviews the works of the major Greco-Roman medical authors, which, she proposes, reveal a greater internal variety than previously realized. She provides full discussions of hysteria, witchcraft, and demonic possession in Western Europe during the late Middle Ages, and she draws on her interest in Asian medicine to include a short, interesting chapter on hysteria, magic, and the supernatural in Japan and China. By general consensus, the

12 Ilza Veith, *Hysteria: The History of a Disease* (Chicago: University of Chicago Press, 1965). See also idem, "Four Thousand Years of Hysteria," *Comprehensive Psychiatry* 12 (1971): 156–64; and idem, "Four Thousand Years of Hysteria," in Mardi J. Horowitz, ed., *Hysterical Personality* (New York: Jason Aronson, 1977), 7–93.

13 For an appreciation, see Harold Merskey, "Hysteria: The History of a Disease: Ilza Veith," *British Journal of Psychiatry* 147 (November 1985): 576–79.

strongest portions of Veith's study deal with the early modern period, in which she details the accomplishments of a series of authors from Harvey and Burton to Cullen and Pinel.

With the nineteenth century, however, Veith's account falters badly. For Veith, the main evolution in the nineteenth-century intellectual history of hysteria involved the Mesmeric tradition. Outside of this, her selection of figures is small and eccentric—it consists of Ernst von Feuchtersleben, Wilhelm Griesinger, and Silas Weir Mitchell—with a number of glaring omissions. Moreover, while earlier histories of hysteria had been designed to highlight Charcot, Bernheim, or Babinski, Veith's study is pervaded by a subtle but strong Freudian historical teleology. Authors are routinely included, excluded, and evaluated according to the degree to which they anticipated psychoanalysis, particularly the themes of psychogenesis and psychosexuality. Veith proves outstanding at ferreting out elements of these ideas in a wide range of texts, and in some instances, this perspective produces favorable results. (For example, she brings to light the work of Baglivi, whom she credits with the first recognition of the emotions as the primary cause of hysteria, and Robert Brudenell Carter's *On the Pathology and Treatment of Hysteria* of 1853.) Elsewhere, however, the perspective blinded her to the contributions of other medical figures and to the presence of important, non-Freudian theoretical trajectories. Veith closes her book with a thoughtful chapter on the early psychoanalytic theory of hysteria. Freud and Breuer's *Studies on Hysteria* of 1895 is the final work to receive consideration. With the advent of psychoanalysis, the author evidently believed that the definitive understanding of the disorder had been achieved, and the history of hysteria effectively came to an end. There is no discussion of Freud's later writings on hysteria (including the Dora case) nor of any Freudian or non-Freudian literature in the twentieth century.[14]

Almost immediately upon its appearance in 1965, Veith's study became the "definitive" history of hysteria for a generation of British and North American readers. In 1973, the influence of the book was extended with the appearance of a French translation.[15] The vast majority of the new hysteria studies rely on Veith for a basic factual grounding in the subject, oftentimes citing her book with unqualified praise. For this reason, it is especially important to keep an eye on the challenges to Veith's work, and to the intellectual-historical tradition generally, that have begun to accu-

[14] In fairness, it should be observed that in 1964, while completing her book, Veith fell seriously ill, which may explain the decline in quality in the later portions of her book. Veith has recently reflected poignantly on her illness in a personal memoir entitled *Can You Hear the Clapping of One Hand? Learning to Live with a Stroke* (Berkeley: University of California Press, 1988).

[15] Ilza Veith, *Histoire de l'hystérie* (Paris: Seghers, 1973).

mulate recently and that today are calling into question the authoritative status of her account.

In 1986, Veith's influential volume was joined by a second major intellectual history, Étienne Trillat's *Histoire de l'hystérie*.[16] Trillat is a prominent practicing psychiatrist in France who served for a decade as editor of the periodical *L'évolution psychiatrique*. He is the first senior clinician to write at book length about the subject. With a different national and professional background than Veith, Trillat not surprisingly nominates a substantially different gallery of authors and texts for his canonical tradition. Trillat's study is also far more heavily weighted toward the modern period.

Trillat opens conventionally with Plato and Hippocrates and in the first quarter of his book moves swiftly through the centuries to the late 1700s. He then devotes the remainder of his work to a close and quite original handling of the nineteenth and twentieth centuries. The reader senses no theoretical bias in Trillat's selection or interpretation of texts. But in place of Veith's Freudian *telos*, we detect a distinct Gallocentrism that consistently causes him to ignore the achievements of foreign, particularly British, authors as compared with French writers. Nevertheless, the French contribution to the history of the disorder has been so exceptionally rich that on the whole Trillat's approach serves him well. There are many delightful passages in the book: for instance, on the image of *la vaporeuse* in eighteenth-century high society and on the effects of the new Romantic image of Woman on medical thinking about hysteria.[17] Also, Trillat presents a sequence of texts that was left out entirely of Veith's study, namely the French alienist tradition of writing on hysteria—the treatises of Louyer-Villermay, Brachet, Dubois d'Amiens, Georget, Cerise, and Landouzy—from the first half of the nineteenth century.[18] His chapters on Charcot and Janet are superb.

Trillat writes as a physician-cum-historian. His presentation is less scholarly and systematic than Veith's. Throughout the book, the footnoting is skimpy, and there is no bibliography or index. Nevertheless, Trillat's study is far more informed and sensitive clinically than any of its predecessors. Throughout the account, Trillat remains cognizant of the unique nature of the doctor/patient relation in cases of hysteria. He includes a separate chapter on the elusive and continually shifting nosographical relationship between hysteria and neighboring disorders, such as hypochondriasis, epilepsy, melancholia, and neurasthenia. And he makes many perceptive observations about the impact of medical specialization on theorizing about the disorder.

[16] Étienne Trillat, *Histoire de l'hystérie* (Paris: Seghers, 1986).
[17] Ibid., 55–60, 98–100.
[18] Ibid., 100–111.

Perhaps most significantly, Trillat resists the temptation to conclude his work with Freud. After a lengthy and well-informed analysis of the hysteria concept in the complete psychoanalytic corpus, he devotes eighty pages to medical thinking about hysteria in the twentieth century up to the 1960s. Trillat brings to light a number of episodes that are most likely unfamiliar even to professional historians of psychiatry. Included are the assault on the Salpêtrian theory of hysteria following Charcot's death by Babinski, P. C. Dubois, and Jules Déjerine; the psychoanalytic writings of Karl Abraham and Sándor Ferenczi on *Kriegshysterie*; the relation of hysteria to Anglo-American psychosomatic medicine of the mid-1920s; and the resurgence of a neurological model of the disease in France and Romania during the interwar period.[19] At a time when it has become de rigueur to denigrate linear intellectual histories of science and medicine as Whiggish and old-fashioned, Trillat's volume establishes that, when the level of analysis remains high, and the story is told well, this older approach remains intellectually exciting. Furthermore, by constructing a partially alternative historical canon of authors and texts and integrating clinical concerns into his account, Trillat broadens this tradition significantly.[20]

Ancient Classical Hysteria

The history of ideas about diseases may develop in other ways too, such as through studies of individual figures, texts, and episodes. Historical scholarship in this vein is by nature specialized but may carry implications for the general intellectual history of the subject as well as the historiographical genre as a whole.

Recent writings about hysteria in the ancient Greco-Roman world provide a case in point. As we learned above, the colorful Greek origins of the term and concept "hysteria" form a standard part of nearly every historical account of the malady. In 1990, this view was ratified yet again in a full-length study of the disorder in ancient Greek and Roman medicine.[21] However, the accuracy of the conventional historical picture of classical hysteria has now been called deeply into question by the writings of Helen King.

A young British classicist, King combines in her work scrupulous lin-

---

[19] Ibid., 196–212, 243–52, 263–70, 252–60.

[20] For a third general history, important principally for its extended excerpts from the original sources, consult George Randolph Wesley, *A History of Hysteria* (Washington, D.C.: University Press of America, 1979).

[21] Roccatagliata, *Isteria*, which includes chapters on the Hippocratic texts, Plato, Aristotle, Celsus, Soranus, and Galen. See also R. Pons Bartran, "La histeria clasica y su large agonia," *Revista de Psiquiatria de la Facultad de Medicina de Barcelona*, 16, no. 5 (September–October 1989): 233–42.

guistic analysis and imaginative cultural interpretation.[22] Suspicious of traditional accounts of "Hippocratic hysteria," King returned to the pertinent Hippocratic texts. These sources consist of an entry in the Hippocratic *Aphorisms* and extended passages from two major Hippocratic treatises, *The Nature of Women* and *Diseases of Women*. The texts were originally written in the fifth century B.C., most likely by a number of authors, and then reappeared in Greek, Latin, Arabic, and Byzantine editions during the sixteenth century. The results of King's investigation are startling. King discovers that the actual term "hysteria"—that is, a noun used to designate a disease entity—never appears in these sources at all. Instead, she locates only statements regarding the *hystera*, signifying simply the uterus, and descriptions of a very loose collection of physical symptoms characterized adjectivally as *hysterikos*, meaning "of the womb" or "from the womb." The primary manifestation of the disorder as presented in these passages, King shows, is a sensation of suffocation due to pressure from an ascending uterus on the heart, liver, and lungs. This respiratory discomfort is accompanied irregularly by miscellaneous symptoms that may also appear in many different combinations and in conjunction with other sicknesses. The main sufferers from these complaints are recently widowed adult women deprived of the sexual intercourse to which they had been accustomed. There are no case histories of the illness.[23]

Moreover, these passages in the ancient texts, King continues, consist primarily of narrations of bodily events and lists of therapeutic recipes. They are not concerned with projecting causes, proposing pathogeneses, or formulating diagnostic categories. "In the [Hippocratic] gynaecological texts," she observes, "disease entities are rarely distinguished and named, but disorders are referred to by the part of the body most affected (e.g., 'When the womb moves to the liver'), or simply by the listing of their symptoms."[24] Of hysteria specifically, she remarks that "there is no attempt in the Greek text to provide a single term to cover what are largely different combinations of symptoms for which entirely different remedies are recommended."[25] In other words, according to King's analysis, we find in these writings no sense of hysteria as an integrated disease entity with a distinct nosographical identity. Nor, King establishes fur-

---

[22] Helen King, "From Parthenos to Gynē: The Dynamics of Category" (Ph.D. diss., University College London, 1985), esp. 103–118; idem, "'Accuse Not Nature': The Diagnosis of Hysteria in the Hippocratic Corpus" (Paper delivered at the Triennial Meeting of the Combined Classical Associations, Oxford, July 1989); idem, "Once Upon a Text: Hysteria from Hippocrates," in Gilman et al., *Hysteria Beyond Freud*, 3–89.

[23] Ibid., 3–11, 14–28.

[24] King, "From Parthenos to Gynē," 103.

[25] Ibid., 107.

ther, did later Greek or Roman medical writers, who spoke of *hysterike pnix*, or "suffocation caused by the womb," have such a notion in their conceptual vocabularies. "The most consistently, and inaccurately, applied disease category found in work on ancient gynecology," she concludes, "is that of hysteria."[26]

In place of the received wisdom, King meticulously reconstructs "the textual tradition of hysteria." This proves to be a series of complex, often internally contradictory ideas, images, and terminologies that accumulated through centuries of antique and medieval texts. By the sixteenth century, she shows, something with the ontological status of a disease category and a descriptive profile discernibly similar to our own clinical picture of hysteria emerged.[27] The term itself, King finds, emerged extremely late. King's researches in medical and etymological dictionaries reveal that the French adjective *hystérique* first appeared in 1568 and its English counterpart "hysterical" in 1615. The terms "hysterick," meaning a medication for the symptoms, and "hysteric," applied to a person prone to the symptoms, made their respective appearances in 1649 and 1657. *Hystérie*, the French noun for the disease, cannot be found before 1731. The first known usage of the English noun "hysteria," in a London medical journal, dates from 1801![28]

How, we ask, could such a basic historical misreading occur? King explores the question in an interesting historiographical excursus based on some impressive textual detective work. She begins by tracing the error to Veith's *Hysteria: The History of a Disease*. At the outset of her chapter on Greece and Rome, Veith stated explicitly that the appellation "hysteria" appeared for the first time in the Hippocratic *Aphorisms*.[29] Veith continues in many places in her book nonchalantly to employ modern diagnostic terminology in her discussion of texts from the fifth century B.C.[30] And where did Veith get *her* version of Hippocrates? By training, Veith was a skilled linguist with several languages at her command, but unfortunately Greek was not among them. Moreover, the full *Corpus Hippocraticum* has never been translated into English. Consequently, Veith was compelled, as her footnotes indicate, to rely on the mid–nineteenth-

[26] Ibid., 103.

[27] King, "Once Upon a Text," 28–61.

[28] Ibid., 73, n. 74; idem, "From Parthenos to Gynē," 108. In all of hysteria studies—old and new, historical and medical—I know of only a single other acknowledgement of the very late linguistic appearance of the term "hysteria." See W. Russell Brain, "The Concept of Hysteria in the Time of William Harvey," *Proceedings of the Royal Society of Medicine* 56, no. 4 (April 1963): 323, which cites dates somewhat different from King's.

[29] Veith, *Hysteria*, 10.

[30] Harold Merskey and Paul Potter lodge a similar complaint against Veith's handling of the Egyptian literature on hysteria in "The Womb Lay Still in Ancient Egypt," *British Journal of Psychiatry* 154 (June 1989): 751–53.

century French translation of the complete Hippocratic works. This translation was the work of Émile Littré, the nineteenth-century linguist, physician, and philosopher of science. King returns to Littré's ten-volume *Oeuvres complètes d'Hippocrate* and locates the gynecological treatises in volumes 7 and 8, which appeared in 1851 and 1853. These she then compares closely to earlier Greek editions of the texts.

From this exercise, King discovers that Littré's rendition of the texts themselves is reasonably accurate, but that Littré took the liberty of adding section headings over many of the passages in question and that these headings read "Hysteria." Littré's reconstruction then served as the basis for both an abridged English translation of Hippocrates in an American medical journal of the 1890s and for Veith's study in 1965.[31] King proceeds to show that, over the past thirty years, one writer after another—physician and historian, modernist and classicist alike—has depended unsuspectingly on either Veith or Littré for their knowledge of the Hippocratic doctrine of hysteria.[32] According to King's analysis, then, the Greek "theory" of hysteria as it has come down to us today is the result of a series of historical mediations: it consists of the original Hippocratic descriptions, filtered through the Galenic commentaries, recorded in sixteenth-century Greek, Latin, Arabic, and Byzantine editions, interpreted by a nineteenth-century critic/translator, and reinforced by present-day doctors and historians.[33]

The Greek texts concerning hysteria, or what Littré alleged was hysteria, are as inaccessible to me as to Veith. But King's rereading was sufficiently subversive to take me back both to Littré's volumes (which King reports are relatively reliable as descriptive symptomatology) and to the late nineteenth-century American abridgement of them, as well as to a partial rendition into English from the Greek documents which appeared in 1985 in an American medical periodical.[34] I came away persuaded by

[31] Dr. Robb, "Hippocrates on Hysteria," *Johns Hopkins Hospital Bulletin* 3 (June 1892): 78–79.

[32] Significantly, in their commentaries on Hippocrates, the early French histories of hysteria cite from Littré's translations too. See Gilles de la Tourette, *Traité clinique et thérapeutique de l'hystérie*, 2–3; Abricossoff, "L'hystérie aux XVIIe et XVIIIe siècles," 7–8; and Cesbron, *Histoire critique de l'hystérie*, 32–39.

[33] King, "Once Upon a Text," 11–14.

[34] *Aphorismes* (1851), in *Oeuvres complètes d'Hippocrate*, trans. from the Greek by Émile Littré (Paris: J. B. Baillière, 1839–61), 4, 545, no. 35; *De la nature de la femme* (1851), in *Oeuvres complètes d'Hippocrate*, 7, 312–431, paragraphs 3, 48, 49, 62, 68 73, 75, 87; *Des maladies des femmes* (1853), in *Oeuvres complètes d'Hippocrate*, vol. 8, book 1, paragraph 7; book 2, paragraphs 123–27, 151, 152, 201; Robb, "Hippocrates on Hysteria"; and James Palis, Evangelos Rossopoulos, and Lazaros Triarhou, "The Hippocratic Concept of Hysteria: A Translation of the Original Texts," *Integrative Psychiatry* 3, no. 3 (September 1985): 226–28.

her analysis. As King claims, the reader finds in these pages no coherent clinical syndrome of hysteria in the modern sense but only the most casual enumeration of symptoms, including labored breathing, loss of voice, neck pain, heart palpitations, dizziness, vomiting, and sweating.

Perhaps most surprising is to discover what is *not* described in these sources. There are no clear references to convulsions, to an arching of the back, or to the *globus hystericus*. There is no mention of hyperesthesias nor, with the exception of "a numbness of head and tongue," of anesthesias. Similarly, the only statements regarding mental or emotional states are two sentences concerning "confusion" and "anxiety." In other words, what today we see as the typical motor and sensory somatizations of hysteria and as a hysterical personality structure are almost totally absent from the Hippocratic texts. Moreover, a number of recorded symptoms, such as "a blackening of the skin," appear incoherent to the modern reader. The largest amount of space is devoted to an exotic pharmacopoeia of antidotes, all of which are intended to alleviate individual symptoms rather than any disease as a whole.[35]

To be sure, King's rereading of the classical sources is open to debate. Generations of post-Hippocratic readers have doubtlessly modernized the meaning of these writings, and it is useful to be reminded that the texts become fully intelligible only in the context of early classical Greek gynecology. At the same time, King's argument does not square with the fact that many seventeenth- and eighteenth-century commentators, long predating Littré, also ascribed the initial conception of the disorder to Hippocrates. Moreover, if the imposition of twentieth-century diagnostic models onto earlier medical systems is ahistorical, the simple noting of descriptive clinical continuities between past and present texts is surely a defensible exercise.[36] Nevertheless, the revisionist potential of King's work is profound. Her findings remind us that faulty translations can lead to interpretive error and that a historical "fact," recorded in an influential secondary source, may be endlessly replicated in subsequent scholarship. More importantly, her research suggests a reconceptualization of the ori-

[35] Furthermore, in one of those coincidences that makes us believe in a scholarly Zeitgeist, King's discoveries have received simultaneous support from other quarters. In his *Histoire de l'hystérie*, published in Paris six months after the completion of King's thesis, Trillat comments of the Hippocratic texts that "the word 'hysteria' figures nowhere in it. It has been added by Littré in the subtitles everywhere that Hippocrates devotes a paragraph to the 'suffocation of the uterus.'" Reflecting on the rudimentary symptomatology set down in these writings, Trillat suggests that the Hippocratic texts represent "a pre-history" of hysteria (*Histoire de l'hystérie*, 14 and 20.)

[36] For two recent discussions that incorporate King's findings, see Jean-Philippe Catonné, "L'hystérie Hippocratique," *Annales médico-psychologiques* 150, no. 10 (December 1992): 705–19; and Harold Merskey and Susan J. Merskey, "Hysteria, or 'Suffocation of the Mother,'" *Canadian Medical Association Journal* 148, no. 3 (1993): 399–405.

gins of the history of hysteria itself. In the long run, it may prove more accurate to see in the history of the disorder less a single, dramatic, inaugural moment worked out over two millennia than a slow accretion of meanings across the centuries, coalescing by the seventeenth and eighteenth centuries (just prior to the linguistic emergence of "hysteria") to form the full-fledged clinical picture we recognize today.

In addition, King's work highlights the ideological functions that the writing of intellectual history may serve. In a polemical passage, King argues that the systematic misreading of the classical texts over the past century and a half has not been without its motives. Littré, she proposes, who was trained medically and was a leading philosopher of positivist science during the Second Empire, wrote at a time when the medical profession in France was anxious to establish its scientific and professional credentials. "Littré read Hippocrates in his own image and in the image of the medicine of his time . . . with the explicit intention of using Hippocratic wisdom to improve the medical practice of his own day."[37] Seeking intellectual support for their own projects, King contends further, contemporary physicians have been equally eager to father the notion of hysteria onto the Greeks. In short, creating a remote and venerable historical heritage for a disease entity—especially one as elusive and mysterious as hysteria—implies the universality of the disorder, establishes the validity of the diagnostic category, and bolsters the scientific status of psychiatric medicine itself.[38]

Finally, by extension, King's findings call into question the validity of all existing narrative intellectual histories of the disease. The linear textual reconstructions of Amselle, Cesbron, Veith, and Trillat are based on the notion of a continuous, long-term record of medical texts about something called hysteria. King, however, powerfully problematizes this premise. If the Hippocratic origins of the hysteria concept cannot be confirmed, and if the received wisdom about classical hysteria is partly a latter-day positivist creation, and if the clinical syndrome can only be identified reliably beginning two and a half centuries ago, then is not the long diagnostic lineage on which these histories are predicated in danger? In ways the author herself may not realize, her work deconstructs the traditional intellectual-historical idea of "the history of a disease."

The Renaissance and Early Modern Periods

In contrast to the classical centuries, the history of ideas about hysteria during the Christian Middle Ages has received comparatively little atten-

---

37 King, "'Accuse not Nature,'" 10 and 11.
38 King, "Once Upon a Text," 64.

tion from scholars. The relative absence of occidental texts during the medieval millennium reflects of course the change in conceptualization of hysteria from a morbid natural phenomenon to a supernatural visitation. As we learned above, discussion of the subject was submerged in clerical commentary on religious ecstasy, demonic possession, and exorcism.[39] The most spectacular document to emerge from the long reign of demonological psychiatry in Europe was the *Malleus Maleficarum* of 1494. A kind of textbook of medieval misogyny, the book expounds the many physical and mental behaviors in women believed to indicate bewitchment and therefore to require punishment. Many of these behaviors have subsequently been labeled hysterical by modern, clinically oriented historians.[40]

A second focal point of recent intellectual-historical study of hysteria has been the remedicalization of the malady after the long dominance of the demonological model. A key secularizing text is Edward Jorden's *A Briefe Discourse of a Disease Called the Suffocation of the Mother*, which has recently been reissued with a superb historical introduction by Michael MacDonald.[41] Jorden (1578–1632) was a prominent member of the London College of Physicians. His book was occasioned by a highly controversial legal case that took place in 1602. A certain Mary Glover, the fourteen-year-old daughter of a London alderman, had suddenly been

[39] Paula Fredriksen, "Hysteria and the Gnostic Myths of Creation," *Vigiliae Christianae* 33, no. 3 (September 1979): 287–90; Danielle Jacquart and Claude Thomasset, *Sexualité et savoir médical au moyen âge* (Paris: Presses universitaires de France, 1985), 236–42; Hope Phyllis Weissman, "Margery Kempe in Jerusalem: Hysterica Compassio in the Late Middle Ages," in M. J. Carruthers and E. D. Kirk, eds., *Acts of Interpretation: The Text in Its Context, 700–1600: Essays on Medieval and Renaissance Literature in Honor of E. Talbot Donaldson* (Norman, Okla.: Pilgrim Books, 1982), 201–17; William B. Ober, "Margery Kempe: Hysteria and Mysticism Reconciled," in W. B. Ober, *Bottoms Up! A Pathologist's Essays on Medicine and the Humanities* (Carbondale, Ill: Southern Illinois University Press, 1987), 203–20; Phyllis R. Freeman, Carley Rees Bogarad, and Diane E. Sholomskas, "Margery Kempe, A New Theory: The Inadequacy of Hysteria and Postpartum Psychosis as Diagnostic Categories," *History of Psychiatry* 1, no. 2 (June 1990): 169–90; Helen Monica Green, "The Transmission of Ancient Theories of Female Physiology and Disease through the Early Middle Ages" (Ph.D. diss., Princeton University, 1985), chap. 1.

[40] F. A. Whitlock and J. V. Hynes, "Religious Stigmatization: An Historical and Psychophysiological Enquiry," *Psychological Medicine* 8, no. 2 (May 1978): 185–202; Nicholas P. Spanos and Jack Gottlieb, "Demonic Possession, Mesmerism, and Hysteria: A Social Psychological Perspective on Their Historical Interrelations," *Journal of Abnormal Psychology* 88, no. 5 (October 1979): 527–46; Gilbert H. Glaser, "Epilepsy, Hysteria and 'Possession': A Historical Essay," *Journal of Nervous and Mental Disease* 166, no. 4 (April 1978): 268–74.

[41] Edward Jorden, *A Briefe Discourse of a Disease Called the Suffocation of the Mother* (London: John Windet, 1603); Michael MacDonald, ed., *Witchcraft and Hysteria in Elizabethan London: Edward Jorden and the Mary Glover Case*, (London and New York: Tavistock/Routledge, 1991).

smitten by a battery of nervous symptoms, including convulsions, loss of sight and speech, and a lack of sensation on the entire left side of her body. Young Glover had recently had a violent argument with an eccentric and ill-tempered neighbor, Elizabeth Jackson, and as Glover's convulsions worsened, Jackson was accused by the Glover family of being a witch who had cast a spell over the afflicted girl. Glover and Jackson had several dramatic courtroom confrontations, in which Glover flew into hysterical fits and spoke in a bizarre nasal voice. As her symptoms became ever more theatrical, the case attracted the attention of powerful authorities in the church, the legal profession, and the government.

Jorden's *Discourse* runs to only fifty-five compact pages. Hunter and Macalpine single the text out as the work that, "for better or worse," introduced the concept of hysteria into English medicine.[42] In his prefatory remarks, made with the governmental authorities in mind, Jorden cautiously declares his belief in the reality of witchcraft. However, like Weyer, whose book he had read, he goes on to argue that many phenomena typically interpreted as signs of demonic seduction were signs of medical illness.[43] The full title of Jorden's tract reads *A briefe discourse of a disease called the suffocation of the Mother. Written uppon occasion which hath beene of late taken thereby, to suspect possession of an evill spirit, or some such like supernaturall power. Wherein is declared that divers strange actions and passions of the body of man, which in the common opinion, are imputed to the Divell, have their true naturall causes, and do accompanie this disease.* Nonetheless, Jorden's argument was unsuccessful, and Jackson was sentenced to public display in the pillory and a year's imprisonment. In a much publicized event, the Glover girl was later cured through a three-day exorcism conducted by clergymen in the family home.

Jorden's pamphlet, which he wrote in the English vernacular for public enlightenment, is a clear defense of the naturalness of hysterical phenomena in the midst of the witchcraft craze. Like Weyer, Jorden has subsequently been lauded as a pioneering medical rationalist and his book canonized in the history of hysteria. Veith also argues that Jorden pointed the way toward an ideogenic theory of hysteria and that he was the first author to recommend something like psychotherapy as treatment for the ailment.[44]

MacDonald, however, an American social, cultural, and medical historian of early modern England, offers a significant rereading of what the Mary Glover case and Jorden's little book were all about. In his extensive

---

[42] Hunter and Macalpine, *Three Hundred Years of Psychiatry,* 69.

[43] Jorden, *Briefe Discourse,* chap. 1, 1a–5a.

[44] Veith, *Hysteria,* 123.

introduction to the document, MacDonald reconstructs in scrupulous detail the social, political, legal, and religious circumstances surrounding the case. He determines that in its motives and intentions, Jorden's work was anything but a general, disinterested tract against unreason. During the late sixteenth century and the early seventeenth, the Church of England was being challenged from within by Puritan extremists and from without by Catholic critics who claimed to have the independent power to cast out devils from the possessed. The Glovers, MacDonald finds, were intensely pious Puritans, and their daughter's legal case was part of a bitter struggle that raged during the final years of Queen Elizabeth's rule between the Anglican church hierarchy and its Catholic and Puritan opponents. He discovers further that Jorden's conspectus was actually written in 1603, after the loss of the Glover case, in order to provide scientific justification for the Anglican hierarchy to intervene in future possessions and dispossessions, which Catholics and Puritans were then exploiting to win public approval and make converts. With the death of Elizabeth in 1603 and the advent of the Scottish Stuart monarchy, with its feared Catholic sympathies, these issues became still more urgent. Finally, Jorden's was only one of many polemical statements that appeared at this time, and MacDonald reprints two contemporaneous counterpamphlets that provide the immediate argumentative context for Jorden's essay. In short, Jorden's *Discourse on the Suffocation of the Mother* was deeply embroiled in the religious politics of late Elizabethan England and for all intents and purposes was conceived, written, and received as a work of propaganda.

As MacDonald notes judiciously, these facts are not incompatible with earlier readings of Jorden. To establish that Jorden's motives were to a great degree ideological does not detract from his accomplishments as a medical humanitarian or theorist.[45] This said, MacDonald's meticulous reconstruction will almost certainly change permanently our view of Jorden's role in the intellectual history of hysteria. Conventional intellectual-historical accounts have presented ideas about hysteria in a vacuum, lacking historical context of any sort except for anterior medical doctrine. In contrast, MacDonald, by demonstrating the contextual determinants of the ideas in Jorden's essay, provides a much fuller, richer, and more accurate historical picture of a canonical text. He gives us the man and the book in its time. While less radical in its implications than King's work, his writing illustrates beautifully the power of contextualizing his-

---

[45] Jorden's essay provides what is probably the fullest and most systematic symptomatological portrait of hysteria up to that time, including the first description of the *arc de cercle* position, for which the author employed the modern terms "opistotonos"(sic) and "emprostotonos"(sic). (*Briefe Discourse*, 14b).

torical scholarship to enrich and revise traditional intellectual histories of disease.[46]

The Nineteenth and Twentieth Centuries

Aspects of the history of modern medical thought about hysteria are being studied by scholars today too. Currently, nothing exists that even approximates a comprehensive intellectual history of hysteria in the nineteenth century. However, individual figures and texts from the 1800s are being addressed by the new hysteria studies. One such major figure is the French physician Pierre Briquet. Briquet (1796–1881) worked throughout his career at the Hôpital de la Charité in Paris. He was mainly recognized during his lifetime for medical research in the field of infectious diseases. However, in 1859, midway through his career, he published his eight-hundred-page *Traité clinique et thérapeutique de l'hystérie.*[47] Upon publication, P. Briquet's treatise was received respectfully by his Parisian contemporaries. In the 1880s and 1890s, the book was repeatedly praised by Charcot and was cited liberally in the histories of Gilles de la Tourette and Cesbron. However, with the rise of psychoanalysis, the book was eclipsed and has remained so for most of the twentieth century. Amazingly, there is no discussion of Briquet in Veith, and even Trillat's treatment is cursory.[48]

The last ten years, however, has seen a strong revival of interest in Briquet. Ironically, this development is not the work of French medical historians but of a midwestern American psychiatrist. In the early 1970s, Dr. Samuel B. Guze and his colleagues at the Washington Medical School in St. Louis, Missouri, in an effort to find a more workable definition (and less pejorative label) for the disorder, attempted to systematize the clinical content of the hysteria diagnosis and to rechristen it "Briquet's syndrome."[49] Guze and his colleagues define their new category as a stable

---

[46] MacDonald's reinterpretation of the Jorden text is part of a larger movement within historical studies in recent years toward a more contextualist history of ideas. See above all James Tully, ed., *Meaning and Context: Quentin Skinner and His Critics* (Princeton: Princeton University Press, 1988).

[47] Pierre Briquet, *Traité clinique et thérapeutique de l'hystérie* (Paris: J. B. Baillière, 1859). A biographical aside: in many reference works and secondary sources (including Veith and Trillat), Briquet's name is widely miscited as *Paul* Briquet. This is perhaps due to the fact that his name appears on the title page of his book simply as "P. Briquet." For the record, there existed two Briquets of note during the second half of the nineteenth century. Paul Briquet was the author of a well-known work on French educational policy in 1879. Pierre Briquet, a physician, wrote from the 1840s through the early 1880s on a variety of medical topics, including syphilis, cholera, quinine, and hysteria.

[48] Veith, *Hysteria*, 248; Trillat, *Histoire de l'hystérie*, 111–15.

[49] For the history of the concept, consult Slavney, *Perspectives on "Hysteria"*, 35–40.

but chronic polysymptomatic disorder with wide-ranging and recurrent somatic complaints that lack organic explanation; it affects primarily women and begins before the age of thirty.[50] While Guze's neologism was incorporated by the American Psychiatric Association into the third edition of the *Diagnostic and Statistical Manual of Psychiatric Disorders* (1980), it remains controversial, and currently the concept behind it is being swallowed up by the category "somatization disorder." Moreover, the term, which in fact approximates Briquet's characterization of hysteria only very roughly, is something of a historical misnomer.[51] Nevertheless, this belated, eponymous recognition of Briquet has served to arouse a new and much-needed historical interest in his work.

Chiefly as a result of the psychiatric debate over Briquet's syndrome during the 1980s, a full and linguistically accessible edition of the complete *Traité clinique et thérapeutique de l'hystérie* is now being prepared for publication.[52] With this translation into English, it is likely that Briquet will increasingly be granted a prominent place in the history of hysteria. Most of what has been discovered thus far about Briquet comes from a number of highly informative articles by François Mai and Harold Merskey. Mai and Merskey are Canadian psychiatrists with extensive first-hand experience of hysterical patients in a variety of institutional settings. In 1980, they presented in the *Archives of General Psychiatry* a detailed summary of Briquet's monograph, including sections on the etiology, symptomatology, pathogenesis, diagnosis, and prognosis of hysteria.[53] A year later, they provided a translation of selections from the *Traité*.[54] Then, in March 1982, they organized a symposium at the University of Western Ontario for the centenary of Briquet's death, out of which emerged a third paper placing Briquet in his biographical and medico-historical contexts.[55]

[50] After formulating clinical criteria for the syndrome in a number of articles during the 1960s, Guze formally proposed the term in 1970 in "The Role of Follow-up Studies: Their Contribution to Diagnostic Classification as Applied to Hysteria," *Seminars in Psychiatry* 2, no. 4 (November 1970): 401. Subsequent elaborations appeared in a series of papers in the *American Journal of Psychiatry* from 1972 to 1975.

[51] Léon Chertok, "Hysteria versus Briquet's Syndrome," *American Journal of Psychiatry* 132 (1975): 1087; Maurice Dongier, "Briquet and Briquet's Syndrome Viewed from France," *Canadian Journal of Psychiatry*, 28 (October 1983): 422–27.

[52] Pierre Briquet, *Clinical and Therapeutic Treatise on Hysteria*, trans. from the French by Dr. David V. Sheehan and C. Eugene Scruggs (work in progress).

[53] Francois M. Mai and Harold Merskey, "Briquet's *Treatise on Hysteria*: A Synopsis and Commentary," *Archives of General Psychiatry* 37, no. 12 (December 1980): 1401–5.

[54] Francois M. Mai and Harold Merskey, "Briquet's Concept of Hysteria: An Historical Perspective," *Canadian Journal of Psychiatry* 26, no. 1 (February 1981): 57–63.

[55] Francois M. Mai, "Pierre Briquet: Nineteenth-Century Savant with Twentieth-Century Ideas," *Canadian Journal of Psychiatry* 28, no. 6 (October 1983): 418–21. See also idem, "The Forgotten Avant Garde," *Trends in Neurosciences* 5, no. 3 (March 1982): 67–68.

From a reading of the *Traité* as well as from the studies of Mai and Merskey, Briquet emerges as a figure of premier importance in the history of hysteria. Briquet dismissed most previous medical commentary on hysteria as arrant nonsense. He argued strenuously against the historical association of hysteria with the female reproductive apparatus, and he reacted with angry incredulity to the revival of the uterine doctrine in the writings of Pinel, Louyer-Villermay, and their followers. In contrast, Briquet maintained that the seat of hysterical pathology was in the encephalon. He characterized the disorder as "a neurosis of the brain . . . consist[ing] principally of a perturbation . . . of the affective sensations and the passions."[56] He believed that the disorder was caused by the complex and highly individual interaction of many disparate factors, including age, gender, emotional disposition, family history, mode of education, previous physical illness, and psychological stress. He observed that the malady developed temperamentally most often in individuals with an "affective predominance." Among emotional causes, he emphasized traumatic domestic events, such as the death of a spouse, anxiety over the health of children, or physical spousal abuse. He distanced himself from what he regarded as past prejudices about the disease by repeatedly downplaying any possible etiological association with sexuality. With this in mind, he opened his study with seven extended clinical reports of hysteria in adult men, and he sprinkled his narrative with dozens of cases involving prepubertal children. In the long, piecemeal process of the declassicalization of hysteria, Briquet's book is a cardinal document.

Briquet's methodology in the *Traité* also represents a significant departure from earlier medical writing on hysteria. Previous authors had floated theories of the disorder derived from dominant medical philosophies or from only one or two representative cases. Briquet, in contrast, conducted what can only be called epidemiological research. Drawing on statistical techniques he had developed in his earlier work on cholera and syphilis, he gathered information over a ten-year period about some 430 clinical histories of hysteria. He analyzed this material for medical and sociological correlations involving age, gender, occupation, family background, social class, educational level, sexual behavior, and prior physical and mental health. With many of his patients, he collected follow-up data on their condition from six months to four years after date of discharge. Regarding the symptomatology of hysteria, Briquet believed the disorder could affect any organ system. He studied most closely abnormalities of motion and sensation. He noted the marked predilection for hysterical contractures, paralyses, and anesthesias to occur on the left side of the

[56] Briquet, *Traité de l'hystérie*, 3.

body and then calculated the percentage of lateral distributions for each category of symptom. He speculated too on the link between hysterical neuroses and social and national background. He even assembled information on the mental and physical health of the children of hysterical mothers.

The nature of Briquet's achievement is less controversial than Weyer's or Jorden's. We sense in the *Traité clinique et thérapeutique de l'hystérie* a modern medical method and worldview. Briquet brought to the subject a new clinical richness, and, with his extensive quantitative studies of hysteria, he was a pioneer of twentieth-century epidemiological and cross-cultural psychiatry. One hundred and thirty years later, physicians can agree with a remarkable number of his observations and conclusions. The recovery of his treatise represents a significant and unambiguous enlargement of the canon of texts in the intellectual history of hysteria. Within the new hysteria studies, the discovery of Briquet's work is probably the single most valuable acquisition from the clinician's perspective.

A final recent addition to the intellectual-historical tradition is Martha Noel Evans's *Fits and Starts: A Genealogy of Hysteria in Modern France*, published in 1991.[57] Around the turn of the last century, psychiatry in France, confronted simultaneously with the rise of Freudian psychoanalysis and Kraepelinian institutional psychiatry, separated from mainstream European psychological medicine. Psychiatric historiographies have reflected this secession and have been written along rather nationalistic lines. As we have seen, English-language histories tend to end with the coming of psychoanalysis, and the last French figure familiar to Anglophonic readers is typically Janet. However, in 1986 Trillat, as we have seen, extended the field of hysteria studies into the twentieth century. Now Evans, an American critic and historian of French literature and women's studies, has produced a full intellectual history of hysteria in France from the age of Charcot to the end of the 1980s.

The French, Evans notes bemusedly, have conducted something like a national love affair with the great neurosis. In the twentieth century, hysteria "has played a consistently central role in the evolution of modern psychiatry and psychoanalysis" in France, to a degree unmatched in other countries.[58] The story of hysteria in France during this period has had its own dynamic, largely untouched by contemporaneous theoretical developments in other places, except for the Freudian psychoanalytic tradition, which was itself Frenchified by Jacques Lacan. Evans discusses dozens of figures and over a hundred texts from a century of theorizing—all in all,

---

[57] Martha Noel Evans, *Fits and Starts: A Genealogy of Hysteria in Modern France* (Ithaca and London, Cornell University Press, 1991).

[58] Ibid., 6.

as interesting and substantial as any period in the intellectual history of the disease. To her great credit, in exploring these subjects she repaired personally to France for a year, where she interviewed authors, followed university seminars and lectures, and even accompanied clinical rounds.

In *Fits and Starts*, Evans serves as a well-informed guide for the reader experiencing for the first time an alien and exotic intellectual landscape. She begins with Charcot and his museum of performing hysterical women at the Salpêtrière. She continues with the early twentieth-century psychological theories of Bernheim, Janet, Paul Sollier, and Paul Hartenberg. The interwar years brought the first French psychoanalytic writings about hysteria, by A.L.N. Hesnard, René Laforgue, Marie Bonaparte, and Édouard Pichon, as well as the work of Ernest Dupré, Henri Ey, and Henri Codet. French medicine after World War II attempted to apply new somatic psychotherapies, including psychosurgery and electroconvulsive treatments, to severely hysterical patients. And Daniel Widlocher, Jean Delay, Charles Brisset, Julian Ajuriaguerra, and P. C. Racamier formulated their own theories of the neurosis during the 1950s. Evans discusses Lacan's "hysterization of psychoanalysis" during the 1950s and 1960s as well as the spate of books Lacan inspired by authors such as Monique David-Mesnard, Anne Chateau, Charles Melman, Marie-Claire Boons, and others. Following the 1968 uprisings in Paris, as Evans also shows, a large and boisterous body of writing, mostly by lay analysts, academic philosophers, literary critics, and women's studies scholars, combined feminist, Lacanian, and post-Lacanian ideas in a thoroughgoing critique of traditional psychoanalytic thinking about the disorder. And in the late 1980s French physicians created "spasmophilia," the latest and most fashionable reformulation of the hysteria concept, which is now generating a medical literature of it own. Far from having disappeared, hysteria, she establishes conclusively, is alive and well and living in the imagination of contemporary French physicians and the avant-garde Parisian intelligentsia.

Fits and Starts represents a first attempt to organize a history of hysteria in twentieth-century France. From my reading, the later sections of Evans's book, dealing with subjects close to the present, lose the admirably detached, intellectual-historical quality of earlier chapters and lapse at times into coarse politicizing. Similarly, the author's conception of hysteria history as a gendered and one-directional power exchange between helpless female patients and vindictive male physicians is overdrawn ideologically and seems to me to be undermined by many of the texts presented in her book.[59] Furthermore, Evans apparently lacks the sense of irony that many readers will feel is appropriate to her subject, in

[59] See "The Doctor/Patient Relationship" below.

view of the sensationalism and sheer loopiness of some of the theories canvassed in her book. Nevertheless, Evans's study is a singular addition to the new hysteria studies. Her innumerable, detailed, and intelligent expositions of dozens of texts by twentieth-century authors are enormously informative. And the story she relates amounts to a long, rich, and independent national history of hysteria that previously failed utterly to make it into history writing outside of France. Attuned to the subject by her professional training and political interests, Evans has reconstructed a previously unknown, or ignored, textual subtradition within the overall intellectual history of hysteria.[60]

In summation, it is likely that intellectual histories of disease will continue to retain their interest and value. They tend to be readable and chock full of factual information. Moreover, they perform the indispensable pedagogical task of setting out the basic ideational content of the history of diseases. At the same time, and despite the initial appearance of being the stablest and most consensual genre of writing, histories in this mode have been substantially enlarged, qualified, and revised over the past ten years. In particular, the roster of writers, texts, and topics projected to constitute the intellectual-historical canon has been continually reworked.

Reviewing the interpretive tradition in full, it is clear that undergirding each historical account has been a particular theoretical orientation. This orientation provides a means for authors to appraise, privilege, and prioritize themes, figures, and texts. As psychiatry itself evolves, and with it the perceived cognitive content of the discipline, the retrospective process of canon construction changes too. Behind each history of ideas is an implicit or explicit medical teleology, and behind each recovery of a new historical text is a development in contemporary medical theory that endows special precursory status on an author's writings. No doubt other figures in the history of hysteria are waiting for an appropriate contemporary context in which to be rediscovered.[61] In this regard, it is interesting to speculate on the eventual impact of the new neurosciences on hysteria studies. Despite an initial appearance to the contrary, intellectual histories of disease are no less interpretive, no less "constructed," than works in other scholarly traditions.

[60] For more on Evans's book, see "Feminist Histories of Hysteria" below.

[61] A case in point is the twentieth-century German alienist Ernst Kretschmer. Kretschmer's biological interpretation of hysteria, as an adaptive, ontogenically determined pattern of reaction, is interesting and highly original, but thus far has been excluded from historical coverage, most likely because it does not connect with any subsequent school or movement. See Kretschmer, *Über Hysterie* (Leipzig: Georg Thieme, 1923; trans. 1926), later enlarged as *Hysterie, Reflex und Instinkt* (Stuttgart: Georg Thieme, 1944).

PSYCHOANALYTIC HYSTERIA

More has been written about hysteria in the late nineteenth century than about any other segment of its history. This is due overwhelmingly to Freud and Charcot. While Freud's work certainly is not synonymous with the history of the disease in its entirety, as some psychoanalytic historians in the past believed, he is easily the single most important theoretician in the long history of the neurosis. Despite many recent critiques of psycho-analytic theory and its scientific status, Freud's place in the history of hysteria remains secure and central. In the new hysteria studies, psycho-analytic hysteria has been studied by biographers, intellectual historians, historians of medicine, philosophers of science, psychiatrists, neurolo-gists, women's historians, and literary critics. The interpretive diversity of their work is enormous.

Freud's historic encounter with hysteria forms a crucial chapter in the early intellectual history of psychoanalysis. As we learned in the short history above, during the final fifteen years of the nineteenth cen-tury Freud discarded the traditional hereditarian model of mental ill-ness, elaborated a concept of conversion symptoms, formulated a theory of the psychosexual origins of neurosis, discovered the processes of repression and defense, probed the realm of unconscious motivation, adopted and abandoned the seduction theory, stumbled toward the con-cept of the Oedipus complex, and grappled with the phenomenon of the therapeutic transference.[62] As previously noted, no medical condition was more important for his thinking on these matters than hysteria. The *Studies on Hysteria* is the first distinctly psychoanalytic text, and psycho-analysis effectively began as a theory of hysteria.[63] Within the history of

[62] Freud accomplished these things in a sequence of publications from 1886 to 1905. These include "Observation of a Severe Case of Hemi-anesthesia in a Hysterical Male" (1886), in *The Standard Edition of the Complete Psychological Works of Sigmund Freud*, trans. and ed. James Strachey, in collaboration with Anna Freud, assisted by Alix Strachey and Alan Tyson, 24 vols. (London: Hogarth Press, 1959), 1, 23–31; "Hysteria" (1888), in *Standard Edition*, 1, 37–59; "Some Points for a Comparative Study of Organic and Hyster-ical Motor Paralyses" (1893), in *Standard Edition*, 1, 155–72; "On the Psychical Mecha-nism of Hysterical Phenomena" (1893), in *Standard Edition*, 3, 25–39; "Extracts from the Fliess Papers" (1892–99), in *Standard Edition*, 1, 173–280; *The Complete Letters of Sig-mund Freud to Wilhelm Fliess, 1887–1904*, trans. and ed. by Jeffrey Moussaieff Masson (London: Harvard University Press, 1985); *Studies on Hysteria* (1895), vol. 2 of *Standard Edition*; "Heredity and the Aetiology of the Neuroses" (1896), *Standard Edition*, 3, 141–156; "The Aetiology of Hysteria" (1896), in *Standard Edition*, 3: 187–221; and *Fragment of an Analysis of a Case of Hysteria* (1901; 1905), in *Standard Edition*, 7: 1–122. For a full listing of Freud's writings on hysteria, see *Studies on Hysteria*, vol. 2 of the *Standard Edi-tion*, appendix B, 310–11.

[63] After an intensive early cultivation of the subject, Freud more or less abandoned hyste-

psychoanalysis, hysteria remains the quintessential neurosis, the primal pathology.

Broadly speaking, the historical study of psychoanalytic hysteria is composed of three subgenres of commentary. First, intellectual-historical studies explore the idea content and evolution of Freud's thinking about the disorder. The major biographies of Freud by Ernest Jones, Marthe Robert, Ronald Clark, and Peter Gay deal amply with Freud's study of hysteria.[64] A significant secondary literature is now available on the origins and early years of psychoanalysis, nearly all of which features discussions of hysteria, at times detailed,[65] while Alan Krohn has chronicled at length the history of psychoanalytic thought about hysteria from Freud to the middle of the twentieth century.[66] In addition, a burgeoning specialized scholarship scrutinizes every conceivable aspect of Freud's thinking about the neurosis, from the methodological foundations of the concept of conversion hysteria to the influence of bacteriological models of disease on psychoanalysis to the reception of *Studies on Hysteria* in the contemporary medical press.[67] As we approach the centenary of the pub-

---

ria at the turn of the century for work on other topics. ("Toute la théorie psychanalytique est née de l'hystérie," comments Trillat. "Seulement, la mère meurt après l'accouchement.") On the theoretical decentering of hysteria within twentieth-century psychoanalysis, see Daniel Widlöcher, "L'hystérie dépossédée," *Nouvelle revue de psychanalyse* 17 (Spring 1978): 73–87.

[64] Ernest Jones, *Sigmund Freud: Life and Work*, 3 vols. (London: Hogarth Press, 1953), vol. 1, *The Young Freud, 1856–1900*, chaps. 11 and 12; Marthe Robert, *The Psychoanalytic Revolution: Sigmund Freud's Life and Achievement* [1964], trans. from the French by Kenneth Morgan (New York: Avon, 1968), chaps. 4 and 6; Ronald W. Clark, *Freud: The Man and the Cause* (London: Jonathan Cape, 1980), 72–92, 130–33, 228–31; Peter Gay, *Freud: A Life for Our Time* (New York: Basic Books, 1988), 63–74, 246–55.

[65] Ola Andersson, *Studies in the Prehistory of Psychoanalysis* (Stockholm: Svenska Bokförlaget, 1962), passim; Hannah S. Decker, *Freud in Germany: Revolution and Reaction in Science, 1893–1907*, monograph 41 of *Psychological Issues* 11, no. 1 (New York: International Universities Press, 1977), chap. 2; Raymond E. Fancher, *Psychoanalytic Psychology: The Development of Freud's Thought* (New York: Norton, 1973), chap. 2; Kenneth Levin, *Freud's Early Psychology of the Neuroses: A Historical Perspective* (Hassocks, Sussex: Harvester Press, 1978), chaps. 3 and 4; Walter A. Stewart, *Psychoanalysis: The First Ten Years, 1888–1898* (New York: Macmillan, 1967), passim; Jacques Nassif, *Freud: L'inconscient: Sur les commencements de la psychanalyse* (Paris: Gailiée, 1977), part 1; Elisabeth Roudinesco, *La bataille de cent ans: Histoire de la psychanalyse en France*, 2 vols. (Paris: Éditions Ramsay, 1982), 1, 21–84; Malcolm Macmillan, *Freud Evaluated: The Completed Arc* (Amsterdam: Elsevier Science Publishers, 1990), chaps. 1–7.

[66] Krohn, *Hysteria: The Elusive Neurosis*.

[67] Michel de Certeau, "Ce que Freud fait de l'histoire: À propos de 'Une névrose démoniaque au XVIIe siècle," *Annales: Économies, sociétés, civilisations* 25, no. 3 (May–June 1970): 654–67; J. Biéder, "La 'communication préliminaire' de 1893," *Annales médicopsychologiques*, année 130, 1, no. 3 (March 1972): 401–6; Jacqueline Lubtchansky, "Le point de vue économique dans l'hystérie à partir de la notion de traumatisme dans l'oeuvre de Freud," *Revue française de psychanalyse* 37 (1973): 373–405; John E. Gedo, Melvin

lication of *Studies on Hysteria* in 1995, and therefore the beginning of the second century of Freud studies, professional interest in "the historical Freud" is stronger than ever.

The widest-ranging and most creatively conceptualized recent study of the intellectual origins of psychoanalysis is *Freud's Discovery of Psychoanalysis: The Politics of Hysteria*, by William McGrath.[68] A psychoanalytically informed cultural historian, McGrath takes as his inspirations Carl Schorske's well-known essay on politics and patricide in *The Interpretation of Dreams* and Peter Loewenberg's psychobiographical studies of political and cultural figures in nineteenth-century central European history.[69] What interests McGrath is "the interplay between [Freud's] inner world of dreams and phantasies and the outer influences of family situation, religious tradition, educational background, and sociopolitical environment."[70] Exploring these forces, McGrath peruses Freud's published and private writings on hysteria with the textual thoroughness of the literary critic. He painstakingly reconstructs the chronology of ideas, experiences, and circumstances that surrounded Freud's thinking about hysterical neurosis during the 1890s, paying particular attention to the circumstances of Freud's pivotal reformulation of the seduction theory in 1896–97. For Freud's private emotional life during

---

Sabshin, Leo Sadow, and Nathan Schlessinger, "*Studies on Hysteria*: A Methodological Evaluation," in John. E. Gedo and George. H. Pollack, eds., *Freud: The Fusion of Science and Humanism*, monograph 34/36 of *Psychological Issues* 9, nos. 2/3 (New York: International Universities Press, 1976), 167–86; Frank J. Sulloway, *Freud, Biologist of the Mind: Beyond the Psychoanalytic Legend* (New York: Basic Books, 1979), 51–69; M. B. Macmillan, "Delboeuf and Janet as Influences in Freud's Treatment of Emmy von N.," *Journal of the History of the Behavioral Sciences* 15, no. 4 (October 1979): 299–309; K. Codell Carter, "Germ Theory, Hysteria, and Freud's Early Work in Psychopathology," *Medical History* 24, no. 3 (July 1980): 259–74; Bercherie, *Genèse des concepts freudiens*, 18–101, 239–66; Benjamin B. Rubinstein, "Freud's Early Theories of Hysteria," in R. S. Cohen and Larry Laudan, eds., *Physics, Philosophy and Psychoanalysis: Essays in Honor of Adolf Grünbaum*, (Dordrecht: D. Reidel, 1983), 169–90; Isabel F. Knight, "Freud's 'Project': A Theory for *Studies on Hysteria*," *Journal of the History of the Behavioral Sciences* 20, no. 4 (October 1984): 340–58; Léon Chertok, "À l'occasion d'un centenaire Charcot: L'hystérie et l'hypnose," *Perspectives psychiatriques* 21, no. 2 (1983): 81–89; Norman Kiell, *Freud without Hindsight: Reviews of His Work (1893–1939)*, with translations from the German by Vladimir Rus and from the French by Denise Boneau (Madison, Conn.: International Universities Press, 1988), chaps. 1, 3, and 7; M. B. Macmillan, "Freud and Janet on Organic and Hysterical Paralyses: A Mystery Solved?" *International Review of Psycho-Analysis* 17, part 2 (1990): 189–203; Mace, "Hysterical Conversion I."

[68] William J. McGrath, *Freud's Discovery of Psychoanalysis: The Politics of Hysteria* (Ithaca, N.Y.: Cornell University Press, 1986).

[69] Carl E. Schorske, "Politics and Patricide in Freud's *Interpretation of Dreams*," *American Historical Review* 78, no. 2 (April 1973): 328–47; Peter Loewenberg, *Decoding the Past: The Psychohistorical Approach* (New York: Knopf, 1983), esp. 161–204.

[70] McGrath, *Freud's Discovery of Psychoanalysis*, 16.

these years, he draws on Freud's dreams from the late 1890s as recorded in *The Interpretation of Dreams* and Freud's correspondence with his close personal friend and professional confidant Wilhelm Fliess.

McGrath establishes that Freud's basic explanatory strategy in creating a new theory of the neuroses involved the use of architectural metaphors, especially metaphors drawn from Catholic medieval architecture.[71] He traces this symbolic language to a variety of public and private arenas in Freud's life. As a young and ambitious Jewish doctor in Catholic Vienna, McGrath proposes, Freud believed that his political and professional aspirations were blocked. On the cultural level, Freud connected the Catholic Church with religious, emotional, and sexual suppression. These conscious and unconscious associations in Freud's mind were reinforced by the overtly anti-Semitic clerical party of Karl Lueger, which came to municipal power in Vienna in April 1897. In McGrath's view, these realities combined in Freud's psyche with his increasing clinical familiarity with hysterical patients and his pressing need to resolve intrapsychic conflicts aroused by the death of his father late in 1896. It was these disparate observations and experiences that sensitized the future founder of psychoanalysis to the themes of neurotic defense, hysterical repression, and the role of sexuality in the etiology of the neuroses. For McGrath, the psychoanalytic theory of hysteria represents an intellectual rationalization in the most constructive sense of the word: a long and theoretically consequential effort to resolve on the level of scientific theory the oppressive personal and political circumstances of the theoretician. In place of a purely intellectual history of the origins of psychoanalysis, then, McGrath provides a provocative psychocultural portrait in which empirical observation, medical and national politics, generational rebellion, and personal neurosis conspired in the formation of Freud's thought.

A second genre of scholarship about psychoanalytic hysteria is that of speculative retrospective rediagnosis. This work, which is necessarily restricted to medical writers, takes as its object the individual hysterical patient of the past. The literature in this category is large and rather repetitive. We might take as a sample the commentary on the celebrated Anna O.—in the words of Philip Rieff, "the ur-patient of psychoanalysis."[72]

In their original presentation of Anna O.'s case in 1895, Breuer and Freud stressed the patient's motor and sensory disturbances. In their view, Anna O. suffered centrally from scattered tactile anesthesias, sporadic loss of hearing, shifting contractures of the extremities, and bizarre visual

---

[71] McGrath presents the crux of his argument in the fourth chapter of his book titled, after one of Freud's scientific drafts, "The Architecture of Hysteria" (152–96).

[72] Philip Rieff, *Freud: The Mind of the Moralist* (London: Victor Gollancz, 1959), 11.

aberrations. They interpreted these symptoms as bodily expressions of repressed traumatic memories and without hesitation diagnosed the case as conversion hysteria.[73] A number of subsequent readers have endorsed Freud and Breuer's diagnosis.[74] However, in 1952 the New York psychiatrist Charles Goshen, writing at a time when the schizophrenia diagnosis was rapidly gaining ground, published an influential article in the *American Journal of Psychiatry* proposing that all five cases in the *Studies on Hysteria* were actually misdiagnosed schizophrenic illnesses.[75] Moreover, Suzanne Reichard and Frederick Bram, in 1956 and 1965, respectively, followed Goshen in emphasizing the quasi-psychotic manifestations of Anna O.'s case.[76]

In the past two decades, Freud's classically hysterical cases have been open to continual medical reassessment along the lines of Goshen, Reichard, and Bram. In 1970, Henri Ellenberger noted the radical mood shifts of Anna O. and hinted strongly at a multiple personality disorder.[77] In 1980, Marc Hollender, a sociologically oriented psychologist, departed from the standard intrapsychic interpretations of the case to offer "an essentially person-oriented, interpersonal and psychosocial" approach. In Hollender's view, the long clinical encounter between doctor and patient had resulted from Breuer's infatuation with his young and attractive patient and Anna O.'s desire to achieve an intimate relationship with a charismatic figure from outside the family circle.[78] Around the same time, a prominent Chicago psychoanalyst decided that Anna O. had actually suffered from a toxic psychosis, probably as the result of a morphine addiction.[79] In 1981, the authors of the *DSM-III Casebook* judged Anna O.'s case a "diagnostic enigma" and proposed a series of categories for different stages of the illness, including conversion disorder, major depression, and atypical dissociative disorder.[80] And in 1982, Lind-

---

[73] Breuer and Freud, *Studies on Hysteria*, 21–47.

[74] Ola Andersson, "A Supplement to Freud's Case History of 'Frau Emmy v. N.' in *Studies on Hysteria* 1895," *Scandinavian Psychoanalytic Review* 2, no. 1 (1979): 5–16.

[75] Charles E. Goshen, "The Original Case Material of Psychoanalysis," *American Journal of Psychiatry* 108 (May 1952): 829–34.

[76] Suzanne Reichard, "A Re-examination of 'Studies in Hysteria,'" *Psychoanalytic Quarterly* 25, no. 2 (1956): 155–77; Frederick M. Bram, "The Gift of Anna O.," *British Journal of Medical Psychology* 38, part 1 (March 1965): 53–58.

[77] Henri F. Ellenberger, *The Discovery of the Unconscious* (New York: Basic Books, 1970), 482; and Adam Crabtree, *From Mesmer to Freud: Magnetic Sleep and the Roots of Psychological Healing* (New Haven: Yale University Press, 1993), Postscript.

[78] Marc H. Hollender, "The Case of Anna O.: A Reformulation," *American Journal of Psychiatry* 137, no. 7 (July 1980): 797–800.

[79] George H. Pollock, "The Possible Significance of Childhood Object Loss in the Josef Breuer—Bertha Pappenheim (Anna O.)—Sigmund Freud Relationship," *Journal of the American Psychoanalytic Association*, 16, no. 4 (October 1968): 711–39.

[80] Robert L. Spitzer et al., *DSM-III Case Book: A Learning Companion to the Diagnos-*

say Hurst, writing in the *Journal of the Royal Society of Medicine* and accentuating still a different set of symptoms, argued that Anna O. suffered most likely from either tubercular meningitis or spontaneous disseminated encephalomyelitis.[81] Other commentators have tended either to confirm the initial diagnosis of hysteria, rediagnose the case organically, or relabel it a borderline or psychotic condition.[82]

The practice of retrospective rediagnosis culminated in 1984 with *Anna O.: Fourteen Contemporary Reinterpretations*, a collection of articles contributed mainly by American psychiatrists and psychoanalysts.[83] They work from many different theoretical perspectives, and each casts a brief diagnostic *pensée arrière* on the famous proto-patient of psychoanalysis. From the vantage point of group process theory, Melvin Muroff sees the origin of Anna O.'s illness in a conflicted relationship with her father.[84] Joseph Noshpitz, a child psychiatrist, discusses the patient's developmental history, which he projects was marked by sexual inexperience and affective immaturity.[85] Taking the object relations approach popular among English psychiatrists, Gerald Gargiulo traces Anna O.'s difficulties to a disturbed relationship with her mother rather than the oedipal father.[86] Walter Stewart stresses her rivalry with her brother, who was able to escape from the closed world of the family for a fulfilling university career,[87] while Joseph Martorano, a clinical psychopharmacologist, brings out the likely biochemical bases of the patient's hysteria.[88] John P. Spiegel, a professor of

---

tic and Statistical Manual of Mental Disorders (Third Edition) (Washington, D.C.: American Psychiatric Association, 1981), 328–32.

[81] Lindsay C. Hurst, "What was Wrong with Anna O?" *Journal of the Royal Society of Medicine* 75, no. 2 (February 1982): 129–31. See also E. M. Thornton, *Freud and Cocaine: The Freudian Fallacy* (London: Blond and Briggs, 1983), chap. 8.

[82] W. W. Meissner, "A Study on Hysteria: Anna O. *Rediviva*," in *The Annual of Psychoanalysis*, vol. 7 (New York: International Universities Press, 1979), 17–52; John Wykert, "Anna O.—A Re-evaluation," *Psychiatric News* 15 (May 2, 1980): 5, 22; Else Pappenheim, "A Postscript to the Case of Anna O.," *Bulletin of the Psychoanalytic Association of New York* 18, no. 8 (1981): 15; Christopher Reeves, "Breuer, Freud and the Case of Anna O: A Re-examination," *Journal of Child Psychotherapy* 8, no. 2 (1982): 203–14; Slavney, *Perspectives on "Hysteria,"* chap. 14.

[83] Max Rosenbaum and Melvin Muroff, eds., *Anna O.: Fourteen Contemporary Reinterpretations* (New York: Free Press, 1984).

[84] Melvin Muroff, "Anna O.: Psychoanalysis and Group Process Theory," in Rosenbaum and Muroff, *Anna O.*, 71–84.

[85] Joseph D. Noshpitz, "Anna O. as Seen by a Child Psychiatrist," in Rosenbaum and Muroff, *Anna O.*, 65, 67.

[86] Gerald J. Gargiulo, "Anna O.: An English Object Relations Approach," in Rosenbaum and Muroff, *Anna O.*, 149–60.

[87] Walter A. Stewart, "Analytic Biography of Anna O.," in Rosenbaum and Muroff, *Anna O.*, 47–51.

[88] Joseph T. Martorano, "The Psychopharmacological Treatment of Anna O.," in Rosenbaum and Muroff, *Anna O.*, 85–100.

social psychiatry, discusses the twisted social and familial aspects of Anna O.'s upbringing and pronounces the patient "essentially . . . a victim of the Viennese Jewish Princess syndrome."[89] The collection continues in this vein.[90]

Even as a nonphysician, I confess to enjoying these second guesses. They require considerable diagnostic ingenuity. And for clinicians, it is probably inevitable that they reflexively make these reappraisals as they read historical psychiatric materials. However, I want to suggest that in the specifically historical study of hysteria, this line of commentary is of limited value. From my reading, the cumulative effect of this literature is neither to impress the reader with the accuracy of medical language nor to convince us of the superiority of new over old diagnostic systems, but rather to call into question the analytical procedure itself. Doctors today, no less than a hundred years ago, tend to see what they have been trained to see, and in the end, the essays in this latest anthology primarily reflect the professional training and prior theoretical persuasion of the diagnostician. In the absence of either reliable follow-up information or "hard" clinical data on Anna O.'s medical history, the debate over "what Anna O. really had" is unresolvable. Moreover, historians will bristle at the implication of a number of these articles that nineteenth-century patients such as Anna O. were initially misdiagnosed. Certainly, with changes in diagnostic nomenclature, the contemporary medical interpretation of these cases will differ from that of 1895; but the focus of historical inquiry must remain on the theory and practice of medicine a century ago, and by the shared medical criteria of the time, Anna O.'s was a classic case of hysteria. Ultimately, in my view, the recent vogue for the medical reinterpretation of Freud's famous case reports reveals more of the current and constantly fluctuating state of the diagnostic art in psychiatric medicine than about that remote and elusive target, the historical patient.

The third and final scholarly genre of psychoanalytic hysteria concerns what we might call historico-biographical reconstructionism. In 1953,

[89] John P. Spiegel, "The Case of Anna O.: Cultural Aspects," in Rosenbaum and Muroff, *Anna O.*, 57.

[90] For exercises in retrospective rediagnostics in regard to Freud's other hysterical patients, see Pierre Marty et al., "Der Fall Dora und der psychosomatische Gesichtspunkt," *Psyche* 33, nos. 9–10 (September/October 1979): 888–925; Lindsay C. Hurst, "Freud and the Great Neurosis," *Journal of the Royal Society of Medicine* 76, no. 1 (January 1983): 57–60; Clemens de Boor and Emma Moersch, "Emmy von N.—eine Hysterie?" *Psyche* 34, no. 3 (March 1980): 265–79; Else Pappenheim, "Freud and Gilles de la Tourette: Diagnostic Speculations on 'Frau Emmy von N.,'" *International Review of Psycho-analysis* 7, part 3 (1980): 265–77; W. W. Meissner, "Studies on Hysteria—Frau Emmy von N.," *Bulletin of the Menninger Clinic* 45, no. 1 (January 1981): 1–19; and idem, "Studies on Hysteria—Katharina," *Psychoanalytic Quarterly* 48, no. 4 (October 1979): 587–600.

Ernest Jones, in the first volume of his great biography of Freud, disclosed the real-life identity of Anna O. as Bertha Pappenheim.[91] Jones went on to indicate a number of new facts about the case, including that Pappenheim's treatment with Breuer had ended badly and that during their final session the patient had suffered a phantom pregnancy. Since Jones's revelations, it has become increasingly apparent that much additional information of importance can be unearthed concerning the patients in Freud's case histories. Because the scientific claims of psychoanalysis rest in large part on Freud's clinical writings, and because the number of his published case histories is small, and because the stories they relate are of high inherent interest, these works have attracted intense scholarly study. In recent years, some outstanding detective work has gone into establishing the actual identities of Freud's hysterical patients and reconstructing their social, medical, and familial worlds. With one exception—the English governess "Miss Lucy R." in *Studies on Hysteria*—the identities of all Freud's patients in his published case histories have been established. Much fascinating material is being uncovered.[92]

Remaining with the case of Anna O., the most authoritative work in this mode is Albrecht Hirschmüller's *Physiologie und Psychoanalyse in Leben und Werk Josef Breuers* (1978).[93] Building on the previous re-

[91] Ernest Jones, *The Life and Work of Sigmund Freud*, 3 vols. (New York: Basic Books, 1953–57), vol. 1, *The Formative Years*, 223.

[92] If American psychiatrists have predominated in the practice of retrospective rediagnostics, German historians have led the way with historico-biographical reconstructionism. In addition to Hirschmüller's book, see Gerhard Fichtner and Albrecht Hirschmüller, "Freuds 'Katharina'—Hintergrund, Entstehungsgeschichte und Bedeutung einer frühen psychoanalytischen Krankengeschichte," *Psyche* 39, no. 3 (March 1985): 220–40; Oskar Wanner, "Die Moser vom 'Charlottenfels,'" *Schweizer Archiv für Neurologie, Neurochirurgie und Psychiatrie* 131, no. 1 (1982): 55–68; and Oskar Wanner, "Sigmund Freud und der Fall Emmy von N.," *Schaffhauser Nachrichten* 105 (May 6, 1977): 17–19. In addition to his article on Anna O., Ellenberger, a pioneer in this genre, wrote "L'histoire d'"Emmy von N.,'" *L'Évolution psychiatrique* 42, no. 3 (July–September 1977): 519–41. Among other scholars, see the resourceful psychoanalytic sleuthing of Peter J. Swales in "Freud, His Teacher, and the Birth of Psychoanalysis" in Paul Stepansky, ed., *Freud: Appraisals and Reappraisals*, vol. 1 (Hillsdale, N.J.: Analytic Press, 1986), 3–82; and idem, "Freud, Katharina, and the First 'Wild Analysis,'" in Stepansky, ed., *Freud: Appraisals and Reappraisals*, vol. 3 (1988), 80–164. L. Z. Vogel's "The Case of Elise Gomperz," *American Journal of Psychoanalysis* 46, no. 3 (Fall 1986): 230–38 contains biographical information about a hysterical patient of Freud's who does not appear in the *Studies*. For a lively and highly literate synthesis of this scholarship, consult Lisa Appignanesi and John Forrester, *Freud's Women: Family, Patients, Followers* (New York: Basic Books, 1992), chaps. 3–5.

[93] Albrecht Hirschmüller, *Physiologie und Psychoanalyse in Leben und Werk Josef Breuers* (Bern and Tubingen: Hans Huber, 1978), now finally available in English as *The Life and Work of Josef Breuer: Physiology and Psychoanalysis* (New York: New York University Press, 1989). Hirschmüller, arguably the leading scholar of early psychoanalytic history today, is professor of medical history at the University of Tübingen.

searches of Ellenberger, Hirschmüller discovered that Pappenheim, far from regaining full health after her private treatment, as Breuer and Freud contended, had suffered serious relapses and required institutionalization at the Bellevue Sanatorium in Kreuzlingen, Switzerland.[94] In Swiss medical archives, he unearthed over a dozen previously unknown documents—including Breuer's handwritten medical report and family letters to the Bellevue hospital director—that have allowed him to piece together much of Pappenheim's later medical history.

Hirschmüller has found that Pappenheim later displayed a much severer pathology than appears in Breuer's original account. Following her sessions with Breuer in 1881–82, the patient developed mild convulsions, muscular jerks, and a severe facial neuralgia. As her mental condition deteriorated and the neurological symptoms persisted, she was placed, against her will, in the Bellevue Sanatorium. At Kreuzlingen, where she resided for four months in 1882, she received increasingly large doses of morphine and chloral hydrate. She became addicted to the drugs, and efforts to wean her from them resulted at least once in an attack of delirium tremens. Moreover, from 1883–88, following a number of attempts at suicide, Pappenheim required hospitalization four more times at a second sanatorium in the Vienna suburbs. Her primary diagnosis throughout this period remained hysteria.[95] Far from being the prototype of a successful cure of hysteria by the cathartic method, then, Anna O.'s case involved a long, painful, and protracted recuperation, punctuated by serious relapses. Psychoanalytic historians have varied widely in their reception of Ellenberger's and Hirschmüller's findings. But one thing is clear: the historical reconstruction of medical biographies has considerable potential for modifying our understanding of the origins of psychoanalysis as well as the history of hysteria.

The historical detective work of Hirschmüller and other scholars carries implications in other directions too. Despite my critical remarks above, historico-biographical reconstructionism may unearth new information that contributes to the medical comprehension of historical cases. Within recent hysteria studies, at least one piece of scholarship has combined diagnostic revisionism and biographical reconstructionism in a successful and sophisticated synthesis.

Writing in 1987 in the *Journal of the American Psychoanalytic Association*, Alison Orr-Andrawes, an American neuropsychiatrist, offers her

---

[94] Henri F. Ellenberger, "The Story of 'Anna O.': A Critical Review with New Data," *Journal of the History of the Behavioral Sciences* 8, no. 3 (July 1972): 267–79, repr. in Mark S. Micale, ed., *Beyond the Unconscious: Essays of Henri F. Ellenberger in the History of Psychiatry* (Princeton: Princeton University Press, 1993), chap. 9.

[95] Hirschmüller, *Physiologie und Psychoanalyse*, 131–71, with documents concerning the case on 348–82.

own reading of the case of Anna O.[96] Orr-Andrawes' essay integrates materials from the original case report of Freud and Breuer with the archival sources disinterred by Ellenberger and Hirschmüller, as well as with contemporary neuropsychiatric research. Orr-Andrawes begins by noting the large number of strange and acute neurological symptoms in Anna O.'s case. These symptoms, she points out, have not been explained adequately by previous psychiatric interpretations, and they suggest to her an undisclosed organic factor. She then attempts to piece together the precise symptomatological evolution of the case. She proposes that Anna O.'s peculiar periods of diurnal somnambulism—her *absences*—in fact represented the complex partial seizure activity of psychomotor epilepsy. This is a diagnosis that was unknown to European medicine in the 1880s and for which the indispensable diagnostic procedure, the electroencephalogram, was not available for another fifty years. These mild seizures, Orr-Andrawes suggests, may have been caused by a focal cerebral lesion that had previously been subclinical but was brought to symptomatological level with the death of the patient's father and her abandonment by Breuer. This syndrome, Orr-Andrawes continues, may well have been compounded by metabolic changes due to nutritional deficiencies from the patient's anorectic behavior and by a dependency on chloral hydrate. Contemporary medical research, Orr-Andrawes indicates further, has established the abnormal psychological and neurological behaviors that may follow temporal lobe epilepsy. Drawing fluently on these findings, Orr-Andrawes demonstrates that many of Anna O.'s most "psychological" symptoms may result from a mild epileptic psychosis. Alternating personality states, Orr-Andrawes notes, are also strongly associated today with temporal lobe epilepsy. Anna O.'s idiosyncratic inability to recognize faces, she adds, was in all likelihood an example of the rare neurological syndrome of prosopagnosia.

Orr-Andrawes is careful to insist that her neuropsychiatric interpretation of Anna O. does not contradict but rather complements previous psychodynamic interpretations. Citing the contemporary medical literature on the interaction of organic and psychological elements in convulsive disorders, she proposes that the most unstable but recurrent of Anna O.'s symptoms probably represented hysterical "derivatives," i.e., originally epileptic phenomena that (in symbolically meaningful ways) were prolonged or amplified functionally. As for Anna O.'s distinctive language abnormalities, the author reasons that these initially developed as a true Brocan aphasia appearing in association with an epileptic discharge but over time became functionally fixed by the patient and "incorporated

---

[96] Alison Orr-Andrawes, "The Case of Anna O.: A Neuropsychiatric Perspective," *Journal of the American Psychoanalytic Association* 35, no. 2 (1987): 387–419.

into her repertoire of conversion symptoms."[97] In conclusion, where Breuer and Freud saw a pure conversion hysteria, and latter-day commentators a random assortment of neurotic and psychotic phenomena, Orr-Andrawes presents a complicated but "intelligible and consistent neurological picture" in which a large number of pieces of the clinical puzzle fall into place.[98]

Of course, Orr-Andrawes' formulation, like the others, remains speculative. We are unable to evaluate her hypothesis definitely because, again, we do not possess drug charts, an autopsy report, or electroencephalographic printouts for the patient. In the long run, her essay too may only reflect current medical enthusiasms—in this instance, for the neurobiological reinterpretation of psychodynamic material.[99] However, while previous writing in this category has been exclusionary—that is, has been designed to correct or cancel earlier interpretations—Orr-Andrawes' work is integrative. Other writers have tended toward the mechanical application of preselected diagnostic labels. In contrast, Orr-Andrawes draws selectively on the three extant subtraditions of research about psychoanalytic hysteria to provide an intricate, symptom-by-symptom reconstruction of the case that combines classic psychoanalytic concepts, the latest available historical data, and the most up-to-date findings of psychopharmacology and the neurosciences. Hers is an example of the sort of exciting new work in hysteria studies that may be accomplished through a careful, cross-disciplinary combination of materials and methodologies.

FEMINIST HISTORIES OF HYSTERIA

To a very great extent, the history of hysteria is composed of a body of writing by men about women. Inherent in this simple historical fact is the basis for the largest, most active, and most transformative interpretive tradition within the new hysteria studies, the feminist tradition.

In earlier historical writings, the fundamental male-female dimensions of hysteria went unexamined. Astonishing as it seems in retrospect, the element of gender in this most gendered of psychodiagnostic categories was entirely absent from prefeminist historical narratives. Even early hysteria historians who were women—Abricossoff, Wettley, and Veith—said little or nothing about the intersexual aspects of the disorder. Equally significant, intellectual histories of disease have rested on a number of

---

[97] Ibid., 408.

[98] Ibid., 412.

[99] Furthermore, her study is open to reinterpretation by other physicians using her own methods. See Harold Merskey, "Anna O. Had a Severe Depressive Illness," *British Journal of Psychiatry* 161 (August 1992): 185–94.

methodological and conceptual premises that implicitly eschewed a sociological approach to the subject. They construed hysteria as a real pathological entity that was fixed and universal in the natural world through time. And they envisioned the history of the disorder as an accumulation of clinical observations and theoretical ideas about that entity. In addition, histories of medical thought presented the work of doctors in strictly internalist terms. Physicians were regarded as the objective recorders of empirical data and, unlike nonscientific intellectuals, were thought to be immune from social, cultural, and political contamination. Present latently in intellectual-historical accounts was also the belief that advances over time in understanding the disease as a matter of course brought benefits to individuals afflicted with it. Over the past two decades, these assumptions have been called deeply into question by the feminist historiography of medicine.

Feminist scholarship entails a fundamental reconceptualization of medical history. Historians and critics in this tradition challenge the internalist historiographical model of previous generations as intellectually uninteresting and ideologically self-serving. They contend that an array of subjective, extraneous, nonscientific factors has been decisively at work in the making of past medical theories and practices and that an account of these factors is best rendered by nonmedical specialists. According to their revisionist sociological analyses, many theories of disease have masqueraded rhetorically as objective, empirical science while in fact serving functions of social control. Moreover, many feminist commentators reject what they perceive as the elitist emphasis of earlier history writing about great doctors and their theories and seek in its place the historical experience of the common (female) patient. As an alternative reading of the medical-historical record, the feminist interpretive tradition functions implicitly as a critique of all previous scholarly literatures (themselves the product of another male-dominated profession) and the often masculinist assumptions embedded in that writing.

From the mid-twentieth century onward, feminist theoreticians and women's historians have been drawn to the history of psychiatry and women's mental health as meaningful sites for revisionist historical study. Significantly, several foundational texts of modern European feminism, such as Viola Klien's *The Female Character: History of an Ideology* (1946) and Simone de Beauvoir's *The Second Sex* (1949), addressed the historical role of science and medicine, with specific attention to psychiatry, in providing intellectual justification for female subordination.[100] The

---

[100] Viola Klein, *The Female Character: History of an Ideology* (London: Kegan Paul, Trench, Trubner, 1946), chaps. 3, 4, 5, 7; Simone de Beauvoir, *The Second Sex* [1949], trans. H. M. Parshley (New York: Knopf, 1976), chap. 2.

same theme was sounded in influential American feminist writings during the 1960s, including Betty Friedan's *The Feminine Mystique* (1963), Kate Millett's *Sexual Politics* (1969), and Germaine Greer's *The Female Eunuch* (1970).[101] Similarly, within the university, the first wave of writings by women's historians seized upon topics such as birth control, medical attitudes toward sexuality, obstetrics and gynecology, and the nervous and mental diseases of women. Today, a full-fledged feminist historiography of psychiatry has developed while feminist scholarship on other branches of the history of science and medicine is growing rapidly.[102]

As the most dramatic and infamous of "women's diseases," hysteria in particular seems to cry out for sociological analysis. At the core of the feminist reinterpretation is the view of the disorder and its history as a kind of cross-gender portraiture. From its alleged origins in the writings of ancient Egypt and Greece to present-day psychiatric writings, hysteria may be interpreted as a key medical metaphor for *la condition féminine*.[103] Through centuries of medical writing, the disorder represented in the descriptive language of the clinic everything that men found irritating or irascible, mysterious or unmanageable, in the opposite sex. The wildly shifting physical symptomatology of the disease was thought by many observers to mirror the irrational, capricious, and unpredictable nature of Woman. The exaggerated emotionality of the hysterical female was viewed as a pathological intensification of natural feminine sensibility itself, and the hysterical fit was perceived as a sort of spasm of hyperfemininity, mimicking both childbirth and the female orgasm. Throughout much of medical history, hysteria has represented, quite literally, an *embodiment* of female nature in the eyes and minds of male observers.[104]

If feminist scholars interpret the record of hysteria itself as a reading of femininity, precisely what that reading consists of has varied greatly. In ancient medicine, hysteria (if hysteria it be) took its very name from the uterus. Paola Manuli has argued that classical gynecological theorists, reasoning synecdochically, achieved social and sexual domination over women by reducing them in scientific theory to a single reproductive organ. The *donna matrice*, or "womb woman," of ancient Greece and

[101] Betty Friedan, *The Feminine Mystique* (New York: Norton, 1963), chap. 5; Kate Millett, *Sexual Politics* (Garden City: Doubleday, 1969), 176–220; Germaine Greer, *The Female Eunuch* (London: Paladin Grafton Books, 1970), passim.

[102] For an intelligent and informative account of this scholarship, see Nancy Tomes, "Feminist Histories of Psychiatry," in Mark S. Micale and Roy Porter, eds., *Discovering the History of Psychiatry* (New York: Oxford University Press, 1993), chap. 19.

[103] Beret E. Strong, "Foucault, Freud, and French Feminism: Theorizing Hysteria as Theorizing the Feminine," *Literature and Psychology* 35, no. 4 (Winter 1989): 10–17.

[104] On the body of the female hysteric as a "semiotic body" whose gestures and physical symptoms can be "read," see the provocative analysis in Peter Brooks, *Body Work: Objects of Desire in Modern Narrative* (Cambridge: Harvard University Press, 1993), chap. 8.

Rome was little more than a characterless appendage of her most unruly anatomical organ.[105] In demonological psychiatry, the image took on more aggressively misogynistic forms. The historical witch/hysteric was pictured as innately and actively evil—a sinister and sexually rebellious creature who threatened the social and moral order and demanded official censorship.[106] And in Jorden's tract of 1603, hysteria appeared as "the suffocation of the Mother," again linking the disease primarily, and primordially, with disturbed female generative power.

During the modern period, the pathological portrait shifted again. Canvassing German-language medical writing on hysteria during the nineteenth century, Regina Schaps detects a fluctuation between the representations of Woman as *femme fatale* and *femme fragile*.[107] In contemporaneous French writings, Jacqueline Carroy-Thirard locates four recurrent images of the hysterical female: the treacherous and deceitful woman, the victim of excessive emotional sensibility, the fanatical *religieuse*, and the hysteric as nymphomaniac.[108] Similarly, Wendy Mitchinson examines the Canadian medical press during the same period and finds a highly biologized depiction of the hysteric. Here, the female body was imaged as an exquisite set of structures and processes that with many sexual behaviors and at every stage of the life cycle—puberty, pregnancy, childbirth, menopause—was prone to malfunction. All women were hysterics *in potentia*, the victims of overly evolved and hypersensitive nervous and reproductive systems who by natural endowment could at any moment slide into sickness.[109] The derogatory diagnostic delineation of women extends into our own century too. Feminist psychologists have argued plausibly that the category of the "hysterical personality type," which was prevalent in mid–twentieth-century American psychiatric discourse, functioned in part as a vehicle of gender ideology.[110] From the

[105] Paola Manuli, "Donne mascoline, femmine sterili, vergini perpetue. La ginecologia greca tra Ippocrate e Sorano" (1983), cited in King, "From Parthenos to Gynē," 113. See also Aline Rousselle, "Images médicales du corps: Observation féminine et idéologie masculine: Le corps de la femme d'après les médecins grecs," *Annales: Économies, sociétés, civilisations* 35, no. 5 (September–October 1980): 1090 and 1109–11.

[106] Carol F. Karlsen, *The Devil in the Shape of a Woman: Witchcraft in Colonial New England* (London: Norton, 1987), 253–57; Barbara Ehrenreich and Deirdre English, *Witches, Midwives, and Nurses*, Glass Mountain Pamphlets (Old Westbury, N.Y.: Feminist Press, 1973).

[107] Regina Schaps, *Hysterie und Weiblichkeit: Wissenschaftsmythen über die Frau* (Frankfurt: Campus, 1982), 138–44.

[108] Jacqueline Carroy-Thirard, "Figures de femmes hystériques dans la psychiatrie française au 19e siècle," *Psychanalyse à l'université* 4, no. 14 (March 1974): 313–23.

[109] Wendy Mitchinson, "Hysteria and Insanity in Women: A Nineteenth-Century Canadian Perspective," *Journal of Canadian Studies* 21, no. 3 (Fall 1986): 87–105.

[110] Bart and Scully, "The Politics of Hysteria: The Case of the Wandering Womb," in Edith S. Gomberg and Violet Franks, eds., *Gender and Disordered Behavior: Sex Differ-

technical world of medical terminology, these images spread to other areas of popular culture.[111]

In each of these instances, disease pictures of hysteria have served as representations by men of women in a state of ill health. But where, feminist scholars inquire today, does the pathology lie? In the neurotic and suffering female? Or in the defensive and pathologizing male diagnostician? It may well lie in the relationship between the two. The British neurologist Eliot Slater observes that the hysteria diagnosis denotes "a disorder of the doctor-patient relationship. It is evidence of noncommunication, of a mutual misunderstanding" between the main figures in the clinical encounter.[112] Likewise, the French classicist Danielle Gourevitch defines hysteria as "the disease . . . of women in their relationship to men."[113] And was it perhaps with hysteria in mind that Jacques Lacan once observed gnomically that "la femme est le symptôme de l'homme?"[114] Past medical writing about hysteria, feminist analyses emphasize, has been a rich projective screen for male feelings of anger and anxiety toward women. Equally, the history of such writing expresses the immense incomprehension between the sexes through the ages. Hysteria is at once a sign of the powerful stigmatizing potential of medical science directed toward a disempowered social group and a symbol of the limit of male knowledge about the opposite sex.

Early Studies: The History of Hysteria as Medical Victimology

Insofar as I have been able to determine, the first piece of palpably feminist writing about the history of hysteria appeared in an article by the Swiss-German medical historian Esther Fischer-Homberger in 1969.[115] Possibly reacting against Veith's 1965 study, Fischer-Homberger sets out simply to document what she perceives as the heritage

---

ences in Psychopathology (New York: Brunner/Mazel, 1979), 366–78; Harriet E. Lerner, "The Hysterical Personality: A 'Woman's Disease,'" *Comprehensive Psychiatry* 15, no. 2 (March/April 1974): 157–64; and Marcie Kaplan, "A Woman's View of DSM-III," *American Psychologist* 38, no. 7 (July 1983): 786–92, with critical discussion of Kaplan's article on 793–803. For an informed defense of the diagnosis, see Slavney, *Perspectives on 'Hysteria,'* chaps. 8 and 9.

111 For instance to film. On the cinematic representation of the hysterical woman, consult Charles E. Wells, "The Hysterical Personality and the Feminine Character: A Study of Scarlett O'Hara," *Comprehensive Psychiatry* 17, no. 2 (March/April 1976): 353–59.

112 Eliot Slater, "What Is Hysteria?" in Roy, *Hysteria*, 40.

113 Danielle Gourevitch, *Le mal d'être femme: La femme et la médecine dans la Rome antique* (Paris: Société d'édition "Les Belles Lettres," 1984), 127.

114 Cited in Gérard Wajeman, "Psyché de la femme: Note sur l'hystérique au XIXe siècle," *Romantisme: Revue du dix-neuvième siècle* 13–14 (1976): 65, n. 7.

115 Esther Fischer-Homberger, "Hysterie und Misogynie—ein Aspekt der Hysteriegeschichte," *Gesnerus* 26, no. 1/2 (1969): 117–27.

of misogynistic sentiment embodied in medical writings about the disease.

The antiwoman bias in the history of hysteria, Fischer-Homberger estimates, has ebbed and flowed through the ages, reaching high points in Platonic and Hippocratic theory, medieval and early modern writing about witchcraft, and late nineteenth-century medical literature from the Continent. In an idea that later social historians would return to, Fischer-Homberger proposes that the swell of medical interest in hysteria during the later nineteenth century was a hostile response, in the realm of diagnostic theory, to the emergent women's movement. She also advances the idea that the hysteria diagnosis through the generations has served simultaneously to stigmatize women as weak or wicked and to protect them from blame or malice by explaining their undesirable traits as the result of an illness beyond the control of the individual.[116] As elsewhere in the history of psychiatry, protection and pathologization have gone hand in hand. Fischer-Homberger speculates further that the past application of the hysteria label has frequently functioned as a channeling into "rationalized" theoretical form of older, more active and persecutory forms of the male hatred of women. Written on the verge of the feminist and Foucauldian transformations in historical studies, Fischer-Homberger's essay offers a kind of capsule intellectual history of medical misogyny written by a professional medical historian.[117]

The first feminist writing about hysteria's history in the English-speaking academic world appeared early in the 1970s, as growing numbers of women graduate-schooled in the activist sixties acquired faculty positions and began to publish. Without exception, the first wave of women's historians concentrated on the experience of middle-class females in Victorian Britain and America, a period and social class in which the genderization of the diagnosis was believed to be especially pronounced.

Ann Douglas Wood's "'The Fashionable Diseases': Women's Complaints and Their Treatment in Nineteenth-Century America" is emblematic of this early phase.[118] Wood's essay, which came out of the first Berk-

[116] Fischer-Homberger writes of "diese beschimpfend-entschuldigende soziologische Doppelfunktion der Diagnose Hysterie," "this insulting-excusing sociological double-function of the hysteria diagnosis" (117).

[117] This article initiated a sharp turn to feminist medical history writing within Fischer-Homberger's career. See her later collection of essays, *Krankheit Frau und andere Arbeiten zur Medizingeschichte der Frau* (Bern: Hans Huber, 1979).

[118] Ann Douglas Wood, "'The Fashionable Diseases': Women's Complaints and Their Treatment in Nineteenth-Century America," *Journal of Interdisciplinary History* 4, no. 1 (Summer 1973): 25–52, repr. in Mary S. Hartman and Lois Banner, eds., *Clio's Consciousness Raised: New Perspectives on the History of Women* (New York: Harper and Row, 1974), 1–22.

shire Conference on Women's History in 1973, was cast in what two women's historians at the time called the "male oppression model."[119] Scholarship in this mold emphasizes the manifold ways in which bourgeois women in the 1800s were victimized by "the male medical establishment." It tends to reject the knowledge claims and therapeutic rhetoric of nineteenth-century doctors and to interpret the very idea of hysteria as a self-serving, sex-role stereotype designed to maintain the social and sexual status quo. Several themes recur in this literature: the condescending authoritarianism of male doctors toward their female patients; the tacit collusion of doctors, husbands, and fathers in controlling rebellious womenfolk; the combination of fear, desire, and hostility in the male response to women; and the widespread reality of abusive practices, most egregiously gynecological violence, in the treatment of female nervous disorders. Methodologically, Wood, drawing on the new social-historical techniques of her day, integrates printed medical texts with the letters, diaries, and fictional and autobiographical writings of female patients. Furthermore, she concentrates on a group of well-known female authors, including Charlotte Perkins Gilman, Alice James, and Jane Addams, who suffered from hysteria and neurasthenia and were either institutionalized psychiatrically or treated by well-known private nerve doctors.[120]

In Wood's 1973 study, writing historically about hysteria is essentially an exercise in unmasking the hidden sexist dimension in past medical writings and practices. This is doubtless a necessary preliminary stage for a new revisionist methodology. Nevertheless, almost immediately upon its appearance, the victimization model was crisply criticized from within the feminist camp.[121] Responding directly to Wood in the same periodical, Regina Markell Morantz disputes the idea that all medical thinking about women's nervous and mental illnesses in the nineteenth century can be reduced to covert or unconscious woman-hating. Wood's work, Morantz argues, introduces valuable historical themes and sources but by and

---

[119] Hartman and Banner, *Clio's Consciousness Raised*, vii.

[120] Other writings from the seventies in this category include Barbara Ehrenreich and Deirdre English, *For Her Own Good: 150 Years of the Expert's Advice to Women* (New York: Anchor Press/Doubleday, 1978); G. J. Barker-Benfield, *The Horrors of the Half-Known Life: Male Attitudes toward Women and Sexuality in Nineteenth-Century America* (New York: Harper Colophon, 1976); and Ben Barker-Benfield, "Sexual Surgery in Late Nineteenth-Century America," *International Journal of Health Services* 5, no. 2 (1975): 279–98.

[121] Regina Markell Morantz, "The Perils of Feminist History," *Journal of Interdisciplinary History* 4, no. 4 (Spring 1973): 649–60. See, too, Morantz's review of Barker-Benfield's book in *Bulletin of the History of Medicine* 51, no. 2 (Summer 1977): 307–10, as well as Gail P. Parsons, "Equal Treatment for All: American Medical Remedies for Male Sexual Problems: 1850–1900," *Journal of the History of Medicine and Allied Sciences* 32, no. 1 (January 1977): 55–71.

large is overstated ideologically. Moreover, Morantz, a social historian with a background in medical history, challenges several components of Wood's argument; specifically, that doctors rather than patients were to blame for their nervous suffering, that male patients were treated better than female patients, and that female physicians practiced a more humane and effective therapeutics than their male counterparts. Despite its evident ideological gratifications, Morantz polemicized in 1973, historical victimology tends to constrict interpretation. "Surely to view the existence of Victorian women solely from the perspective of male domination has become a sterile and tedious line of inquiry," she concludes.[122]

Scholarship occasionally continues to appear, even today, in the male oppression mode.[123] In the main, though, most women's historians, learning from the Wood-Morantz exchange, abandoned this approach and have been much more prone to take the gender bases and biases of past medical literature less as the conclusion of their work than as a working premise for other lines of inquiry. Barely launched, feminist hysteria studies engaged in a sharp internal debate that reoriented its course at the outset.

Hysteria, Social History, and the Social Sciences

In 1972, the American psychologist Phyllis Chesler published her scorching antipsychiatric critique *Women and Madness*.[124] That same year, the social historian Carroll Smith-Rosenberg singlehandedly elevated the feminist historiography of hysteria to a more sophisticated analytical level. Smith-Rosenberg accomplished this with her highly influential article "The Hysterical Woman: Sex Roles and Role Conflict in Nineteenth-Century America."[125] Smith-Rosenberg's contribution, in what may still be the single most significant piece of feminist writing on hysteria, was to redefine the basic terms of the historical debate. More than Fischer-Homberger or Wood, Smith-Rosenberg firmly brought the discussion of

[122] Regina Morantz, "The Lady and Her Physician," in Hartmann and Banner, *Clio's Consciousness Raised*, 50–51.

[123] For a recent and particularly heavy-handed example, there is Jeffrey M. Masson, *A Dark Science: Women, Sexuality, and Psychiatry in the Nineteenth Century* (New York: Farrar, Straus and Giroux, 1986), with a preface by Catharine MacKinnon. In the introduction to his book, Masson likens nineteenth-century writing on women's nervous afflictions to latter-day pornography, equates the pelvic examination of female patients to rape, and characterizes the labels "witch" and "hysteric" as "yet another example . . . of the unrestricted violence that men have unleashed against women throughout history" (14).

[124] Phyllis Chesler, *Women and Madness* (New York: Avon Books, 1972).

[125] Smith-Rosenberg, "The Hysterical Woman: Sex Roles and Role Conflict in 19th-Century America," *Social Research* 39, no. 4 (Winter 1972), 652–78, recently reprinted with minor changes in Smith-Rosenberg, *Disorderly Conduct*, 197–216, 330–35.

hysteria from medical and literary history into the new domain of social history. She shifted the focus of analysis from the professional diagnostician and his malevolent motives to the patient's behavior and its contemporary social and psychological meanings. She also highlighted the importance and distinctive nature of the relationship between doctor, hysterical patient, and family.

Smith-Rosenberg's essay consists of three interlocking theses. Freud had located the origins of Victorian hysteria in the restrictive social and sexual codes of the day, while the first feminist critics traced it to the direct social, legal, and political oppression of women.[126] As her subtitle suggests, Smith-Rosenberg conceptualizes the source of the problem more complexly, in the discontinuity of gender roles foisted upon middle-class women in the nineteenth century. In contrast to Wood, Smith-Rosenberg concurs with Victorian physicians that hysteria a century ago involved real neurotic suffering on the part of women, but she sees these maladies as the result of a pathogenic disparity between the prevailing ideals of Woman as delicate and feminine object of courtship and strong, pain-bearing, and self-sacrificing wife and mother.[127] In the spirit of the new interdisciplinary history of the 1970s, Smith-Rosenberg deepened her analysis by drawing on ideas from the social and psychological sciences of the day, particularly psychoanalytic ego psychology, which she had studied professionally.

In the second level of her argument, Smith-Rosenberg applies the concepts of "the sick role" and "illness behavior," borrowed from recent American sociology, to a concrete historical setting. She maintains that, while hysteria was the outcome of an unbearable ambivalence of gender roles, the disorder also functioned as a passive form of resistance against this same sex/gender system. In psychoanalytic terms, the hysterical illness of the Victorian middle-class woman had an evident, if unconscious, "secondary gain." It was a desperate "flight into illness" that allowed women to resist prescribed gender roles by moving literally within the space of the *domus* from the kitchen, nursery, and marital bedroom to the sickroom. Making an interpretive move that would appear often in later feminist literature, Smith-Rosenberg viewed hysteria as double-edged: the Victorian hysterical female was both "product and indictment of her culture."[128]

[126] Sigmund Freud, "'Civilized' Sexual Morality and Modern Nervous Illness" (1908), in *Standard Edition*, 9: 177–204.

[127] For a later statement of this view by a nonhistorian, see Krohn, *Hysteria*, 156–211.

[128] Thus the French feminist critic Catherine Clément describes hysteria as "femininity in revolt . . . along with the historical fetters that enclose it on all sides" ("Enclave/Esclave," in Isabelle de Courtivron and Elaine Marks, eds., *New French Feminisms: An Anthology* [Amherst: University of Massachusetts Press, 1981], 133). Juliet Mitchell likewise observes

Following her analysis of the hysterical victim, Smith-Rosenberg turns to the social and professional place of the physician. This is the third element of her argument and one that has subsequently received less attention. At a time when other scholars were dwelling on the exploitative nature of the doctor/patient relationship, Smith-Rosenberg envisioned the role of the medical man as more complicated and conflicted. Doctors at the time responded to hysterical women, she suggests, with frustration, since they were generally unable to treat these cases successfully, and with insecurity, as a threat to their professional authority. At the same time, she perceives that doctors were "unwitting accomplices" in the game. By officially diagnosing the complaints of women as medical illnesses and attentively ministering to them, Victorian physicians were in a real sense valorizing the chosen sick role of the hysterical woman and, as it were, siding with the female patient against husband and family.[129] Drawing selectively and imaginatively, then, on new methodological perspectives within Anglo-American historical studies and social sciences of the 1960s and early 1970s, Smith-Rosenberg's essay provides the first full psycho-sociological portrait of the nineteenth-century hysteric and her doctor. It is a portrait that is sensitive, discerning, and somewhat tragic.

Hysteria and Anglo-American Feminist Literary History

In Britain and the United States, the second half of the 1970s was marked by the widespread citation of Smith-Rosenberg's article and the progressive attenuation of the victimization model. This was followed by the appearance of a number of new disciplinary perspectives on the feminist study of hysteria. Up to this time, feminist scholars had united medical history, social history, psychoanalytic studies, and the social sciences. The 1980s brought the fusion of hysteria studies and Anglo-American literary history.

To date, the most substantial work along these lines is Elaine Showalter's *The Female Malady: Women, Madness, and English Culture, 1830–1980*.[130] Showalter's book, which appeared in 1985, has received a wide readership and introduced many English-language readers to the feminist

---

that "hysteria is the woman's simultaneous acceptance and refusal of the organisation of sexuality under patriarchal capitalism. It is simultaneously what a woman can do both to be feminine and to refuse femininity" (*Women: The Longest Revolution* [London: Virago, 1984], 289–90).

[129] Smith-Rosenberg, "The Hysterical Woman," in *Disorderly Conduct*, 209ff.

[130] Elaine Showalter, *The Female Malady: Women, Madness, and English Culture, 1830–1980* (New York: Pantheon, 1985). Showalter is a prominent literary historian at Princeton University with interests in women's literature and the social and cultural history of psychiatry.

reinterpretation of psychiatry's past. It is the first attempt to address the subject broadly and synthetically. Showalter's goals are to write "a feminist history of madness," by which she means an account of the actual experience of women suffering mental maladies, and "a cultural history of madness as female malady," or the representational history of mad and nervous women as recorded in literary and visual texts.

The Female Malady ambitiously surveys these subjects across a century and a half. For Showalter, hysteria is "the quintessential female malady," reflecting changing gender prejudices through successive epochs.[131] In the writings of nineteenth-century British institutional psychiatrists, she finds that ostensibly objective commentary about hysteria, chlorosis, neurasthenia, and anorexia was in fact powerfully prescriptive of social and moral values. Professional discourses on the nervous disorders painted a picture of the sexes as having fundamentally different human natures, which in turn provided the theoretical underpinning for a society of "separate spheres." Showalter also introduces the idea that the hysteria diagnosis was employed during this period as a sort of punitive psychopathological labeling. Women in Victorian and Edwardian England who flouted conventional gender roles by, say, agitating for the vote, seeking advanced education, or filing for divorce were frequently subjected to the diagnosis. Construing these "aberrant" gender behaviors as psychological sickness was a way of explaining and controlling them. As for the hysterical patients themselves, Showalter interprets their actions as passive antipatriarchal protests in the symbolically encoded language of the physical symptom.[132]

Showalter also considers Freud's hysterical patients. Departing from earlier feminist critics, she interprets *Studies on Hysteria* as an innovative and progressive statement in the history of hysteria. The work of Freud and Breuer, she points out, evinced at least partial awareness of the social genesis of neurotic illness. And while other medical accounts retailed images of hysterical women as weak-willed and contemptible figures, the cases in *Studies on Hysteria* offered full and sympathetic clinical portraits of believable, individualized, and intellectual women. Furthermore, she argues, these early psychoanalytic explorations specifically refuted one of the great intellectual evils of Victorian psychological medicine, the deterministic doctrine of degeneration. In so doing, Showalter claims, Freud and Breuer contributed decisively to a transition from the highly moralized and gender-differentiated psychologies of the time to the "psychiatric modernism" of the twentieth century. However, Showalter interestingly proposes a split in Freud's work between the compassion and

131 Ibid., 129.
132 Ibid., 129–34, 162–64.

intellectual openness of the *Studies on Hysteria* and the forced theorizing and abusive treatment on display in the case of Dora six years later.[133]

Since 1985, Showalter's main thesis concerning the feminization of madness in nineteenth-century Britain has been challenged persuasively by medical historians.[134] In a related criticism, it has been pointed out that Showalter often makes the mistake of equating literary representations of female insanity with the actual lived experiences of historical women. Still, her literate, intelligent, and elegant synthesis clearly provides the next step in the development of the feminist historiography of hysteria. Far more successfully than any text before it, *The Female Malady* integrates medical and nonmedical sources, and subsequent historical studies of gender, medicine, and science complement the book beautifully.[135] Perhaps most important in the long run, the bold chronological sweep of Showalter's study points the way toward a full feminist history of hysteria, which henceforth becomes an increasingly feasible project.[136]

The History of Hysteria and Lacanian Psychoanalysis in France

Concurrent with, but wholly independent of, the work of American feminist critics and historians during the 1970s and 1980s were developments in France. Avant-garde Parisian intellectual life during the 1960s and 1970s centered around the postmodernist trio of the psychoanalyst Lacan, the philosopher Foucault, and the linguist Jacques Derrida. Lacan formulated seductive nativist readings of psychoanalysis—"French Freud"—that integrated psychoanalytic theory with structuralist and poststructuralist linguistics. Foucault provocatively explored the covert political contents and operations of knowledge systems in "the human sciences" of the past. And Derrida reoriented literary criticism away from questions of the writer's biography, historical context, and authorial motivation and intent to the study of autonomous texts and the linguistic

---

[133] Ibid., 155–62.

[134] Andrew Scull, *Social Order/Mental Disorder: Anglo-American Psychiatry in Historical Perspective* (Berkeley: University of California Press, 1989), chap. 11; Nancy Tomes, "Historical Perspectives on Women and Mental Illness," in Rima Apple, ed., *Women, Health, and Medicine in America: A Historical Handbook* (New York: Garland, 1990), 154–58.

[135] Lynne Nead, *Myths of Sexuality: Representations of Women in Victorian Britain* (Oxford: Basil Blackwell, 1988); Cynthia Eagle Russett, *Sexual Science: The Victorian Construction of Womanhood* (Cambridge: Harvard University Press, 1989); Mary Poovey, *Uneven Developments: The Ideological World of Gender in Mid-Victorian England* (London: 1989); Mary Jacobus, Evelyn Fox Keller, and Sally Shuttleworth, eds., *Body/Politics: Women in the Discourses of Science* (London: Routledge, 1990).

[136] For a discussion of Showalter's later work on the cultural history of hysteria, see below, 249, 253–54.

and symbolic systems that constitute them. By the mid-1970s, Lacanian, Foucauldian, and Derridian ideas and ideologies had combined in turn with French academic feminism, itself radicalized by the political upheavals of May 1968. In many French universities, a new theoretical project emerged: the unsparingly critical analysis of medical and scientific texts and the discourses of power and subjectivity that, beneath the rhetorical surfaces of objectivity and empiricism, subtend these texts.

By the mid-1970s, these new teachings were articulated within hysteria studies by a number of Lacan's feminist followers.[137] Most prominently, the journalist Catherine Clément and the novelist and feminist theorist Hélène Cixous published conjointly *La jeune née* in 1975, followed by Cixous's *Portrait de Dora* in 1976.[138] For Cixous and Clément, psychoanalytic psychology represents the most influential model today for the normative psychological evaluation of the sexes. They also observe that psychoanalysis was for all intents and purposes formulated between 1890 and 1900 on the basis of Freud's clinical encounters with a group of hysterical women. *Portrait de Dora* is an experimental theatrical reenactment of events, memories, fantasies, and dreams borrowed from Freud's case histories of hysterics, while *La jeune née* offers a high-spirited, clashing dialogue between the two authors about the nature of female hysteria.

With Cixous and Clément, hysteria becomes a means of studying in historical microcosm the construction of female gender within psychoanalytic science and, by extrapolation, of images of Woman in patriarchal scientific and medical discourses. Responding to Lacan's romanticization of hysteria, they identify themselves with the hysterical patient both as a clinical type and a historical figure. It is the hysteric, they assert, who down through the ages has embodied the illness of her sex by struggling against the distorted and controlling images of femininity forced on her. "We might say that the Absolute Woman, in culture, the woman who really represents femininity most effectively, who is closest to femininity as *prey* to masculinity, is actually the hysteric," Cixous writes.[139]

During these same years, Luce Irigaray, a psychoanalytically trained philosopher, highlighted the pathologization of femininity in many theoretical structures of Western science, medicine, and philosophy. In *Speculum of the Other Woman* (1974) and *The Sex Which Is Not One* (1977),

---

[137] E. Grosz, *Jacques Lacan: A Feminist Introduction* (New York: Routledge, Chapman and Hall, 1990).

[138] Cixous and Clément, *La jeune née* (Paris: Union générale d'édition, 1975); Cixous, *Portrait de Dora* (Paris: Éditions des femmes, 1976). See also Clément, *Les fils de Freud sont fatigués* (Paris: B. Grasset, 1978).

[139] Hélène Cixous, "Castration or Decapitation?" trans. Annette Kuhn, in *Signs* 7, no. 1 (Autumn 1981): 47. This article originally appeared as "Le sexe ou la tête?" *Les cahiers du GRIF* 13 (1976): 5–15.

Irigaray argues that a credible construction of female sexuality in Freudian theory is not simply subordinated to male sexuality but absent altogether. It is this lack of presence that has permitted the hysterization of the female through history.[140] In 1976, Janine Chasseguet-Smirgel underscored once more the phallocentrism of Freud's psychosexual ideas,[141] and in 1979, Monique Schneider deepened the French Lacanian debate historically by probing the political, cultural, and psychological homologies between the witch and the hysteric.[142] By the early 1980s, hysteria and its history had become part of a far-reaching critique among French intellectuals of patri-archal cultures and one of the most controversial subjects within French feminist studies. In content and style, this was what Martha Noel Evans dubs "the hysterical phase of French psychoanalytic feminism."[143]

Feminism, Lacanian Psychoanalysis, and American Deconstructive Literary Criticism

During the early 1980s, post-Lacanian feminist hysteria studies were brought to the American university. This transmission took place through the writings of the British feminist psychotherapist Juliet Mitchell and the American literary critic Jane Gallop, assisted by translations into English of Cixous, Clément, Irigaray, and Schneider.[144] The latest methodological synthesis in the feminist historiography of hysteria combines these French imports with American literary deconstructionism. By the mid-1980s in America, it was literary critics and theorists, rather than medical and social historians, who were writing hysteria's history.

A transitional position within hysteria studies between the Anglo-American literary history of Showalter and French Lacanian analyses may

---

[140] Luce Irigaray, *Speculum de l'autre femme* (Paris: Éditions de minuit, 1974); and idem, *Ce sexe qui n'en est pas un* (Paris: Éditions de minuit, 1977).

[141] Janine Chasseguet-Smirgel, "Freud and Female Sexuality: The Consideration of Some Blind Spots in the Exploration of the 'Dark Continent,'" *International Journal of Psycho-analysis* 57 (1976): 275–86.

[142] Monique Schneider, *De l'exorcisme à la psychanalyse: Le féminin expurgé* (Paris: Retz, 1979).

[143] Evans, *Fits and Starts*, 220. The seventh chapter of Evans' book provides a more detailed account of the work of Cixous, Clément, and Irigaray.

[144] Juliet Mitchell and Jacqueline Rose, *Feminine Sexuality: Jacques Lacan and the École Freudienne* (London: Macmillan, 1982); Jane Gallop, *The Daughter's Seduction: Feminism and Psychoanalysis* (Ithaca, N.Y.: Cornell University Press, 1982), esp. chap. 9; Cixous, "Castration or Decapitation?"; Cixous and Clément, *The Newly Born Woman*, trans. Betsy Wing (Minneapolis: University of Minnesota Press, 1986); Clément, *Portrait of Dora*, trans. Anita Barrows (London: John Calder, 1979); idem, *The Weary Sons of Freud* (New York: Verso, 1987); Irigaray, *Speculum of the Other Woman*, trans. G. C. Gill (Ithaca, N.Y.: Cornell University Press, 1985); idem, *This Sex Which Is Not One*, trans. C. Porter and C. Burke (Ithaca: Cornell University Press, 1985).

be found in a lively study by Dianne Hunter. Writing in an academic feminist periodical in 1983, Hunter takes up the familiar case of Anna O. but with a novel approach.[145] From Breuer's case report Hunter selects a single, symbolically charged group of symptoms and subjects them to close cultural, linguistic, and psychological analysis. Anna O.'s condition, it will be recalled, was marked by bizarre language disorders. For long periods, the patient forgot her native German and was able to communicate only in foreign languages. At other times, she appeared to lose all knowledge of grammar and syntax and either spoke in a childish gibberish or lapsed into muteness. Breuer thought these episodes resulted from a terrifying hallucination undergone by the patient one day as she sat at the bedside of her ailing father.

Hunter, however, tenders a feminist interpretation. Following an observation of Breuer's, she makes much of Anna O.'s talent and intelligence. She surmises that Anna O. deeply resented her inferior position as daughter in an Orthodox Jewish family and felt stifled by the prospect of a lifelong existence of domestic monotony. Hunter then interprets the patient's repression of speech as a regressive refusal to speak the patriarchal language of the closed world around her. Drawing adeptly on contemporary work in developmental psychology and language theory, and in particular on the Lacanian concept of the psychological analogues to linguistic structures, she explains that modes of communication and periods of parental identification are paired in the emotional and cognitive life of the child. "In patriarchal socialization," she specifies, "the power to formulate sentences coincides developmentally with a recognition of the power of the father."[146] From this perspective, Anna O.'s hysterical inability to speak in her native tongue—her linguistic misbehavior, if you will—represented an unconscious rejection of the oppressive cultural order of her upbringing and an effort to return to the earlier and more emotionally gratifying world of preoedipal communication with the mother.

Hunter then extrapolates from Anna O.'s case to the meaning of hysteria within psychoanalytic theory as a whole. Pursuing a kind of feminist-Szaszian line of analysis, she depicts hysteria as an alternate nonverbal body language used by women to address an uncomprehending, male-dominated society a hundred years ago. "Hysteria is a self-repudiating form of feminine discourse in which the body signifies what social conditions make it impossible to state linguistically."[147] Individual symptoms, she adds, such as the classic *globus hystericus*, signify the choked-off

---

[145] Dianne Hunter, "Hysteria, Psychoanalysis, and Feminism: The Case of Anna O.," *Feminist Studies* 9, no. 3 (Fall 1983): 464–88.

[146] Ibid., 474.

[147] Ibid., 485.

words of women in constraining patriarchal society. The work of Freud, she proposes further, is an attempt by a male observer to decode theoretically this pseudosomatic form of surrogate communication. "Psychoanalysis," concludes Hunter, "entered the history of consciousness in dialogue with the subjectivity of women. Freud's discovery of the unconscious was a response to the body language of nineteenth-century hysterics. Psychoanalysis can be seen as a translation into theory of the language of hysteria."[148]

A full exemplification of the synthesis of Lacanian and post-Lacanian feminist psychoanalytic theory with American literary-critical deconstructionism is the anthology *In Dora's Case: Freud—Hysteria—Feminism.*[149] Published in 1905 under the title *Fragment of an Analysis of a Case of Hysteria*, the Dora case is Freud's last, longest, and most complex clinical report on the disorder.[150] The case involves a feisty and intelligent eighteen-year-old woman who developed a panoply of psychosomatic symptoms, including heart palpitations, spells of nervous coughing, and right-sided migraines. In the course of the case history, we learn that Dora had become the hapless victim of a torrid, triangular psychodrama involving her father, a close male friend of the family named Herr K., and the friend's wife, Frau K. Unsatisfied sexually by his own wife, Dora's father was carrying on an affair with Frau K. In an effort to placate the husband and continue the illicit liaison, Dora's father had allowed Herr K. to make advances to his adolescent daughter. As the painful reality of the situation became obvious to Dora, the young woman was clearly in need of a confidant. Early in the analysis, Freud became convinced of the veracity of his patient's account of these events, but he offered little sympathy. Instead, he rather extravagantly interpreted Dora's rejection of the amorous advances of Herr K. as an unconscious mask of her own passionate feelings for the older man and, beyond this, of a secret attraction to both her father and Frau K. Freud's handling of Dora is widely regarded as harsh and authoritarian.[151] For his own theoretical purposes (above all, as an illustration of his recently completed dream theory), he seems to have browbeaten his young patient. The clinical encounters between doctor and patient were openly and mutually antagonistic, and, after three months, Dora defiantly terminated the treatment. Up to the time of her death in 1945, and following a long and miserable

---

[148] Ibid.

[149] Charles Bernheimer and Claire Kahane, eds., *In Dora's Case: Freud—Hysteria—Feminism* (New York: Columbia University Press, 1985). A second edition of the book, published in 1990, includes three additional essays.

[150] Freud, *Fragment of an Analysis*, in *Standard Edition*, 7: 1–122.

[151] See the judicious discussions of the case in Gay, *Freud*, 246–55 and Appignanesi and Forrester, *Freud's Women*, chap. 5.

marriage of her own, Dora (Ida Bauer in real life) lived unhappily, and hysterically, ever after.[152]

Given Freud's undisguised hostility to this patient as well as the patently novelistic quality of his case histories, it is probably inevitable that this text should occasion sharp feminist and literary-critical rereadings. *In Dora's Case* is a compilation of twelve essays by literary critics teaching in American and English universities. A premise of the book is that Freud's writings may be studied as modernist literature, using the same literary-critical techniques as are applied to novels, plays, and poems.[153] Methodologically, the essays reconstruct minutely the language, narrative techniques, and rhetorical strategies employed by Freud to achieve his intellectual (and emotional) aims. The ideological goals of the volume are the same as those of the French post-Lacanian feminists: to unveil the hidden gender prejudices of psychoanalytic theory and display and disrupt male systems of knowledge generally. Earlier British and American feminist writers, such as Smith-Rosenberg, drew theoretical inspiration from psychoanalysis in their study of hysteria; in contrast, the authors of this collection are deeply antagonistic to Freud. Moreover, whereas previous writers employed lucid expository styles and analytical modes, these authors traffic in the poststructuralist feminist terminology of "the Lacanian Other," "symbolic inscription," "the Law of the Father," and "the problematic of sexual difference."

Throughout *In Dora's Case*, it is taken for granted that Freud's work with Dora was in every sense a failure and that his system of psychology as a whole has proven profoundly inadequate to the exploration of female sexuality. Psychoanalysis is by definition "a phallocentric epistemology," and the Dora case is an instrument of something called "the phallic order." In the relentlessly critical pursuit of these points, the authors, in a paradox they do not resolve, employ Freud's own ideas and terminology against him in tones that are alternately playful and pugnacious. A favorite theme in these discussions is Freud's unacknowledged emotional and sexual attraction to the young and vivacious but difficult Dora. Claire Kahane, an editor of the volume, describes the case as "a paradigmatic text of patriarchal assumption about female desire." Suzanne Gearhart

---

152 The literature on Dora is large and cannot be reviewed here. For critical, cultural readings of the case, see the bibliography in Bernheimer and Kahane, *In Dora's Case*, 277–80. A useful summary of medical writings on the subject is available in Jerry. L. Jennings, "The Revival of 'Dora': Advances in Psychoanalytic Theory and Technique," *Journal of the American Psychoanalytic Association*, 34, no. 3 (1986): 607–35. For social, cultural, and medical perspectives on the case, refer to Hannah Decker, *Freud, Dora, and Vienna, 1900* (New York: Free Press, 1990).

153 The model for this approach was provided by Steven Marcus in "Freud and Dora: Story, History, Case History," *Partisan Review* 41, no. 1 (Winter 1974): 12–23, 89–108, repr. in Bernheimer and Kahane, *In Dora's Case*, chap. 3.

examines Freud's unconscious bisexual identification with his patient. Toril Moi sees the case as "Freud's masculine protest against the implications of his own femininity"; while Maria Ramas describes it as "a pervasive patriarchal fantasy of sadomasochistic sexual relations in which the feminine position is fixed as masochistically submissive." Madelon Sprengnether characterizes it as Freud's "defense against his own orality, passive desire, and femininity"; the unfinished, fragmentary nature of the work gets interpreted as an expression of his castration anxiety.[154] As the book proceeds, its real subject becomes less Dora's hysteria than Freud's neuroses. In the end, psychoanalytic hysteria emerges as a failed effort at cross-sexual gender representation and the perfervid product of one man's fascinating, conflicted imagination.

I can think of no good reason not to enjoy this latest collection of studies about the history of hysteria. A microanalysis of texts and an emphasis on linguistic usage are valuable. Throughout the book, the wordplay is fun, and the self-conscious display of avant garde theoretical ideas is often clever.[155] Freud's *Fragment of an Analysis of a Case of Hysteria* undoubtedly contains autobiographical elements in addition to many assumptions about female sexuality and evidence of his manipulations of a young and vulnerable patient. While these facts were previously established, it is useful, I suppose, to have them documented in greater textual detail than before. Conservative, in-house psychoanalytic readings of the case have certainly now been demolished.[156]

Nevertheless, I question whether *In Dora's Case*—and the American academic institutionalization of post-Lacanian psychoanalytic feminism generally—represents an intellectual advance for feminist hysteria studies. Earlier scholars such as Wood, Smith-Rosenberg, Hunter, and Showalter employed the methods of their disciplines to achieve an understanding of a given historical reality. In contrast, *In Dora's Case*, similar in this regard to the recent volume of medical essays about Anna O., is frankly ahistorical. It tells us less about any aspect of the history of hysteria than about the inbred and overintellectualized state of so much literary criticism and literary theory today. As the theoretical layerings in the

---

[154] In Bernheimer and Kahane, *In Dora's Case*: Kahane, "Introduction, Part Two: Why Dora Now?" 24, 27, 28; Suzanne Gearhart, "The Scene of Psychoanalysis: The Unanswered Questions of Dora," 105–27; Toril Moi, "Representation of Patriarchy: Sexuality and Epistemology in Freud's Dora," 181–99; Maria Ramas, "Freud's Dora, Dora's Hysteria," 149–80; Madelon Sprengnether, "Enforcing Oedipus: Freud and Dora," 267–71.

[155] For a second, still trendier example of this sort of work, check out Arthur and Marilouise Kroker, eds., *The Hysterical Male: New Feminist Theory* (New York: St. Martin's Press, 1991).

[156] These qualities of the book have been appreciated by Janet Malcolm in a review for the *New Yorker*, reprinted as "Dora" in *The Purloined Clinic: Selected Essays* (New York: Knopf, 1992), 8–15.

essays accumulate, and the jumble of jargons multiply, the book moves further and further from hysteria as any kind of lived historical experience or clinical reality. What's more, the lapses into incomprehensibility, so common among second-generation deconstructionists, combined with the strictly linguistic conceptualization of textuality in the literary-deconstructive project as a whole, to my mind dilute and trivialize the genuine revisionist potential of earlier feminist work, with its roots in the women's movement of the 1960s.[157] Most importantly, one comes away from this anthology with the strong suspicion that, despite its pretense to sophisticated linguistic and psychological analysis, the contributors have set out above all to do to Freud today what Freud did to Dora ninety years ago. In a real sense, *In Dora's Case* returns us, under altered theoretical circumstances, to two earlier interpretive modes: amateur psychobiography and the victimization model of history writing.[158]

The Debate over Hysteria as Protofeminism

The feminist critique of hysteria and its heritage that began to take shape in the late 1960s has concentrated on topics such as the theoretical content of the diagnosis, the motivations of the medical profession, and the psychological economy of the patient. Running through this writing is also a subsidiary theme concerning the historical relation between nineteenth-century hysteria and the emergent women's movement. This is among the most internally contested ideas within the feminist literature, and it has been addressed by French, British, and North American authors.

Once again, it is the example of Anna O. that provides material for irresistible speculation on this point. Following her psychotherapy, as we have seen, Breuer's patient endured a long period of sickness and convalescence. However, after her recovery, Pappenheim went on to become a prominent exponent of German feminist social and political causes. She

[157] These same reservations have been voiced by the "new historicists" in their critique of the linguistic turn within the humanities generally. On the transition from the literary-critical formalism of the 1970s and 1980s to the more historicized methodology of the so-called new cultural studies, see Lynn A. Hunt, "Introduction: History, Culture, and Text," in Hunt, ed., *The New Cultural History* (Berkeley: University of California Press, 1989), 1–22.

[158] This contrasts with the more constructive enterprise of certain Anglo-American feminists, who acknowledge elements of scientific sexism in Freud but are concerned to retain what remains theoretically valid and powerful in his thinking in an effort to achieve a new and more satisfactory psychology of women. See Juliet Mitchell, *Psychoanalysis and Feminism* (London: Lane, 1974); Nancy Chodorow, *Feminism and Psychoanalytic Theory* (New Haven: Yale University Press, 1989); and Elisabeth Young-Bruehl, ed., *Freud on Women: A Reader* (London: Hogarth Press, 1990), Introduction.

directed an orphanage in Frankfurt, cofounded the League of Jewish Women, fought against prostitution, translated writings by Mary Wollstonecraft, and authored a play entitled *Women's Rights*.[159] In a real sense, her later career emerged in opposition to the values of her Orthodox Jewish patriarchal background. Other women during this period who had nervous breakdowns, such as Charlotte Perkins Gilman and Jane Addams, also managed to recover by forging for themselves unconventional lives as creative and productive women.

In 1979, the French psychoanalyst Luçien Israël commented suggestively that Pappenheim was an outstanding example of "the successful hysteric."[160] One could almost claim that her career was a brilliant sublimation of her earlier neurosis. Generalizing from Pappenheim's experience, Israël proposes that a life of self-abnegating social good works represents "one of the possible evolutions of hysteria."[161] Israël's observations have also received a number of feminist formulations. Cixous historicizes and heroicizes the female hysteric as "a suffering and sumptuous sister of modern feminists."[162] Underscoring the contributions of Pappenheim to the origins of both psychoanalytic theory and the women's movement, Hunter throws out the idea that "feminism is transformed hysteria, or more precisely, that hysteria is feminism lacking a social network in the outer world."[163] Showalter expands on this notion by postulating a far-reaching cultural and psychological parallelism between the two entities: both feminism and hysteria, she contends, are violent reactions against male-dominated societies—feminism in the world of organized public politics, hysteria in the realm of private psychopathologies.[164] Showalter moreover proposes that the movement between feminism and hysteria was two-directional: physicians and laymen often branded voluble members of the women's movement hysterical while militant suffragettes employed quasi-medical strategies such as hunger strikes, a sort of willful collective anorexia, in the pursuit of their political goals. In this

---

[159] Dora Edinger, *Bertha Pappenheim: Freud's Anna O.* (Highland Park, Ill.: Congregation Solel, 1968); Ellen M. Jensen, *Streifzüge durch das Leben von Anna O./Bertha Pappenheim: Ein Fall für die Psychiatrie—Ein Leben für die Philanthropie* (Frankfurt am Main: ZTV, 1984).

[160] Lucien Israël, *L'hystérique, le sexe et le médecin* (Paris: Masson, 1979), 4, 196–205. Israël discusses Mary Baker Eddy, founder of the Christian Science Movement, as a second "successful" hysteric.

[161] Ibid., 205.

[162] Evans, *Fits and Starts*, 215.

[163] Hunter, "Hysteria, Psychoanalysis, and Feminism," 485.

[164] Showalter, *Female Malady*, 161. See also Diane Price Herndl, "The Writing Cure: Charlotte Perkins Gilman, Anna O., and 'Hysterical' Writing," *NWSA Journal* 1 (1988): 53–54.

view, the patients of Freud and Charcot emerge as historical heroines in what Showalter calls "the 'protofeminism' of hysterical protest."[165]

Other feminist scholars have provided alternative readings. Joan Jacobs Brumberg, the leading American feminist historian of anorexia nervosa, expressly rejects the idea that hysteria and feminism exist on a kind of psychopolitical continuum.[166] To the same effect, Anne Steinmann, a psychoanalytically-oriented clinical psychologist, reacts against what she sees as feminist idealizations of Pappenheim. In their place, Steinmann provides a picture of the mature Pappenheim as a partially failed and unfulfilled figure.[167] For their part, Clément and Moi countenance the view that Victorian hysteria was a feminine "anti-language" of the body; but, like Steinmann, they interpret the hysterical mode of response as a tragic one. "It may be gratifying to see the young, proud Dora as a radiant example of feminine revolt," Moi responds to Cixous, "but we should not forget the image of the old, nagging, whining, and complaining Dora she later becomes, achieving nothing. Hysteria is not . . . the incarnation of the revolt of women forced to silence but rather a declaration of defeat, the realization that there is no other way out. Hysteria is . . . a cry for help when defeat becomes real."[168] Clément's and Moi's hysteria is a suffering in silence, an unthreatening and apolitical expression of social discontent without the power to effect change. A failed feminism.

Finally, Juliet Mitchell provides a characteristically perceptive set of observations. In *Women: The Longest Revolution*, Mitchell reflects on the subject in broad historical terms and projects a more or less unbroken connection through time between forms of male oppression and female counterresponse. She discusses European witchcraft as a "pre-political manifestation of hysteria" and an "unconscious feminism."[169] And she accedes to the idea of nineteenth-century hysteria and feminism as divergent reactions—one unconscious and internalized, the other conscious and extroverted—to identical social realities.[170] At the same time, she is

---

[165] Showalter attributes the term "proto-feminist" in regard to the hysteric to an unpublished paper by Jane Gallop (*Female Malady*, 160, 275).

[166] Joan Jacobs Brumberg, *Fasting Girls: The Emergence of Anorexia Nervosa as a Modern Disease* (Cambridge: Harvard University Press, 1988), 37–38.

[167] Anne Steinmann, "Anna O.: Female, 1880–1882: Bertha Pappenheim: Female, 1980–1982," in Rosenbaum and Muroff, *Anna O.*, 118–31.

[168] Moi, "Representations of Patriarchy," in Bernheimer and Kahane, *In Dora's Case*, 192.

[169] Mitchell, *Women: The Longest Revolution: Essays on Feminism, Literature and Psychoanalysis* (London: Virago, 1984), 117.

[170] If I understand her correctly, Mitchell suggests further that in the struggle against dominant gender stereotypes, women often unconsciously internalized these behaviorial models: "It was, among other things," she observes, "against their definition as hysterics that nineteenth-century feminists protested—no doubt, they often did so hysterically" (ibid., 120).

chary of a direct and romantic equation of public politics and personal pathology. Instead, Mitchell proffers a wholly different historical antithesis, not between witchcraft and hysteria, failed and successful patients, or hysteria and feminism, but between hysteria and motherhood. In the history of women, she reflects, hysteria—passive, paralyzing, and unproductive—finds its true negation in the full, positive, (pro)creative life of the mother.[171]

To sum up, considerable continuity exists within the feminist tradition of hysteria studies. However, in perusing the literature as a whole, the internal intellectual diversity is at least as striking. The subjects of inquiry within the feminist literature on hysteria range widely, from the professional male theoretician to the suffering female patient, from the clinical relationship between doctor and patient to the disembodied medical diagnosis. Some feminist writers conceptualize hysteria as a "real" disease involving genuine mental pathology while other authors see it solely as a social and cultural construction. Some scholars emphasize the secondary gain of women in a sick role; others focus on the primary losses of women subjected to stigmatizing medical definitions. Victorian neurosis figures both as a heroic protest with political ramifications and as a pathetic collapse into private, maladaptive illness. And Freud appears alternately as villain and liberator. During the past twenty-five years, feminist historians and critics have deployed a multiplicity of methodologies, drawn from intellectual history, cultural history, social history, the history of science and medicine, psychoanalytic studies, literary history and criticism, and language theory. Their work has drawn on and contributed to an impressive number of developments within political and intellectual modernism and postmodernism.

The greatest contribution of feminist medical history writing has no doubt been the discovery and exploration, in great empirical and analytical detail, of the role of gender in the history of disease. Considered cumulatively, the feminist interpretive tradition suggests the indispensability of the hysteria concept in the representation of Woman within Western patriarchal societies. It also establishes powerfully the influence of gender on the making of psychological medicine. By any standards, these are signal contributions. Conversely, the greatest weakness of feminist hysteria studies to date is most likely an unquestioned and uncritical analytical centrality granted to a category—gender reductionism—that remains, after all, only one of several major components in disease history. In the end, feminist histories of medicine hugely qualify and complicate earlier interpretive approaches but do not invalidate them.

[171] Ibid., 312–13.

Finally, the pattern of evolution of the feminist interpretive tradition has been notably more complex than that of other historiographical schools. From its inception right up to the present, the feminist study of medicine, while retaining its basic interpretive identity, has been characterized by rigorous self-revision. The tradition has drawn ideological sustenance from general feminist theory. At the same time, it has managed regularly to broaden itself intellectually by embracing the ideas, methods, and sources of neighboring, nonfeminist fields of inquiry. Also, after resourcefully drawing on these more established areas and methods to constitute itself, it has then repeatedly doubled back to enrich and revise these same fields. Moreover, as the feminist tradition grows in substance and self-confidence, it has itself begun to contribute in important ways to the formation of new subdisciplines, such as the history of sexuality, the history of the body, gay and lesbian studies, and cultural studies. There is every reason to expect this evolution to continue.

Within the new hysteria studies, the feminist interpretive tradition is easily the most controversial; it is also the most dynamic and vibrant. Enormous critical energy has been displayed in the field over the past twenty-five years. One need only compare the state of hysteria studies in the early 1960s and the early 1990s to realize the great difference it has made.

CHARCOT AND THE HISTORY OF HYSTERIA

As we have seen, the prominence of the late nineteenth century in the history of hysteria is due partly to Freud. It is equally owing to Charcot, the second major figure dominating the story of the disease during its famous fin-de-siècle phase. But, interestingly, the historical, and therefore historiographical, fates of Freud and Charcot could not be more divergent. Psychoanalytic hysteria emerged in obscurity, remained intensely controversial for years, and afterward dominated psychiatric thinking for half a century. In contrast, Charcot's theories succeeded brilliantly during his lifetime, attracting countless adherents within the medical profession as well as international popular attention. The first histories of hysteria, we have seen, were written by Charcotian protégés who featured his teachings prominently. Charcot's fame, however, was followed by a radical posthumous decline. In the twentieth century, a deep split formed in the evaluation of his life's work. For his neurological researches, he was crowned "the father of neurology." In contrast, his later so-called psychological writings, on topics such as hysteria, hypnosis, somnambulism, ambulatory automatisms, and dissociation, were attacked as sensationalistic and charlatanish. At the same time, Charcot's ideas in this domain were obscured by the early twentieth-century rise of Kraepelinian institutional psychiatry, Freudian psychoanalysis, and Pavlovian behavioralist psychology. By 1900, the age of Charcot, and with it the *belle époque* of French hysteria, had effectively come to a close.

One consequence of the twentieth-century eclipse of Charcot's reputation has been an almost complete lack of professional medical-historical scholarship about him. Despite the fame and flamboyance of his work on hysteria—indeed, perhaps *because* the popular historical rendition of his work was so patently and pleasingly dramatic—scholars for many years were disinclined to take up the subject. Between his death in 1893 and 1980, none of Charcot's writings about hysteria were translated into other languages, and no authoritative "life-and-times" biography appeared. Georges Guillain's valuable *J. M. Charcot (1825–93): Sa vie, son oeuvre* (1955) includes only a single short chapter on hysteria. And A.R.G. Owen's *Hysteria, Hypnosis and Healing: The Work of J.-M. Charcot* (1971), while more informative on hysteria, is written from the standpoint of the occult sciences and draws only on those writings of Charcot available in English translation.[172] Likewise, Veith's chapter on Charcot is quite thin, relying on Guillain and a handful of case histories. No one as yet has traced systematically the origin and development of Charcot's ideas on hysteria, and we lack a sophisticated sociological analysis of the school of the Salpêtrière. Similarly, there has been very little retrospective rediagnosis or biographical reconstruction of Charcot's hysterical patients.[173]

In lieu of the detailed and original historical scholarship that exists for Freud, two types of literature about Charcot appeared. Much of the commentary has been descriptive and anecdotal. It relies on a large but limited body of material, comprised chiefly of student reminiscences and literary accounts of Charcot that were written with equal uncriticalness by contemporary admirers and adversaries and then copied over the years from one secondary source to another. These commentaries typically reveal little familiarity with Charcot's collected medical works.

A second body of writing has been the product of the Freud factory. Because Freud, at a pivotal point in his career, studied briefly with Charcot, Charcot's theories of hysteria appear routinely in the scholarly literature about psychoanalysis. This approach has yielded some intelligent work drawing on at least a portion of Charcot's clinical writings, but the image of Charcot as primarily a precursor of psychoanalysis has also led

[172] Georges Guillain, *J.-M. Charcot (1825–1893): Sa vie, son oeuvre* (Paris: Masson, 1955), trans. Pearce Bailey (1959); A.R.G. Owen, *Hysteria, Hypnosis and Healing: The Work of J.-M. Charcot* (London: Dennis Dobson, 1971).

[173] An exception to the lack of original research on Charcot during this period is Henri F. Ellenberger's "Charcot and the Salpêtrière School," *American Journal of Psychotherapy* 19, no. 2 (April 1965): 253–67.

to serious interpretive distortions. Over the past fifty years, psychoanalytic historians in search of "the origins of the unconscious" have badly overstated the psychogenic component in Charcot's medical thinking, isolated artificially the themes of hypnosis and hysteria from the body of his work, and obscured the real nature of his interest and achievement in studying the disorder.

Happily, with the coming of the new hysteria studies in the early 1980s, this situation began to change dramatically. The general development of the neurosciences, the increase of attention to medical history, the growth of psychiatric interest in dissociative psychological phenomena, and the decline of the psychodynamic paradigm that consigned Charcot to the secondary status of Freudian forerunner have contributed to a brisk scientific and historical renewal of interest in Charcot. In recent years, these forces have been accelerated by the 1993 centenary celebrations of Charcot's death.

In retrospect, the revival of Charcot studies began in 1982 with an exhibition held at the Salpêtrière devoted specifically to Charcot's place in the history of hysteria. This event marked a kind of official reinstatement of this aspect of his work within the Parisian medical community.[174] In 1984, two well-established British neurologists offered a thoughtful, scientific defense of Charcot's theories of the neuroses.[175] In 1987, André Brouillet's celebrated canvas, Une leçon clinique à la Salpêtrière, which had languished for decades in a museum storage room in the provinces, was exhibited in Paris.[176] In 1988, the first translation into English of a selection of Charcot's Leçons du mardi, accompanied by an extensive scholarly commentary, appeared.[177] A year later, the historic correspondence between Charcot and Freud was published in French and English,[178] and in 1991 a nineteenth-century British edition of Charcot's lectures on hysteria was reissued.[179] Similarly, in France Charcot's theo-

[174] J.-M. Charcot et l'hystérie au XIXe siècle, catalogue de l'exposition par Jacqueline Sonolet, Chapelle de la Salpêtrière, June 2–18, 1982 (Paris: Beba, 1982).

[175] E.M.R. Critchley and H. E. Cantor, "Charcot's Hysteria Renaissant," British Medical Journal 289, no. 6460 (December 22–24, 1984): 1785–88.

[176] La leçon de Charcot: Voyage dans une toile, exhibition organized by the Musée de l'assistance publique de Paris, September 17–December 31, 1986 (Paris: Tardy Quercy, 1986).

[177] Charcot the Clinician: The Tuesday Lessons: Excerpts from Nine Case Presentations on General Neurology Delivered at the Salpêtrière Hospital in 1887–88 by Jean-Martin Charcot, translated with commentary by Christopher G. Goetz (New York: Raven Press, 1987), esp. lesson 5.

[178] "'Mon Cher Docteur Freud': Charcot's Unpublished Correspondence to Freud, 1888–1893," annotations, translation, and commentary by Toby Gelfand, Bulletin of the History of Medicine 62, no. 4 (Winter 1988): 563–88.

[179] J.-M. Charcot, Clinical Lectures on Diseases of the Nervous System vol. 3, trans. Thomas Savill (1889), ed. Ruth Harris, Tavistock Classics in the History of Psychiatry (London: Routledge, 1991).

ries were defended medically by a Salpêtrière psychiatrist in 1982.[180] A historical novel about Charcot appeared in 1990, followed by two popular, book-length accounts of his life.[181] As part of the commemoration of Charcot's death, a major exhibition was sponsored by the American Academy of Neurology; the World Congress of Neurology sponsored an official recognition of his achievements; French physicians prepared a contemporary overview of his medical work; and a three-day conference at the Pitié-Salpêtrière hospital complex, bringing together an international cast of doctors and historians, was held.[182]

While some of these developments have been popular and commemorative, others indicate a substantial revival of professional scholarship about Charcot's life and work. Jacques Gasser, for instance, has established an authoritative and scrupulously comprehensive chronology of Charcot's medical writings and clinical lessons.[183] Alain Lellouch has studied definitively Charcot's geriatric writings.[184] Bernard Brais has intricately reconstructed the world of medical politics in which Charcot and his students worked.[185] The remnants of the Bibliothèque Charcot are now being preserved and catalogued. A major intellectual biography by a distinguished team of researchers is in progress.[186] Throughout this period, a steady stream of publications on specialized aspects of Charcot's life and work has also appeared.[187] After generations of neglect, a full-

---

[180] Daniel Widlöcher, "L'hystérie, cent ans après," *Revue neurologique* 138, no. 12 (1982): 1053–60.

[181] Philippe Meyer, *Sommeils indiscrets: Roman* (Paris: Olivier Orban, 1990); Wanda Bannour, *Jean-Martin Charcot et l'hystérie* (Paris: Éditions Métailié, 1992); Jean Thuillier, *Charcot de la Salpêtrière* (Paris: Laffont, 1993).

[182] "Charcot's Life; Charcot's Scientific Career," Forty-Fifth Annual Meeting of the American Academy of Neurology (History of Medicine Section), New York, April 25–May 1, 1993; Symposium on Charcot, Fifteenth World Congress of Neurology, Vancouver, Canada, September 5–10, 1993; Michel Bonduelle, Dominique Laplane, André Perret, *Jean-Martin Charcot: Points de repères* (Paris: Sanofi Pharma, 1993); "La neurologie de l'aube à demain: Charcot et son temps", Pitié-Salpêtrière, Paris, June 9–11, 1993. The proceedings of the Paris conference are forthcoming in the *Revue neurologique*.

[183] J. Gasser, "Jean-Martin Charcot (1825–1893) et le système nerveux: Étude de la motricité, du langage, de la mémoire et de l'hystérie à la fin du XIXième siècle," (Ph.D. diss., École des hautes études en sciences sociales, 1990), Annexe A, 610–775; Annexe B, 805–61.

[184] Alain Lellouch, *Jean-Martin Charcot et les origines de la gérontologie* (Paris: Payot, 1992).

[185] Bernard Brais, "The Making of a Famous Nineteenth Century Neurologist: Jean-Martin Charcot (1825–1893)" (Masters thesis, University College London, 1990).

[186] Christopher Goetz, Michel Bonduelle, and Toby Gelfand, *Constructing Neurology: Jean-Martin Charcot, 1825–1893* (New York: Oxford University Press, forthcoming).

[187] Gladys Swain, "L'âme, la femme, le sexe et le corps: Les métamorphoses de l'hystérie à la fin du XIXe siècle," *Le débat* 24 (March 1983): 107–27; Paul Bercherie, "Le concept de la folie hystérique avant Charcot," *Revue internationale d'histoire de psychiatrie* 1, no. 1

scale revival of professional interest, led by French, Swiss, Canadian, and American physicians and historians, is under way.

To date, the new Charcot studies are disparate and specialized. They do not thus far constitute a distinct interpretive tradition in the manner of the feminist, psychoanalytic, or intellectual-historical traditions. Rather they form a new focal point of scholarly interest and one of the most active and promising research sites within the historiography of hysteria. For this reason, it is unnecessary to review the literature comprehensively. Rather, in order to flesh out an emergent subfield, I would like to consider in somewhat greater detail four pieces of recent scholarship that employ different methodologies to illuminate different aspects of Charcot's work on "la grande névrose."

In a previous chapter, I discussed Étienne Trillat's *Histoire de l'hystérie*. Included in Trillat's history is a desultory but highly discerning thirty-page chapter on Charcot.[188] Trillat reconstructs in roughly chronological order the "clinical inventory" of Charcotian hysteria. He shows that to a large extent Charcot defined hysteria negatively, in opposition to a num-

---

(1983): 47–58; Wayne E. Massey and Lawrence C. McHenry, "Hysteroepilepsy in the Nineteenth Century: Charcot and Gowers," *Neurology* 36, no. 1 (January 1986): 65–67; Joseph Aguayo, "Charcot and Freud: Some Implications of Late 19th-Century French Psychiatry and Politics for the Origins of Psychoanalysis," *Psychoanalysis and Contemporary Thought* 9, no. 2 (1986): 223–60; William Parry-Jones, "'Caesar of the Salpêtrière': J.-M. Charcot's Impact on Psychological Medicine in the 1880s," *Bulletin of the Royal College of Psychiatrists* 11, no. 5 (May 1987): 150–53; Christopher G. Goetz, "Charcot at the Salpêtrière: Ambulatory Automatisms," *Neurology* 37, no. 2 (June 1987): 1084–88; idem, "The Salpêtrière in the Wake of Charcot's Death," *Archives of Neurology* 45, no. 4 (April 1988): 444–47; Mark S. Micale, "The Salpêtrière in the Age of Charcot: An Institutional Perspective on Medical History in the Late Nineteenth Century," *Journal of Contemporary History* 20, no. 4 (October 1985): 703–31; idem, "Diagnostic Discriminations: Jean-Martin Charcot and the Idea of Masculine Hysterical Neurosis" (Ph.D. diss., Yale University, 1987); A. Lellouch, Cl. Villard, L. Corman, "La personnalité de J.-M. Charcot (1825–1893)," 2 parts, *Histoire des sciences médicales* 22, no. 2 (1988): 97–113; Toby Gelfand, "Réflexions sur Charcot et la famille névropathique," *Histoire des sciences médicales* 21, no. 3 (1987): 245–50; idem, "Charcot's Response to Freud's Rebellion," *Journal of the History of Ideas* 50 (April–June 1989): 293–307; Alain Lellouch, "La méthode de J.-M. Charcot (1825–1893)," *History and Philosophy of the Life Sciences* 11, no. 1 (1989): 43–69; Mary James, "The Therapeutic Practices of Jean-Martin Charcot (1825–1893) in Their Historical and Social Context" (Ph.D. diss., University of Essex, 1990); J. Gasser, "J.-M. Charcot et la découverte des localisations motrices chez l'homme," *Gesnerus* 45, nos. 3/4 (1988): 501–20; Daphne de Marneffe, "Looking and Listening: The Construction of Clinical Knowledge in Charcot and Freud," *Signs* 17, no. 1 (Autumn 1991): 91–112. From slightly earlier studies, see Georges Haberberg, "De Charcot à Babinski: Étude du rôle de l'hystérie dans la naissance de la neurologie moderne" (Ph.D. diss., University of Paris, Créteil, 1979); and *J.-M. Charcot: L'hystérie*, ed. E. Trillat (Toulouse: Privat, 1971).

[188] Trillat, *Histoire de l'hystérie*, chap. 6.

ber of stubborn clinical stereotypes of the disorder. He emphasizes that in both the etiological and symptomatological realms, Charcot's thinking moved from the neurological to the psychological,[189] and he underscores the great impulse to order driving Charcot's scientific work. In the second half of the nineteenth century, to establish the laws of the development of a disease was, all-importantly, to render the subject scientifically comprehensible and respectable. As a consequence, everything in Charcot's disease model had its place: a uniform etiology, a clear hierarchy of symptoms, and a paroxysm that followed a prescribed developmental sequence. Any untoward manifestations that did not conform to the picture were classified as *formes frustes*.[190] As a disease construct, Charcot's hysteria was highly pleasing to contemplate in its symmetry—a stately classical façade enclosing a wild, baroque interior—but it was clinically impractical.[191]

Trillat also draws attention to the important place of experimentation in the Salpêtrian research program. Between 1872 and 1878, Charcot formulated the basic nosographical outlines of hysteria according to the principles of classic French clinical medicine. However, after 1878, Trillat establishes, his methodology shifted from close observation in the wards to physiological experimentation in the laboratory and amphitheater. Trillat traces Charcot's "experimental itinerary" through the 1880s. By testing patients with electrical devices for sensory stigmata, transferring hysterical symptoms with magnets from one side of the body to the other, and hypnotizing subjects to demonstrate their mental impressionability, Charcot and his colleagues, Trillat implies, were imitating the techniques of the new physiological medicine of their day. But despite the semblance of science, these endless procedures were circular, self-reinforcing, at times simply silly, and not infrequently humiliating and even harmful to patients. Moreover, the most meaningful theoretical implication of this work—that many of the symptoms in these cases were of ideogenic origin—was articulated not by Charcot himself but by his pupils, a decade later.[192]

Trillat includes in his discussion several paragraphs on Charcot's experimental use of magnets and metals. This subject has been ably expatiated upon by the American historian of the mental sciences, Anne Harrington. In two densely researched studies appearing in British publications, Har-

[189] Ibid., 135.

[190] The "scientification" of hysteria in Charcot's work is also the subject of Gérard Wajeman's *Le maître et l'hystérique* (Paris: Navarin, 1982), chaps. 6 and 7.

[191] Trillat, *Histoire de l'hystérie*, 132–38. See also Gasser, "Jean-Martin Charcot et le système nerveux," chap. 5.

[192] Trillat, *Histoire de l'hystérie*, 138–47. See also Gasser, "Jean-Martin Charcot et le système nerveux," 467–504.

rington has explored the nineteenth-century French medical interest in "metalloscopy," "metallotherapy," and "magnetotherapy."[193] Specifically, she relates the story of Victor Jean-Marie Burq. A doctor working in Paris at mid-century, Burq believed he had discovered that particular metals, such as gold, silver, copper, and iron, possessed the uncanny power to remove or alleviate hysterical symptoms, including fits, spasms, and anesthesias. In Burq's view, each individual had a distinctive "metallic idiosyncrasy," a personal physiological pattern of response to these substances when placed on the surface of the body or ingested in mineral form.

Drawing on journal articles, medical dissertations and monographs, and academic committee reports, Harrington reconstructs the spread of Burq's ideas throughout the Parisian scientific community during the final three decades of the century, when the scientific literature on magnetotherapy and metalloscopy was in flower. She shows that as research on the subject continued during the 1880s, the scope of natural powers attributed to these magnetic materials became increasingly extravagant. More and more "aesthesiogenic" agents were discovered, and more and more hysterical symptoms were said to yield to these agents. Investigators also formulated a concept of "the metallic transfer," according to which sensory-motor symptoms could be moved from one side of the body to the other, emotional moods could be reversed, and mental and physical states could be transferred from one individual to another, even at a distance.[194] Near the end of his life, Burq was awarded the Légion d'Honneur by the French government for his contributions to medical science.

Following the so-called Edinburgh school of the sociology of science, with its emphasis on "explanatory symmetry," Harrington resists the temptation to find this episode in medical history merely amusing.[195] She reviews nineteenth-century explanations for these metallic phenomena, and she demonstrates the intellectual coherence of the theories of Burq and Charcot within the context of contemporary chemical, molecular, and electrophysiological models of the nervous system. She underscores the

[193] Anne Harrington, "Metals and Magnets in Medicine: Hysteria, Hypnosis and Medical Culture in *fin-de-siècle* Paris," *Psychological Medicine* 18, no. 1 (February 1988): 21–38; idem, "Hysteria, Hypnosis, and the Lure of the Invisible: The Rise of Neo-mesmerism in *fin-de-siècle* French Psychiatry" in W. F. Bynum, Roy Porter, and Michael Shepherd, eds., *The Anatomy of Madness: Essays in the History of Psychiatry*, 3 vols. (London: Routledge, 1988), 3: 226–46.

[194] See also Harrington *Medicine, Mind, and the Double Brain: A Study in Nineteenth-Century Thought* (Princeton: Princeton University Press, 1987), 171–82.

[195] According to the members of this school, the same analytical historical procedures that direct our accounts of what seem to us true, progressive, and successful scientific theories should be applied to allegedly non-, pre- or pseudoscientific conceptual systems from the past that have fallen by the historical wayside.

historical continuities between the Mesmeric cults of the 1780s and 1790s, Burq's mid-century ideas on metals and magnets, and the "neo-Mesmerist" writings of Jules Bernard Luys, Alfred Binet, Charles Féré, and Victor Dumontpallier. She notes too the presence of "vitalist" and "fluidist" ideas during this golden age of positivism. In closing, she proposes that the French metalloscopic enterprise provided a major impetus to the renaissance of interest in hysteria and hypnosis during the closing decades of the century.[196] Harrington's work, which brings the empirical and analytical standards of professional science historiography to Charcot studies, reminds us how much of the basic intellectual history of hysteria, even during its "heroic period," remains to be explored.

Lastly, with the work of Georges Didi-Huberman and Sander Gilman, we have something quite different. Didi-Huberman is a professional art historian interested primarily in visual representations of hysteria. More than any category of psychopathology short of out-and-out insanity, hysteria boasts a rich iconographical heritage, and a number of the most dramatic materials came out of Charcot's Salpêtrière. Didi-Huberman's *Invention de l'hystérie: Charcot et l'Iconographie photographique de la Salpêtrière* is at once difficult and indispensable.[197] Unfortunately, the work suffers from the French disease: it is written in an irritatingly affected style, replete with gratuitous literary and philosophical allusions from Dante to Derrida, and darkened by an obfuscating jargon, much of which only conceals statements of the obvious. Also, for a book-length study, it tells us disappointingly little about the actual history of medical photography. At the same time, as an assemblage of rare and fascinating documents with an evocative running commentary, the book is invaluable.

The three-volume *Iconographie photographique de la Salpêtrière* was compiled by D.-M. Bourneville and P. Régnard, two of Charcot's disciples, and was published between 1876 and 1880.[198] The volumes are a kind of illustrated nosographical atlas of French hysteria a century ago. The text of the "photographic iconography" relates at length the extraordinary medical biographies of Geneviève B., Célina, Rosalie Ler., Blanche Wittmann (the notorious "Queen of the Hysterics"), Madeleine W., Thérèse L., and, Didi-Huberman's favorite, Augustine, described by the author as "a masterpiece" of human pathology. The photographs accompanying the text—120 in all—record indelibly the familiar stages of the full hysterical attack as formulated by Charcot in the 1870s.[199]

[196] Harrington, "Metals and Magnets," 27–31; idem, "Rise of Neo-Mesmerism," 227–30.

[197] Georges Didi-Huberman, *Invention de l'hystérie: Charcot et l'Iconographie photographique de la Salpêtrière* (Paris: Macula, 1982).

[198] D.-M. Bourneville and P. Régnard, *Iconographie photographique de la Salpêtrière*, 3 vols. (Paris: Delahaye et Lecrosnier, 1876–1880).

[199] Extended excerpts from the source are reprinted in D.-M. Bourneville and P. Ré-

The drama here is high, and Didi-Huberman does not fail to capitalize on it. As literary critics today treat Freud's case histories as clinical "narratives," so Didi-Huberman discusses the volumes of the *Iconographie photographique* as "visual texts." The stylized sculptural positions assumed by the women in these documents, he points out, mimic the emotions of terror, disgust, lust, and surprise. With an exposure time of up to twenty minutes, these photographs were in every sense poses; it is never clear here who is deceiving whom. Are the patients putting the doctors on? Are the doctors exploiting the patients in order to document pet theories? Or are the doctors fooling themselves? The erotic component in these *gestes corporels* is overwhelming. Medical students, still all men at the time, probed their patients with specula, tested for hysterogenic zones with manual pressure to the ovarian area, and started and stopped hysterical seizures with the use of amyl nitrate. For their part, the patients were scantily clad, their postures provocative, and what the photographs only suggest their lascivious conversation under hypnosis made explicit. In what Didi-Huberman sees as a kind of licensed medical voyeurism, doctors recorded every sight and sound of the presumably afflicted patient.[200] Didi-Huberman's work exposes the ways in which hysteria, in its most flamboyant form a hundred years ago, emerged as a mixed scientific, sexual, and aesthetic construction. His book unites, for the scholarly gaze, one of the most compelling sets of documents in the history of hysteria.[201]

The sophisticated art-historical and cultural-historical analysis of these images that is absent from Didi-Huberman's glossy compilation was provided in 1993 by Sander Gilman. A medical, cultural, and literary historian with a specialty in modern Germany, Gilman in the last decade has emerged as the leading authority on the visual representation of disease and insanity.[202] In a recent monograph-length essay, he studies in particular the role of photography in shaping the medical and cultural "idea" of the hysteric in fin-de-siècle Europe.[203]

gnard, "Première observation de Célina (1876–1877)" and "Seconde observation de Célina (1879–1880)," *Revue internationale de psychopathologie* 4 (1991): 281–322.

[200] The strong erotic undercurrent in the Salpêtrière's study of hysteria has been remarked upon by numerous scholars. See, for instance, Michel Foucault, *Histoire de la sexualité*, vol. 1, *La volonté de savoir* (Paris: Gallimard, 1976), 74–76; and Carroy-Thirard, "Figures de femmes hystériques," 313–23.

[201] In 1984, Didi-Huberman repeated this service with a reissue of Jean-Martin Charcot and Paul Richer, *Les démoniaques dans l'art*, Introduction by Pierre Fédida, Postscript by Georges Didi-Huberman (Paris: Macula, 1984).

[202] Sander L. Gilman, ed., *The Face of Madness: Hugh W. Diamond and the Origins of Psychiatric Photography* (New York: Brunner-Mazel, 1976); Sander Gilman, *Seeing the Insane: A Cultural History of Psychiatric Illustration* (New York: Brunner-Mazel, 1982); idem, *Disease and Representation: Images of Illness from Madness to AIDS* (Ithaca, N.Y.: Cornell University Press, 1988).

[203] Sander L. Gilman, "The Image of the Hysteric," in Gilman et al., *Hysteria beyond Freud*, 345–452.

Gilman's is an exciting and searching analysis that coordinates a mass of visual and written materials. As Freud commented in an often-cited remark from his obituary of Charcot, his mentor was preeminently a *visuelle*: in studying, conceptualizing, diagnosing, and depicting hysterical pathology, Charcot privileged visual modalities. (This contrasts with Freud's more aural, analytical, and etiological enterprise.) For such a cognitive termperament, the discovery of medical photography during the mid-nineteenth century was highly gratifying. Gilman demonstrates that a parallel developed between the epistemology of positivist medicine, which Charcot championed, and the myth of the absolute realism of photographic representation.[204] Furthermore, Charcot's generation lacked a firm understanding of the causes of hysteria and instead lavished its attention on the descriptive neurosymptomatology of the disease. Consequently, as Gilman perceives, hysteria in effect became Charcot's visualization of it. Symptoms were interpreted not simply as signs of some deeper, unknown dysfunction but as the "meaning" of the disease itself. Equating essence and iconography, pathology and physiognomy, the disease entity hysteria was construed as the visible surface of the patient's body and behavior, with its schematized postures, hysterical stigmata, and hysterogenic zones.[205] Like Trillat, Gilman also brings out the psychological and cultural circularity of these images within nineteenth-century culture: doctors first created an appropriate visual idea of the hysteric; then hospitalized patients learned to fulfil this ideal, which further taught the medical profession how to "see" the disease. Finally, widely publicized documents like the *Iconographie photographique* made these images available culturally, which in turn influenced the formation of illness behaviors throughout society.

During many past periods, hysteria was as much seen as heard and read about. Through the work of Didi-Huberman and Gilman, this visual dimension of the history of the disease is being recovered.

Nonfeminist Social and Political Histories

Finally, I wish to discuss three scholars, whose work might well have been absorbed into the traditions discussed above but who, mainly on methodological grounds, may more advantageously be considered under separate cover. The methodological and conceptual frameworks employed by these three authors are quite different, but all three are North American

[204] Ibid., 353–79. On this general subject, see also George Levine, ed., *Realism and Representation: Essays on the Problem of Realism in Relation to Science, Literature, and Culture* (Madison: University of Wisconsin Press, 1992).

[205] Ibid., 345–53, 379–402.

historians with strong interests in European social and medical history, and all three focus on the nineteenth-century experience of hysteria.

Jan Ellen Goldstein is a historian of modern Europe with a strong interest in the history of the professions and Foucauldian theory. In recent years, Goldstein has carved for herself a distinctive niche within hysteria studies by formulating a specifically political interpretation of nineteenth-century hysteria. She first presented her carefully worked out ideas in 1982 in a widely cited article published in the *Journal of Modern History*. She has subsequently elaborated these views in *Console and Classify: The French Psychiatric Profession in the Nineteenth Century* (1987).[206] In Goldstein's work, the history of hysteria forms a chapter in a larger book-length project devoted to "an intellectual history of psychiatry in social and political context."[207]

Goldstein begins her analysis with a historical conundrum: how today are we to understand the well-known phenomenon of a dramatic, almost epidemic, increase in the number of recorded cases of hysteria during the final quarter of the nineteenth century? She judges insufficient past Freudian and feminist responses to the question, with their unicausal emphases on social, psychological, and genderal factors. In contrast, Goldstein explores the political and professional dimensions of hysteria's history.

Throughout the nineteenth century, Goldstein indicates, the French medical profession, and not least the fledgling specialty of psychiatry, underwent a process of rapid and aggressive disciplinary expansion. Key aspects of this development involved securing a reliable patient population for clinical practice and an area of unchallenged technical expertise for scientific research. From her earlier researches on the Esquirolian diagnosis of monomania, Goldstein had discovered the ways in which an entity as specialized and seemingly objective as a psychiatric diagnosis can serve the professional interests of diagnosticians (in that case, French asylum doctors during the 1820s and 1830s).[208] The hysteria diagnosis, she reasons by extension, operated in much the same way half a century later. However, in contrast to monomania, which was associated with the insanities, the hysteria diagnosis, Goldstein observes, laid claim to the large and intermediate range of psychopathologies between a state of full health and complete lunacy. This is an area of mental life that was being medicalized for the first time in the late nineteenth century and

---

[206] Jan Goldstein, "The Hysteria Diagnosis and the Politics of Anticlericalism in Late Nineteenth-Century France," *Journal of Modern History* 104, no. 2 (June 1982): 209–39; idem, *Console and Classify: The French Psychiatric Profession in the Nineteenth Century* (New York: Cambridge University Press, 1987), chap. 9.

[207] *Console and Classify*, 6.

[208] Ibid., chap. 5.

that would be successfully claimed in the twentieth century by the neuroses.

Charcotian hysteria, Goldstein continues, in conjunction with Beardian neurasthenia, broadened the field of pathological phenomena over which psychiatrists prevailed. It also provided for the specialty respectable subject matter for scientific exploration and a large and expanding patient clientele. Nineteenth-century physicians employed military and geographical metaphors in describing their relationship to these nervous disorders, and Goldstein adopts their language: hysteria, she writes, offered a rich and fertile "territory" to be "conquered" and "annexed" to the "domain" of professional mental medicine. "Charcot's interest in hysteria," Goldstein sums up, "can be seen as part of—and one of the most stunningly successful sallies in—an expansionist movement in French psychiatry to capture this 'intermediary zone.'"[209]

In the second level of her argument, Goldstein observes that in the competitive professional marketplace the growth of one discipline inevitably entailed loss for another. In extending their intellectual jurisdiction over hysteria and neurasthenia—a process Goldstein describes aptly as "the appropriation of the *demi-fous*"—physicians inevitably came into conflict with other professional bodies traditionally holding authority over matters of the mind. In nineteenth-century France, this meant, above all, the Catholic Church. Goldstein documents at length the antagonistic relations of the psychiatric profession with the various ruling groups and political regimes in France from the July Monarchy to the Third Republic. Wending her way through an extraordinary range of printed and archival sources, she reconstructs a history of controversy and confrontation between the Church, the state, and the medical profession. During the second half of the 1860s and the early 1870s, the conservative Bonapartist government, in alliance with the Church, had on numerous occasions intervened in the operations of the Paris Faculty of Medicine to suppress state-funded teaching activities deemed subversively atheistic. Charcot and his students pursued a highly organic approach to the study of mind and were also known for their liberal-republican allegiances. By the end of her analysis, Goldstein succeeds in establishing that within the medical politics of the late Second Empire and the early Third Republic, Charcot's aggressively materialized model of the mind and his freshly positivized theory of hysteria carried a high ideological charge.[210]

By the late 1870s, the forces of French republicanism had consolidated their power, and a strong ideological alliance was forged between scientific psychiatry and the new government. Not surprisingly, it was during

[209] Ibid., 333.
[210] Ibid., 339–61.

the 1880s that the study of hysteria flourished most vigorously in Parisian hospitals. Charcot and his followers, Goldstein continues, now operating in an atmosphere that was politically more congenial, seized the intellectual initiative. They spearheaded a campaign for the laicization of nursing staffs in the capital, and Charcot occupied a newly created academic chair devoted to the study of nervous diseases. Most relevantly, Goldstein maintains that a number of salient features of the Salpêtrian theory of hysteria—such as the description in quasi-religious language of stages of the attack and the diagnosis of medieval demoniacs and religious convulsionaries in terms of medical pathology—reflected a strong anticlerical agenda. Goldstein sees the work of the school of the Salpêtrière, then, as part of a more or less self-conscious secularizing strategy designed to present the Church as ignorant, irrational, and old-fashioned and the medical community as a force for reason, humanity, and modern science.[211] It was essentially the great political and professional serviceability of the hysteria concept, in Goldstein's interpretation, that explains its widespread adoption at this particular historical moment.

Goldstein's work reveals interesting similarities to, and differences from, that of Edward Shorter. After a controversial early career in the fields of women's studies and the history of the family, Shorter moved into the history of medicine, with an emphasis on nineteenth-century psychiatry and neurology. Among his many recent publications are four essays on the history of hysteria and the first installment in a two-volume study of the history of nervous disorders in the nineteenth and twentieth centuries.[212]

As with Goldstein, Shorter begins by dissenting from feminist historians of the previous two decades who envision the history of hysteria as "a sort of socio-psychological transaction."[213] In response to the social constructionist interpretations that dominated medical historiography during the 1980s, Shorter seeks to write a kind of clinical history of nervous disease. A social historian of modern Europe with medical training, he is interested in "the history of hysteria as a genuine psychiatric

---

[211] Ibid., 361–77.

[212] Edward Shorter, "Les désordres psychosomatiques, sont-ils 'hystériques'? Notes pour une recherche historique," *Cahiers internationaux de sociologie* 76, special number (January–June, 1984): 201–24; idem, "Paralysis: The Rise and Fall of a 'Hysterical' Symptom," *Journal of Social History* 19 (Summer 1986): 549–82; idem, "Women and Jews in a Private Nervous Clinic in Vienna at the Turn of the Century," *Medical History* 33, no. 2 (April 1989): 149–83; idem, "Mania, Hysteria and Gender in Lower Austria, 1891–1905," *History of Psychiatry* 1, no. 1 (March 1990): 3–31; idem, *From Paralysis to Fatigue: A History of Psychosomatic Illness in the Modern Era* (New York: Free Press, 1992); idem, *From the Mind into the Body: The Cultural Origins of Psychosomatic Symptoms* (New York: Free Press, 1994).

[213] Shorter, "Les désordres psychosomatiques," 204.

disorder"—that is, hysteria as an actual disease entity whose past evolution, including changes in clinical presentation and rates of occurrence, can be charted meaningfully.[214] In the reconstruction of this subject, he consults a large volume of medical-historical data. While Goldstein relies for her theoretical underpinning on Foucault, the historical sociology of science, and the Anglo-American sociology of the professions, Shorter draws on contemporary ethnopsychiatry and epidemiological psychiatry.

Shorter predicates his approach to the history of psychosomatic sickness on the concept of "the symptom pool" or "symptom repertoire."[215] He maintains that the basic mechanism of hysterical conversion (i.e., the expression of acute emotional anxiety through physical symptom formation) has existed with the same relative frequency across time and across cultures. However, the specific bodily signs or syndromes through which the mechanism has operated have varied greatly and have largely been socially and culturally determined. "A range of physical symptoms [are] available to the unconscious mind for the physical expression of psychological conflict . . . and what interests the cultural historian is *why* certain symptoms are selected in certain epochs."[216] Shorter notes, for instance, the prevalence of swooning and convulsive fits in the eighteenth century, which are rare today. In their place, we have witnessed a surge in the number of psychogenic eating disorders among adolescent and young adult women.[217] Shorter also observes that in the nineteenth century the central form of somatization involved sensorimotor disorders, including hysterical paralyses. His most engaging passages are those he devotes to the idea of studying "the social history of a . . . hysterical symptom."[218] Taken together, his work suggests the possibility of writing not only a history of psychiatric ideas but a historical psychology.

Cognizant of the methodological problems inherent in this task, Shorter nonetheless attempts to chronicle such a symptomatological history. Before 1800, he posits, psychogenic motor paralyses were relatively uncommon. However, from a chronological reading of German, French,

---

[214] Ibid., 202; Shorter, "Rise and Fall of a 'Hysterical' Symptom," 549.

[215] Shorter, "Les désordres psychosomatiques," 201–6; idem, "Rise and Fall of a 'Hysterical' Symptom," 549–51; idem, *From Paralysis to Fatigue*, chap. 1.

[216] Shorter, "Rise and Fall of a 'Hysterical' Symptom," 549.

[217] For similar speculations from a medical perspective, refer to C. Stefanis, M. Markidis, and G. Christodoulou, "Observations on the Evolution of the Hysterical Symptomatology," *British Journal of Psychiatry* 128 (March 1976): 269–75 and Jacques Frei, "Contribution à l'étude de l'hystérie: Problèmes de définition et évolution de la symptomatologie," *Schweizer Archiv für Neurologie, Neurochirurgie und Psychiatrie* 134, no. 1 (1984): 93–129.

[218] Shorter, "Rise and Fall of a 'Hysterical' Symptom," 551; *From Paralysis to Fatigue*, 95–128; 267–73.

British, and American medical periodicals, he finds a dramatic increase in these infirmities over the course of the nineteenth century. He reviews the scope of the disturbances (monoplegias, paraplegias, hemiplegias, gait disturbances, articular aches and pains, and muscle contractures of all types) and sprinkles his narrative with dozens of illustrative case histories. Shorter finds the culmination of this pattern in the phenomenon of the chronic nervous invalid, a stock figure in the social histories of Victorian Britain and New England. He provides a memorable historical portrait of what he calls "the couch cases" of the nineteenth century: those innumerable middle- and upper-middle-class ladies of London, Boston, and Philadelphia, confined for months if not years to their bedrooms, endlessly attended by family, friends, and physicians, and shuffling from private nervous clinic to hydropathic establishment to seaside resort. "No historian will be able to account for 'hysteria',," he observes, "who is unable to explain why these women took to their beds and stayed there."[219] Shorter maintains further that, after the turn of the last century, the symptom content of the hysterical neuroses shifted again. After 1900, these high rates of functional paralytic disabilities in women, he reports, vanished "as swiftly and mysteriously as they arose."[220]

What, then, caused these striking changes from generation to generation in the symptomatological content of hysteria? Shorter's ideas on this point are preliminary and speculative. In one place, he proposes a "triangle" of factors, corresponding roughly with biological, sociological, and psychological conditions, which govern the unconscious selection and formation of psychiatric symptoms in every individual.[221] Elsewhere, he observes that the increase in the number of hysterical infirmities was coincident with a period of accelerated industrialization and conjectures that the rise in hysterical paralyses is somehow related to "the logic of capitalism."[222] And in *From Paralysis to Fatigue*, Shorter subsumes the history of hysteria into a larger "history of psychosomatic illness" that stretches continuously from the beginnings of modern medicine three hundred years ago to the present. The ideology of medicine was in a constant state of flux, and Shorter proposes that patients continually changed the manifestations of their psychological anxieties to accord unconsciously with the reigning medical paradigms of the day. For Shorter, the whole smorgasbord of nervous symptoms and eccentricities—from eighteenth-century fainting to the hysterical tics and fits of Charcot's time to the psychogenic pain and fatigue syndromes of

---

[219] Shorter, "Rise and Fall of a 'Hysterical' Symptom," 564.
[220] Ibid., 550.
[221] Shorter, "Mania, Hysteria and Gender in Lower Austria," 1–2, 31–33.
[222] Shorter, "Rise and Fall of a 'Hysterical' Symptom," 573.

today—results from complex codes of illness behavior subtly inculcated by physicians and internalized unconsciously by patients.[223]

The ideas and interpretations put forth by Goldstein and Shorter are controversial. In her purely political analysis of the hysteria diagnosis in nineteenth-century France, Goldstein ignores a number of key clinical and medical-scientific factors. Her argument concerning the relation between hysteria and anticlericalism rests mainly on collateral primary sources (e.g., the writings of Richer, Charles Richet, and Bourneville) rather than the work of Charcot himself; and, as I will discuss below, her thesis does not account adequately for Charcot's most important and personal statement on Catholicism, the essay "La foi qui guérit." For his part, Shorter is most likely to arouse opposition on methodological and epistemological grounds. Diagnostic language between the nineteenth and twentieth centuries has shifted greatly, and many cases Shorter describes from a hundred years ago would doubtless be diagnosed differently today. Past epidemiological data is notoriously unreliable, and, as Goldstein and others show, any number of factors may create the retrospective illusion of an epidemiological rise or decline. Much of what Shorter takes for increases in the incidence of hysterical symptoms may result from other factors, including the growth of neurological knowledge, fashions in diagnostic labeling, the expansion of the popular and professional medical presses, and the greater willingness of middle-class individuals to seek medical consultation. The obstacles to writing historical psychiatric epidemiology may well be insurmountable.

In the final analysis, however, the writings of Goldstein and Shorter are surely among the most important and original within the new hysteria studies. Goldstein brings the latest French and American scholarship on the theme of medicalization to the subject of hysteria. Like MacDonald in his work on Jorden, she presents us with hysteria in situ, deeply and complexly enmeshed in the historical situation of a particular place and time without which it remains incomprehensible. Furthermore, her meticulously researched and carefully crafted interpretations set high scholarly and intellectual standards for the investigation of a subject that is all too susceptible to faddish and sensationalistic treatment. On the other hand, Shorter does not offer us detailed and polished readings but rather a series of highly suggestive general propositions. The idea of writing the history of a single psychogenic physical symptom is most interesting. His attempt to write a history of hysteria from an informed clinical perspective is a notable contribution to the conceptualization of the subject, and he has plumbed the printed medical literature of the past two centuries more deeply than other hysteria historians. Finally, Shorter's concept of cultur-

[223] Shorter, *From Paralysis to Fatigue*, chap. 1.

ally determined and socially sanctioned "styles of somatization" in different cultures and eras may well provide the best conceptual bridge constructed to date between medical and historical approaches to the history of hysteria.

Finally, Janet Oppenheim's *"Shattered Nerves": Doctors, Patients, and Depression in Victorian England* (1991) deserves special mention.[224] Goldstein studies hysteria as an expression of evolving relations between psychiatrists and the French state, and Shorter presents it as a chapter in the history of mind-body relations. For Oppenheim, hysteria is a key component in what she labels "the nervous culture of Victorian England."[225]

Nineteenth-century Britons exhibited an extraordinary preoccupation with nervous and mental disease. From the beginnings of Victoria's reign to the First World War, they generated a large and largely alarmist medical literature about nervousness, neurasthenia, hysteria, nerve prostration, nervous degeneration, and the like. Oppenheim conceptualizes her subject broadly to provide a multidimensional historical portrait of these neuroses in a single cultural, chronological, and geographical setting. She is interested equally in the theoretical, therapeutic, and institutional aspects of the subject and in the history of hysteria from the doctor's and the patient's perspectives. In the course of her analysis, she synthesizes an outstanding array of sources, including medical textbooks, monographs, and periodicals; physicians' casebooks, memoirs, and correspondence; popular medical magazines and public hygiene literature; patients' diaries, letters, and autobiographies; and novels and short stories. She places psychiatric topics in the larger contexts of lay and medical attitudes toward health, disease, the body, love, marriage, sexuality, and maternity.

The lengthiest chapter of *"Shattered Nerves"* deals with "Neurotic Women" in Victorian Britain.[226] Hysteria, Oppenheim observes here, was "the archetypal feminine functional disorder in the nineteenth century."[227] Two contradictory readings of the hysterical female, she finds, emerge from Victorian medical literature: the willess hysteric, who lacked the ability to control her emotional impulses and fell into childish and self-indulgent invalidism, and the willful hysteric, who insubordinately asserted her demands in the face of societal imperatives. Buttressing these views of the hysterical woman, Oppenheim discovers, was general Victorian medical ideology, which depicted women as delicate, decorative, and fundamentally idle creatures, with volatile reproductive apparatuses and a lower position on the scale of cerebral evolution than men. In this view,

---

[224] Janet Oppenheim, *"Shattered Nerves": Doctors, Patients, and Depression in Victorian England* (New York: Oxford University Press, 1991).

[225] Ibid., 14.

[226] Ibid., chap. 6.

[227] Ibid., 181.

the well-known female proclivity to hysterical breakdown resulted from the combination of small brains and large reproductive organs. Despite glaring logical and empirical shortcomings in these ideas and the presence of a great deal of counterevidence, most Victorian physicians, Oppenheim shows, adhered to these beliefs axiomatically. At the same time, Oppenheim emphasizes the diversity of beliefs within the medical profession and reviews the minority opinions of dissenting male doctors, early female doctors, political feminists, and nonfeminist intellectual women.

In retrospect, Oppenheim argues, Victorian and Edwardian psychiatry was a failure both in its theoretical and therapeutic aspirations. Most physicians genuinely, even desperately, wanted to help their hysterical patients, Oppenheim believes. But the doctors envisioned recovery as the restoration of women to the restrictive domestic lives that their society deemed normal for them rather than their achievement of a new emotional strength and self-reliance. Behind this view, Oppenheim argues, rested a highly moralized vision of the nature, causes, symptoms, and cure of psychological sickness generally. With little sense of the social or psychological determinants of many of these cases, it is not surprising that Victorian and Edwardian alienists failed to alleviate the suffering of their patients. As Oppenheim indicates, the moralization of the neuroses in nineteenth-century Britain also had a retarding effect on psychiatric science. Preoccupied with their role as moral authorities, British doctors were consistently surpassed by the French and German medical communities in somatic and psychodynamic psychiatry. In Oppenheim's account, physicians, patients, and families alike are the victims of the Victorian sociosexual system.[228]

A unique feature of *"Shattered Nerves"* is its attention to the life of individual patients. Oppenheim is skeptical of the view of hysteria as a diagnostic construction of malevolent male physicians; in its place, she explores the real mental and emotional anguish of women in Victorian times. She accomplishes this principally by integrating into her narrative a series of poignant biographical vignettes.[229] She relates the life stories of well-known women, such as Beatrice Webb, Olive Schreiner, Maria Sharpe, Eleanor Marx, and Amy Levy, as well as many lesser-known or anonymous figures. Real human faces emerge from the past: intelligent, intellectual women, beleaguered by crippling stereotypes of femininity and struggling to find stimulation and meaning in their personal and professional lives within Victorian bourgeois society. Oppenheim also brings out how the gender codes of the day were internalized. Even strong, independent-minded women who were gifted with sharp critical

---

[228] Ibid., 293–318.
[229] See especially 215–25.

insights into the contemporary social world were deeply troubled by unresolved conflicts about their lives as wives, mothers, and lovers. Their final struggle—which in more than one case eventuated in suicide—was often not with family, physician, or husband but with themselves. If Goldstein provides a political reading of the history of hysteria and Shorter a clinical history, Oppenheim gives us an existential, experiential account that reconstructs the inner histories of hysteria in the lives of individuals from the past.

Of additional relevance in *"Shattered Nerves"* is its relation to the feminist historiographical tradition. Oppenheim is thoroughly versed in the feminist scholarship of the preceding two decades, and she too takes the Victorian hysteric as her subject. Yet, interestingly, she uses her book as an occasion to evaluate the accumulated ideas and interpretations of feminist historical accounts against a mass of new empirical data. As *Shattered Nerves* amply documents, Victorian mental medicine was deeply prejudiced against women. At the same time, Oppenheim contends that many earlier feminist formulations have been skewed for ideological purposes and require qualification, complexification, and in some cases rejection. The view that Victorian hysterical sickness was a mass flight into illness and a passive-aggressive rebellion against the patriarchal order, a staple of feminist scholarship, is a good example. Despite the emotional satisfactions of this claim for late twentieth-century feminists, Oppenheim avers, the idea is only one of several possible explanations for the disorder among middle-class women a century ago. Other backgrounds for nervous collapse, she insists, included disappointment at failed marriages, loneliness and isolation, depression from the death of a spouse or children, and loss of religious faith, as well as organic, especially neurochemical, disorders. Oppenheim also argues that the rebellion hypothesis ignores the many constructive, resourceful, non-neurotic ways in which women managed to navigate through the constraints of Victorian society and lead productive, self-expressive lives.[230] Elsewhere, Oppenheim, in the tradition of Regina Morantz, stresses the diversity of relations between doctors and patients, the limitations imposed on medical practice by the state of scientific knowledge, and the vulnerability of both men and women to the social tensions and cultural anxieties of the time.

For me, Oppenheim's *"Shattered Nerves"* is among the most intellectually satisfying works to appear within the new hysteria studies. Not coincidentally, the book is also among the most interdisciplinary. The author appears to be universally well-read in her subject. She integrates the perspectives of medical, social, and cultural history and draws on

---

[230] Ibid., 226ff.

both scientific and nonscientific sources. In a body of scholarship dominated by specialized studies, her book (like Showalter's) moves ambitiously toward synthesis. Moreover, Oppenheim achieves throughout her narrative the admirable feat of discussing the emotional life and sexuality of an earlier age completely without condescension. Perhaps most welcome is Oppenheim's thoughtful interpretive eclecticism. She resists the appeal of single, overarching explanations for complex historical realities: "We are far better served by the flexibility of an empirical approach to the remaining evidence than by a theoretical rigidity that insists on building explanatory models, even where the foundations are too slight to bear the load."[231] In this spirit, her book repeatedly establishes the sophisticating and particularizing power of detailed empirical research. One comes away from this volume with the impression that there were nearly as many experiences of hysteria in the nineteenth century as there were doctors and patients. It is probably a correct impression. More than any work that has appeared thus far, *"Shattered Nerves"* is the critical beneficiary of the full heritage of hysteria studies.

[231] Ibid., 11.

Chapter 2

THEORIZING DISEASE HISTORIOGRAPHY

THE NEED FOR DEFINITIONAL CLARITY

THE REVIEW of scholarship in the long foregoing chapter establishes the range and richness of the new hysteria studies. With this background, I would now like to move from past and present writing and thinking to future prospects. What are the strengths and weaknesses of the new hysteria studies as a whole? How can we begin to move from the five full but disparate existing traditions of commentary toward a more integrated interdisciplinary discourse on the subject? What is needed for the future intellectual and disciplinary development of the field? And how can we work toward a more comprehensive understanding of the history of disease generally?

All historical inquiry begins with an act of definition, and the history of disease is no exception. The well-known directionalist intellectual histories of hysteria, which have provided generations of readers with an intellectual framework for understanding the subject, give the impression that their subject is a single, unchanging disease entity, recognizable across twenty centuries. For Gilles de la Tourette, Abricossoff, Amselle, and Cesbron, hysteria was one, indivisible, and universal. Similarly, Ilza Veith in 1965 confidently subtitled her study "the history of a disease" and spoke elsewhere of "four thousand years of hysteria."[1] For her, hysteria was an identifiable morbid entity with an ascertainable etiology that remained the same from prehistory to the present and across Europe, Asia, and the Americas. Medical comprehension of the disease evolved through long periods of ignorance and enlightenment, to be sure; but the disease, the pathological object itself, remained stable.

It is becoming increasingly apparent today that these appealing, positivist assumptions are unwarranted. In reading through past medical texts, we realize early on that hysteria through the ages has been characterized in exceedingly various ways. Indeed, it would be difficult to think of another medical category that has proven so capacious over such a long expanse of time. In lay parlance, the word has traditionally denoted a common form of emotionally excessive behavior. In many literary works, it has appeared as a metaphor for a general emotional malaise, a vague

---

[1] Veith, *Hysteria*; idem, "Four Thousand Years of Hysteria."

"hysteria of the heart."[2] Past medical meanings have been no less various and nebulous. In the sixteenth and seventeenth centuries, hysteria was frequently subsumed under the rubric of melancholia. In the eighteenth century, it slid imperceptibly into hypochondria, the vapors, and the spleen. And in nineteenth-century medical discourses it overlapped with nervousness, neurasthenia, and nerve prostration, while "hysterical insanity" was often interpreted as a form of "degeneration" and out-and-out madness. Many physicians through the generations have used the word loosely in reference to any nervous malady with spastic or convulsive complications. In fact, except for the 1870s and 1880s, when Charcot succeeded in imposing a significant degree of semantic and nosographical stability on the concept, doctors have always disagreed about the basic symptomatological composition of the disorder. Throughout history, physicians have complained vociferously about the vagueness and indefinability of hysteria.[3]

The chronic imprecision of the hysteria concept results in part from the nature of the subject itself. Hysteria may assume the form of a great many other diseases, and volatility of temperament is often part of the clinical picture. But the broad diversity of definitions most likely reflects more

[2] Edna Steeves, "Hysteria of the Heart: A Recurrent Theme in Novel Writing" (Paper delivered at the Seventeenth Annual American Society of Eighteenth-Century Studies, Williamsburg, Virginia, March 13–16, 1986).

[3] Writing in his *Epistolary Dissertation* of 1685, Sydenham characterized hysteria as "a farrago of disorderly and irregular phenomena. . . . Hence it is exceedingly difficult to describe a history of the disease" (*The Works of Thomas Sydenham*, 2 vols. [London: Sydenham Society, 1850], 2: 90). A generation later, Bernard de Mandeville, in an imaginary dialogue between a doctor and patient, has the patient exclaim in frustration: "You Gentlemen of Learning make use of very comprehensive Expressions: the word HYSTERICK must be of a prodigious latitude, to signify so many Different Evils, unless you mean by it a Disease, that, like the Sin of Ingratitude, includes all the rest. . . . The very name is become a joke" (*Treatise on Hypochondriack and Hysterick Diseases* (1711), 2d. ed. [1730], 267). "The many and various symptoms which have been supposed to belong to a disease under the appellation," William Cullen observed a century later, "render it extremely difficult to give a general character or definition of it" (*First Lines of the Practice of Physic*, with notes by John Rotherham, 2 vols. [Philadelphia, Parry Hall, 1792], 1:257). And in 1853, Robert Brudenell Carter complained that hysteria, as a diagnostic concept, had "an inexactness unparalleled in scientific phraseology" (*On the Pathology and Treatment of Hysteria* [London, John Churchill, 1853], 1). In 1875, Silas Weir Mitchell described hysteria as "the nosological limbo of all unnamed female maladies. It were as well called mysteria for all its name teaches us of the host of morbid states which are crowded within its hazy boundaries" ("Rest in Nervous Disease: Its Use and Abuse," in E. C. Seguin, ed., *A Series of American Clinical Lectures*, vol. 1, [New York: 1875], no. 4, 94). Three years after Mitchell, the French alienist Charles Lasègue offered his well-known verdict on the disorder: "The definition of hysteria has never been given and never will be. The symptoms are not constant enough, nor sufficiently similar in form or equal in duration and intensity that one type, even descriptive, could comprise them all" ("Des hystéries périphériques," *Archives générales de médecine*, 7th ser., 1 [June 1878]: 655).

than the inherent clinical variability of the phenomenon. Traditional intellectual histories claim that the "basic features [of hysteria] have remained more or less unchanged," an epistemological precondition for the longitudinal reconstruction of a disease concept.[4] But in fact, even on the most literal, phenomenological level, the *differences* in past recorded symptomatologies are at least as striking as the similarities.

Helen King, we learned above, has established that, popular historical expectations notwithstanding, the only features appearing consistently in ancient Hippocratic descriptions of what is reputed to have been hysteria are a moving womb and a sensation of suffocation. A reading of the pertinent Hippocratic texts reveals other symptoms, such as pain in the nostrils, coldness in the limbs, and a blackening of the skin that today are clinically incoherent. Pierre Pomme's *Traité des affections vaporeuses des deux sexes*, the most popular work on the nervous disorders in eighteenth-century France, lists among the commonest signs of hysteria difficulty in breathing, sleepiness, toothache, and a deathlike immobility.[5] In the 1680s, Sydenham, with his fabled powers of clinical observation, considered the only pathognomonic sign of hysteria to be a clear and abundant discharge of urine following a fit.[6] The French alienist Brachet, writing in the 1840s, believed the sensation of a moving ball in the throat and convulsive muscular contractions were emblematic of the disorder.[7] In the 1870s, Charcot concluded that motor and sensory abnormalities—anesthesias, hyperesthesias, paralyses, and contractures—were the most important manifestations of the malady. Many earlier authors interpreted the paroxysm as a key feature; but hysterical attacks scarcely figure at all in the theories of Freud, Janet, and Babinski.

No less divergent have been the mental manifestations projected as part of the disease. Most medical observers have stressed hyperemotional states. Yet Sydenham believed that despair and anxiety were more typical, and the early nineteenth-century British alienist George Burrows emphasized delirium.[8] Burrows's contemporary, Thomas Laycock, argued that a tendency to pathological lying and deceit was the central defining mark.[9] And Janet emphasized "la belle indifférence" of the hysteric. Not without justice, the French psychoanalyst Gérard Wajeman has commented that

---

[4] Veith, *Hysteria*, viii.

[5] Pierre Pomme, *Traité des affections vaporeuses des deux sexes*, 4th ed., 2 vols. (Lyon: Benoit Duplain, 1769), 1: 1–9.

[6] Thomas Sydenham, *Epistolary Dissertation* (1685), in *Works of Thomas Sydenham*, 2, 88.

[7] Brachet's ideas are cited in J. Corraze, "La question de l'hystérie," in Jacques Postel and Claude Quétel, eds., *Nouvelle histoire de la psychiatrie* (Toulouse: Privat, 1983), 403.

[8] George Man Burrows, *Commentaries on Insanity* (London: Underwood, 1828), 191.

[9] Thomas Laycock, "On Anomalous Forms of Hysteria," *Edinburgh Medical and Surgical Journal* 50 (July 1838): 64–65.

"there doesn't seem to be anything that medicine has not said about hysteria: it is multiple, it is one, it is nothing; it is an entity, a malfunction, an illusion; it is true and deceptive; organic and perhaps mental; its exists, it does not exist."[10]

This situation severely complicates the task of the prospective historian of hysteria. Given the wildly diverse descriptions of the subject under study, it is likely that many different morbid phenomena have from time to time been gathered under the umbrella of "hysteria".[11] In fact, as noted earlier, much of the case material that constitutes "the history of hysteria" would almost certainly be reclassified today either as organic disease, psychotic or borderline disorders, nonhysterical neurosis, or perhaps as no sickness at all. With hysteria, the role of organicity demands special attention. Unique among disorders, hysteria (at least as post-Sydenhamian doctors have understood it) is defined by a remarkable ability to simulate other disorders, most often physical and particularly neurological, disorders. It is that disease whose essence lies in imitating other diseases. Moreover—and the point cannot be emphasized strongly enough—hysteria, throughout the greater part of its history, has been interpreted by medical observers as a wholly *somatic* derangement. Currently, we view the disorder as an intensely psychological condition; but until the turn of the last century it was understood as a physical infirmity with a specific projected pathophysiological mechanism: a wandering womb, ascending uterine vapors, irritable ovaries, digestive or menstrual turmoil, a spinal or cerebral lesion, and so forth. In 1965, Eliot Slater and E. Glithero of the National Hospital in Queen Square, London made a documented argument that many cases labeled hysteria in current psychiatric practice were in fact misdiagnosed organic disorders, including epilepsy, head injury, multiple sclerosis, and cerebral vascular disorders.[12] This claim has not gone uncontested, but the general thrust of the criticism sent a collective shudder through the psychiatric profession. What if a large number of diagnosed cases have not been hysteria at all?

Scholars have recently begun to apply this same line of analysis to hysteria's famous past. Working with the ancient Egyptian papyri, Harold

[10] Gérard Wajeman, "The Hysteric's Discourse," in Helena Schulz-Keil, ed., *Hystoria: Lacan Study Notes*, special issue, nos. 6–9 (New York: New York Lacan Study Group, 1988), 1.

[11] Irvine Loudon makes a similar point in regard to a related diagnostic category in "The Diseases called Chlorosis," *Psychological Medicine* 14, no. 1 (February 1984): 27–36.

[12] E.T.O. Slater and E. Glithero, "A Follow-up of Patients Diagnosed as Suffering from 'Hysteria,'" *Journal of Psychosomatic Research* 9, no. 1 (September 1965): 9–13; Slater, "Diagnosis of 'Hysteria,'" *British Medical Journal* 1, no. 5447 (May 29, 1965): 1395–99. See also F. A. Whitlock, "The Aetiology of Hysteria," *Acta Psychiatrica Scandinavica* 43, no. 2 (1967): 144–62; H. Merskey and N. A. Buhrich, "Hysteria and Organic Brain Disease," *British Journal of Medical Psychology* 58, part 4 (December 1975): 359–66.

Merskey and Paul Potter have argued eruditely that the conditions described in these early documents cannot be distinguished from a range of gynecological problems, such as uterine prolapse, puerperal fever, and perimenstrual difficulties.[13] Along the same lines, Phyllis Freeman, Carley Bogarad, and Diane Sholomskas have emphasized the connections between Margery Kempe's "hysteria" and postpartum psychosis.[14] In a study of seventeenth-century English medical writings on hysteria, Katherine Williams has found that many cases appeared in conjunction with fevers, chills, hematuria, pelvic inflammations, and, in one case, a uterine malignancy.[15] And Guenter Risse, working with late eighteenth-century case records from the Royal Edinburgh Infirmary, has discovered that many instances of hysteria were brought on by amenorrhea in young working women.[16] Medical historians have often noted the deep confusion between hysteria and epilepsy that existed until the early twentieth century.[17] My point here is not that all cases recorded as hysteria in the past have been misdiagnosed organic disease, or that historians must begin with an act of diagnostic reassessment. Nor is it that hysteria as we know it has not existed continuously through the centuries. It very well may have. I want rather to suggest that the historical record simply does not allow us to judge with any certainty and accuracy on this point.

Other conceptual obstacles also exist to positing a single, transhistorically valid definition of hysteria. Today, a majority of nonmedical scholars, as well as a fair number of physicians, interpret hysteria less as a discrete psychopathology than as a sort of social communication in the symbolic language of the bodily symptom. In this view, the content and significance of the hysterical communication derive from the ambient social, cultural, and medical milieux. Therefore, the "meaning" of hysteria is substantially different in the worlds of classical Greek paganism, sixteenth-century Catholic demonology, Victorian bourgeois society, and our own post-Freudian late twentieth century. Viewed sociologically, it proves difficult, if not impossible, to compare phenomena from such divergent times and places.[18] At least since the late seventeenth century, medical observers

[13] Merskey and Potter, "The Womb Lay Still in Ancient Egypt," 753.

[14] Freeman et al., "Margery Kempe, A New Theory," 177–81.

[15] Katherine E. Williams, "Hysteria in Seventeenth-Century Case Records and Unpublished Manuscripts," *History of Psychiatry* 1, no. 4 (December 1990): 383–401.

[16] Guenter Risse, "Hysteria at the Edinburgh Infirmary: The Construction of Hysteria, 1876–1895," *Medical History* 32, no. 1 (January 1988): 8–9, n. 32 and 16.

[17] Temkin, *The Falling Sickness*, 2d ed., 351–59; C. Muller, "Épilepsie et hystérie (Problème historique et d'actualité)," *Revue médicale et la Suisse Romande* 82, no. 2 (February 1962): 98–102; E. M. Thornton, *Hypnotism, Hysteria and Epilepsy: An Historical Synthesis* (London: William Heinemann, 1976).

[18] Analogously, Joan Jacobs Brumberg has argued against the clinical or cultural equation of the fasting practices of medieval saints, or morbid and prolonged self-denial of food

have noted in hysteria an extraordinary, chameleon-like capacity to reflect the environment in which it develops. More recently, Sander Gilman, Charles Rosenberg, Janet Golden, and Edward Shorter have underscored the innumerable social and cultural determinants of disease forms.[19] From this perspective, if hysteria is the psychopathology, or disorder, or behavioral phenomenon, that is most likely to change in content over time, that offers the greatest number of sickness presentations, and that is the most reactive to and reflective of changing external circumstances, are we justified in retrospectively imposing on it a single psychiatric interpretation from the late twentieth century?

Confronted with these prodigious conceptual and epistemological problems, historians may pursue a number of strategies. We might, for example, attempt to determine what past patients diagnosed as hysterical "really had," in order to exclude those cases that sound like something else and to assemble a body of genuine instances of the malady. This line of analysis has produced some interesting work; but retrospective rediagnosis, as I tried to show above, is a notoriously slippery exercise. Given the highly fragmentary nature of past medical records, as well as major shifts in diagnostic categorization over the generations, I am less than sanguine about the possibility of writing a meaningful clinical history of hysteria.[20] Alternatively, we might employ a twentieth-century model of the disorder—say, the Freudian theory of conversion hysteria—to determine which cases should be included and excluded in a historical account. But, besides the obvious presentism of such an approach, contemporary psychiatric criteria of hysteria, no less than those from earlier times, are fiercely controversial and provide no consensual standard for judging past writings. Many physicians today question if hysteria even constitutes a bona fide disorder. Still again, we might attempt modestly to limit ourselves to a history of those people labeled hysterical in the past. But even an attempt to establish this sort of simple linguistic continuity proves impossible. A plethora of terms ("the fits," "suffocation of the Mother," "uterine epilepsy," "clonus hysteria," "neurospasmania," "pithiatism," "psychasthenia"), that may or may not have designated medically equivalent phenomena, have been used through the centuries.

---

in a religious context, and the modern medical concept of anorexia nervosa. See *Fasting Girls: The Emergence of Anorexia Nervosa as a Modern Disease*, (London: Harvard University Press, 1988), 2–3, 41–47.

[19] Gilman, *Disease and Representation*; Charles E. Rosenberg and Janet Golden, eds., *Framing Disease: Studies in Cultural History* (New Brunswick, N.J.: Rutgers University Press, 1992); Shorter, *From Paralysis to Fatigue* and *From the Mind into the Body*.

[20] Jacques Revel and Jean-Pierre Peter share my skepticism on this point. See "Le corps: L'homme malade et son histoire," in Jacques Le Goff and Pierre Nora, eds., *Faire de l'histoire*, 3 vols. (Paris: Gallimard, 1974), 3: 169–91.

Furthermore, as King and Russell Brain have determined, the noun "hysteria" did not even enter the English language until the late eighteenth century.[21]

At the current stage of our understanding, I believe that the most satisfactory approach to these problems is twofold. First, at the outset of our work we should pause to reflect on the nature of the available historical evidence and its limitations. We then need to acknowledge the conceptual, interpretive, and methodological complexities inherent in writing "the history of a disease" and to work toward formulating a thoughtful historical epistemology.[22] Such a working epistemology will vary for different historical subjects. For diseases with known organic etiologies and clear and consistent symptom profiles, the epistemological conditions for historical inquiry will be simpler and less confining. Generally speaking, the history of organic medicine will be easier to approach than psychological medicine, although here too viruses may mutate over time, immunological responses evolve, and so forth. Within the history of psychiatry, where the causes of so many disorders remain unknown, the task of historical reconstruction will necessarily be more difficult. While Stanley Jackson has demonstrated persuasively that the symptom profiles of what we now call the depressive disorders appear consistently and continuously in records reaching from ancient times down to our own day, though of course under varying names (e.g., melancholia), this cannot be claimed for many other psychodiagnostic categories.[23] The intricacies and indeterminacies of writing the history of hysteria in particular are great and must be confronted. In turn, these matters rest on the larger, thornier questions of the meaning and definition of "disease" and "illness" generally.[24]

[21] Some of these same points about the difficulties inherent in writing linear intellectual histories of disease are discussed in regard to another diagnostic category by John Gabbay in "Asthma Attacked: Tactics for the Reconstruction of a Disease Concept," in Peter Wright and Andrew Treacher eds., *The Problem of Medical Knowledge: Examining the Social Construction of Medicine* (Edinburgh: Edinburgh University Press, 1982), 29–35.

[22] One of the chief strengths of Oppenheim's *"Shattered Nerves"* in my opinion is that it opens with a lengthy discussion of precisely these matters.

[23] Stanley W. Jackson, *Melancholia and Depression: From Hippocratic Times to Modern Times* (New Haven: Yale University Press, 1986), esp. chaps. 1 and 5.

[24] From a large literature on this topic, see Henry Cohen, "The Evolution of the Concept of Disease," in Brandon Lush, ed., *Concepts of Medicine: A Collection of Essays on Aspects of Medicine* (Oxford: Pergamon Press, 1961), 159–169; F. K. Taylor, "A Logical Analysis of the Medico-Psychological Concept of Disease," *Psychological Medicine* 50 (1971): 356–64; Jean-Pierre Peter, "Les mots et les objets de la maladie," *Revue historique* 399 (July–September 1971): 13–38; C. Boorse, "On the Distinction between Disease and Illness," *Philosophy and Public Affairs* 5 (1975): 49–68; Robert E. Kendell, "The Concept of Disease and Its Implications for Psychiatry," *British Journal of Psychiatry* 127 (1975): 305–15; Guenter Risse, "Health and Disease: History of the Concepts," in Warren T. Reich, ed.,

Second, I believe that our analytical approach must be thoroughly and conscientiously contextualist. It is only by establishing as fully and accurately as possible the range of contemporary medical, social, and cultural meanings of hysteria in particular past settings that we can talk in historical terms about the subject. If we pick up a piece of medical writing on hysteria today, we are likely to find ourselves plunged at the outset into a detailed and seemingly pedantic debate over terminology. Is hysteria a personality structure, a mechanism of psychoneurotic illness, a psychogenic symptom reaction, or a pattern of collective behavior? How does the condition relate nosographically to conversion disorder, Briquet's syndrome, somatization disorder, and abnormal illness behavior? After decades of clouding their discussions with usages that were unclear and contradictory, physicians now acknowledge the need to begin with a set of clearly defined criteria.[25] Historians do not have to formulate a viable clinical model of hysteria. Nor need we struggle to determine if hysteria is a "real" disease. But we do need to establish a valid *historical* definition of the concept within our writings: How was hysteria characterized in the medical doctrines of the authors and periods under consideration? What was the general scientific system from which these definitions derived their contemporary cognitive meaning? What were the popular and cultural meanings and associations of the concept? And how did these associations operate socially and culturally within their own time?

A large volume of hysteria studies, old and new, are in my view vitiated by their lack of a preliminary definition of the subject under discussion. Disease formulations of hysteria have been so radically different through the ages, and the ontological status of the concept is so uncertain, that to refer to the disorder as a single historical phenomenon may be primarily a convenient fiction. At our current level of knowledge, the Veithian project of writing a single, synthetic, diachronic history is probably unmanageable. In its place, however, it is possible to reconstruct the multiple past

---

Encyclopedia of Bioethics, 4 vols. (New York: Free Press, 1978), 2: 579–85; F. Kraüpl Taylor, *The Concepts of Illness, Disease and Morbus* (Cambridge: Cambridge University Press, 1979); Ruth Macklin, "Mental Health and Mental Illness: Some Problems of Definition and Concept Formation," in Arthur L. Caplan, H. Tristram Engelhardt, Jr., and James J. McCartney, eds., *Concepts of Health and Disease: Interdisciplinary Perspectives* (Reading, Mass.: Addison-Wesley, 1981), 391–418; and Jerome C. Wakefield, "The Concept of Mental Disorder," *American Psychologist* 48, no. 3 (March 1992): 373–88. The classic medical-historical discussion of this issue is Owsei Temkin's "The Scientific Approach to Disease: Specific Entity and Individual Sickness," in A. C. Crombie, ed., *Scientific Change* (New York: Basic Books, 1963), 629–47.

[25] On the enduring diversity of hysterias in medical theory and the need to decide among them, see Micheline Castaigne, "Les confins de l'hystérie," *Reuve du praticien* 32 (1982): 922–24; and Russell Meares et al., "Whose Hysteria: Briquet's, Janet's or Freud's?" *Australian and New Zealand Journal of Psychiatry* 19, no. 3 (1985) 256–63.

languages of hysteria and their many local contexts and meanings. If these epistemological issues are not to undermine the possibility of writing about hysteria altogether, then we need to begin with a careful act of definition and to respect the historical specificity of disease concepts.

BEYOND THE "HISTORICAL HYSTERICS"

A second requirement for the future historical study of hysteria is to broaden the empirical foundation of our knowledge. As readers may have noticed from the review above, a remarkably large amount of what we think we know about hysteria in the past rests on a very slender evidential base. This base is composed primarily of what the French psychoanalyst Lucien Israël has called the "historical hysterics" of the nineteenth century:[26] the early patients of Freud, the women in Charcot's *Iconographie photographique*, and cultural and literary figures like Charlotte Perkins Gilman, Alice James, Eleanor Marx, and Virginia Woolf. That these cases should have seized our attention is altogether understandable. They involve the lives of famous doctors and celebrated patients, and they are recorded in interesting and easily accessible documents that portray what Roy Porter has called "articulate sufferers."[27] The problem lies with generalization. Even taken together, these twenty or so individuals comprise only a minuscule fraction of the overall number of cases diagnosed as hysterical in the past. The information they offer is insufficient for broad conclusions; and they may in fact provide a picture of the diagnosis that in important ways is unrepresentative of larger historical realities.

There are a number of ways in which we might broaden our historical knowledge. We can first conduct fresh empirical researches on the "historical hysterics" themselves. This has been the approach, as we have seen, of scholars such as Ola Andersson, Henri Ellenberger, Albrecht Hirschmüller, and Peter Swales, who have unearthed new information about the personal and medical biographies of the patients discussed in the *Studies on Hysteria*.[28] No less interesting are those of Freud's patients whom he does *not* discuss in his publications. In some of the most engaging pages of Hirschmüller's monograph on Breuer, we get a glimpse of two women diagnosed as hysterical—Emma L. and Clara B.—who were treated by Breuer in the 1880s but not included in the *Studies on Hysteria*.[29] Elsewhere, he has uncovered a third case of a severely hysterical woman, Nina R., who was seen by both Breuer and Freud over a five-year

[26] Israël, *L'hystérique, le sexe et le médecin*, 196.

[27] Roy Porter, "The Patient's View: Doing Medical History from Below," *Theory and Society* 14, no. 2 (March 1985): 176.

[28] See the discussion of these texts above, 62–64.

[29] Hirschmüller, *Physiologie und Psychoanalyse*, 183–94, 383–89.

period in the same sanatorium in which Anna O. was treated.[30] The letters and drafts exchanged between Freud and Fliess from the 1890s contain references to over a dozen hysterical patients who have never been investigated by modern scholarship.

What seems particularly urgent at this point, however, is the need to unrivet our gaze from the figures of Freud and Charcot. To be sure, the study of psychoanalytic hysteria will continue to flourish, and a serious book-length study of Charcot's hysterical patients has yet to be written. But these medical giants were only two among a great many theoreticians whose work deserves study in its own right and sheds light on the intellectual working environments of Charcot and Freud.

The fact that the world of late nineteenth-century hysteria extended far beyond the walls of the Salpêtrière and Berggasse 19 is borne out by a reading of two recent French dissertations: Philippe Miloche's "Un méconnu de l'hystérie: Victor Dumont Pallier" (1982) and Béatrice Auvray-Escalard's "Un méconnu de l'hystérie: Jules Bernard Luys" (1984).[31] Victor Alphonse Amédée Dumont Pallier (1826–99) worked at La Pitié hospital in Paris from 1870 to 1886 and at the Hôtel-Dieu from 1886 until the end of his life. He gathered around him a group of students to conduct extensive research on the hypnotic psychology and physiology of hysteria. In 1886, he founded the *Revue de l'hypnotisme expérimental et thérapeutique* and in 1889 served as president of the first international congress on hypnosis in Paris. Like Charcot, Dumont Pallier conceptualized hypnosis as an artificial neurosis that could only be induced in hysterical individuals. However, he showed little interest in Charcot's *grande hystéro-épilepsie*, with its rigid four-part attack, and studied the less histrionic physical and mental manifestations of the disorder. He was particularly interested in hysterical disorders of the peripheral vasomotor system and the bilateral distribution of hysterical symptoms. Combining Charcot's notion of the hysterogenic zone with his own research on cerebral hemispheric function, he developed a theory of hysterical "reflexogenic motor zones." In a similar vein, Jules Bernard Luys, as Auvray-Escalard shows, worked at La Charité hospital in Paris during the final decades of the century, where he pursued his own laboratory studies of hysteria, developing a number of new theories about the disorder and conducting dramatic public demonstrations.

It is probably no coincidence that the new studies of Luys and Dumont

[30] Hirschmüller, "Eine bisher unbekannte Krankengeschichte Sigmund Freuds und Josef Breuers aus der Entstehungszeit der 'Studien über Hysterie,'" *Jahrbuch der Psychoanalyse*, vol. 10 (Bern: Hans Huber, 1978), 136–68.

[31] Philippe Miloche, "Un méconnu de l'hystérie: Victor Dumont Pallier (1826–1899)" (Ph.D. diss., University of Caen, 1982); Béatrice Auvray-Escalard, "Un méconnu de l'hystérie: Jules Bernard Luys (1828–1897)" (Ph.D. diss., University of Caen, 1984). For assistance in securing these sources, I thank Dr. Pierre Morel.

Pallier have issued from French provincial medical faculties. As Bernheim and the Nanceans attacked the medical dominance of Paris in the 1880s, so a young generation of scholars in the French provinces a century later is challenging the historiographical hegemony of Charcot and the Salpêtrière.[32] No doubt beyond the capital cities that have monopolized our historical perceptions of hysteria thus far there exist other *méconnus*. To cite one further example: Dr. Joseph Grasset of Montpellier. Grasset (1849–1918) was born, educated, and passed virtually his entire career in the southern French city of Montpellier. By all accounts, he was a brilliant physician with exceptionally wide-ranging medical interests. He occupied in turn the professorships of therapeutics, clinical medicine, and general pathology on the Montpellier faculty. In a long and prolific career, Grasset wrote on many neurological and psychological topics (he is probably best known for his *Traité pratique des maladies du système nerveux*), but from the mid-1880s to the mid-1890s, he concentrated on hysteria. Grasset presented his ideas in a series of writings in local medical publications. During the peak of European interest in the subject, it was Grasset, rather than Charcot or one of the Salpêtrians, who furnished the book-length entry on hysteria for the largest of the nineteenth-century French medical encyclopedias.[33]

In the first three editions of his *Traité* as well as his encyclopedia article, Grasset presented hysteria in classically Charcotian terms, as a neurodegenerative disease with an array of physical manifestations that required treatment by medical electricity and hydrotherapy.[34] With the fourth edition of his treatise in 1893–94, however, published a year after Charcot's death, he adopted a more psychological formulation.[35] In this edition, Grasset, now under the sway of Lasègue and Janet, added a lengthy section on the "mental stigmata" of hysteria, including amnesias, abulias, and "subconscious fixed ideas." After 1896, he broke free from the ideas of other practitioners and struck out on his own, concocting a

---

[32] The theses of Miloche and Auvray-Escalard were supervised by Dr. Pierre Morel of the Department of Psychiatry at the University of Caen. Morel has embarked upon a project to reconstruct the history of hysteria in France outside the work of Charcot.

[33] Joseph Grasset, "Hystérie," in Amédée Dechambre and Léon Lereboullet, eds., *Dictionnaire encyclopédique des sciences médicales*, 100 vols. (Paris: Asselin et Houzeau, 1889), 4th ser., 15: 240–352.

[34] Joseph Grasset, *Maladies du système nerveux*, 2 vols. (Montpellier: C. Coulet, 1879), 2: 549–623; idem, *Traité pratique des maladies du système nerveux*, 2d ed. (Montpellier: C. Coulet, 1881), 921–72; idem, *Traité pratique des maladies du système nerveux*, 3d ed. (Montpellier: Coulet, 1886), 973–1029.

[35] Joseph Grasset and G. Rauzier, *Traité pratique des maladies du système nerveux*, 4th ed., 2 vols. (Montpellier: C. Coulet, 1899–94), 2: 715–831, esp. 715–24, 787–808, and 823–25. See also Grasset, "La théorie psychologique de l'hystérie," *Nouveau Montpellier médical* 36, nos. 44–45 (November 1893): 866–79, 885–98.

kind of anatomo-metaphysical model of the disorder. He proposed a "theory of the two psychisms," in which the human mind consists of a superior, conscious level of functioning (which Grasset designated as "the Letter O.") and an inferior, "polygonal" level of unconscious operation. Grasset postulated that both mental levels reveal anatomical and physiological correlatives and that hysteria results from a lack of coordination between the strata.[36] Until the end of his life, Grasset subscribed to his theory of dual psychisms, reminiscent of Meynert's "brain mythology" of the 1880s and Freud's later structural model of the psyche.

The interpretive significance of the work of these physicians is considerable. The standard view today of hysteria theory in France during the nineteenth century pits Charcot and the school of the Salpêtrière against Liébeault and Bernheim of Nancy; no other worthy contenders are acknowledged. But in fact, we can see that the period gave rise to several major *chefs d'écoles*, both inside Paris and outside, with evolving allegiances among members of the groups. Each of these figures had a theory or model of the disease, a program of experimental research, a following of students and patients, and strong popular appeal. A full history of hysteria in France during the fin de siècle, then, should include all of the major theoreticians of the disorder—Janet, Dumont Pallier, Luys, Grasset, Lasègue, Pitres, and Babinski, as well as Charcot and Bernheim —and their coteries of followers. The fog beyond Paris and Vienna is just beginning to clear, and the view beyond these capital cities is revealing a rich and variegated historical landscape.

Even with this enlargement, however, our picture will remain incomplete. The Charcots, Bernheims, and Grassets of the world were elite urban practitioners. Beyond this, we know almost nothing of the ideas and practices of the general mass of doctors. For this dimension of the story, the most satisfactory means of investigation is most likely quantitative. We get an excellent idea of the type of understanding this approach may impart by looking at the 1987 study of Francis G. Gosling, *Before Freud: Neurasthenia and the American Medical Community, 1870–1910.*[37]

George Beard's fashionable diagnostic creation from the American Gilded Age is a familiar historical item; yet, as with hysteria, nearly everything we know about neurasthenia has come down to us from the practices of a few famous physicians—chiefly from Beard and Mitchell— and the fictional and autobiographical writings of their best-known pa-

---

[36] Grasset, *Leçons de clinique médicale faites à l'hôpital Saint-Eloi de Montpellier*, 3d ser. (Montpellier: Coulet et fils, 1895–98), 122–248; 4th ser. (1898–1902), 724–40; idem, "Le psychisme inférieur," *Revue des deux mondes* 26, no. 2 (March 15, 1905): 314–47.

[37] Francis G. Gosling, *Before Freud: Neurasthenia and the American Medical Community, 1870–1910* (Chicago: University of Illinois Press, 1987).

tients. In contrast, Gosling offers a comprehensive content analysis of the remarks on neurasthenia that appeared in American medical journals from Beard's first pronouncement on the topic in 1869 to the waning of the diagnosis around 1910. In all, this literature consists of some 322 articles, written by 262 physicians, presenting 387 cases of the disorder. Gosling investigates the use of the neurasthenia label in private medical practices, municipal hospitals, public dispensaries, private sanatoria, and state-operated asylums. He explores the development of the etiological theories and symptom profiles of the diagnosis over a forty-year period. He provides a collective biography of the medical practitioners who wrote on the subject and supplies a composite social and medical portrait of the neurasthenic population by looking at the age, sex, occupation, social class, and marital status of patients. He traces the spread of the diagnosis from prestigious northeastern neurologists to doctors in small towns and rural areas of the United States and to members of an increasing variety of medical specialties.

Gosling's study provides the sort of indispensable body of data about a past diagnostic concept that we urgently need for other psychodiagnostic categories and that can serve as the basis for social and cultural interpretation. Up to this point, our understanding of hysteria has been selective and impressionistic. By moving beyond canonical medical and literary texts, by reading comprehensively, and by simple counting, we can achieve a much fuller historical picture of the doctors, the patients, and the diagnosis involved.

FROM THEORY TO PRACTICE

As we saw in chapter 1, the largest quantity of historical writing in hysteria studies concerns the intellectual history of the disorder. Writing a formal history of medical concepts remains a useful and defensible exercise, and, when dealing with earlier historical periods in which primary materials are scarce, this may be all that is possible. However, an exclusively intellectual-historical methodology has two implications: it places the scientific enterprise of the physician above the existential experience of the patient (of which more below), and it privileges medical ideas over medical practice.

In 1967, Erwin Ackerknecht, the preeminent senior medical historian in the world at the time, penned a three-page article in the *Journal of the History of Medicine and Allied Sciences* titled "A Plea for a 'Behaviorist' Approach in Writing the History of Medicine."[38] Here, Ackerknecht

---

[38] Erwin H. Ackerknecht, "A Plea for a 'Behaviorist' Approach in Writing the History of

underscored the frequently large discrepancies between the scientific ideas recorded by elite practitioners in printed texts and what the majority of the medical profession actually did in daily practice. Ackerknecht's admonition makes us realize that most of our historical knowledge about hysteria concerns etiological theory—that is, ideas about the nature and causes of the malady—and avant-garde medical theory at that. Even with the most famous physicians, we know little about how they treated the patient once the diagnosis of hysteria was established. As for lesser-known physicians, whether in private or institutional settings, their therapeutic regimens remain entirely obscure.

The value of combining the history of medical theory with the history of medical practice is evident in a smattering of the new hysteria studies. Katherine Williams has investigated the hysteria diagnosis in seventeenth-century English medical practice.[39] She begins by detailing the theories of hysteria held by the most prominent medical men of the sixteenth and seventeenth centuries, such as Harvey, Jorden, Burton, Willis, and Sydenham. She then moves beyond printed medical texts to explore manuscript sources from two major repositories—the Sloane Collection of the British Library and the Manuscript Collection of the Wellcome Institute for the History of Medicine—that include the case records of several lesser-known doctors working in London, Yorkshire, and Stratford-on-Avon during the 1670s, 1680s, and 1690s.

From these unpublished medical logs, Williams is able to determine that these doctors applied the label of hysteria (or diagnostic terms which Williams believes are congruent with latter-day hysteria) to between six and ten percent of their patients. These patients were invariably women in their twenties and thirties, a majority of whom were married at the time they fell ill. Several were or had recently been pregnant, and most are listed as "Miss" or "Mrs.," which Williams surmises signifies a middle-class background. These doctors did not expatiate on theoretical views about hysteria; but, as Williams points out, the terminologies and remedies they employ reveal their beliefs about disease etiology. They referred to "furor uterinus," "the vapours," and "suffocation of the Mother," and they often wrote about the disorder in tandem with urogenital difficulties, reproductive irregularities, and menstrual problems. To combat the malady, they prescribed a small arsenal of "antihystericals"; one physician

Medicine," *Journal of the History of Medicine and Allied Sciences* 22, no. 3 (July 1967): 211–14. See also idem, "Nonideological Elements in the History of Psychiatry," in George Mora and Jeanne L. Brand, eds., *Psychiatry and Its History: Methodological Problems in Research* (Springfield, Ill.: Charles C. Thomas, 1970), 223–28, which elaborates on this theme in the history of psychiatry.

[39] Williams, "Hysteria in Seventeenth-Century Records and Unpublished Manuscripts."

applied a sweet-smelling pessary to the vulvar area to secure the uterus in its place.[40]

On first reading, Williams's article appears unremarkable, and her sources at this stage are too few to permit generalizations about seventeenth-century English medical practice. Nevertheless, her study establishes that hysteria three hundred years ago was not simply a theoretical entity but a real, workaday diagnosis for doctors. Moreover, her discovery of a large number of "middle-class" patients calls into question the image of the nervous disorders at this time as the preserve of the aristocratic classes. Most importantly, her study uncovers glaring discrepancies between the writings of the best-known medical authors of the age and the everyday practices of the rank and file of the profession. Despite the new and widely publicized theories of the neurophysiological nature of hysteria in the 1670s and 1680s, theories that have repeatedly been foregrounded in the ideocentric historiography of the subject, professional contemporaries of Willis and Sydenham clung tenaciously to Hippocratic and Galenic conceptualizations of the disorder.[41]

A second relevant piece is Guenter Risse's study of the hysteria diagnosis at the Royal Infirmary of Edinburgh in the late eighteenth century.[42] Risse examines the theories and practices of some of the most eminent medical men of the time, including Whytt, Blackmore, Cheyne, and Cullen, who served as academic physicians at one of Europe's most prestigious medical centers. However, his analysis rests on the published writings of these figures and two rich collections of clinical materials from hospital archives. The surviving folios of the General Registry of Patients at the Royal Edinburgh Infirmary present a detailed profile of the hysterical population between 1770 and 1800. From this thirty-year period, Risse locates 157 cases of "hysteria" or "hysteric complaint." Examining this historical data at five-year intervals, he finds that between .2 percent and 3.5 percent of the total number of yearly admissions were so diagnosed. Ninety-eight percent of the patients (that is, all but three) were women, and a majority (63 percent) were unmarried. In age, they ranged from fourteen to sixty-two, and all of them at this municipal facility were from the lower social orders. The average length of hospitalization was twenty-six days.[43]

The medical casebooks from the Infirmary, consisting of cases pre-

---

[40] Ibid., 387–90, 391–99.

[41] Williams's study may profitably be read in conjunction with Michael MacDonald's introductory essay in *Hysteria and Witchcraft in Elizabethan London*; and George S. Rousseau's, "'A Strange Pathology': Hysteria in the Early Modern World, 1500–1800," in Gilman et al., *Hysteria Beyond Freud*, chap. 2.

[42] Risse, "Hysteria at the Edinburgh Infirmary."

[43] Ibid., 5–6.

sented by professors during their daily rounds in the teaching wards and recorded by medical students, provide another window onto the daily clinical practice of eighteenth-century Scottish doctors. For the period 1771–99, Risse locates thirty clinical histories of hysterical female patients that include detailed information about therapeutics.[44] A regular and wholesome manner of living, with no excesses of eating, drinking, or sexuality, was believed to be the best prophylactic measure against hysterical sickness. For patients with mild hysterical symptoms, Drs. Cullen, Gregory, Home, Hope, and Rutherford prescribed restorative regimens of a nourishing diet, moderate physical exercise, iron-based tonics, and warm footbaths. For severe cases, they intervened with opiate-based, antispasmodic medications. Risse finds further that 42 percent of the hysterical patients were given blisters; 25 percent underwent "electric sparks" applied to the throat or lower abdominal area; 17 percent were subjected to regular bloodletting; and 12 percent were treated with leeches.[45] He also calculates that an annual average of 58 percent of the hysteria patients left the Infirmary with the classification of "cured," 33 percent were discharged as "relieved," and 9 percent departed without the doctor's approval.[46] Risse's sources thus provide a historical picture not of etiological ideas or general therapeutic ideals but of the actual hands-on treatment administered to a particular clinical population in a concrete historical institutional setting.

A third work of this kind is *Évolution de la conception de l'hystérie de 1870 à 1930 dans un service de l'asile de Maréville*, by Frédérique Menzaghi, Annie Millot, and Michèle Pillot.[47] The Maréville asylum, currently the Centre hospitalier spécialisé de Nancy, is located several kilometers southwest of Nancy in the department of the Meurthe-et-Moselle in eastern France. With a patient population of between 1,400 and 1,950, Maréville was the largest mental hospital in France during the closing decades of the nineteenth century. The authors of the study, one of whom is a psychiatric nurse at the institution, gained access to the hospital's past annual administrative statistics and the medical dossiers for the admissions department. For the sixty-year period under review, Menzaghi, Millot, and Pillot locate 173 dossiers pertaining to hysteria.

Probably the most notable feature of the diagnosis in these records is that it almost always appears in a secondary or adjectival capacity. At

[44] Risse reproduces one of these cases in "Hysteria at the Edinburgh Infirmary," 21–22.
[45] Ibid., 10–13.
[46] Ibid., 6 and 14.
[47] Frédérique Menzaghi, Annie Millot, and Michèle Pillot, *Évolution de la conception de l'hystérie de 1870 à 1930 dans un service de l'asile de Maréville*, 2 vols. (Master's thesis, University of Nancy II, 1987). My grateful thanks to Jacqueline Carroy for her help in obtaining a copy of this work.

Maréville, hysteria rarely took the form of a disease entity per se but rather of a kind of behavioral gloss that could be applied to an array of more severe, primary psychopathologies. For the period between 1870 and 1930, Menzaghi, Millot, and Pillot report the following diagnostic headings and numbers of cases: "folie hystérique"—49; "manie hystérique"—25; "hystéro-épilepsie"—11; "mélancolie hystérique"—7; "hystérie simple"—6; "lypémanie avec symptômes hystériques"—4; "hystéro-névropathique"—3; "pithiatisme"—2; "imbécilité hystérique"—1; and "démence hystérique"—1.[48] From 1910 to 1930, more elaborate hybrid diagnoses appeared, such as "hystéro-mélancolie avec préoccupations hypocondriaques" and "crises hystériformes très nettes accompagnées d'idées fixes de persécution."

What did hysteria represent to Maréville alienists that it could combine freely with so many psychiatric categories? Above all, the cases to whom the label was affixed were characterized by an impulsive or irrational emotivity: the patients laughed or cried without reason; they talked too much (a condition one doctor dubbed "hysterical logorrhea"); or they were excessively sentimental or self-dramatizing. Several women were said to display "the hysterical temperament," which seems to have meant they lied habitually or faked physical sickness. Sexual behaviors also figured prominently in the profiles of patients. Despite the polemicizing of Briquet and Charcot, the age-old association of hysteria and hypersexuality remained strong in the minds of these provincial doctors. Finally, exaggerated religiosity was noted in a surprising number of cases. In other words, any of the basic psychotic disorders, as we would say today, occurring with behaviors that were erratic, or erotic, or ecstatic, were liable at Maréville to receive the hysteria label.[49]

The Maréville study, combined with the writings of Williams and Risse, present hysteria in three different national, chronological, and institutional settings. Williams investigates differences in theoretical attitudes between the medical avant-garde and the mainstream of the profession; Risse concentrates on quotidian clinical realities, with an emphasis on therapeutic practice; and Menzaghi, Millot, and Pillot focus on the evolution of diagnostic language and systems. The kinds of knowledge generated by a "behaviorist approach" to psychiatric history are limited only by the content of the sources and the analytical ingenuity of the historian. In each historical setting, the author or authors find that hyste-

[48] Ibid., 1: 22.

[49] A study similar in scope and methodology to that of Menzaghi, Millot, and Pillot is Giel Hutschemaekers's *Neurosen in Nederland: Vijfentachtig jaar psychisch en maatschappelijk* (Nijmegen: S.U.N., 1990), esp. chaps. 10 and 11. Hutschemaekers examines the evolution of the hysteria diagnosis from 1900 to 1985 as recorded in 5,450 patient files from seven mental health care facilities in the Netherlands.

ria was recognized widely, diagnosed routinely, and treated regularly. Williams and Risse discover that the concept was fully operative one to two hundred years before the age of Charcot and Freud. Williams, Menzaghi, Millot, and Pillot examine their subjects during well-known periods in the history of ideas about hysteria; but both studies provide a picture that is considerably at variance with that in standard intellectual histories. All three works locate the disorder in substantial numbers outside the age groups and social classes previously postulated as typical. The modest studies of Williams, Risse, and Menzaghi, Millot, and Pillot represent tentative moves beyond a purely textual history of hysteria and indicate that the revisionist potential of such an approach is considerable.

BEYOND THE FREUDIAN HISTORICAL TELEOLOGY

From its earliest days right up to the present, the history of psychiatry has been marked by the existence of competing, if not bitterly opposing, schools. Most conspicuously, since the eighteenth century the field has been convulsed by a deep, dichotomous debate between the somatic and mentalist philosophies of mind. The historiographical ramifications of this division have been great. With every dialectical change in the dominant psychiatric paradigm, the vantage point for the retrospective construction of the history of the discipline has changed. Each generation of practitioners has produced a historical account that privileges those past ideas and practices anticipating its own formation and that consigns to marginal status competing ideas and their heritages. In this process, individual figures and texts—sometimes entire epochs—have been excluded from the historical record.

Psychiatric history writing as a field of professional study came into existence primarily during the first half of the present century. This period corresponds with the ascent of the so-called depth or dynamic psychiatries of Freud, Jung, Adler, and Janet. Not unexpectedly, the most influential general historical studies from these years, such as Gregory Zilboorg's *A History of Medical Psychology* (1941) and Franz Alexander and Sheldon Selesnick's *The History of Psychiatry* (1966), are structured around a kind of Freudian historical teleology.[50] In these texts, Freud becomes the central event in the history of the psychological sciences, while other figures and themes are either eulogized or criticized according to their degree of anticipation of, or divergence from, the psychoanalytic model of the mind.

[50] Zilboorg, *A History of Medical Psychology*; Franz G. Alexander and Sheldon T. Selesnick, *A History of Psychiatry: An Evaluation of Psychiatric Thought and Practice from Prehistoric Times to the Present* (New York: Harper and Row, 1966).

The Freudocentrism of the mid-twentieth century has also been reflected in the field of hysteria studies. The history of medical thinking about hysteria includes a line of medical research in Britain extending from the second quarter of the nineteenth century to the First World War. In 1837, Sir Benjamin Brodie, a surgeon at St. George's Hospital in London, published *Lectures Illustrative of Certain Local Nervous Affections*.[51] In his study, Brodie reported a number of perplexing cases from his practice in which the patient suffered long-term articular pain and swelling but in whom postmortem examination revealed no deterioration of the bone or cartilage. He traced the precise innervation of the nerves and muscles in these cases and found that they failed to conform to known anatomy. He noticed further that these conditions were often preceded in the life of the patient by a minor physical injury or an emotional trauma. Brodie eventually interpreted these cases as "local nervous affections" that were patterned, often in exquisite detail, on neurological diseases. Brodie's initial perception involved deformities of the joints— "hysterical knee," "hysterical hip," and so forth—but he went on later in his career to present what he regarded as hysterogenic cases of paralysis, back pain, chorea, edema, torticollis, loss of voice, and urinary retention. This kind of case, Brodie contended, was much more common than most doctors realized, and he wrote his book in an effort to prevent unwarranted surgical interventions on the part of his colleagues.

Brodie's unassuming lectures from the 1830s initiated a tradition within the British medical community of studying the differentiation of organic and functional disorders based on the absence of structural pathology. In 1842, Edward O. Hocken, an eye surgeon, explored visual disorders with hysterical complications.[52] In the mid-1850s, the London neurologist Robert B. Todd investigated the phenomenon of "emotional paralyses" that lacked ascertainable neuropathy but assumed "quasi-neurological" forms.[53] A decade later, Julius Althaus, at Queen Square Hospital, studied the subtle clinical differences between hysterical and nonpsychiatric convulsive disorders.[54] In 1867, the surgeon Frederic C. Skey delivered a set of lectures at St. Bartholomew's Hospital stating unequivocally that every part of the human body could be the site of hysterical symptom formation.[55]

[51] Sir Benjamin C. Brodie, *Lectures Illustrative of Certain Local Nervous Affections* (London: Longman, Rees, Orme, Brown, Green, and Longman, 1837).

[52] Edward Octavius Hocken, *An Exposition of the Pathology of Hysteria* (London: S. Highley, 1842).

[53] Robert Bentley Todd, *Clinical Lectures on Paralyses, Diseases of the Brain, and Other Affections of the Nervous System* (London: J. Churchill, 1854).

[54] Julius Althaus, *On Epilepsy, Hysteria and Ataxy* (London: Churchill, 1866).

[55] Frederic Carpenter Skey, *Hysteria: Local or Surgical Forms of Hysteria: Six Lectures* (London: Longmans, Green, Reader, and Dyer, 1867).

Subsequently, Russell Reynolds, professor of medicine at University College Hospital in London, published a short but highly suggestive article in the *British Medical Journal* in 1869. Reynolds brought forward several examples of what he called "paralysis dependent on idea."[56] By this phrase, Reynolds designated the clinical phenomenon known today as the "glove and stocking" paralysis or anesthesia: a regional motor or sensory deficit that follows the popular segmental understanding of anatomy rather than the actual distribution of the nerves and muscles. Like Brodie, Reynolds found that the onset of "psychical paralysis" was often preceded by an incident establishing in the mind of the patient the belief that he or she was paralyzed. Reynolds emphasized the great diagnostic value of these observations.

Francis Anstie extended Reynolds's line of investigation to another category of symptom in *Neuralgia and the Diseases that Resemble It* (1871),[57] and in 1873, John Chapman elaborated on the "neurodynamic" element in the cases discussed by Anstie.[58] In the same year, Sir James Paget, one of the most distinguished physicians of his age and, like Brodie and Skey, a surgeon, published perhaps the most elegant statement in this tradition, his well-known articles in *The Lancet* on the concept of "neuromimesis."[59] Synthesizing the findings of his countrymen from the previous four decades, Paget maintained that nervous disorders could in fact imitate any local disorder. He observed that these "nervous mimicries" were often repetitions or exacerbations of previous physical illnesses in the medical biography of the patient but noted as well that such symptoms, in their severity and tenacity, often bore little relation to the physical injury that elicited them. He observed that symptoms unaccompanied by organic impairment sometimes disappeared as spontaneously as they had arisen; relief might come in a matter of hours, or after months or even years of suffering. In 1883, Herbert Page, a corporate physician for a major British railway company, published his *Injuries of the Spine and Spinal Cord without Apparent Mechanical Lesion*, which explored the pathology of "nervous shock" in victims of train accidents.[60] In 1891, Thomas Buzzard, another London neurologist, considered the obverse phenomenon of the misdiagnosis of organic disorders as psychological in

---

[56] Russell Reynolds, "Paralysis, and Other Disorders of Motion and Sensation, Dependent on Idea," *British Medical Journal* (1869): 483–85.

[57] Francis E. Anstie, *Neuralgia and the Diseases That Resemble It* (London: Macmillan, 1871).

[58] Chapman, *Cases of Neuralgia and Kindred Diseases of the Nervous System* (London, J. and A. Churchill, 1873).

[59] Sir James Paget, "Nervous Mimicry," *The Lancet* (1873), reproduced conveniently in Stephen Paget, ed., *Selected Essays and Addresses by Sir James Paget* (London: Longmans, Green, and Co., 1902), chap. 7.

[60] Herbert W. Page, *Injuries of the Spine and Spinal Cord without Apparent Mechanical Lesion* (London: J. and A. Churchill, 1883).

On the Simulation of Hysteria by Organic Disease of the Nervous System.[61] Further work on the subject was conducted around the turn of the century by the neurophysiologist Henry Charlton Bastian and the internist Thomas Savill.[62]

Nineteenth-century British research on the hysterical replication of local neurological symptoms is an interesting and scientifically quite significant stream of thought in the history of hysteria. Yet the tradition, spanning-three quarters of a century, is entirely absent from the historical literature about hysteria. This includes Veith's account, which limits its discussion of British physicians in the nineteenth century to Robert Brudenell Carter, and Trillat's, which cites no British authors at all after Sydenham. How are we to understand these omissions? No historical study of course can be truly comprehensive, and British work in the 1800s may in part have been obscured by the French school, from Briquet to Charcot, with its greater flamboyance. What's more, the physicians listed above at times employed alternative terminology—"local nervous affection," "paralysis dependent on idea," "neuromimesis"—in their discussions of hysteria, which may have hidden their work from the historian's view. Yet, it is likely that another factor has been at work too.

From Brodie to Buzzard and beyond, these medical authors worked within a firmly organicist tradition. They were not institutional alienists or private-practice psychiatrists but internists, neurologists, and surgeons. Furthermore, their work has not been perceived retrospectively as contributing to the growing mentalist heritage within the history of the psychological sciences that culminated in "the psychodynamic revolution" of the twentieth century. Still more to the point, their writings conduced less to psychoanalytic theory than to late twentieth-century neuropsychiatry. Veith wrote *Hysteria: The History of a Disease* in 1965, at the close of the hegemonic period of psychoanalysis. Her book shares many of the characteristics of the general histories of psychiatry by Zilboorg, Alexander, and Selesnick. Throughout her history, psychogenic theories of hysteria are assumed to be valid while somatogenic ones are either criticized as wrong or excluded altogether. In her account, Veith expends considerable energy and space locating "prefigurations" of the Freudian model of hysteria, with its theoretical ingredients of psychogenesis, sexual determinism, and unconscious mentation. And, as noted before, her book ends with the *Studies on Hysteria*. Veith's only general references to the work of British physicians after Sydenham speak of "the

[61] Thomas Buzzard, *On the Simulation of Hysteria by Organic Disease of the Nervous System* (London: J. and A. Churchill, 1891).

[62] Henry Charlton Bastian, *Various Forms of Hysterical or Functional Paralysis* (London: Lewis, 1893); Thomas D. Savill, *Lectures on Hysteria and Allied Vaso-Motor Conditions* (London: Glasher, 1909).

static quality of British thinking and writing on hysteria" and "the increasingly sterile and repetitive neurological basis that had emanated from Great Britain for nearly two hundred years."[63]

I do not want to be misunderstood on this point: Freud's contribution to the history of hysteria, as I acknowledged above, is singular. His writings on the neurosis retain great originality and power, and it is difficult to imagine any future historical account in which they will not figure prominently. Nor has the study of Freud's place in that history been exhausted. However, precisely because Freud looms so large, and because his intellectual and cultural impact have been so immense, he has tended to dominate the imagination of historians to the exclusion of other contributors, and in particular to dwarf important *nonpsychoanalytic* developments within the history of hysteria and the history of psychiatry generally. In particular, the view that sees centuries of medical writing merely as a kind of extended psychoanalytic prologue has become obstructionist.[64] With the waning of the orthodox psychoanalytic paradigm within the mental sciences over the past generation, historians today are in an excellent position to explore these other intellectual trajectories, which in the long run will enrich their historical accounts.

All history writing is of course perspectival; there are no universal, value-neutral vantage points from which to write about hysteria, or any other disease. For exactly that reason, it behooves historians to be aware of the many interpretive perspectives that can be taken on their subject and to acknowledge as explicitly as possible the perspectives they have chosen. The more inclusive the perspective adopted, the more complete the historical picture that results.

Toward Sociosomatic Synthesis

"Internal" versus "external": the relation between these two analytical categories has bedeviled the historical study of science and medicine from the start. As Charles Rosenberg has noted, the issue, despite a plethora of prescriptive statements, is far from being settled today.[65] For reasons that are themselves historical, the cleavage between the two approaches has been especially wide within the historiography of psychiatry—wider per-

---

[63] Veith, *Hysteria*, 174, 183.

[64] For thoughts on "psychoanalytic imperialism" in psychiatric history writing generally, see Henri Baruk, "Quelques réflexions sur l'histoire de la psychiatrie," *Histoire des sciences médicales* 18 (1984): 205–7. On hysteria in particular, see Gilman et al., *Hysteria Beyond Freud*, which takes this line of thinking as its premise.

[65] Charles Rosenberg, "Science in American Society: A Generation of Historical Debate," *Isis* 74, no. 273 (September 1983): 364–65. See also idem, "Woods or Trees? Ideas and Actors in the History of Science," *Isis* 79, no. 299 (December 1988): 565–70.

haps than in any other area of study. The field of psychiatric history as it exists today began to take shape during the mid-twentieth century in a powerful, ideologically charged clash between "Whig" historians, most of whom were practicing psychiatrists with an interest in the history of their profession, and "antipsychiatrists," many of whom were sociologists and social historians working within a revisionist, debunking tradition. These two camps corresponded more or less directly to internalist and externalist methodologies. One undesirable effect of this development has been the enduring tendency to pursue, in polemical forms, one methodology at the expense of the other.

Presently, the social-historical school is ascendant. Over the past twenty years or so, the sociological approach, broadly conceived, has been powerfully bolstered by the emergence of social history and women's studies within mainstream historical studies and by the Mertonian and then Kuhnian sociologies of knowledge within the history of science. To these factors should be added the nature of the subject itself. Dealing as it often does with states of mind, sexuality, and emotional behavior, rather than clear cut organic diseases, psychiatry is especially susceptible to mirroring a range of subjective, nonscientific forces. Moreover, it is here that the scientific credentials of medicine appear flimsiest. Psychiatry, as Michel Foucault observed, maintains "a low epistemological profile,"[66] and its therapeutic pretensions all too often in the past have been ludicrously inflated. The subject seems virtually to demand rigorous externalist interpretation.

Particularly prevalent today among social historians of psychiatry, especially in France and the United States, is what the science historian Steven Shapin, in a somewhat different sense, has termed "the coercive model" of the sociology of science.[67] The chief features of this approach are the tendencies 1) to equate the social with the exploitative, 2) to view psychiatry and its components—doctors, patients, and institutions—monolithically, with little internal diversity or disagreement, 3) to judge contemporary statements of humanitarianism and scientific objectivity as rhetorical camouflage for a deeper nonmedical program, 4) to advance the sociological origin of medical theories against their validity as scientific knowledge, and 5) to present social-historical arguments in order to supplant rather than supplement conventional internalist accounts.

It is the last two features of the list that are of particular interest here. Since the mid-1980s, scholars in many branches of the history of science have successfully pursued the rapprochement of internalist and external-

[66] Michel Foucault, "Truth and Power," in Meaghan Morris and Paul Patton, eds., *Michel Foucault: Power, Truth, Strategy* (Sydney: Feral, 1979), 29.

[67] Steven Shapin, "History of Science and Its Sociological Reconstructions," *History of Science* 20, no. 56 (1982): 194–98.

ist methodologies. In 1992, Rosenberg and Janet Golden tentatively announced the arrival of "a post-relativist moment" in which "neither biological reductionism nor exclusive social constructionism constitute viable intellectual positions."[68] Nevertheless, this achievement cannot be claimed for the field of psychiatric history. For a surprising number of scholars today, the historical Whiggism of the 1940s and 1950s, long since in retreat, continues to serve as the imagined adversary of their own line of thought. Through much of the recent writing in the area, a sociological methodology is characterized definitionally as new, critical, and sophisticated while an intellectual-historical approach, studying "rational," scientific questions in their own right, is presented as naive, conservative, and anachronistic.[69] Analogously, in much recent scholarship about the history of psychiatric diagnoses, a strict social-constructionist procedure has become critically correct.[70] Thirty years after the initial clash of ideologies and methodologies, the idea has somehow become established that a serious concern with the idea content of past psychiatric systems is uninteresting and unnecessary, a methodological regression to an old-fashioned internalism, a concession to the dreaded "positivist" historiography of the past.[71]

[68] Rosenberg and Golden, *Framing Disease*, xxiv.

[69] For a clear enunciation of these valuations, see Christopher Lawrence, "Cognitive Issues: Having It Both Ways," *Social History of Medicine* 2, no. 2 (August 1989): 87–92.

[70] Karl Figlio, "Chlorosis and Chronic Disease in Nineteenth-Century Britain: The Social Constitution of Somatic Illness in a Capitalist Society," *Social History* 3 (1978): 167–97; Christopher Lawrence, "The Nervous System and Society in the Scottish Enlightenment," in Barry Barnes and Steven Shapin eds., *Natural Order: Historical Studies of Scientific Culture* (Beverly Hills/London: Sage, 1979), 19–40; Goldstein, "The Hysteria Diagnosis and the Politics of Anticlericalism;" Ian Hacking, "The Invention of Split Personalities (An Illustration of Michel Foucault's Doctrine of the Constitution of the Subject)," in Alan Donagan, Anthony N. Perovich, Jr., and Michael V. Wedin, eds., *Human Nature and Natural Knowledge* (Dordrecht: D. Reidel, 1986), 63–85.

[71] The literature on this controversial subject is large. For the history of science generally, see Imre Lakatos, "History of Science and Its Rational Reconstructions" in Yehuda Elkana, ed., *The Interaction between Science and Philosophy* (Atlantic Highlands, N.J.: Humanities Press, 1974), 195–241; Larry Laudan, *Progress and Its Problems: Toward a Theory of Scientific Growth* (Berkeley: University of California Press, 1977), chaps. 6 and 7; Shapin, "History of Science and Its Sociological Reconstructions"; idem, "Discipline and Bounding: The History and Sociology of Science as Seen through the Externalism-Internalism Debate," *History of Science* 30 (1993): 333–69; Mary Hesse, "Hermeticism and Historiography: An Apology for the Internal History of Science," in Roger H. Stuewer, ed., *Historical and Philosophical Perspectives on Science* (Minneapolis: University of Minnesota Press, 1970), 134–62; Barry Barnes, "'Internal' Versus 'External' Factors in the History of Science," in Barnes, ed., *Scientific Knowledge and Sociological Theory* (London: Routledge and Kegan Paul, 1974), chap. 5; and Karin D. Knorr-Cetina and Michael Mulkay, eds., *Science Observed: Perspectives on the Social Study of Science* (London: Sage Publications, 1983), chaps. 1, 2, 4 and 5.

For the issue within medical history, there is John Harley Warner's highly discerning

Now, beyond question, the social history of psychiatry has produced much of the most exciting scholarship in the field over the past fifteen years. Social historians of science have repeatedly shown themselves adept at retrieving from past intellectual artifacts those elements that reflect prevailing social and cultural conditions. Regarding the history of psychiatry in particular, one study after another has demonstrated the social and political interests served by past theories and practices. This approach has been particularly successful in scholarship dealing with the history of the "moral treatment," degeneration theory, sexology, and the psychiatric treatment of women.

However, on this point I would like to argue against the current. Given the contemporary state of psychiatric historiography, taken as a whole, I believe that the sociologizing impulse, with its implicit but programmatic anti-internalism, has become problematic. Within psychiatric historiography, a necessary and justifiable reaction against the old, one-sided internalist methodology is in danger of producing an opposite excess which, with its emphasis on the hidden social and political agendas of medicine, is as lopsided and distortive as the original approach. The source of this new counter-reductionism is not sociological interpretation as such but rather the persistent prioritizing of the social over all other explanatory categories. When a new factor is discovered in the realm of historical causation, there often follows for some time a tendency to ascribe to that factor an exaggerated importance, a kind of causal sovereignty, rather than to see it as one of a range of integrated factors. This appears to be the situation at present within the historiography of psychiatry. In avid pursuit today of the social, political, and economic determinants of past medical thinking and practice, some critics and historians, including a good portion of those writing about hysteria, are neglecting detrimentally the role of other crucial factors, especially clinical and cognitive ones. In the future, if we are to work toward a more complete understanding of the history of disease, it will be necessary to overcome this stubborn and unproductive dichotomy.[72]

"Science in Medicine," in *Osiris*, 2d ser., 1 (1985): *Historical Writing in American Science*, 37–58 and "The History of Science and the Sciences of Medicine," in *Osiris*, 2d ser., (forthcoming), as well as S. E. D. Shortt's "Clinical Practice and the Social History of Medicine: A Theoretical Accord," *Bulletin of the History of Medicine* 55, no. 4 (Winter 1981): 533–42. Reflections on the subject in the history of psychology may be found in John Cerullo, "Epistemological Problems and the Character of Social Science: Toward an Historical Perspective on Contemporary Issues" (Lecture delivered to the Wellesley College Colloquium on the History of Psychology, Wellesley College, April 15, 1989).

[72] In the words of a wise man writing fifty years ago: "Il est évident que l'histoire de la médecine ne se fera jamais ni par des historiens qui ne sont pas médecins, ni par des médecins qui ne sont pas historiens—mais par une collaboration d'historiens, rompus aux méthodes érudites et connaissant les milieux sociaux d'autrefois—de médecins ayant étudié

To defend the writing of hysteria history in particular from an internalist perspective may seem a futile and unenviable task; but there are in fact several reasons to include an informed medical-scientific approach to the subject. To begin with, the study of hysteria and its allied mental and physical states has produced through the ages a great deal of significant scientific work. In the late seventeenth century, Willis and Sydenham provided shrewd and detailed clinical portraits of the disorder that remain valid today. In the nineteenth century, we have just seen, British surgeons and neurologists probed the functional imitation of local neurological symptoms by investigating hysteria. Through his twenty-year study of the neurosis, Charcot sharpened the clinical differentiation between epileptic and psychogenic seizures, explored the ideogenic component in the functional nervous disorders, identified astasia-abasia and Tourette's syndrome, and investigated the mental effects of toxic chemical exposure. Similarly, in the work of Freud and Janet hysteria presided at the birth of twentieth-century dynamic psychiatry. And through the study of specialized hysterias, labeled variously as posttraumatic neurosis, traumatic neurasthenia, shell shock, and accident neurosis, physicians have learned a great deal about the neuropsychology of trauma. The list could easily be extended. Hysteria's history, in short, consists of an admixture of misogyny, sensationalism, and mistreatment on the one hand with astute clinical observation, pioneering neuropathological research, and brilliant psychological theorizing on the other. It would be foolish to allow the dubious aspects of this history to blind us to its real achievements.

Next, studying hysteria historically demands a sensitivity to the distinctive clinical conditions under which medicine was practiced in each epoch. "To ignore the clinical context in which disease is identified is to miss the distinguishing feature of medical practice," Barbara Sicherman warned a decade and a half ago. "For it is in the consulting room, the hospital clinic, and at the bedside that the daily drama of diagnosis and treatment takes place."[73] Sicherman's admonition in regard to neurasthenia applies with added force to hysteria. We will consider shortly the nature of the doctor/patient relationship in the history of the neuroses.

---

spécialement les doctrines médicales anciennes—et, j'ajoute, de philosophes. . . . Tant que nous n'aurons pas des études fortement basées sur une telle collaboration (je dis collaboration et non juxtaposition), nous aurons des histoires sur la médecine, plus ou moins sérieuses, plus ou moins pénétrantes et documentées; nous n'aurons pas d'histoires de la médecine" (Lucien Febvre, review of Paul Delaunay, *La vie médicale aux XVIe, XVIIe et XVIIIe siècles*, in *Annales d'histoire économique et sociale* 8, no. 37 [January 1936]: 180–81).

[73] Barbara Sicherman, "The Uses of a Diagnosis: Doctors, Patients, and Neurasthenia," *Journal of the History of Medicine and Allied Sciences* 32 (1977): 33–54.

Suffice it to say here that the relationship of physician to hysterical patient is highly distinctive. The ability of the doctor to manipulate an impressionable patient and in turn to be impressed by a talented and manipulative hysteric is utterly unique. Moreover, as Trillat perceives, the differentiation of hysteria from a multitude of other physical and psychological conditions has been a pressing concern throughout the clinical and intellectual history of the disorder. These factors, among others, have played a crucial role in shaping medical theory and practice through the years and cannot responsibly be ignored by the historian.

There is, moreover, the continual need in the history of science and medicine to understand our subjects "on their own terms." The precise scientific merits or demerits of past writing on hysteria will remain a matter of debate. But ultimately the historian will be less concerned to assess the truth value of this work than to puzzle out the ways in which past theories and practices have operated within their own medical and cultural milieux. Recent scholarship on such scientifically dubious topics as alchemy, astrology, occultism, and phrenology has demonstrated that this aim can be achieved only with a serious effort to get inside the "scientific" mind of the age. With hysteria, this is particularly important for the nineteenth century, which was the most self-consciously scientific period in the history of the disorder. At times, this goal requires a relatively simple effort to place the beliefs of the past in their contemporary theoretical context. Even seemingly silly ideas usually reveal an intellectual integrity, an "internal logic," of their own. At other times, such knowledge can only be obtained, as Nancy Tomes has commented, by reconstructing "the internal, intellectual dilemmas" of medical professionals in the past.[74]

These considerations, it seems to me, argue for a flexible, "multifunctional" reading of psychiatric history, including the history of diagnostics.[75] The fact that a given scientific artifact can be shown to have served as social ideology neither precludes its simultaneous operation on other levels nor establishes that the social function represents its "true," or most essential, meaning. A theory of disease may be mediated by gender, class, race, or other nonscientific variables and still represent a legitimate intellectual effort and a successful piece of medical science. Diagnostic categories may be internally as well as extrinsically determined, and a theory of hysteria may be "constructed" clinically and

---

[74] Nancy Tomes, "The Anatomy of Madness: New Directions in the History of Psychiatry," *Social Studies of Science* 17, no. 1 (February 1987): 367.

[75] Chris Lawrence refers to multifunctionality in medical historiography in "The Nervous System and Society in the Scottish Enlightenment," in Barry Barnes and Steven Shapin, eds., *Natural Order: Historical Studies of Scientific Culture* (London: Sage Publications, 1979), 34–36.

scientifically as much as socially and culturally.[76] And what balance should scientific and social considerations occupy in future psychiatric historiographies? This depends obviously on the historical episode in question as well as the disciplinary background and analytical proclivity of the individual scholar. There is no single prescription. Nor do I want to argue that historians of disease must necessarily be trained in contemporary clinical medicine. However, what is apparent is that one must at least be conversant with the basic language of those individuals who were trained medically in the past, even when this requires mastery of a foreign and technical theoretical system.

There is at least one other reason for obtaining knowledge about the medical science of diseases in the past, too. Such a perspective, I believe, is imperative for the project of a social history of psychiatry itself. A selection of the new hysteria studies illustrates both positively and negatively that an integrated internalist and externalist approach is something more than a remote interdisciplinary ideal or a pleasing gesture toward methodological catholicity. Earlier, we saw that Carroll Smith-Rosenberg, in her influential article of 1972, reflects on the unique role of clinical and psychological mediation played by family physicians in nineteenth-century British and American households. Smith-Rosenberg then uses this observation as the basis for a social interpretation of hysterical neurosis in Victorian America. In a like manner, Trillat, seeking to explain the revival of genital theories of hysteria in the late eighteenth century, highlights the dual influences of a new Romantic image of Woman and the discovery of ovulation by physiologists, which emphasized anew the active generative role of the female body.[77] Risse's study of the Edinburgh Infirmary probably provides the best example. Attempting to analyze the working-class identity of the hysterical population in eighteenth-century Edinburgh, Risse notes a seasonal pattern of admissions for many patients, the frequency of amenorrhea and dysmenorrhea in the symptom profiles, and an emphasis in medical casebooks on treatment with warm shelter and adequate diet. Combining these observations, he surmises that a significant portion of cases of "hysteria" at the Infirmary were in fact associated with severe nutritional deficiencies among poor working women during the long winter months.[78] In each of these instances, historically sensitive physicians, or medically informed historians, were able to offer analyses that contributed to an understanding of the "social" history of the disease.

---

[76] For a historical illustration of this point, see Mark S. Micale, "On the 'Disappearance' of Hysteria: A Study of the Clinical Deconstruction of a Diagnosis," *Isis* 84 (October 1993): 496–526.

[77] Trillat, *L'histoire de l'hystérie*, 99.

[78] Risse, "Hysteria at the Edinburgh Infirmary," 8–9, n. 32; 13, 15, 16, 17.

On the opposite side of the issue, we might consider at greater length a single example. In an earlier context, I reviewed the work of the historian Jan Goldstein concerning the hysteria diagnosis in France during the early Third Republic.[79] I tried to show that Goldstein has made some of the most important and sophisticated contributions to the new hysteria studies, work that ranks among the finest in the historical sociology of science today. In this context, however, Goldstein's approach is noteworthy in that it combines refined sociological analysis with a conspicuous lack of attention to clinical and scientific matters.

Goldstein's 1987 book *Console and Classify* studies a series of individuals and episodes pertinent to the rise of the psychiatric profession in France. In the first three-quarters of the book, Goldstein discusses the major French alienists of the first half of the century, including Pinel, J.-E.-D. Esquirol, Étienne Georget, Jean-Pierre Falret, J.-G.-F. Baillarger, Félix Voisin, Ulysse Trélat, A.-L. Foville, and J.-J. Moreau de Tours. In separate chapters, she considers the origins of Pinel's moral treatment, the growth of the Esquirol circle of psychiatrists, the nature of the monomania diagnosis, and the struggle over the law of 1838 for asylum reform.[80] In the final quarter of her work, Goldstein considers at length the hysteria diagnosis in the work of Charcot and his students. In this section, she assimilates Charcot's work into the earlier tradition of French institutional alienism. Comparing him with such figures as Falret, Trélat, and Moreau de Tours, she describes Charcot variously as an *"aliéniste,"* "a mad-doctor," one of "the Salpêtrière psychiatrists," and "the last of the great nineteenth-century French psychiatrists." In accordance with this view, she interprets the accomplishment of the Salpêtrière school as "the psychiatric capture of hysteria."[81] Moreover, throughout her narrative, she discusses hysterical disorders as *névroses*, which she takes to mean the milder, nonpsychotic forms of psychopathology and which she proposes were cultivated by psychiatrists in an effort to claim a new and lucrative clientele for themselves.

Now despite Goldstein's illumination of the political aspects of her subject, an examination of the medical-historical record reveals the inaccuracy of these characterizations. In truth, Charcot was never a *médecin aliéniste*, and while he was occasionally, and increasingly after the mid-1880s, a timid psychological theorist, he was not a psychiatrist in any past or present sense of the term. Charcot was indeed entrenched in the rich nineteenth-century French medical heritage, but not as the product of Pinelian alienism. Rather, his work continued two other illustrious

[79] Chap. 1, 98–100, 103.
[80] Goldstein, *Console and Classify*, chaps. 3–8.
[81] Ibid., 328, 329, 359, 382, 334.

national traditions, the Laennecian and Cruveilhierian tradition of pathological anatomy and the more recent Bernardian school of experimental physiology.[82] Between 1873 and 1882, while he was formulating his theory of hysteria, Charcot occupied the chair of Pathological Anatomy on the Paris Medical Faculty. He may most accurately be described as a physician of general internal medicine with a specialty in clinical neurology.

In this same vein, it is true that Charcot classified hysteria as a *névrose*, but he used this term in the strictly neurological, late nineteenth-century sense of an organic disorder of the higher nervous system believed to have an anatomical and physiological substratum of unknown nature and location. Accordingly, he classified hysteria not with the mental pathologies but with the other "functional nervous disorders," such as epilepsy, tabes, chorea, multiple sclerosis, general paralysis, and Parkinson's Disease.[83] Charcot's methodology for the study of the nervous disorders was an organic-pathological one in which the essential scientific exercise consisted in the correlation of antemortem clinical observations with autopsical data. Finally, in his daily clinical practice, Charcot saw, treated, and theorized about a category of patient that was fundamentally different from those of Pinel, Esquirol, and Georget two generations earlier—namely, cases of chronic and progressive neurological disease as opposed to severe psychiatric disability.[84] In other words, in his medical education, scientific methodology, clinical activities, academic affiliations, and patient populations, Charcot belonged to a tradition within French medicine substantially separate from the classic French alienism of the first half of the century.

To be sure, these facts do not invalidate Goldstein's basic argument concerning the politicization of the hysteria diagnosis, but their interpretive ramifications are nonetheless significant. Among other things, they cause the author to conflate the practices of the neurologist and the asylum physician and to misconstrue the historical relationship between *maladies mentales* and *maladies nerveuses*. These oversights in turn lead her to project a misleading disciplinary continuity between two substan-

[82] Toby Gelfand has recently made this point in "Réflexions sur Charcot et la famille névropathique," *Histoire des sciences médicales* 21, no. 3 (1987): 245–46.

[83] The exact list of neuroses varied from author to author. For the status of the debate on this subject in the French medical community during the 1880s, see Alexandre Axenfeld and Henri Huchard, *Traité des névroses*, 2d ed., enl. (Paris: Germer Baillière et Cie, 1883), esp. 1–31 and 919–1154; and "Névrose," in Émile Littré, *Dictionnaire de médecine, de chirurgie, de pharmacie, de l'art vétérinaire et des sciences qui s'y rapportent*, 16th ed. (Paris: J.-B. Baillière, 1886), 1070.

[84] This important distinction was first made by Georges de Morsier in "Jean-Martin Charcot 1825–1893," in Kurt Kolle, ed., *Grosse Nervenärzte*, 3 vols. (Stuttgart: Georg Thieme, 1956), 1, 39–40.

tially different cognitive and professional enterprises and to select as a representative of the psychiatric profession in the second half of the century an inappropriate figure and episode.[85] Goldstein may view Charcot as a psychiatrist partly because Freud was briefly one of Charcot's students, and he practiced in the same hospital as many earlier French alienists. However, the misunderstanding also results from methodological factors. If we return to Goldstein's chapter on hysteria with this question in mind, we find that the bulk of her discussion is devoted to a reconstruction of the political and professional context surrounding Charcot and that only in the final pages does she turn to the theory of hysteria proper. Even here, she explores the covert ideological dimension of the theory but does not consider the content and structure of the diagnosis itself. Her understanding of Salpêtrian hysteria derives largely from a range of nonmedical sources. She has only occasionally consulted the nine volumes of Charcot's collected scientific works, and none of Charcot's more than 120 case histories of hysteria appear in her analysis.

My intention here is not to criticize a scholar who has contributed importantly to our understanding of the history of hysteria. I want rather to illustrate the dangers inherent in a pure and autonomous social constructionism. Historians, of course, need not discuss every causal factor at work in a given situation but may focus for added analytical power on a single element. However, they do need to remain cognizant of the full range of variables in operation and particularly of those elements that impinge on the factor chosen for analysis. Such an approach by no means forecloses a political or professional interpretation. In fact, a reading of Charcot's writings suggests that the hysteria diagnosis in France a century ago was indeed formulated in part for ideological, "nonscientific" purposes, but not only in the way proposed by Goldstein.

Placed in its broad medical-historical context, the salient feature of the Salpêtrian theory of hysteria is probably its highly neurological character. Two centuries earlier, Sydenham and Willis advanced a nervous model of hysteria; but while they made a purely theoretical statement, Charcot's ideas, in an age of rapid specialization, represented a strong intraprofessional assertion. As Trillat has observed astutely, the history of medical thought about hysteria since the time of Briquet has been divided decisively along intraprofessional lines, with each group of specialists advocating the model of the disease that enhances their own explanatory authority over the subject.[86] Between 1860 and 1880, the fastest-growing

[85] W. F. Bynum has pointed out that Morelian degeneration rather than Salpêtrian hysteria furnishes a plausible diagnostic sequel to the work of Pinel and Esquirol (See Bynum's review of Goldstein's *Console and Classify* in *British Journal of the History of Science* 21, no. 3 [July 1988]: 370).

[86] Trillat, *Histoire de l'hystérie*, 121–25.

medical specialty in French medicine was not institutional alienism, which was then among the least prestigious and most vulnerable fields,[87] but clinical neurology. The sharp rivalry between neurology and institutional psychiatry that Bonnie Blustein has documented for American medicine at this time also obtained in Britain and on the Continent.[88] Charcot took an eager and aggressive part in the major intraprofessional disputes of his day, and integral to his efforts was his model of hysteria, with its neuropathic theory of etiology, a symptomatology that emphasized paralyses, anesthesias, and contractures, and a highly physicalistic regimen of therapy. Seen in this light, then, the success of Charcot and his students was not the psychiatric appropriation of hysteria (that would be the achievement of Freud and Janet a generation later) but rather the *neurologization* of the disorder. The hysteria diagnosis of the late nineteenth century, in other words, was indeed a valuable tool in the process of discipline-building; but it was instrumental not only against the Catholic Church but also within the medical profession too, on the *intra*professional as well as *inter*professional level. In short, we have here an instance in which an informed medical-scientific and medical-historical perspective in psychiatric history leads to an alternative sociological reading of a subject.

I have written polemically in this section that there are many reasons for historians of hysteria, as well as of other disease categories, to take seriously the internalities of their subject. On balance, it appears that exclusive methodological allegiances to either externalism or internalism invite interpretive error and ideological overstatement. In order to achieve a fuller and more accurate historical understanding in the future, we need to work toward an integrated *sociosomatic* model of disease that draws selectively and comfortably on both categories of causality.

THE "DOCTOR-PATIENT RELATIONSHIP"

Investigation of the clinical encounter between physicians and their patients represents one of the richest new dimensions of disease history. Until recently, this encounter has been construed rather simply. Paradoxically, the figure of the patient is absent equally from older, internalist

[87] A point well established in Ian R. Dowbiggin, *Inheriting Madness: Professionalization and Psychiatric Knowledge in Nineteenth-Century France* (Berkeley: University of California Press, 1991), chap. 1.

[88] Bonnie Ellen Blustein, "'A Hollow Square of Psychological Science': American Neurologists and Psychiatrists in Conflict," in Andrew Scull, ed., *Madhouses, Mad-Doctors, and Madmen: The Social History of Psychiatry in the Victorian Era* (Philadelphia: University of Pennsylvania Press, 1981), 241–70.

histories of psychiatry and from the more recent social-historical literature. Accounts of psychiatric ideas produced by physicians have tended to
present patients as the raw and inert "clinical material" from which
medical scientists gathered their observations, derived their conclusions,
and demonstrated their theories. In revisionist, sociologically oriented
writings of the past two decades, the patient has been no less anonymous.
Here, patients typically assume the role of victims in an exploitative
process, the undifferentiated objects of social or sexual control. With both
approaches, the link between patient and practitioner is envisioned as
direct and one-directional—passive on the part of the patient and preda-
tory or parasitical on the doctor's side.

Over the decades, a number of scholars have in passing proposed a less
iatrocentric historiography.[89] Then in 1985 a major programmatic call
was sounded for a new and more "patient-centered" medical history.[90]
Roy Porter's important proposal immediately raises further questions:
What exactly should a patient-oriented history consist of? And how can
the historian best pursue such an elusive and sensitive project? Most to
the point for present purposes, what might a patient-focused approach
look like specifically in the history of hysteria, where such an assignment
offers special problems and challenges? So far, the first writings in this
direction have taken as their subjects lay medical beliefs and practices,
popular attitudes toward disease and death, subjective perceptions of
illness, and images of the medical professional in the lay population.[91] In
addition to these, I believe that one theme psychiatric historians may
profitably explore concerns the role of the individual patient in the production of scientific theory.

If we examine the major breakthroughs in medical history, we find that
they were often made in the presence of a patient but that the patient
played almost no active part in the formation of the new concept or
technique. We do not bother to study the patients on whom W.T.G.
Morton and J. C. Warren demonstrated the first anesthetic agent, or
whom Pasteur first inoculated against rabies, or whom Christiaan Barnard used in the first cardiac transplant. Not so with the history of

[89] Douglas Guthrie, "The Patient: A Neglected Factor in the History of Medicine," *Proceedings of the Royal Society of Medicine* 38 (April 4, 1945): 490–94; Thomas S. Szasz,
William F. Knoff, and Marc H. Hollender, "The Doctor-Patient Relationship and Its Historical Context," *American Journal of Psychiatry* 65 (December 1958): 522–28.

[90] Porter, "The Patient's View," 175–98. See also Porter's introductory remarks to *Patients and Practitioners: Lay Perceptions of Medicine in Pre-Industrial Society* (Cambridge:
Cambridge University Press, 1985), 1–22; idem, *Mind-Forg'd Manacles: A History of Madness in England from the Restoration to the Regency* (London: Athlone, 1987), chap. 5; and
idem, "The Patient in England, c. 1660–c. 1800," in Andrew Wear, ed., *Medicine in Society*
(Cambridge: Cambridge University Press, 1992), 277–307.

[91] See the ten essays in Porter, *Patients and Practitioners*.

psychiatry. In critical ways, the historical and psychological structure of relations between doctors and patients in psychiatry is very different from that in other branches of medicine. More perhaps than in any other specialty, the formulation of a psychiatric diagnosis relies on the patient's subjective descriptions of his or her symptoms to the practitioner. And in no other branch of medicine does the course and therapeutic outcome of a case rest so firmly on the subtle and subjective therapist-patient relationship.

In particular, if we move within psychiatric history beyond the study of the insanities and the experience of institutionalization, which has dominated the attention of scholars since the 1960s, to the history of the neuroses, we find that a flexible, interactionist model of physician/patient relations is necessary. In fact, it is precisely in the history of the neuroses, more than any other area of organic or psychological medicine, that the patient has often played a highly active and creative role. Psychiatric clinicians are thoroughly familiar with the dynamic participation of the patient in the medical encounter, and there exists by now a large literature, informed by the precedents of psychoanalytic ego psychology, on the concepts of transference, countertransference, and the therapeutic alliance. However the *historical* aspects of this phenomenon have yet to be considered.

At many times and places in the history of hysteria, the connection between suffering individuals, or "patients," and the figures from whom they have sought assistance, doctors, has been complex, evolving, and two-directional. Ideas, information, and insights to this effect currently lie scattered in the medical and historical literature of hysteria where they are waiting to be united into a research program. The point of departure for this perception is yet again Anna O.

In *Studies on Hysteria*, Breuer went out of his way to establish the talent and intellectual capacity of his twenty-one-year-old patient. He referred to Pappenheim's "powerful intellect," which revealed "an astonishingly quick grasp of things and penetrating intuition," and he later described her as "bubbling over with intellectual vitality."[92] We also know that in the course of her illness Pappenheim manifested an exceptional range of symptoms, including a hysterical pregnancy and the remarkable mnemonic talent of reliving the day-to-day events of exactly a year before. Biographers have related the story of Pappenheim's subsequent career as a translator, playwright, social reformer, and cultural critic. Also, rereading Anna O.'s case, we notice what historians of psychoanalysis have previously pointed out: namely, that it is Pappenheim herself who arrived at a method of removing symptoms through the

[92] Breuer and Freud, *Studies on Hysteria*, in *Standard Edition*, 2: 21, 22.

exploration of past emotional experiences during a state of self-induced hypnosis and that it was she who presented her "findings" to the doctor. The famous "talking cure" was in a real sense the invention of the patient, with Freud and Breuer theorizing their way from it to the concept of catharsis.[93]

If we continue to the other cases in *Studies on Hysteria*, we find that a similar situation prevails. The early analysands of Freud presented an extraordinary collection of symptoms. Frau Emmy von N., who, Freud noted, possessed "an unusual degree of education and intelligence," stammered spastically and emitted strange clacking sounds in mid-conversation.[94] Miss Lucy R. experienced two specialized olfactory hallucinations—the smells of cigar smoke and burnt pudding—accompanied by depressive episodes. And Frau Cäcilie M., whose case Freud presents in the running footnotes to the book, instantaneously converted insults or anxiety into facial neuralgias. These symptoms may be seen as inventive and highly individualized bodily metaphors for the expression of acute psychological distress.

Significantly, in each of these cases, the "creative" illnesses of the hysterical patient led to an intellectual creativity on the part of the physician. In fact, considered cumulatively, Freud's intellectual debt to the "sick" women in the *Studies on Hysteria* is staggering. Anna O. led the way to the discovery of the cathartic method. Emmy von N. encouraged Freud to abandon the practice of hypnosis and pointed toward the technique of free association. Fräulein Elisabeth von R., the fifth and final patient in the book, provided Freud with his first glimpse of unconscious resistance. As for Cäcilie M., Freud held her in the highest esteem. In his autobiography, he saluted the young woman as "a very highly gifted hysteric," whom he sent to Charcot's clinic for observation.[95] Further, it was Cäcilie M.'s case that convinced Freud "that hysteria of the severest type can exist in conjunction with gifts of the richest and most original kind."[96] On two occasions, Freud characterized this patient as his "Lehrmeisterin,"—his "teacher" or "instructress."[97] The exact comparative roles played by doc-

---

[93] Reflecting as early as the 1920s on the decisive role of the patient in the origins of psychoanalytic theory, Sándor Ferenczi remarked that psychoanalysis represented "the shared discovery of an ingenious neurotic and a clever doctor" ("Relaxationsprinzip und Neokatharsis" (1929), in *Bausteine zur Psychoanalyse*, 2d ed., [Bern: Hans Huber, 1964], 3: 469). More recently, Peter Gay has referred to "an epoch-making collaboration between a gifted patient and her attentive physician" (*Freud*, 65).

[94] Freud, *Studies on Hysteria*, in *Standard Edition*, 2: 49.

[95] Freud, *An Autobiographical Study* (1925), in *Standard Edition*, 20: 17–18. Anthony Stadlen has pointed out to me that Freud's original German description—"eine vornehme, genial begabte Hysterika"—is stronger still than the standard English translation.

[96] *Studies on Hysteria*, 103.

[97] This striking term appears twice in Freud's writings, separated by a forty-year inter-

tor and patient in the creation of psychoanalytic theory are impossible to determine, and, however noteworthy the contributions of these individuals, psychoanalysis as we know it was finally the product of Freud's mind. But plainly, Freud learned a great deal from his hysterical patients, knew that he learned from them, and was in a real sense led to many of his early discoveries by a remarkable gallery of hysterical women.[98]

This view of an interactive doctor/patient relationship derives from early psychoanalytic history and may on first glimpse appear limited to that sphere. But this train of thought may be applied to other segments of psychiatric history too. In a little-known essay written in 1961, Henri Ellenberger generalized brilliantly from the experience of Anna O. to the history of dynamic psychiatry over a two-hundred-year period.[99] During the 1950s, Ellenberger conducted the research for *The Discovery of the Unconscious*, his encyclopedic nine-hundred-page history of Western psychiatry from prehistorical times to the twentieth century. After gathering the many threads for his historical tapestry, Ellenberger stood back to examine the pattern. Among the phenomena he detected was "that of the psychiatrist who has for an object of study a certain patient, most often a female patient, generally a hysteric, with whom he establishes unconsciously a rather long, complicated, and ambiguous relationship, of which the final issue will turn out to be highly fruitful for science."[100] The hysterical women in these cases, Ellenberger elaborated, were usually ill for a single stage of their lives, most often during a vulnerable youthful period. They tended to encounter their physicians at important, intellectually formative periods of the doctors' career, and they often served as the clinical model—the founding case—of the doctors' theoretical work. The encounters between doctors and patients, he continued, were typically based on an emotional and psychological manipulation that was mutual, undeclared, and often unrecognized. Moreover, after these early

---

val, and both times in reference to Cäcilie M.: letter to Wilhelm Fliess, February 8, 1897, in Sigmund Freud, *Briefe an Wilhelm Fliess 1887–1904*, ed. Jeffrey Moussaieff Masson, assisted by Michael Schröter and Gerhard Fichtner (Frankfurt am Main: S. Fischer, 1986), 243; and letter to Hubertus Prinz zu Löwenstein, July 23, 1938, repr. in Ella Lingens, "Sigmund Freud und die Deutsche Akademie im Exil," *Sigmund Freud House Bulletin 5*, no. 1 (Summer 1981): 28.

[98] Other scholars have also emphasized the initiative of the hysterical patient in the beginnings of psychoanalysis. See Jacques Nassif, *Freud: L'inconscient: Sur les commencements de la psychanalyse* (Paris: Galilée, 1977), part 3; Roudinesco, *Histoire de la psychanalyse en France*, 1: 29–33; Showalter, *Female Malady*, 157–58; and Gay, *Freud*, 69–74.

[99] Henri F. Ellenberger, "La psychiatrie et son histoire inconnue," *L'union médicale du Canada 90*, no. 3 (March 1961): 281–89, repr. in English translation in Mark S. Micale, ed., *Beyond the Unconscious: Essays of Henri F. Ellenberger in the History of Psychiatry* (Princeton: Princeton University Press, 1993), chap. 8.

[100] Ellenberger, "La psychiatrie et son histoire inconnue," 281.

neurotic illnesses, the hysterical patients frequently went on to lead independent and self-expressive lives.

Ellenberger then illustrated this important insight with seven cases drawn from the late eighteenth to the early twentieth centuries. These are the cases of Maria Theresia Paradis, an Austrian aristocrat who suffered from hysterical blindness, served as the source of Mesmer's theory of the universal magnetic fluid, and later became a prominent concert pianist; Fredericke Hauffe, a village girl who was treated by the German Romantic psychiatrist Justinus Kerner and became the subject of the first monograph on a single patient in psychiatric history; Léonie B., a clairvoyant peasant girl from Normandy who served as the centerpiece of Janet's *L'automatisme psychologique*; Carl Gustav Jung's patient Helene Preiswerk, who became the subject of his dissertation; Hélène Smith, a patient of the early twentieth-century Swiss psychologist Flournoy, who inspired the book *Des Indes à la planète Mars*; Blanche Wittmann, the clinical prototype for Charcot's theories; and Anna O.[101] In other words, Ellenberger located on a large historical scale the phenomenon that Freud and Breuer experienced in their early hysterical patients. His findings suggest that in many different times and cultures a complex and unconsciously collaborative relationship has evolved between hysterical patients and their physicians. It would be most interesting to have a close and comparative history of the major paradigmatic patients in the history of psychiatry.

Following the lead of psychoanalytic biographers, Ellenberger thus underscored one relationship that appears repeatedly in the history of hysteria. A second recurrent relationship finds its classic expression in a visual source, Brouillet's *Une leçon clinique à la Salpêtrière* of 1886. Brouillet's canvas portrays Charcot as the great *maître d'école*, professing to a serious and attentive gathering of medical students, while a hysterical female patient (Wittmann) stands dramatically before the audience, fists clenched, shoulders bared, and head thrown back as she faints into Babinski's arms. The scene, one of the most popular icons of psychiatry's past, is familiar to us today through a widely reproduced etching by Pirodin, a copy of which hung famously in Freud's consulting room in Vienna. Today we stare at this compelling and mysterious image, which seems to overflow with subtextual meanings, and try to determine what is really going on. Where in the scene does the central drama lie? Is positivist science, in the figure of Charcot, sternly demonstrating its power on a suffering and vulnerable patient? Or is Wittmann, her dramatic and voluptuous presence carefully cultivated, giving a seasoned performance for an impressionable audience of young medical students? The mixture of scientific sobriety and erotic seduction in the scene is overwhelming.

[101] Ibid., 283–88.

In the past decade, a number of French psychiatrists have philosophized provocatively about the therapeutic interrelationships between hysterical patients and their doctors and in the process have provided a kind of extended theoretical gloss on Brouillet's representation. Taking "l'ensemble des relations hystériques-médecins" as their subject, Lucien Israël and Gérard Wajeman have explored the elusive but powerful network of sexual, emotional, and intellectual ties that bind doctor and patient in the therapeutic relationship.[102] According to Israël and Wajeman the hysterical patient, usually a female, reveals herself to the psychiatrist, most often a male. With verbal encouragement, she offers the most intimate autobiographical revelations, presents a panoply of real and simulated symptoms, and entices him with physically suggestive behaviors. The doctor responds to this spectacle by manipulating the patient therapeutically and by erecting theoretical structures. The patient, with her mimetic gifts and erotic charisma, can inspire, deceive, and arouse the physician. In contrast, the physician's authority is largely interpretive: he has the ability to formulate diagnoses, pathologize at random, and theorize in print, with or without the consent of the hysterical patient. For the medical scientist, the behavior of the hysterical patient represents his scientific data, the empirical moment, from which he derives the ideas and information for his work. And from this intense emotional microenvironment, the patient receives—what? A cure? Consolation? A confidant? A sexual admirer? A permanent caretaker?

Martha Evans, who has brought these French ideas to Anglophonic readers, speaks of "the paradigm of hysteria as a heterosexual love story" in which the medical man is teased into an act of theory.[103] But within the doctor/hysteric relationship, how is the sexualized psychodrama of the clinical encounter translated into scientific discourse? Does theory represent an expression of the clinical partnership? Is it a communication, coded on both sides, between physician and patient? Or does it operate perhaps as a sublimation of the relationship into licit, rationalized form? Evans interestingly interprets the process of theorizing about hysteria as an intellectual defense on the part of the male physician against the sexual

---

[102] This line of thinking was first laid out in the 1950s by J. Ajuriaguerra, "Le problème de l'hystérie," *L'encéphale* 40, no. 1 (1951): 50–87 and P. C. Racamier, "Hystérie et théâtre," *L'évolution psychiatrique* 17, no. 2 (April–June, 1952): 257–89. The major recent explorations are Israël, *L'hystérique, le sexe et le médecin*; Wajeman, *Le maître et l'hystérique*, part 2; and Charles Melman, *Nouvelles études sur l'hystérie* (Paris: Joseph Clims Denoël, 1984).

[103] Martha Noel Evans, "L'hystérie et la séduction de la théorie," *Frénésie: Histoire, psychiatrie, psychanalyse* 4 (Autumn 1987): 51–61, trans. from the French with minor changes as "Hysteria and the Seduction of Theory," in Dianne Hunter, ed., *Seduction and Theory: Readings of Gender, Representation, and Rhetoric* (Chicago: University of Illinois Press, 1989), 73–85.

allurements of the patient.[104] From a somewhat different angle, Jean Guetta has written that the doctor and the hysterical patient form a kind of "neurotic couple": the patient challenges the doctor's characteristically obsessional need to control his anxieties about the patient through knowledge, certainty, and a code of objectivity, while the patient refuses to conform to the rules of good behavior and seeks to unmask the doctor's ignorance and insecurity.[105] Whatever the psychodynamics, the fruits of this coupling, ideally, again appear to be theory: systematized, scientific knowledge for the doctor and self-knowledge for the patient.

The ruminations of Israël, Wajeman, Evans, and Guetta have emerged from contemporary psychiatric situations, but these ideas might be applied, à l'Ellenberger, to earlier periods. The notion that a highly gendered confrontation between doctor and patient may be scientifically engendering has also been touched upon by historians. Jacqueline Carroy-Thirard has noted that the scientific voyeurism of Charcot and his students, who attempted to capture photographically the convulsive eroticism of the hysteric, is mirrored by the strong clinical exhibitionism of the hysterical patient. Writing about Briquet's patients a generation earlier, Carroy-Thirard has also observed "the connivance of the hysteric and the doctor, in which it is unclear who is leading the game, the woman who complains or the physician who theorizes from her complaint."[106] In the same vein, Trillat has mused on "the reciprocal seduction in which doctor and hysterical patient are at once victims and beneficiaries."[107] In how many other times and places has this secret clinical romance transpired?

A third and final pattern of patient/physician interaction in the history of hysteria finds its prototypical expression in another Freudian text, the Dora case. This interaction is based on the sentiment of hostility, and it reveals (as Fischer-Homberger realized) a long, if ignoble, history stretching back at least to the witch persecutions of the sixteenth century. A fascinating, pre-Freudian illustration of this configuration may be found in *On the Pathology and Treatment of Hysteria*, written by the midnineteenth British internist Robert Brudenell Carter.[108] Carter's slender volume has been commented upon by scholars as an anticipation of psy-

---

[104] Evans, "Hysteria and the Seduction of Theory," 8 (cited from the typescript).

[105] Jean Guetta, *Un type de couple névrotique: L'hystérique et l'obsessionnel* (Paris: Mémoire pour le CES de psychiatrie, 1985).

[106] Carroy-Thirard, "Figures de femmes hystériques dans la psychiatrie française au 19e siècle," 316; see also 321 and 323. Carroy-Thirard mentions as well that it was the patient Geneviève from the *Iconographie photographique* who "discovered" on her own body hysterogenic ovarian points and then first brought this phenomenon to Charcot's attention.

[107] Trillat, *Histoire de l'hystérie*, 273.

[108] Robert Brudenell Carter, *On the Pathology and Treatment of Hysteria* (London: Churchill, 1853).

choanalytic psychology and psychosomatic medicine.[109] However, the work is also highly pertinent as a document in the history of patient/therapist relations.

To be specific, in the middle of a long chapter on therapeutics, Carter provides a twenty-page excursus on the handling of hysterical patients; it provides one of the most detailed accounts of doctor/patient relations in the history of the neurosis.[110] At the beginning of the discussion, Carter, only twenty-five years of age at the time of writing and perhaps daunted by the prospect of encountering a more experienced opponent, warned his fellow physicians about the challenge of confronting female neurotic patients:

> [This] first conversation with an hysterical girl, is a thing that must not be hastily or lightly undertaken, for upon the method of its performance will chiefly depend the success of after management. However much the practitioner may possess of firmness, coolness, and tact; however much knowledge of human nature generally, and of the character of the individual under his charge, he will have commenced a task in which none of these powers or acquirements will be found either redundant or superfluous. He will be called upon to place unwavering trust in his own professional opinion, and to act upon his faith; to express himself with such determination as to show the hopelessness of a contest with him.[111]

Carter then goes on to discuss the doctor's encounter with the hysterical patient as a titanic power struggle between two combatants equally matched in skill, resourcefulness, and determination to fight. For his colleagues in the profession, Carter obligingly details the rules of the game and the strategies for success. The patient, he warns, may deploy every possible strategy of evasion and deceit at her disposal, including using a repertoire of simulated symptoms. She may respond to the doctor's actions with anger or incredulity, with reasoned denial or embarrassed admission, with temper tantrums, fits of sobbing, or convulsive seizures. Carter cites instances of doctors inexperienced in the clinical art who were fooled by these performances and reviews "the rules for the detection of malingerers."[112] In the end, he claims, the strong and determined medical man will prevail. Carter conveys this conviction in metaphorical language that is unambiguously military:

[109] Veith, *Hysteria*, 199–210; Alison Kane and Eric T. Carlson, "A Different Drummer: Robert B. Carter and Nineteenth-Century Hysteria," *Bulletin of the New York Academy of Medicine* 58, no. 6 (September 1982): 519–34.

[110] Carter, *On the Pathology and Treatment of Hysteria*, 108–30.

[111] Ibid., 110.

[112] Note the similarity between Carter's guidelines and the instructions in early modern witchcraft manuals for the interrogation of bewitched women.

No hysterical woman can by any possibility hold out for a long time against this kind of treatment; but the length of the siege which she is able to maintain, will depend quite as much upon the amount of her trust in her own powers, as upon the actual ingenuity and cunning which she calls to her aid. A traitor in the camp is as mischievous in mental, as in physical, warfare; and doubt is the most dangerous of traitors, not only admitting the enemy, but also rendering inefficient the weapons of defence.[113]

Ellenberger construed the doctor/patient relationship as an ongoing scientific collaboration, and contemporary French psychoanalysts have envisioned it as a love story. For Carter, it was war, and his book a plan of battle from a young soldier at the front.

Through the generations, the relationships between patients and doctors have no doubt been as diverse as the cases themselves. Nevertheless, within the new hysteria studies it is possible to isolate at least three forms of engagement in which patients operated as active forces in the process of theory production. In these three structured relationships, the hysterical patient inspires, or seduces, or angers the physician into an act of theory. No doubt other modes of interaction exist as well.[114] Conversely—and this side of the issue merits investigation too—the hysterical patient may call a halt to the theoretical process. She may, for instance, deceive, either through the stories she tells about herself or through counterfeit symptomatologies. Charcot, Dumont Pallier, and Luys were in a real sense defeated by their hysterical patients, so shrewd were the patients' performances and so great the doctors' eagerness to theorize from their behavior. Similarly, the hysteric may behave badly during public demonstration or she may remain silent. Like Dora, she may terminate treatment willfully. As a last resort, the hysterical patient may simply refuse to get well.

Over the past two decades, a sizable medical and historical body of writing has appeared about doctor/patient relationships in contemporary psychodynamic settings. We have also begun to acquire a valuable general sociology of doctor/patient relations.[115] We need now to work as well

---

[113] Carter, *On the Pathology and Treatment of Hysteria,* 117.

[114] One such pattern is based on iatrogenic symptom formation. Here the physician, through verbal interrogation and physical examination, unwittingly provides medical information to the hysterical patient that the patient, with her superb suggestibility and histrionic skill, translates into the vocabulary of the psychogenic physical symptom. The doctor then reconverts this coded body language into theoretical discourse.

[115] Michael Balint, *The Doctor, His Patient, and the Illness* (New York: International Universities Press, 1957); Pedro Lain Entralgo, *Doctor and Patient,* trans. from the Spanish by Frances Partridge (London: Weidenfeld and Nicolson, 1969); Ann Cartwright, *Patients and Their Doctors* (London, 1967); Martin. S. Staum and Donald E. Larsen, eds., *Doctors, Patients, and Society: Power and Authority in Medical Care* (Waterloo, Ontario: Wilfred Laurier University Press, 1982); J. Katz, *The Silent World of Doctor and Patient* (New York: Free Press, 1984). A useful guide to the literature in this area is also now available in Michael

toward a *historical psychology* of the doctor/patient relationship. Then it will be possible to integrate the existing social and intellectual histories of disease with a new patient-centered account of the subject. Then we can have a history of hysteria that combines the stories of the pioneering patients with those of the pioneering doctors.

THE DE-DRAMATIZATION OF HYSTERIA

The history of hysteria is nothing if not dramatic. This flamboyance proceeds mainly from the colorful symptomatology of the disorder. The kaleidoscopic clinical content of the condition has made a powerful impression on the imagination of people in the past—and on the scholarly imagination today. Generally speaking, the history of hysteria is most likely to bring to mind the gross motor and sensory conversions of the Victorian invalid, the erotic exhibitionism of Charcot's *grandes hystériques*, and the elaborate and idiosyncratic neurotica of Freud's patients. Above all, it conjures up a picture of the female hysteric *en pleine crise*: hair disheveled, head tossed back, limbs contorted, eyes rolling, and body rigid and writhing.

If psychoanalysis has given us the most influential twentieth-century theory of hysteria, Charcot provided the most compelling symptomatological portrait. Charcot, as we have seen, found method in the madness of the disorder by reducing the hysterical attack to a series of uniform stages and universal laws. It was an intellectual gesture— imposing order on what was inherently chaotic—that contemporary Frenchmen found immensely appealing, and in return they offered a number of dramatic memorializations of *his* hysterical attack. Foremost among these representations are the *Iconographie photographique de la Salpêtrière* of 1876–80, Brouillet's *Une leçon clinique à la Salpêtrière*, and the drawings and etchings of Charcot's student Paul Richer.[116] Recent hysteria studies, especially those by nonmedical scholars in France and the United States, have done much to highlight the theatrical aspects of historical hysteria. Didi-Huberman's *Invention de l'hystérie* is devoted in full to the *Iconographie photographique*, and during the 1980s both Brouillet's canvas and Richer's etchings were the subjects of public exhibitions in Paris.[117] In the historical scholarship on hysteria today, these

---

Glasser, ed., *Physician-Patient Relationships: An Annotated Bibliography* (New York: Garland Publishing, 1991).

[116] The best sampling of Richer's visual work is scattered through the second enlarged edition of his *Études cliniques sur l'hystéro-épilepsie ou grande hystérie* (Paris: Delahaye et Lecrosnier, 1885).

[117] Didi-Huberman, *Invention de l'hystérie* and *La leçon de Charcot*; Sonolet, J.-M. *Charcot et l'hystérie au XIXe siècle.*

images are reproduced endlessly. They are often discussed as the central—at times, the sole—materials giving us knowledge of hysteria in the nineteenth century. Furthermore, a common tendency is to treat the hysterical fit, in all its drama, as the most significant or characteristic aspect of the malady or to equate it with a given author's general theory of the disease.[118]

It is not surprising that our historical understanding of the subject should have developed in this way. Hysteria in its everyday meaning denotes excessive or uncontrollable emotionality. By its nature, it is a highly corporealized pathology in which psychological anxieties are played out on the stage of the human body. Self-dramatization is an inherent part of it, and the works of Régnard, Bourneville, Brouillet, and Richer capture this element of theater powerfully. Clearly, theirs are key documents in the history of medical photography, in nineteenth-century French popular culture, and in the iconographical history of women.

Nevertheless, I believe that this has become a limiting and misleading feature of the new hysteria studies, and again I would like to propose a small corrective. On this topic, as with many others in the history of disease, it is imperative to maintain a distinction between medical-historical and cultural-historical conceptualizations of a subject. Regarding hysteria, I believe that in recent years a false centrality has been imposed on the documents named above, while a mass of other relevant primary source materials has been ignored. The result has been an excessive emphasis on the most spectacular aspects of hysteria's history that trivializes the subject and distorts historical understanding.

Within the intellectual history of hysteria, the relative ranking of symptoms—which ones are deemed central, which of secondary and tertiary significance—has changed greatly over time. Comparing these symptomatological hierarchies, we discover that over the past two centuries the hysterical fit has increasingly been subordinated first to nonconvulsive physical symptoms and then to psychological behaviors. In demonological theories of psychiatry, the attack was seen as the central manifestation of the disorder. However, with the increasing secularization of the disease, this changed. Gaston Amselle cites Charles Lepois, in the

---

[118] Didi-Huberman, *Invention de l'hystérie*; Wajeman, "Psyché de la femme"; Carroy-Thirard, "Figures de femmes hystériques dans la psychiatrie française au 19e siècle," 317–23; George F. Drinka, *The Birth of Neurosis: Myth, Malady, and the Victorians* (New York: Simon and Schuster, 1984), 74–107; Showalter, *Female Malady*, 147–54; Ruth Harris, *Murders and Madness: Medicine, Law, and Society in the Fin de Siècle* (Oxford: Clarendon Press, 1989), chap. 5; Michelle Perrot, ed., *A History of Private Life*, 4 vols., trans. from the French by Arthur Goldhammer (Cambridge, Mass.: Belknap Press, 1990), vol. 4, *From the Fires of Revolution to the Great War*, 624–33; Evans, *Fits and Starts*, chap. 1; Bannour, *Jean-Martin Charcot et l'hystérie*, passim.

early seventeenth century, as the first theorist to question the centrality of the fit in the clinical definition of hysteria.[119] Later in the seventeenth century, Sydenham initiated the practice of studying hysteria by individual bodily symptom, and by 1800 the hysterical attack had begun to lose its pathognomonic status. In his study of Scotland in the late eighteenth century, Risse finds "that only a minority of females labelled as suffering from hysteria actually displayed the characteristic fits."[120] During the nineteenth century, some authors, such as Carter, continued to interpret the paroxysm as the defining mark of the disorder, but a growing percentage of doctors privileged gynecological, neurological, or psychological symptoms. Of the 430 cases in Briquet's treatise of 1859, roughly a third include no spastic or convulsive symptoms at all. A generation later, Charcot often reminded his readers that a seizure was not necessary for the diagnosis of a case as hysterical. As noted previously, the attack scarcely figures at all in the writings of Freud and Janet. This progressive clinical decentering of the fit continued through twentieth-century theorizing about the neurosis.[121]

Related to the long-term symptomatological evolution of the disorder is the fact that case-historical literatures from earlier times in fact often display a disease picture that is considerably out of kilter with the popular view today. Despite the retrospective emphasis placed on this part of his work, Charcot in fact wrote comparatively little about the hysterical attack.[122] He constructed his model of the fit in the 1870s and made few changes in it during the remainder of his career. He formulated the theory primarily to establish that the attack followed a coherent developmental sequence and to differentiate the hysterical *attaque* from the epileptic *accès*. He did not show a greater interest in the attack than in other manifestations of hysteria—he published much more, for instance, on hysterical paralyses, hysterical contractions, and hysterical language disorders —and his overall description of the malady covered an enormous nosographical range.

The *Iconographie photographique de la Salpêtrière* has received much scholarly attention lately, but the information for properly contextualiz-

---

[119] Amselle, *Conception de l'hystérie*, 12.

[120] Risse, "Hysteria at the Edinburgh Infirmary," 9–10.

[121] See, for instance, Hutschemaekers's *Neurosen in Nederland*, 187, fig. 10.2, which charts the increasing scarcity of the epileptiform fit in Dutch medical records from 1900 to 1985.

[122] The main writings are "Description de la grande attaque hystérique," *Progrès médical* 7, no. 2 (January 11, 1879): 17–20; "De l'hystéro-épilepsie," in *Leçons sur les maladies du système nerveux* (Paris: Adrien Delahaye, 1872–73), lecture 13, 321–37; Charcot and Paul Richer, *Les démoniaques dans l'art* (Paris: Delahaye et Lecrosnier, 1887), 96–106; and "Hystérie à grandes attaques," in *Leçons du mardi à la Salpêtrière: Policlinique 1887–1888*, 2d ed., 2 vols. (Paris: Louis Battaille, 1892), 1, 103–5.

ing the source within both Charcot's oeuvre and late nineteenth-century medicine is rarely provided. In fact, in number and content, the cases in the *Iconographie photographique* were unrepresentative of the majority of hysterical patients at this time. As Janet wrote in a perspicacious post-humous analysis of Charcot's work, the Salpêtrian depiction of the hysterical attack represented a kind of clinical ideal-type: it integrated a range of physical and emotional behaviors from many medical cases into a single, purified pattern.[123] Such a model, aesthetically pleasing to the orderly mind of Charcot, brought a useful but largely artificial clarity to the subject. As Charcot himself often indicated, the full four-stage attack, with the highly stylized positions, occurred only very infrequently. Far commoner were the attenuated *formes frustes* of the fit: those innumerable partial or imperfect forms consisting of a single stage or posture of the attack—perhaps only a fainting spell, a facial twitch, or language tic. The cases in the *Iconographie photographique* presented those exceptional instances, useful for theoretical and pedagogical purposes, in which the complete cycle of the attack was compressed into one person and performance.

Additionally, even within the context of Charcot's work, these beautiful, baroque hysterias turn out to have been relatively few in number. In 1956, the Genevan psychiatrist Georges de Morsier attempted to calculate the actual number of patients appearing in Charcot's published writings. Morsier found that Charcot's celebrated theory, despite an initial impression of resting on a large empirical foundation, actually drew on no more than twenty-four hysterical patients. Morsier further found, to his surprise, that this small selection of patients was cited time and again by Charcot and his students in lectures, articles, and theses.[124] Likewise, Ellenberger cites Janet claiming that the Charcotian scheme of the hypnotic stages derived from only *three* hysterical women.[125] Morsier's observation was intended to call into question the scientific validity of Charcot's theories at a time when neurophysiological models of hysteria were out of favor. Still, there is an important point here for the historian. The cases recorded by Bourneville, Régnard, Brouillet, and Richer, which are often taken today to reflect widespread medical phenomena a century ago, were remarkable visualizations of historical pathology in extremis; but, even during the heady days of the 1880s and 1890s at the Salpêtrière, the alleged headquarters of the hysteria industry, these cases constituted exquisite clinical rarities.

123 Pierre Janet, "J.-M. Charcot: Son oeuvre psychologique," *Revue philosophique* 39 (June 1895): 572–78.

124 Georges de Morsier, "Jean Martin Charcot, 1825–1893," in Kurt Kolle, ed., *Grosse Nervenärzte*, 2 vols. (Stuttgart: Georg Thieme, 1956), 1: 45, 49.

125 Ellenberger, "Psychiatrie et son histoire inconnue," 284.

If the Blanche Wittmanns of the world represented the royalty of hysteria, so to speak, then what about the rank and file? What did "the average hysterical patient" look like a hundred years ago? Here again, if we move beyond the best-known medical and literary texts, we get a considerably altered historical picture. The nine-volume *Oeuvres complètes de J. M. Charcot* contain eighty-nine case histories carrying the primary or secondary diagnoses of hysteria. Approximately twenty periodical articles by Charcot not appearing in the *Oeuvres complètes* also treat hysterical disorders. While the original three-volume *Iconographie photographique* includes 120 photographs about the cases of eight hysterical women, the *Nouvelle iconographie de la Salpêtrière*, compiled between 1888 and 1918, ran to twenty-eight volumes and generated nearly ten thousand photographic glass negatives.[126] Finally, the Bibliothèque Charcot at the Salpêtrière includes notes and manuscripts for many additional case histories.

Readers versed only in the ubiquitous images of Bourneville, Régnard, Richer, and Brouillet will be surprised by what these sources reveal. It is immediately evident that the large majority of individuals diagnosed as hysterical at the Salpêtrière between 1870 and 1910 suffered not from *la grande hystéro-épilepsie* but from what was variously termed "petite hystérie," "hystérie ordinaire," and "hystérie vulgaire." Hysterogenic zones and the sensation of the esophagian ball appear frequently; but the *grands paroxysmes* with the stylized positions are very uncommon. Within the fifty-one clinical histories of hysteria in the two volumes of *Leçons du mardi*, a symptom count reveals the following percentages: localized or unilateral anesthesias and hyperesthesias, 79 percent; visual abnormalities, 76 percent; paralytic disorders, 35 percent; and loss of pharyngeal reflex, 34 percent. Forty-seven percent of these patients, or twenty-four of them, presented seizure activity of some sort, while 10 percent experienced fainting or dizziness instead of fits, and 37 percent presented no convulsive phenomena at all. Only 16 percent, or eight patients, manifested two or more stages of the classic attack, and only six patients, or 12 percent of the total, received the diagnoses of "hystéro-épilepsie," "hystérie majeure," or "hystérie à grandes attaques." Archival evidence from the Bibliothèque Charcot today offers a still humbler symptomatological picture: loss of sensation and movement in the upper-right extremity of a forty-seven-year-old woman following a violent quarrel with her daughter; recurrent idiopathic headaches, heart palpitations, and lower back pain developing suddenly in a fifty-five-year-old male railway worker; labored breathing associated with fright during a thunderstorm in a fourteen-year-old girl from Brittany.

---

[126] These glass plates are currently housed at the Countway Medical Library in Boston.

Which writings a critic, historian, or biographer sees as central in the corpus of a historical figure is of course a matter of interpretation. But the picture we form finally of the history of a disease should incorporate the widest possible array of available evidence. Thus far, historians of hysteria have given disproportional weight to a smattering of the most popular and picturesque sources and have all but excluded other pertinent materials. At this point, however, the repeated and exclusive emphasis on these vaudevillian images is providing a skewed historical picture and retarding the growth of scholarship on the subject. Aspects of hysteria and its history are intrinsically dramatic, and it is in part this drama that makes the topic so appealing. Nonetheless, for future hysteria studies, we need substantially to desensationalize the subject.

THE QUESTION OF SOCIAL CLASS

The significance of social class as a factor in the history of disease is well established. Within psychiatric history, however, the study of socioeconomic status has centered chiefly on the admission, care, and treatment of the insane in mental hospitals. A few scholars have also reflected on the interconnections between class identity and etiological theory.[127] Very little, however, has been written concerning the complex interactions between social class and diagnostic theory. Regarding hysteria, historians for obvious reasons have concentrated on the theme of gender to the comparative neglect of other sociological variables.

The most common historical association is between nervous disorders and the upper classes. Burtonian melancholia, the hypochondriacal afflictions discussed by Willis, Sydenham, Hoffman, and Boerhaave, and the *maladies nerveuses* discussed by eighteenth-century French writers were attributed to the overrefined sensibilities and idle, extravagant way of life of the upper classes. Moreover, early modern medical literature specifically cited manual labor as an antidote to nervous debility: "For seldom should you see an hired servant, a poor handmaiden, though ancient, that is kept hard to her work and bodily labour, a course country wench, troubled in this kind," intoned Robert Burton in 1621, "but noble virgins, nice gentlewomen, such as are solitary and idle, live at ease, lead a life out of action and employment, are misaffected, and prone to this

---

[127] Charles Rosenberg, "The Bitter Fruit: Heredity, Disease, and Social Thought in Nineteenth-Century America," in Donald Fleming and Bernard Bailyn, eds., *Perspectives in American History*, vol. 8 (Cambridge: Harvard University Press, 1974), 187–235; and S.E.D. Shortt, *Victorian Lunacy: Richard M. Bucke and the Practice of Late Nineteenth-Century Psychiatry* (London: Cambridge University Press, 1986), chap. 4.

disease."[128] A half-century later, Sydenham observed similarly that sooner or later nearly all women were susceptible to hysteria—"except for those who lead a hard and hardy life."[129] And early in the eighteenth century, Mandeville stressed that "the spleen" preyed on the sedentary and luxury-laden classes, sparing "people of lower Fortunes, who have seldom higher Ends, than . . . the getting of their Daily Bread."[130]

During the 1800s, the experience of the nervous disorders extended to the rising middle classes. Psychiatric textbooks by Georget, Laycock, Griesinger and others increasingly located hysteria, hypochondria, and nervousness in the bourgeois and aristocratic classes. In America during the 1870s and 1880s, Beard derived his theory of neurasthenia from the "brain workers" of the American business class while S. Weir Mitchell coaxed and coddled patients from some of the most affluent families in the country. The association between affluence and nervous suffering received further support with the publication of Freud's case histories, drawn as they typically were from patients with wealthy or *haute bourgeoisie* backgrounds. Since the 1960s, this idea has been endorsed indirectly by women's historians who have centered their attention on the middle- and upper-middle-class Victorian woman.

Given this background, one of the most significant findings emerging from the new hysteria studies is the widespread existence of nervous disorders among past working-class populations. In her discussion of English casebooks of the 1670s and 1680s, Williams finds that one out of five patients came from the lower orders. In Risse's study of eighteenth-century Edinburgh, all of the hysterical women are laborers. Goldstein has discovered that the great majority of hysterical patients at the Salpêtrière in the 1870s and 1880s had previously been engaged as laundresses, seamstresses, flower-sellers, and the like; and in their investigation of the Maréville asylum, Menzaghi, Millot, and Pillot find that most entrants receiving the diagnosis were indigents. The one in-depth, quantitative study of this theme in the nineteenth century locates cases of hysteria up and down the social scale.[131]

The discovery of the widespread existence of hysterical disorders among the working classes—or, more accurately, the application of the

[128] Robert Burton, *The Anatomy of Melancholy*, ed. Holbrook Jackson part 1 (New York: Vintage, 1977), 417.

[129] *The Works of Thomas Sydenham*, 2: 85.

[130] Mandeville, *Treatise of Hypochondriack and Hysterick Passions*, 2d ed., 150–51.

[131] Williams, "Hysteria in Seventeenth-Century Primary Sources," 6–7, 11, 19; Risse, "Hysteria at the Edinburgh Infirmary," 1–18; Goldstein, *Console and Classify*, 325; Menzaghi, Millot, and Pillot, *Évolution de la conception de l'hystérie*, 2: 11, Table 3; Susan Ferry, "Lives Measured in Coffee Spoons? A Study of Hysteria, Class, and Women in Nineteenth-Century Britain" (Master's thesis, University of Toronto, 1989).

diagnosis to members of this class—presents a challenge for historians. Much of the extant scholarship on the social history of hysteria, especially British and North American feminist writing, is predicated on the belief that hysteria was a kind of pathological by-product of middle-class Victorian and Wilhelminian society. But, as Goldstein indicates pointedly, Charcot's patients, who provided the material for the best-known model of the disorder in the nineteenth century, "were virtually all working-class women . . . who lived outside the framework of a bourgeois value system."[132] This discrepancy between the reigning social interpretation and the actual demographics of the disorder as we are learning about them calls into question the accuracy, or at least adequacy, of previous sociological readings.

One possible explanation of the discrepancy lies in the doctors, documents, and institutions under inspection. Shorter sees this clearly: "The view has somehow established itself that [hysterical] paralyses were in the nineteenth century a monopoly of 'middle class' women. . . . This view was derived from such sources as the diaries and letters of well-to-do women and the writings of such 'society nerve doctors' as S. Weir Mitchell. But in sources that give lower-class people a chance to appear, such as in case reports from hospitals and doctors with socially diverse practices, it becomes apparent that the great majority of all women striken with these phantom paralyses belonged to the working classes."[133]

Shorter's remarks concerning a single hysterical symptom may well apply generally. Until the early twentieth century, bourgeois and aristocratic people were far likelier than their peasant or proletarian counterparts to go to the doctor, seek the services of expensive specialists, and be treated by the prominent professionals doing the medical writing. However, during the nineteenth century, popular fears of medicine receded, and after 1860 a growing number of dispensaries, public infirmaries, and municipal hospitals administering to the working classes were established.[134] As more physicians came into contact with a wider sector of the population, an increasing number of working-class cases made their way into the medical literature.[135] It is therefore not surprising that scholars

[132] Goldstein, *Console and Classify*, 325–26.

[133] Shorter, "Rise and Fall of a 'Hysterical' Symptom," 572.

[134] Charles E. Rosenberg, "Social Class and Medical Care in Nineteenth-Century America: The Rise and Fall of the Dispensary," *Journal of the History of Medicine and the Allied Sciences* 29, no. 1 (January 1974): 32–54; I.S.L. Loudon, "The Origins and Growth of the Dispensary Movement in England," *Bulletin of the History of Medicine* 55, no. 3 (Fall 1981): 322–42.

[135] Thus the "discovery" of these disorders among working people by one of America's most elitist practitioners: "Many years ago," Silas Weir Mitchell recalled in 1877, "when we first began to sum up and classify the cases which came to my clinic, at the [Philadelphia] Infirmary for Diseases of the Nervous System, my assistants called my attention to the large

are uncovering the first evidence of a working-class presence in the history of hysteria in large urban municipal medical facilities, such as the Edinburgh Infirmary and the Salpêtrière. These early findings suggest, in a point that is pertinent to the history of disease generally, that hysteria among the lower classes was not in fact rare before the nineteenth century, but simply unrecognized, untreated, and unreported.

Conversely, members of the educated and leisured classes have traditionally been more liable to record their subjective experiences of sickness in fictional, autobiographical, and epistolary texts. There are to my knowledge no working-class counterparts to Burton's *Anatomy of Melancholy*, Dr. Johnson's essays and correspondence, or Charlotte Perkins Gilman's *The Yellow Wallpaper*. Shorter establishes this point effectively in a passage concerning two cases of hysterical paralysis from the last century. He first discusses the well-known case of Alice James, the sister of William and Henry, who from the age of nineteen was afflicted with fainting spells, paralysis of the legs, and chronic nervous exhaustion. James traveled from her home in Cambridge, Massachusetts, to one specialist and nerve clinic after another in America and England. She was the classic "New England invalid" who analyzed her condition relentlessly and recorded her emotional and physical sufferings in detailed diaries and letters.[136]

To James's case, Shorter tellingly juxtaposes the story of an anonymous eighteen-year-old wool worker in Rhode Island who suffered from hysterical paraplegia. One day in July 1892, while at work in a textile mill, the young woman fainted and in the fall injured her head and hip slightly. A month after the accident, she began to experience numbness and discomfort in one of her legs, as well as dizziness, weakness, and spells of crying. The girl's parents eventually brought their daughter to the Rhode Island Infirmary in Providence. When a series of blisterings and medications failed to help, the doctor in attendance tried hypnosis, and after several hypnotic sessions the "hysterical hip" improved greatly. The patient was discharged as "cured," and, after two short follow-up visits, was never heard from again.[137] The case of the young woman was congruent symptomatologically and even geographically with that of James—"She, too," Shorter comments, "was a New England invalid"—but James's case inspired a minor masterpiece of psychological autobiography while the

---

number set down as general nervousness. . . . This was the more notable, because of course the persons who seek help at the Infirmary are mechanics and workingmen chiefly, and therefore hardly such as are presumed to suffer from nervousness" ("Clinical Lecture on Nervousness in the Male," *Medical News and Library* 35, no. 420 [December 1877]: 177).

[136] Jean Strouse, *Alice James: A Biography* (London: Jonathan Cape, 1980), esp. chaps. 6, 7, 13 and 14.

[137] Shorter, "Rise and Fall of a 'Hysterical' Symptom," 572–73.

second case produced only a matter-of-fact two-page notice in a local medical journal.[138] Which source is the late twentieth-century scholar more likely to use as a key document in the social history of hysteria?

Once we have established that hysteria has been distributed across the social spectrum—that it is found among the idle rich, the repressed and overwrought bourgeoisie, and the industrious poor—we can inquire further into the meaning of this fact. One answer medical writers may give is that the pattern reflects the universality of hysteria, caused by a particular biological or psychological mechanism. However, if hysteria is partly or primarily sociogenic, then we need to turn for an explanation to the surrounding historical environment. One line of analysis in the recent literature is that hysteria represents "a pathology of powerlessness." In this view, the disorder is a phenomenon of the most helpless and hopeless members of society, to whom the standard modes of self-expression, through education, politics, and the law, are closed and who are therefore compelled unconsciously to employ the desperate nonverbal language of the somatic symptom.[139] By and large, the idea of hysteria as social protest holds up well in the light of the new hysteria studies. Many categories of people to whom the label has been applied (ancient Greek women, Renaissance "witches," Victorian middle-class women, foot soldiers in the First World War) have occupied socially subservient and politically disempowered positions. However, the concept of the "sick role," first applied to the nineteenth-century bourgeois family by Smith-Rosenberg in the early 1970s, is problematic in regard to working-class populations. While the generic psychological pressures on individuals from working-class backgrounds have probably been greater than on other classes, the material exigencies of their lives constrained them. It is difficult to pursue "secondary gain" when one is driven by the primary needs of subsistence.[140]

An additional variable concerns shifts in the social composition of

[138] The relevant sources are Alice James, *Alice James, Her Brothers, Her Journal*, ed. Anna Robeson Burr (Boston: Longwood Press, 1977) and Frank E. Peckham, "A Case of Hysterical Hip-Joint Successfully Treated by Hypnotism," *Boston Medical and Surgical Journal* 129, no. 17 (October 26, 1893): 419–20.

[139] Smith-Rosenberg, "The Hysterical Woman"; G. G. Wallis, "Hysteria Today," *British Medical Journal* 2, no. 6039 (October 2, 1976): 817; Bart and Scully, "The Politics of Hysteria," in Gomberg and Franks, *Gender and Disordered Behavior*, 360ff.; and Showalter, *Female Malady*, chap. 6.

[140] As two American sociologists once put it: "The Victorian lady could dramatize certain emotions in a way that today would be considered silly, if not hysterical. . . . Yet the working girl who was her contemporary was not as likely to faint as was the lady; there would probably not have been anyone to catch the working girl" (Hans Gerth and C. Wright Mills, *Character and Social Structure: The Psychology of Social Institutions* [New York: Harcourt, Brace, 1953], 12–13).

diagnostic populations over time. In a thoughtful essay published in 1977, Barbara Sicherman noted the application of the neurasthenia diagnosis to the American working classes during the closing decades of the nineteenth century.[141] Elaborating on Sicherman's observation, Francis Gosling and Joyce Ray have studied changing patterns in the social epidemiology of neurasthenia from 1870 to 1910. Based on their comprehensive review of the medical-periodical literature, Gosling and Ray pinpoint a process of downward social extension in which the diagnosis was first applied to the overheated "brain workers" in Beard's original writings, then moved in the 1880s to overworked businessmen, and spread finally to the laboring classes, which after 1890 formed the preponderance of the patient population. Gosling and Ray then look comparatively at the application of the diagnosis to men and women from middle- and lower-class backgrounds and formulate a "gender-by-class model." They integrate both factors into a single process of "the democratization of American nervousness."[142]

The analyses of Sicherman, Gosling, and Ray raise the additional question of what exactly is being democratized—diagnostic practice or a psychopathological reality? The second possibility is not as farfetched as it may seem. An interesting snippet of information recurring in recent studies concerns the occupational identities of past hysteria patients. Among working people, one category appears time and again: domestic servant.[143] As early as the eighteenth century, British writers noticed this pattern and contended that domestic staff were beginning to develop the unhealthful living and eating habits of their employers. Modern-day readers will be disinclined to blame the disorder on too much coffee and chocolate, but it may be that bourgeois behaviors were being imitated in other ways. Socially, the lives of domestic servants (and also of nannies and governesses, two other groups appearing conspicuously in the records) are distinguished by close daily contact with their social superiors. Just as certain "aristocratic" ailments of the eighteenth century descended to the middle classes early in the nineteenth, so perhaps a more medicalized self-consciousness began to form later in the century among

[141] Barbara Sicherman, "The Uses of a Diagnosis," *Journal of the History of Medicine and Allied Sciences* 32 (1977): 43–44.

[142] F. G. Gosling and Joyce M. Ray, "The Right to Be Sick: American Physicians and Nervous Patients, 1885–1910," *Journal of Social History* 20 (Winter 1986): 253; Gosling, *Before Freud*, 162.

[143] Risse, "Hysteria at the Edinburgh Infirmary," 5–6, 15; Figlio, "Chlorosis and Chronic Disease in Nineteenth-Century Britain," 181–87; Goldstein, "The Hysteria Diagnosis and the Politics of Anticlericalism," 213. Among primary sources, see Briquet's treatise (121–23), which includes a separate section on hysteria and *domestiques*.

working-class people living in bourgeois environments. A kind of psychological gentrification occurred wherein servants, who attended their bourgeois and upper-class employers in sickness and health, developed the illness behaviors of their social superiors.[144]

The social historian of disease may benefit on this point from a reading of contemporary medical literature. The dominant school of thinking about hysteria in Anglo-American psychiatric circles today interprets hysterical neurosis as a comparatively primitive defense mechanism that is being replaced increasingly by coping strategies that psychologically are more subtle, sophisticated, and inward-looking. This argument is often accompanied by comparative epidemiological data. According to these studies, pockets of hysteria persist in culturally, economically, and educationally deprived environments, while depressive and narcissistic disorders predominate in more urbanized, educated, and medicalized social settings.[145] This view reverses centuries of earlier thinking that associated the malady with a surfeit of civilization and envisioned it as an upper-class phenomenon spreading downward on the social scale. Are the recent findings of historians about class and hysteria reconcilable with contemporary medical research regarding cultural identity and choice of neurosis?

One possible explanation is that hysteria may be specifically a phenomenon of *protomedicalization*. As social populations begin to develop a sensitivity to their emotional health within a secular, naturalistic framework, and as they first become aware that psychological physicians are available to minister to their anxieties, they may employ the most direct and emotionally extroverted method of stress communication (i.e., the formation of psychogenic somatic symptoms). But as the medicalizing process advances, people become cognizant of the rather transparent psychodynamics of hysterical conversion, which thereafter fails to elicit

---

[144] In *The Beaux Stratagem*, written in 1707 by the Irish humorist and playwright George Farquhar, a servant at one point cries "A footman have the spleen!" The servant's employer, Mrs. Sullen, then remarks, "I thought that distemper had been only proper to people of quality." To which an observer responds, "Madam, like all other fashions it wears out, and so descends to their servants." (Cited in Porter, *Mind Forg'd Manacles*, 304, n. 259).

[145] Dewitt L. Crandell and Bruce P. Dohrenwend, "Some Relations among Psychiatric Symptoms, Organic Illness, and Social Class," *American Journal of Psychiatry* 123, no. 12 (June 1967): 1527–38; Henri F. Ellenberger, "Aspects ethnopsychiatriques de l'hystérie," *Confrontations psychiatriques* 1 (1978): 131–45; J. G. Stefánsson, J. A. Messina, and S. Meyerowitz, "Hysterical Neurosis, Conversion Type: Clinical and Epidemiological Considerations," *Acta Psychiatrica Scandinavica* 53, no. 2 (February 1976): 119–38; Myrna M. Weissman, Jerome K. Myers, and Pamela S. Harding, "Psychiatric Disorders in a U. S. Urban Community: 1975–1976," *American Journal of Psychiatry* 135, no. 4 (April 1978): 459–62; and Marvin Swartz et al., "Somatization Disorder in a Community Population," *American Journal of Psychiatry* 143, no. 11 (November 1986): 1403–8.

the desired interpersonal gratification and is abandoned in favor of alternative mechanisms.

The theme of social class in the history of disease is much more complex than at first appears and on closer inspection dissolves into a series of smaller, interrelated questions: What is the meaning of the recent discovery that a high proportion of hysteria cases over the past three hundred years has come from the lower classes? Can traditional feminist interpretations derived from literate middle-class populations be broadened or revised to include new social constituencies? Have genuine evolutions occurred in the social epidemiology of hysteria or only changes in the professional and institutional apparatus for registering the disease in different classes? Is it possible to work toward a general taxonomy of socioeconomic status, psychological behavior, and diagnostic practice? Or in the long run will separate historical accounts for each class be required? Once we have addressed these questions, we need to integrate the element of class with other nonmedical factors, such as age, gender, culture, religious affiliation, and ethnic background, for both the doctors and patients involved. There is much work to do in this domain, too.

HYSTERIA—THE MALE MALADY

With the growth of hysteria studies in recent years, our most familiar images of the subject seem destined for the historiographical dustbin. The vast majority of writing about hysteria has rested on the almost axiomatic assumption that it is and always has been an affliction of adult and adolescent women. Given the etymology of the term, the long involvement of hysteria with the history of witchcraft, and the link between the neurosis and bourgeois Victorian women, the association seems to make sense. Nevertheless, a second discovery emerging from the new hysteria studies is that the diagnosis has been applied in many previous times and places, and in significant numbers, to men, that hysteria is the *male* malady too.[146]

For centuries, the idea of "la maladie de la matrice" in members of the male sex seemed a kind of semantic absurdity, a patent impossibility given the anatomical distinction between the sexes. As the French alienist Louyer-Villermay put it bluntly in 1819: "A man cannot be hysterical; he has no uterus."[147] However, beginning in the seventeenth century, with the change in the projected anatomical seat of the disease from the female reproductive organs to the brain, mind, or nervous system, a gender-

---

[146] I owe this phrase to Nancy Tomes.

[147] Jean-Baptiste Louyer-Villermay, *Traité de maladies nerveuses et en particulier de l'hystérie*, 2 vols. (Paris: J.-B. Baillière, 1816), 1: 116.

neutral model of the disorder became a distinct theoretical possibility. At least as much as the scholarship on hysteria in the working classes, the discovery of the history of masculine hysteria has the ability to enlarge, revise, and subvert earlier traditions of commentary on the topic. It also suggests the complexity of past interactions between medicine, disease, and gender.

Thus far, the study of male hysteria has focused on three historical settings, each of which brings out a different dimension of the topic. As a pendant to Anglo-American feminist writing on neurotic women in the nineteenth century, biographers and historians have of late explored the Victorian neurasthenic male. From his quantitative study of the American periodical literature, Gosling finds that the neurasthenia diagnosis a century ago was applied with rough equivalency to males and females. Howard Feinstein and Tom Lutz have shown that the debilitating nervous invalidism prevalent during the American Gilded Age struck such men as William and Henry James, Louis Agassiz, William Dean Howells, Theodor Dreiser, Frank Norris, and W. E. B. Du Bois;[148] and Suzanne Poirier has pointed out that Silas Weir Mitchell derived his famous rest cure for female patients from the treatment of nervous, battle-fatigued soldiers during the American Civil War.[149] As we will see shortly, a series of nineteenth-century French men of letters—madmen in the attic?—were plagued self-consciously with nerves, neurasthenia, and hysteria.

The history of male nervousness in Britain during this same period turns out to be no less eventful. Characteristically, the subject has been investigated most thoroughly and sensitively by Janet Oppenheim, who devotes a separate chapter of *"Shattered Nerves"* to *"Manly Nerves."*[150] Oppenheim's account of the victims of serious "nervous prostration" during the Victorian years includes John Ruskin, John Addington Symonds, Francis Galton, James Sully, Edmund Gosse, Joseph Lister, and Arnold Toynbee.[151] Oppenheim places the Victorian nervous male in the

[148] Howard M. Feinstein, "The Use and Abuse of Illness in the James Family Circle: A View of Neurasthenia as a Social Phenomenon," in Robert J. Brugger, ed., *Our Selves/Our Past: Psychological Approaches to American History* (Baltimore: Johns Hopkins University Press, 1981), chap. 10; Tom Lutz, *American Nervousness, 1903: An Anecdotal History* (Ithaca, N.Y.: Cornell University Press, 1991).

[149] Suzanne Poirier, "The Weir Mitchell Rest Cure: Doctors and Patients," *Women's Studies* 10 (1983): 15–40.

[150] Oppenheim, *"Shattered Nerves"*, chap. 5.

[151] Oppenheim comments: "The medical profession in these decades never attempted to deny the widespread incidence of nervous breakdown among men. It is utterly erroneous to assume that Victorian doctors perceived the male half of the human race as paragons of health and vigor, while assigning all forms of weakness to women. They could not have done so, even had they wanted to, for the evidence exposing male nervous vulnerability was too familiar to the Victorian public for pretense" (ibid., 141.)

context of evolving attitudes toward masculinity and male emotionality. Accepted and even praised during the Enlightenment and Romantic eras, the lavish display of strong feelings by adult men in public or private became suspect and undesirable during the Victorian years. Oppenheim traces this change to a series of forces growing across the century, including the Evangelical religious impulse, an ethos of aggressive capitalism, strident nationalism and imperialism, the cult of sports, and the doctrine of social Darwinism.

For its part, the medical profession formulated the hypothesis that most cases of nervous breakdown in men resulted from the depletion of finite nervous energies due to excessive work or anxiety. Other projected causes included physical trauma, immoderate diet, sexual excesses, and masturbation. Oppenheim observes that a majority of cases of shattered nerves in men occurred in early adulthood, and she speculates that behind these cases lay other factors, including career indecision, struggles with an authoritarian pater familias, the loss of religious faith, and sexual and emotional repression in gay men. Many of the same social, cultural, and sexual forces constraining women during this period, she shows, operated with deleterious effect on men too.

A second historical setting in which the male variant of hysteria has been probed is late nineteenth-century France. This topic has probably been explored most systematically in my own work.[152] In 1859, Briquet bravely opened his *Traité de l'hystérie clinique et thérapeutique* with seven cases of men, estimating that the disorder occurred between the sexes in a rough ratio of one to twenty.[153] A generation later, Charcot hailed Briquet's treatise and took up the same subject with energy. Between 1878 and 1893, Charcot published over sixty case histories concerning hysterical disorders in men and boys.[154] This constitutes roughly 35 percent of his overall publications on the neurosis. Charcot's work appeared in three phases, each with a specific scientific and professional agenda: from 1878 to 1885, he strove simply to establish the reality of

[152] Mark S. Micale, "Diagnostic Discriminations: Jean-Martin Charcot and the Nineteenth-Century Idea of Masculine Hysterical Neurosis" (Ph.D. diss., Yale University, 1987); idem, "Charcot and the Idea of Hysteria in the Male: Gender, Mental Science, and Medical Diagnosis in Late Nineteenth-Century France," *Medical History* 34, no. 4 (October 1990): 363–411; idem, "Hysteria Male/Hysteria Female: Reflections on Comparative Gender Construction in Nineteenth-Century France and Britain," in Marina Benjamin, ed., *Science and Sensibility: Gender and Scientific Enquiry, 1780–1945* (Oxford: Basil Blackwell, 1991), 200–39; idem, *Hysterical Male: Medicine and Masculine Nervous Illness from the Renaissance to Freud* (New Haven: Yale University Press, work in progress).

[153] Briquet, *Traité clinique et thérapeutique de l'hystérie*, 11–51.

[154] For a selection of these cases, see Jean-Martin Charcot, *Leçons sur l'hystérie virile*, intro. Michèle Ouerd (Paris: S.F.I.E.D., 1984).

male hysteria in the face of longstanding prejudices about the disease within the medical profession; during the middle and latter years of the 1880s, he worked on the subject as part of a heated controversy with German neurologists concerning "post-traumatic nervous disorders"; and from 1887 to 1893, he was engaged in the challenge of differential diagnosis that many of these cases afforded. His research in these areas represents some of the most scientifically significant aspects of his lifework.

Congruent with Goldstein's findings about the social status of female patients at the Salpêtrière, the largest percentage of Charcot's male hysterics were factory workers or members of the traditional *petits métiers* of Paris. Charcot sought to free the diagnosis in these patients from damaging gender stereotypes by arguing repeatedly against the images of the male hysteric as pubescent boy, effeminate or homosexual man, effete aristocrat, or celibate priest. A close and comparative analysis of the Charcotian models of hysteria in males and females reveals a set of similarities and differences between the two conceptualizations. At one time or another, Charcot ascribed virtually the entire range of physical signs found in his hysterical women—including genital hysterogenic zones and hysterical "pseudo-ovarian points"—to his male patients. On this score, his work represents "a very old and gynocentric model of disease imposed with remarkable anatomical literalness onto members of the male population."[155]

At the same time, Charcot's "hysterization of the male body" reflected much more than the simple transposition of an ancient diagnostic category onto a new clinical population.[156] While the basic neuro-symptomatologies described by Charcot in male and female hysterics were the same, the mental manifestations attributed to the two sexes were markedly dissimilar. With cases involving men, Charcot often drained the diagnosis of its affective content by limiting his accounts to purely bodily symptoms. Analogously, in the realm of etiological theory, he applied a primary degenerationist model to his male and female patients alike but posited separate secondary causes for the two sexes, causes that were consonant with prevailing conceptions of male and female nature. In his clinical reports, female patients typically fall victim to hysteria because of an intense emotional experience, occurring most often in private domestic environments. However, men tend to get sick in public settings, because of too much working, drinking, fighting, or fornicating. Likewise, Charcot rarely mentions sexual factors of any sort as relevant to the etiology of

---

[155] Micale, "Charcot and the Idea of Hysteria in the Male," 409.

[156] In the introductory volume of his *Histoire de la sexualité*, Michel Foucault speaks of the "hystérisation du corps de la femme" (137).

his male cases. By thus deemotionalizing and desexualizing the diagnosis, he was effectively able to acknowledge the hysterical neuroses in members of his own sex while avoiding the more delicate and controversial implications of the male hysteria concept.

Following Charcot's professional certification, "hystérie virile" quickly became a popular, even fashionable, topic in scientific circles. During the 1880s and 1890s, a voluminous medical periodical and monographic subliterature appeared in the principal European languages. However, despite its ritualistic prefatory obeisances to Charcot, this later medical writing departed decisively from the views of the master. The authors of these works identified hysterical pathologies in increasingly diverse male populations, including boys, peasants, and soldiers. They also allotted a wider scope to the emotional and sexual causes and symptoms of hysteria in men than had Charcot. Also, in the general European literature, dramatic cases of male hysterics, such as that of Louis Vivé, appeared repeatedly, earning for these patients a notoriety equal to that of the women in the *Iconographie photographique*.

Equally noteworthy is a strong, conservative current running through post-Charcotian European and North American writing about masculine hysteria. Clearly, within medical history the very idea of hysteria in the male sex had the ability to discredit the inherited Hippocratic tradition. If men too could be hysterics, this strongly suggested the need to de-gender the diagnosis. Beyond this, the concept carried implications for the definition of masculinity and femininity in the social world at large, exerting a kind of relativizing effect on the highly polarized sex/gender system of the nineteenth century. Similarly unsettling, the theory of hysteria in the male aroused questions about the stereotyping of femininity by physicians in the past and about the possible emotional or "feminine" component in the male psyche. In a fascinating pattern, late nineteenth-century medical writers creatively, and most likely unconsciously, deployed a series of "strategies of resistance" that allowed them to discuss the subject of hysteria in adult males while avoiding, or at least minimizing, the psychological and sexual ramifications of the idea.[157] Included among these strategies were the use of alternative, technical-sounding terminologies to diagnose male patients, the ascription of unknown organic etiologies to cases involving men, limitation of the label to adolescent boys or effeminate men, and the illustration of the diagnosis with cases drawn from socially and ethnically stigmatized populations. Through the use of these devices, the diagnosis in French, German, and British medical discourses to a great degree became re-gendered by 1900.

This, however, is not quite the end of the story. The line of European

[157] Micale, "Diagnostic Discriminations," part 3; idem, *Hysterical Male*, chap. 4.

medical thinking about the genderization of the neuroses that begins with Briquet and runs through Charcot and his students, culminates, I propose, in Freud's early work. During the winter of 1885–86, it will be recalled, Freud studied with Charcot at the Salpêtrière. This date corresponds precisely with the height of debate within the Parisian medical community about male hysteria, and, upon his return to Vienna, the young Freud delivered a controversial lecture about the topic to the Vienna Society of Physicians.[158] While these episodes are well known, it can plausibly be argued that Freud's exposure to Charcot's work on male hysteria played a larger part in his intellectual and emotional biography than previously recognized. During the next fifteen years, Freud continued to reflect on what he had heard and seen at Charcot's clinic. Unlike his French predecessors, however, he eventually confronted, in both private emotional terms and in the realm of psychological theory, the full implications of the existence of the hysterical neuroses in men. By the turn of the century, his contemplation of the subject contributed to his formulation of a general theory of psychosexuality, including the non–gender-specific idea of universal bisexuality. In short, classic psychoanalytic theory, I believe, represents in part a working out of the heritage of gender indeterminacy implicit in the nineteenth-century French research tradition of masculine hysteria to which Freud was exposed as a young man.[159]

Oppenheim and I both address male hysteria in civilian settings from the past century. A third context studied recently concerns wartime nervous disorders, particularly "shell shock" during the First World War. Eric Leed and Elaine Showalter have reconstructed this painful story from the interestingly different perspectives of the military historian and the feminist literary critic. In No Man's Land: Combat and Identity in World War I, Leed includes a poignant and perceptive chapter on the so-called war neuroses.[160] The conditions of combat confronting soldiers during the First World War, Leed observes, were uniquely destructive: large num-

---

[158] Freud's original lecture to the Viennese Gesellschaft der Ärzte has been lost; however, several firsthand accounts of the meeting from contemporary medical periodicals exist, and these have recently been gathered and reprinted in "Quellentexte," Luzifer-Amor: Zeitschrift zur Geschichte der Psychoanalyse 1, no. 1 (1988): 156–75. See also Jones, Life and Work of Sigmund Freud, 1: 229–32; Henri F. Ellenberger, "La conférence de Freud sur l'hystérie masculine (15 octobre 1886): Étude critique," L'information psychiatrique 44, no. 10 (1968): 921–34; K. Sablik, "Sigmund Freud und die Gesellschaft der Ärzte in Wien," Wiener klinische Wochenschrift 80, no. 6 (February 9, 1968): 107–10; and Kenneth Levin, "Freud's Paper 'On Male Hysteria' and the Conflict between Anatomical and Physiological Models," Bulletin of the History of Medicine 48, no. 3 (Fall 1974): 377–97.

[159] Micale, Hysterical Male, chap. 6.

[160] Eric J. Leed, No Man's Land: Combat and Identity in World War I (Cambridge: Cambridge University Press, 1979), chap. 5.

bers of men, immobile for long periods of time, and in an unprecedentedly mechanized war, witnessed an enormous loss of life all around them. Over time, these circumstances exacted an excruciating psychological toll.

As the war dragged on, the number of cases involving paralysis, blindness, mutism, and amnesia mounted, and physicians were forced to recognize the psychogenic nature of many of these maladies. German and Austrian neurologists conceded the clinical continuity between the "posttraumatic neuroses" of train wreck victims from the 1890s and infantrymen at the battlefront during 1914–18. French doctors acknowledged the similarities between shell shock and the nervous symptoms described by Charcot a generation earlier. And psychoanalytically informed British military physicians, like Freud and Breuer in *Studies on Hysteria*, noted the symbolic correspondence between individual hysterical symptoms and wartime experiences.[161] "The symptoms of shell shock were precisely the same as those of the most common hysterical disorders of peacetime," comments Leed. ". . . What had been predominantly a disease of women before the war became a disease of men in combat."[162] Leed proposes that these breakdowns were to some degree tolerated by the military establishment. Most likely, he conjectures, this was because such disorders were tacitly understood as alternatives to a severer and more permanent psychological break with reality or an organized political protest.[163]

Understandably, feminist historians and critics have had little to say about hysteria in men. However, in an important innovation, Elaine Showalter includes in *The Female Malady* an outstanding chapter that extends feminist interpretive techniques to "male hysteria" in the First World War.[164] It is a big jump from fin-de-siècle Paris, London, and Vienna to the battlefields of Verdun and the Somme, but Showalter finds compelling social and psychological parallels between the two worlds. Like the middle-class women of the 1800s, soldiers on the front lines in

---

[161] "Thus a soldier who bayonets an enemy in the face develops an hysterical tic of his facial muscles; abdominal contractions occur in men who have bayonetted enemies in the abdomen; hysterical blindness follows particularly horrible sights; hysterical deafness appears in men who find the cries of the wounded unbearable, and the men detached to burial parties develop amnesia" (T. W. Salmon, *The Care and Treatment of Mental Diseases and War Neuroses ["Shell-Shock"] in the British Army* (1917), cited in Leed, *No Man's Land*, 179).

[162] Leed, *No Man's Land*, 163.

[163] Ibid., 168, 189.

[164] Showalter, *Female Malady*, chap. 7. See also idem, "Rivers and Sassoon: The Inscription of Male Gender Anxieties," in Margaret R. Higonnet et al., eds., *Behind the Lines: Gender and the Two World Wars* (New Haven: Yale University Press, 1987), 61–69; and Showalter, "Hysteria, Feminism, and Gender," in Gilman et al., *Hysteria Beyond Freud*, 320–26.

1916, she perceives, were trapped in a closed and intolerable situation that was beyond their control. Moreover, like the ill-educated housewives of the previous generation, these men had few psychological skills for expressing directly the unbearable levels of anxiety to which they were subjected. As a result, they too were driven to the primitive language of somatic symptom formation.

In addition, infantrymen in the First World War, Showalter indicates, had undergone a process of gender socialization no less rigorous than that imposed on bourgeois Victorian women. The Edwardian cult of masculinity required a stiff upper lip at all times, unflinching loyalty to country, and no unseemly displays of emotion. From this perspective, rampant mental and physical breakdown on the battlefield was "a disguised male protest not only against the war but against the concept of 'manliness' itself."[165] Showalter also points out that many victims of war hysteria, again like their earlier female counterparts, were contemptuously branded by medical men as simulators and at times forced to undergo painful, aversive treatments designed to restore them as quickly as possible to their prescribed social functions on the battlefield. Sadly, "curing" these victims of hysteria usually meant calming them sufficiently so they could return, suicidally, to the front lines. A strange sense of therapeutics, that.

Recent scholarship about the history of hysteria in men is a microcosm of the new hysteria studies as a whole. The fact that an intellectual historian, social historian, medical historian, military historian, and feminist literary critic have converged simultaneously and independently on the topic suggests its timeliness and interpretive richness. The subject is clearly open to a diversity of approaches. However, whatever the methodology employed and the analysis advanced, a number of things are apparent: the range of patient participants in the history of hysteria has been much wider than previously realized; the disorder has been gendered in ways that are far more various and complex than recognized before; and a fuller and more flexible model of the historical interaction of science, society, disease, and gender than employed thus far is necessary. To be sure, as I stated earlier in the book, the history of hysteria is composed predominantly of a body of writing by men about women. For precisely this reason, the application of the diagnosis to other groups in the past offers a particularly significant area for further investigation.[166]

---

[165] Showalter, *Female Malady*, 172.

[166] For the diagnosis in another understudied population, consult Elisabeth Kloë, *Hysterie im Kindesalter: Zur Entwicklung des kindlichen Hysteriebegriffes*, vol. 9 of *Freiburger Forschungen zur Medizingeschichte* (Freiburg: Hans Ferdinand Schulz, 1979); Elisabeth Kloë and Hildburg Kindt, "Zur Entstehung und Entwicklung des kindlichen Hysteriebegriffes," *Gesnerus* 38, nos. 3/4 (1981): 281–300; and K. Codell Carter, "Infantile Hys-

On the Rise and Fall of Nervous Diseases

Finally, with the exception of several works about France, very little has been written, in either earlier or recent studies, about hysteria in our own century. Books and articles about the disorder in the 1900s are most likely scarce because on first glance the subject appears a nonhistory. Among many physicians nowadays, and nearly all scholars in the humanities, it is a commonplace that hysteria, particularly in its florid, convulsive forms, is a thing of the past. The historiography of hysteria is replete with references to the decline and disappearance of hysteria in our own time.[167] Today, the disorder is most often viewed as a kind of colorful behavioral artifact of fin-de-siècle Europe, while the hysterical patient is considered a specimen of pathology from a bygone era, a kind of clinical endangered species. As Lacan once queried, "Where are the hysterics of earlier times, those magnificent women, the Anna O.s and Emmy von N.'s? . . . What has replaced the former hysterical symptoms today?"[168]

The termination of an entire disease form, especially one that appears to have such a long and venerable history, is surely a noteworthy event. Yet surprisingly, the process by which the alleged disappearance of hysteria occurred has failed to elicit sustained scholarly commentary. A surprising number of historians have been content either to dismiss the question as one of history's unsolved mysteries or to ignore the subject altogether. After charting the history of medical thinking about the malady across two and a half millennia, Veith devotes only two closing paragraphs to the question of "the nearly total disappearance of the illness" in the twentieth century, and then ends her book.[169] Trillat considers the question a bit longer but concludes with a shrug of the scholarly shoulders. The final sentence of his book reads like a historical epitaph: "Hysteria is dead, that is certain. It has taken its secrets with it to the grave."[170] But far from being a nonsubject, the evolution of the hysteria diagnosis in the present century is among the most fruitful topics for historical investigation.

---

teria and Infantile Sexuality in Late Nineteenth-Century German-Language Medical Literature," *Medical History* 27, no. 2 (April 1983): 186–96.

[167] A. Rouquier, "La fin de l'hystérie," *Annales médico-psychologiques*, 118, no. 3 (October 1960): 528; "Eclipse of Hysteria," n.a., *British Medical Journal*, no. 5447 (May 29, 1965): 1389–90; Moustafa Safouan, "Éloge à l'hystérie," in *Études sur l'Oedipe* (Paris: Seuil, 1974), 206–13; and Roberta Satow, "Where Has All the Hysteria Gone?" *Psychoanalytic Review* 66, no. 4 (Winter 1979–1980): 463–77.

[168] Cited in Roudinesco, *Histoire de la psychanalyse en France*, 1: 82–83.

[169] Veith, *Hysteria*, 273–74.

[170] Trillat, *Histoire de l'hystérie*, 274.

In recent years, two explanatory trends have developed in regard to the curious clinical diminution of hysteria. Customarily, if historians address the question, they attribute the phenomenon to psychological and socio-cultural factors. In 1908, in a well-known essay, Freud argued that the prevailing social and moral conditions of the time were exacting an inor-dinately high degree of sexual repression and in the process producing a race of neurasthenic men and hysterical women.[171] During the past twenty-five years, Freud's analysis has been picked up and elaborated on by historians, social scientists, and cultural critics. In their interpreta-tions, hysteria is viewed as a culture-bound pathology of the age of Victo-ria, with its sexual confinement, emotional oppression, and social suf-focation. Conversely, the conspicuous decline in rates of hysterical illness during the twentieth century has attended the passing of those pernicious conditions that generated an increase in nervous complaints during the nineteenth century. In short, the disappearance of hysteria results from de-Victorianization.[172]

Medical authors have posited a second explanation, which might be called the argument from psychological literacy. According to this inter-pretation, people were relatively primitive in their psychological processes before the twentieth century and found it easy to "somaticize" their anxieties, that is, to express emotional distress through psychogenic physical symptom formation. However, through the promulgation of Freudian psychoanalysis, Jungian analytical psychology, American be-haviorism, and the like, individuals have become educated about the nature and operations of the psyche. With the coming of our "psychologi-cal society," and the popularization of such concepts as unconscious motivation and psychosomatic sickness, lay persons began to compre-hend the psychodynamics behind hysterical conversion, which thereafter failed to elicit the desired social response and subjective gratification. As a result, people have been forced to develop more nuanced and inner-directed mental mechanisms for coping with the stresses of life. This line

[171] Sigmund Freud, "'Civilized' Sexual Morality and Modern Nervous Illness" [1908], in *Standard Edition*, 9: 177–204.

[172] Many texts voice this idea, among them Smith-Rosenberg, "The Hysterical Woman"; Wood, "'The Fashionable Diseases'"; John S. Haller, Jr. and Robin M. Haller, *The Physi-cian and Sexuality in Victorian America* (Urbana: University Illinois Press, 1974), chap. 1; Schaps, *Hysterie und Weiblichkeit*, chap. 9; Madeline L. Feingold, "Hysteria as a Modality of Adjustment in *Fin-de-Siècle* Vienna" (Ph.D. diss., California School of Professional Psy-chology, Berkeley, 1983); George Frederick Drinka, *The Birth of Neurosis: Myth, Malady, and the Victorians* (New York: Simon and Schuster, 1984), chaps. 1–6; Mitchinson, "Hys-teria and Insanity in Women"; and Showalter, *Female Malady*, chaps. 5, 6. For articulations by psychologists, see Marc H. Hollender, "Conversion Hysteria: A Post-Freudian Rein-terpretation of 19th-Century Psychosocial Data," *Archives of General Psychiatry* 26 (1972): 311–14; and Krohn, *Hysteria: The Elusive Neurosis*, chap. 4.

of analysis is often coupled with cross-cultural epidemiological data demonstrating that hysterical neuroses currently exist only in rural, lowerclass, or third-world environments and that the decline of hysterical conversion reactions within industrialized, medicalized, and westernized populations has been accompanied by a rise in depressive and narcissistic disorders.[173]

These two hypotheses for the disappearance of hysteria—the arguments from sociosexual emancipation and psychological literacy—assuredly contain an element of truth and will contribute eventually to a full understanding of the subject. At the same time, these explanations, both of which emphasize the role of "external" factors, may be complemented by a third, internal process that to date has remained relatively unappreciated. I am referring to the role of semantic and conceptual paradigm shift within the history of diagnostics. If we examine the medical-historical record closely, we find that the period from 1895 to 1915 was marked by radical nosological and nosographical reformulations; that is, sudden changes in what doctors regarded as the clinical content of the hysteria diagnosis and how they placed the disorder in the overall system of medical classification. The effect of this process was to produce fundamental changes in diagnostic theory and practice, and these changes, in concert with the social and cultural factors named above, may go far toward elucidating the peculiar fortunes of the hysteria concept in our time. By studying closely the evolution of European medical systems, and particularly of French and German psychiatric nosologies in the immediate post-Charcotian era, it is possible to reconstruct this process of diagnostic reconceptualization.

A tentative exercise along these lines suggests that the hysteria diagnosis during the early twentieth century lost ground to three major medical areas. First, new theories of disease causation and advances in diagnostic technique allowed key components of the diagnosis to be incorporated into general organic, especially neurological, medicine. Through centuries of medical history, epilepsy and hysteria were hopelessly confused, and a good quarter of the cases in the French medical

---

[173] Within the American psychiatric world, these ideas seem first to have been enunciated by Paul Chodoff, "A Re-examination of Some Aspects of Conversion Hysteria," *Psychiatry* 17 (1954): 75–81. Subsequent writings include John L. Schimel et al., "Changing Styles in Psychiatric Syndromes: A Symposium," *American Journal of Psychiatry* 130 (1973): 146–55; J. G. Stefánsson, J. A. Messina, and S. Meyerowitz, "Hysterical Neurosis, Conversion Type: Clinical and Epidemiological Considerations," *Acta Psychiatrica Scandinavica* 53 (1976): 119–38; Krohn, *Hysteria*, 174–76; and Marvin Swartz et al., "Somatization Disorder in a Community Population," *American Journal of Psychiatry* 143 (1986): 1403–8. For statements by a medical historian and a sociologist, see respectively Veith, *Hysteria*, 273–74; and Pauline B. Bart, "Social Structure and Vocabularies of Discomfort: What Happened to Female Hysteria?" *Journal of Health and Social Behavior* 9 (1968): 188–93.

literature during the later nineteenth century carried the hybrid label "hystero-epilepsy." However, in a sequence of texts during the twenty years following Charcot's death, including works by Féré (1892), Bonjour (1907), Bouche (1908), Guichard (1908), and Diller (1910), and culminating with Joachim Caspari's *Klinische Beiträge zur Epilepsie und Hysterie* of 1916, physicians developed a much stronger appreciation of the potential psychological aftermath of epileptic seizures. Increasingly, they realized that many cases previously diagnosed as hysteria involved genuine organic pathology. In the late 1920s, with the advent of electroencephalography, it became possible to differentiate much more finely between hysteria and the various epilepsies, including what by the 1950s would be known as temporal lobe epilepsy.

A similar situation obtained with syphilis. While Charcot was aware of many of the neural manifestations of syphilis, he did not perceive the etiological link between syphilitic infections and either tabes dorsalis (syphilis of the spine) or general paralysis of the insane. In the Salpêtrian writing on hysteria, acute paralytic disturbances are among the most common symptoms, and it is now well known that the onset of general paresis, like hysteria, may be characterized by convulsive seizures, double vision, and loss of pain sensation in scattered areas of the body, as well as by exaggerated emotional behaviors. As a consequence, it is likely that a portion of "hysterical" patients at the Salpêtrière actually suffered from "the great imitator."[174] In 1905, Fritz Schaudinn and Erich Hoffmann observed microscopically the spirochete in tissue from a syphilitic sore. The following year August Wassermann developed the first serological test for syphilis, and in 1913, Hideyo Noguchi and J. W. Moore isolated the spirochete in the brain tissue of a paretic patient. In other words, the technical means for distinguishing definitively between advanced neurosyphilis and other central nervous system disorders, and therefore for correcting many previous misdiagnoses, again became available to the generation of doctors immediately following the heroic age of hysteria.

At the same time that the old fortress of hysteria was under siege from mainstream organic medicine, it was being undermined by the psychiatric profession, the second major medical area contributing to the process of diagnostic refashioning. Oddly, it seems not to have been observed previously that the decline of the hysteria diagnosis perfectly corresponded in time with the appearance of a major new classificatory structure in the mental sciences, the Kraepelinian synthesis of the psychoses. Among the new diagnostic concepts emerging from German psychiatric medicine

---

[174] On the widespread diagnostic confusion at the time between hysterical and syphilitic symptoms, see Alfred Fournier, *Les affections parasyphilitiques* (Paris: Rueff et Cie, 1894), 101–22.

in the early twentieth century were Hecker's "hebephrenia" (1869), Kahlbaum's "catatonia" (1874), and Kraepelin's "dementia praecox" and "manic-depressive psychosis" (1896; 1899). The salient feature of Kraepelin's new categories was their relentless expansion. This is demonstrated most clearly in the eight editions of his famous *Lehrbuch der Psychiatrie*, appearing between 1883 and 1916, in which the range of symptoms and syndromes assigned to dementia praecox and manic depressive psychosis widened with each edition. The symptom profiles of Kraepelinian patients include numerous behaviors that almost certainly would have been categorized as hysterical in the preceding generation. All that remained was for Eugen Bleuler of Zurich to publish his monograph *Dementia Praecox or the Group of the Schizophrenias*. In this work of 1911, Bleuler introduced the term "schizophrenia," which immediately began its own highly successful career, incorporating within itself several components of the old hysteria, now signified under new names and camouflaged in different theoretical surroundings.[175]

Contemporaneous with the advance of neurological medicine and the emergence of a new nomenclature of the psychoses was the appearance of the "psychoneuroses" as we know them today, the third medical area absorbing elements of the former hysteria diagnosis. Simply put, those portions of the old hysteria diagnosis that were not claimed decisively at this time by either mainstream organic medicine or institutional alienism were up for grabs by a young generation of doctors eager to theorize anew about the neuroses. Three figures, all former students of Charcot, led the way in this process. Babinski, previously among the strongest adherents to the Salpêtrian credo, repudiated his mentor's teachings bit by bit during the 1890s. In 1901, he proposed a new and much narrower definition of hysteria, to be christened "pithiatism." After years of deliberation, the Neurological Society of Paris voted to adopt Babinski's neologism and officially abandon "hysteria" as a term of French medical terminology. In *La semaine médicale*, Babinski celebrated his linguistic victory in an essay that was tellingly subtitled "On the Dismemberment of Hysteria."[176] In a parallel development, Janet contributed to the process of diagnostic dismantlement with his category "psychasthenia."[177]

[175] To my knowledge, Henri Baruk was the first person to perceive the clinical continuities between Salpêtrian hysteria and the early twentieth-century categories of the psychoses. See Baruk, "L'hystérie et les fonctions psychomotrices," in *Comptes rendus du Congrès des médecins aliénistes et neurologistes de France et de la langue française* [Brussels] (Paris: Masson, 1935), 3–7.

[176] Joseph Babinski, "Démembrement de l'hystérie traditionnelle: Pithiatisme," *Semaine médicale* 29, no. 1 (January 6, 1909): 3–8.

[177] Pierre Janet, "Quelques définitions récentes de l'hystérie," 2 parts, *Archives de neurologie* 26, (1893): part 1, 23–29.

Babinski's pithiatism and Janet's psychasthenia are unfamiliar to Anglo-American readers today, but they remained influential in French psychological medicine until the 1930s. Both concepts illustrate clearly the fluid clinical relationship between the "old" hysteria and the "new" psychoneuroses.

Finally, the period 1895–1910 also brought the coming of psychoanalysis. As is well known, Freud provided some of the best-known clinical representations of turn-of-the-century hysteria in the *Studies on Hysteria* and the Dora case. However, he also introduced a number of theoretical innovations that in the long run contributed to the waning of the diagnosis. With the notion of the "psychoneuroses of defense," and in particular of "angstneurose," *anxiety neurosis,* Freud relabeled several formerly hysterical and neurasthenic patterns of behavior.[178] Moreover, by redefining hysterical neurosis *causally* (i.e., on the basis of the psychological mechanism of conversion), rather than symptomatically, he cut the hysteria concept loose from the age-old idea of a pathognomonic symptom-cluster. This eventually led to a reduction in the clinical scope of the diagnosis. In short, it is this process, of the atomization of the classic hysteria diagnosis three-quarters of a century ago and its reconstitution in many other places and under many different names, that has created the retrospective illusion of a disappearance of the pathological entity itself.[179]

Viewed broadly, the mysterious "disappearance" of hysteria in our own century is part and parcel of the larger historical phenomenon of the "rising" and "falling" of nervous diseases. Melancholia, hypochondria, the spleen, the vapors, chlorosis, and neurasthenia in earlier eras and the functional eating disorders and idiopathic fatigue syndromes in our own age are examples of nervous or mental illness forms that appear to have increased and decreased dramatically in particular times and cultural settings. Doubtless over time other diseases will "rise" and "fall" in the eternal recurrence of ideas, language, and behaviors that is the history of psychiatry. Regarding hysteria's history in the twentieth century, feminist scholars have stressed the role of shifting sociosexual mores; physicians have emphasized changes in the unconscious, learned illness behaviors of patients; Shorter has explored the influence of the medical styling of psychosomatic symptomatologies; and I have highlighted the role of diagnostic drift in the evolution of disease categories. The strange cyclicity of

---

[178] For a good example of this procedure, see Freud, "On the Grounds for Detaching a Particular Syndrome from Neurasthenia under the Description 'Anxiety Neurosis'" [1894], in *Standard Edition*, 3: 84–117.

[179] A more detailed statement of this thesis is available in Mark S. Micale, "On the 'Disappearance' of Hysteria: A Study in the Clinical Deconstruction of a Diagnosis," *Isis* 84 (October 1993): 496–526.

psychopathological forms through time, then, is a final subject deserving investigation by the future historian of psychiatry. Once again, we find that its exploration benefits immeasurably from an integrated internalist and externalist approach and a willingness creatively to combine ideas, evidence, and insights from different fields of knowledge.

Part TWO

HYSTERIA AS METAPHOR

Chapter 3

CULTURES OF HYSTERIA—PAST AND PRESENT TRADITIONS

HYSTERIA'S METAPHORICAL PAST

IN HER beautifully suggestive essay *Illness as Metaphor*, Susan Sontag reminds readers at the outset: "Illness is the night-side of life, a more onerous citizenship. Everyone who is born holds dual citizenship, in the kingdom of the well and in the kingdom of the sick. Although we all prefer to use only the good passport, sooner or later each of us is obliged, at least for a spell, to identify ourselves as citizens of that other place."[1] Precisely because, in the way Sontag observes, the experience of sickness is such a basic component of the human condition, it has never remained confined to the realm of medical discourse. It has also been a powerful, permanent presence in the popular and cultural imagination. In *Illness as Metaphor*, Sontag speaks mainly of tuberculosis and cancer—diseases that have appeared commonly and allegorically in the arts and literature of the past—and, in a more recent work, of AIDS.[2] She warns of the dangers of moralization inherent in the use of disease imagery while also documenting the role of metaphorized illness in some of the strongest works of modern Western philosophy and imaginative literature, from English Romantic poetry, through Nietzsche's writings, to the novels of Thomas Mann and Albert Camus.

From a similar perspective, Sander Gilman has studied searchingly the historical structures of the perception and representation of disease.[3] Gilman establishes that the visual and literary depiction of disease constitutes a more or less continuous tradition from the ancient Greeks to the present, running through nearly every artistic style and cultural setting. Like Sontag, he emphasizes the implicitly punitive function of most disease metaphors: by stigmatizing sick persons as "the Other," figurative representations work to capture and control disease, separating the sane and healthy but vulnerable "Self" from the sick and distancing it from

---

[1] Susan Sontag, *Illness as Metaphor* (New York: Penguin, 1978), 7.

[2] Sontag, *AIDS and Its Metaphors* (New York: Farrar, Straus and Giroux, 1988).

[3] Gilman, *Disease and Representation*; idem, *Seeing the Insane*; idem, "The Image of the Hysteric".

the realization of its own ultimate mortality.[4] In Georges Canguilhem's well-known terminology, these representations serve to demarcate the normal from the pathological.[5] It is the use of disease as a metaphor or figure—and the past, present, and future study of that use—that forms the subject of Part Two of this book.

The history of hysteria in particular has in a real sense been two histories, one medical and the other popular. Sometimes separate, at other times intimately interconnected, these two developments can be traced through nearly the entire textual history of the topic. In certain times and places, it is possible to write separate accounts of these medical-scientific and popular-cultural usages. Hysteria as an icon in the visual arts, a trope in a novel, or a concept in the social sciences, *is* in many ways decisively different from hysteria in medical theory and clinical practice. At other times, however, the standard distinction between scientific and fictional texts dissolves and the traditional division within the history of science and medicine between professional theory, enlightened lay opinion, and popular belief is utterly untenable for hysteria. In these instances, it proves more productive to consider these histories interactively. An understanding of the conceptual and historical relations between the two historical entities—hysteria as a figure or metaphor in extrascientific texts and the nonmetaphorical, medical-historical study of the disorder—will be a major concern of this section.

Hysteria as metaphor has a particularly long and vibrant history.[6] Hysteria's distinctive qualities as a disease have conditioned and complexified its cultural, no less than its medical, history. The inherent drama of many cases of hysterical illness has made its metaphorical potential great. As Nancy Stepan has shown, scientific discourses dealing with sensitive issues of class, race, and gender have typically been especially prone to allegorical rendition.[7] The shapeless and ever-changing clinical phenomenology of the disorder has contributed as well to its inherent metaphoricity.

Hysteria's rich representational history is most likely also connected to its unstable ontological status. Sontag perceives that it is those diseases with murky causes and unknown cures that are most susceptible to sym-

---

[4] Gilman, "Depicting Disease: A Theory of Representing Illness," chap. 1 in *Disease and Representation*.

[5] Georges Canguilhem, *Le normal et le pathologique* (Paris: Presses universitaires de France, 1975).

[6] In the ensuing discussion, I define metaphor according to the second, unabridged edition of *Webster's Third New International Dictionary* (1986), as "a figure of speech in which a word or phrase denoting literally one kind of object or idea is used in place of another to suggest a likeness or analogy between them."

[7] Nancy Leys Stepan, "Race and Gender: The Role of Analogy in Science," *Isis* 77 (1986): 261–77.

bolization.[8] In regard to hysteria, the historical record suggests overwhelmingly that where scientific knowledge has been lacking, imagination, prejudice, and fantasy have flooded in to fill the void. Moreover, precisely because its standing as demonstrable physical or mental disease is so uncertain—because, unlike syphilis and tuberculosis, hysteria may not be a "real" disease at all—it has invited alternative nonmedical renderings. Because the literalness of hysteria is so problematic, discussing the disorder virtually demands analogization.[9]

I suspect that there also exists at least one other reason why hysteria has been so open to metaphorical refashioning at the hands of nonscientific intellectuals through the ages. Sontag addresses the need to demetaphorize illness, to purify medical writing and thinking of its moralizing figures of speech. But we cannot purify hysteria in this way, because in the medical texts themselves hysteria is already a metaphor, a compound of images and associations that are themselves available for subsequent metaphorization. In earlier times, positivist philosophers of science repudiated the role of metaphor in the scientific enterprise; figurative language was regarded as a corrupting, contaminating force in the quest for empirical, value-neutral, and universally valid knowledge. But no domain of thinking is devoid of symbolic forms, including science and medicine. Since the mid-1960s, the role of models, analogies, and metaphors, not just as rhetorical devices but as essential, constitutive elements of science, has been recognized.[10] Unfortunately, we lack today a systematic study of metaphor in the history of medicine, including psychiatry; but metaphorical thinking about the human body and mind in health and sickness has a history going back at least to the ancient Greeks.

The place of hysteria in the history of medical metaphor is a prominent one. In its very name, the disorder is encoded; as soon as the Hippocratic

[8] *Illness as Metaphor*, esp. chap. 8.

[9] Antipsychiatric critics have made this point about psychiatry as a whole. Thomas Szasz, for instance, claims that the very idea of a "mental" (i.e., nonsomatic) disease is a metaphor and that the failure of the profession to acknowledge the metaphorical status of its subject matter is grievously misguided. See Szasz, *The Myth of Mental Illness*; and T. Sarbin, "The Scientific Status of the Mental Illness Metaphor," in Stanley C. Plog and Robert B. Edgerton, eds., *Changing Perspectives in Mental Illness* (New York: Holt, Rinehart and Winston, 1969), 1–16.

[10] Mary Hesse, *Models and Analogies in Science* (Notre Dame, Ind.: University of Notre Dame Press, 1966); Richard Olson, ed., *Science as Metaphor* (Belmont, Calif.: Wadsworth, 1971); W. M. Leatherdale, *The Role of Analogy, Model, and Metaphor in Science* (Amsterdam: North-Holland, 1974); Roger S. Jones, *Physics as Metaphor* (Minneapolis: University of Minnesota Press, 1982); Thomas S. Kuhn, "Metaphor in Science," in Andrew Ortony, ed., *Metaphor and Thought* (Cambridge: Cambridge University Press, 1979), 409–19; David. E. Leary, ed., *Metaphors in the History of Psychology* (Cambridge: Cambridge University Press, 1990).

hystera went from designating the uterus as an organ in classical anatomy to a disease believed to arise from the dysfunction of that organ, it was allegorized.[11] In postclassical medical systems, hysteria was freed from its etymology, and the (literal) womb ceased to be regarded as the origin of the malady. Yet, by metonymic extrapolation, it was often construed as a disease of femininity, maternity, or the female temperament as a whole: hence, popular synonyms such as Edward Jorden's "suffocation of the mother." Later, neurologically oriented theorists in the nineteenth century characterized hysteria as "neuro*mimetic*." To them, it was the masquerading malady that assumed its very identity by taking on the form of other diseases. A similar situation obtains within psychodynamic medicine. In Sándor Ferenczi's phrase, hysterical symptoms are "materializations of psychic conflicts."[12] They represent translations of something psychological into something physical. Psychoanalytic theory introduced yet another mediating metaphor. The twitches, phobias, and paralyses that characterize the cases in Breuer and Freud's *Studies on Hysteria* are not simply emblematic of psychological structures but are complex bodily metaphors cast by the patient's unconscious into subjective, symbolic forms. Even in the Szaszian view, hysteria is not a disease; rather, it is an alternative physical, verbal, and gestural language, an iconic social communication. Within each of these very different theoretical contexts, the role of the physician is that of semiotician: to decode the hysterical symptom, to find out what it "stands for." In short, the analogical impulse that rests at the heart of the cultural history of hysteria begins with the way doctors thought about the disorder, and the cultural history of the disease consists chiefly of social, political, religious, and literary constructions of hysteria superimposed upon previous medical formulations.[13] It is to these multilayered metaphorizations in the nonmedical imagination that we now turn.

THE LITERARY, DRAMATIC, AND VISUAL ARTS

In her wide-ranging study *Madness and Literature*, Lillian Feder demonstrates that a tradition of representing extreme mental states runs within

[11] The same point, I suppose, could be made about all diseases, for which symptoms are by definition only "signs" of a deeper, primary pathology. Cf. the Latin *symptoma*, meaning "something that indicates something else."

[12] Sándor Ferenczi, "The Phenomena of Hysterical Materialization" [1919], chap. 6 in *Further Contributions to the Theory and Technique of Psycho-analysis*, trans. Jane I. Suttie (London: Hogarth Press and Institute of Psycho-analysis, 1926).

[13] This raises the philosophical issue of the general relations between a behavioral entity, an observing author, and the textualization of those observations. Some preliminary discussion of the subject is found in Levine, *Realism and Representation*.

Western literature from Homer, ancient Greek drama, and the Bible to the postmodernist present.[14] The first periods for which hysteria as a metaphor have been investigated in anything like a systematic manner are the Renaissance and the early modern era in England. John Sena, Bridget Lyons, Michael DePorte, and Roy Porter have observed the great prevalence of the themes of mental and nervous debility in the cultural and political life of the British Isles during the sixteenth, seventeenth, and eighteenth centuries. From Robert Burton's *The Anatomy of Melancholy*, through the medical treatises of George Cheyne, Richard Blackmore, and Robert Whytt, to the mid-eighteenth-century writings of the Graveyard Poets, and on to the periodic insanities of George III, extremity or eccentricity of mind has figured as a recurrent motif.[15] While the linkage during these centuries between literature, melancholia, and generic madness has been explored in depth, the study of the literary construction of hysteria is just beginning.

Marie Addyman's "The Character of Hysteria in Shakespeare's England" is the first of the new hysteria studies to deal squarely with the cultural history of the disease in sixteenth-century England.[16] Addyman tracks hysteria, both as term and concept, through the writings of the greatest dramatist of the age, with special reference to *King Lear* and *The Winter's Tale*. She locates a remarkable number of passages in Shakespeare's plays in which the image of hysteria appears. There is a moment, for instance, in act 2 of *King Lear* when the old and failing king anticipates his repudiation by his daughter Regan:

> O! how this mother swells up toward my heart;
> *Hysterica passio*! down, thou climbing sorrow!
> Thy element's below.[17]

Shakespeare here reached into the classical past to use one of hysteria's most powerful images—the swelling uterus lodged in the throat—to convey one of the most intense scenes in his tragedy. Addyman discovers that elsewhere in Shakespeare's oeuvre, as in Elizabethan literature generally, "the rising Mother," "Hysterica Passio," and "Suffocatio"

---

[14] Lillian Feder, *Madness in Literature* (Princeton: Princeton University Press, 1980).

[15] John F. Sena, "The English Malady: The Idea of Melancholy from 1700 to 1760" (Ph.D. diss., Princeton University, 1967); Bridget G. Lyons, *Voices of Melancholy: Studies in the Literary Treatment of Melancholy in Renaissance England* (London: Routledge and Kegan Paul, 1971); Michael V. DePorte, *Nightmares and Hobby Horses: Swift, Sterne and Augustan Ideas of Madness* (San Marino, Calif.: Huntington Library, 1974); Porter, *Mind-Forg'd Manacles*.

[16] Marie E. Addyman, "The Character of Hysteria in Shakespeare's England" (Ph.D. diss., University of York, 1988).

[17] In the Arden edition of the works of Shakespeare, the passage appears in *King Lear*, act 2, sc. 4, lines 54–56 (pp. 80–81).

were common metaphors for acute emotional distress segueing into insanity.[18]

In addition to explicating these passages, Addyman investigates contemporaneous medical, legal, religious, and popular texts about hysteria. These include Jorden's *A Briefe Discourse of a Disease Called the Suffocation of the Mother*, published three years prior to *King Lear*. Addyman finds that the most common image in these seventeenth-century sources, literary and nonliterary, is that of female inarticulacy. The "fluency" of the private body language of the female hysteric contrasts with her silence and inactivity in conventional areas of verbal, social, cultural, and political communication. Probing this idea, Addyman suggestively juxtaposes Shakespeare's plays with three other bodies of writing: sixteenth-century witchcraft manuals, Renaissance tracts on theories of language, and twentieth-century medical writings about linguistic disorders.[19]

Shakespeare has Lear in his moment of anguish cry out in a classical metaphor. With the eighteenth century came the new interpretation of hysteria, hypochondria, and melancholia as nervous distempers. At a time when the arts and sciences were much closer than they now are, this conceptualization of the psyche and its derangement exercised a strong influence on the imaginative literature of the day. The nature and extent of this influence is just beginning to be traced out. John Sena has studied the scene of Belinda's fit in one of the most important pieces of eighteenth-century British literature, Alexander Pope's *The Rape of the Lock* (1712–14).[20] Sena finds that Pope's representation of the fit, which is induced when a lock of Belinda's hair is sheared off, is not simply authorial fantasy but a detailed rendition of a hysterical attack according to the latest theories of Willis and Sydenham. By choosing to describe a hysterical crisis in particular, Pope, Sena proposes, was employing a fashionable icon and displaying familiarity with contemporary medical theory, as well as attempting to heighten the psychological complexity of his characterization. Pope's passage, Sena writes, provides "an artistic rendering of contemporary medical cases."[21]

The role of hysteria in British literary culture has also been examined in John Mullan's 1984 article, "Hypochondria and Hysteria: Sensibility and

[18] See also Isador H. Coriat, *The Hysteria of Lady Macbeth* (New York: Moffat, Yard, 1912); Janet Adelman, *Suffocating Mothers: Fantasies of Maternal Origin in Shakespeare's Plays, Hamlet to the Tempest* (New York: Routledge, 1992); and Heather Ann Findlay, "Madwomen, Witches, and Lady Writers: Hysteria in English Renaissance Texts" (Ph.D. diss., Cornell University, 1993).

[19] Addyman, "Character of Hysteria," esp. 215–37.

[20] John F. Sena, "Belinda's Hysteria: The Medical Context of *The Rape of the Lock*," in Christopher Fox, ed., *Psychology and Literature in the Eighteenth Century* (New York: AMS Press, 1987), 129–47.

[21] Ibid., 137.

the Physicians."[22] Mullan observes the large quantity of medical writing on the nervous disorders emerging from England and Scotland between 1720 and 1770. He ties this medical commentary to the literary "cult of sensibility" then emerging in the novels of Samuel Richardson, Laurence Sterne, and Henry Mackenzie. Mullan notes that personal relations between men of medicine, literature, and philosophy at that time were exceptionally close—Cheyne, for instance, author of *The English Malady*, served as physician to Richardson, correspondent with Samuel Johnson, and medical confidant to David Hume—and he discovers a "quite precise contact between the literary representations of sentiment and sensibility and the physician's models of disorder."[23] Wide employment of the terms "hysteria," "the spleen," "vapors," and "the Hyppo" in the 1700s may be attributed in part to fashion. At the same time, a bookish, reclusive, and sedentary way of life was then believed to conduce to nervous sickness, so that literati were thought to be especially susceptible. As men of education and privilege with a common social and cultural background, doctors and writers alike, Mullan argues, shared a common behavioral vocabulary of "sensibility," "sympathy," "delicacy" and "imagination." Consequently, these nervous conditions could with comparative ease be both diagnosed by physicians in their private clientele and depicted by writers in fictional "middle-class" characters.[24]

Thus far, the most substantial and synthetic study of the literary history of hysteria in early modern Britain has been provided by the American literary historian George Rousseau. In a rich, intricately detailed, monograph-length analysis that appeared in 1993, Rousseau establishes that the hysteria concept was deeply embedded in the general medical, scientific, social, and cultural histories of the period.[25] He shows that after the waning of the demonological model during the late Renaissance, a freshly demystified and explicitly medical definition of hysteria appeared frequently in Jacobean and Restoration drama. The most common association in these texts was with female virginity and widowhood. Later, Rousseau continues, "Enlightenment hysteria" was swallowed up by a larger, monolithic discourse of the nervous distempers.[26] In this guise, it spread far beyond medical treatises, to the letters, diaries, novels,

[22] John Mullan, "Hypochondria and Hysteria: Sensibility and the Physicians," *The Eighteenth Century: Theory and Interpretation* 25, no. 2 (Spring 1984): 141–74.

[23] Ibid., 146.

[24] See also Christopher J. Lawrence, "The Nervous System and Society in the Scottish Enlightenment," in B. Barnes and S. Shapin, eds., *Natural Order: Historical Studies of Scientific Culture* (London: Sage Publications, 1979), 19–40.

[25] George S. Rousseau, "'A Strange Pathology': Hysteria in the Early Modern World, 1500–1800," in Gilman et al., *Hysteria Beyond Freud*, 91–221.

[26] Ibid., 96.

poetry, drama, and dialogues of the day. Rousseau gleans passages from dozens of literary texts, including novels by Tobias Smollet, Henry Fielding, Richardson, Sterne, and Jane Austen. "From the mad hack's attacks of spleen in Jonathan Swift's *Tale of a Tub* to Clarissa Harlowe's persistent bouts with vapors in the Richardson novel of that name, the nervous ailment exists as mundane reality as well as cliché and trope," he writes. "Virtually no author is exempt."[27]

Rousseau finds further that hysteria and its kindred categories operated as much more than merely technical diagnostic dress. Rather, they initiated an entire new way of thinking, feeling, and seeing in Augustan society. Because these concepts were connected with cultural and emotional refinement, they were cultivated by literary intellectuals both in themselves and their fictional creations. "Nervous self-fashioning" occurred in epistolary and autobiographical texts as writers internalized the new nervous codes of behavior. Similarly, the vocabulary of melancholy, hysteria, hypochondria, the spleen, the nerves, and the vapors was deployed to flesh out fictional characters and situations as part of "the new nervous culture of the eighteenth century."[28]

With its preoccupation with the "maladies of the soul," its intense and intimate subjectivism, and its eroticization of the female, the Romantic era seems a highly congenial aesthetic for the exploration of hysteria. Nevertheless, this period in the history of hysteria remains curiously underresearched. In his historical survey, Trillat includes a sizable chapter on "the Romantic epoch" of hysteria. By this phrase, he signalizes the two generations of writings by French physicians from Louyer-Villermay to Briquet.[29] The distinguishing feature of this writing, in Trillat's discussion, is its idealization of Woman as object of love, sexuality, and maternal fertility. Similarly, Alan Bewell has looked closely at the figure of the witch/hysteric in the work of the English Romantic poet William Wordsworth.[30] But there have been almost no other explorations of hysteria during this epoch. Perhaps because "hysterical" themes were subsumed

[27] Ibid., 152.

[28] Ibid., 164, 165. See also Rousseau's earlier studies "Nerves, Spirits, and Fibres: Towards Defining the Origins of Sensibility," *Blue Guitar: Rivista annuale di letteratura inglese e americana* 2 (1976): 125–53; and "Towards a Semiotics of the Nerve: The Social History of Language in a New Key," in Peter Burke and Roy Porter, eds., (Oxford: Polity Press, 1991), 213–75. For some of these themes specifically in Dr. Johnson's work, see Gloria Sybil Gross, "The Development of Samuel Johnson's Theory of Neurosis, 1709–1759" (Ph.D. diss., University of Southern California, 1977).

[29] Trillat, *Histoire de l'hystérie*, chap. 5.

[30] Alan J. Bewell, "A 'Word Scarce Said': Hysteria and Witchcraft in Wordsworth's 'Experimental' Poetry of 1797–1798," *ELH* [*English Literary History*] 53, no. 2 (Summer 1986): 357–90, later repr. in Bewell, *Wordsworth and the Enlightenment: Nature, Man, and Society in the Experimental Poetry* (New Haven: Yale University Press, 1989), chap. 4.

into such brilliant poetic and philosophic forms, critics and historians thus far have failed to take much notice of the interconnections between hysteria and Romantic culture.[31]

The first half of the nineteenth century also witnessed broad cultural evolutions that changed permanently the relation between the medical and literary textual traditions of disease. From the Renaissance to the Romantic era, the arts, medicine, and autobiography, as we have just seen, cohabited comfortably. In contrast, the arts and the sciences during the nineteenth century began to develop radically different epistemological modalities. With the rise of an organized medical profession, physicians sought to define themselves through the progress of the experimental sciences and their privileged access to a body of technical information. Increasingly, they desired to demarcate their enterprise as completely as possible from that of nonscientists, including literary intellectuals. Furthermore, with the rise of a positivist professional ideology, physicians cultivated a specialized and impersonal style of inquiry aimed above all at objectivity (i.e., at producing a discourse written *about* the patient as an object and *for* an expert readership). At roughly the same time, creative writers and artists began to abandon previous classical aesthetic codes, with their universal ideals of beauty. In place of these, they gave themselves over increasingly to a belief in aesthetic individualism and psychological subjectivism. Explicitly contrasting their mode of perception and expression to that of scientists, who "murder to dissect," nineteenth-century poets, novelists, and painters turned to the exploration of extreme emotional and psychological states, including their own.[32] In the history of hysteria, as elsewhere, the world of the "two cultures" was born, and, with one or two notable exceptions (of which more below), the two approaches have not been reunited since.

With the second half of the nineteenth century, the literary history of hysteria comes very much into its own, particularly in the Catholic countries of the European continent. The study of *hystérie littéraire* as a textual tradition in nineteenth-century France was pioneered by the Canadian literary historian Alfred Edward Carter. Carter's highly perceptive and beautifully written study *The Idea of Decadence in French Literature, 1830–1900* was published in 1958 and includes a chapter on nervous and mental maladies in poetry, fiction, and literary criticism.[33] To the best

[31] Susan Wolfson of Rutgers University is currently investigating representations of femininity and masculinity, including hysteria, in English Romantic literature, in a work tentatively titled *Figures on the Margin: The Language of Gender in English Romanticism.*

[32] This theme is developed in J.A.V. Chapple, *Science and Literature in the Nineteenth Century* (Hound Mills, Hampshire: Macmillan, 1986).

[33] A. E. Carter, *The Idea of Decadence in French Literature, 1830–1900* (Toronto: University of Toronto Press, 1958), chap. 3.

of my knowledge, Carter was the first scholar to observe that during the Second Empire the general *Weltschmerz* of the Romantic generation, a vague emotional and spiritual malaise, was transformed into a medicalized concern with specific neuropathologies and psychopathologies. Carter attributes this development to an extension of the Romantic *mal du siècle*, which joined with the growing prestige of the medical sciences. These combined further with new ideas about social, cultural, and biological degenerationism originating with the mid-century alienists Prosper Lucas, J. J. Moreau de Tours, and B. A. Morel. Imaginative writers during the second half of the century who embraced this "neurological Romanticism," Carter states, deployed the nomenclature of the clinic to depict their heros and heroines. This included the languages of insanity, degeneration, sexual perversion, neurosis, and hysteria.[34]

Carter highlights a sequence of authors and texts from 1830 to 1900 in which these terms and themes figure prominently. Jean-Jacques Rousseau, Chateaubriand, Lord Byron, and Edgar Allan Poe provided precedents from both their writings and personal lives. During the middle decades of the century, the poetry and novels of Théophile Gautier, Gustave Flaubert's *Madame Bovary* (1856–57), and the poetry and art criticism of Charles Baudelaire formally initiated the tradition. Flaubert's novel *Salammbô* (1863), followed a year later by Jules and Edmond de Goncourt's *Germinie Lacerteux*—"a study of nymphomania and hysteria in a servant"—elaborated the disease themes found in earlier works.[35]

Then, beginning in the early 1870s, Émile Zola, in his great epical cycle of novels depicting the national decline of France, the twenty-volume Rougon-Macquart series (1870–93), traced the spread of the nervous pathologies through six generations of two French families.[36] In Zola's dynasty of degeneration, the original neurological defect, or "tare nerveuse," comes from Tante Dide, the progenitor of both the Rougon and Macquart lines, who suffered from semi-imbecility and attacks of nerves and convulsions. Zola, who was conversant with the writings of Morel, Lucas, and Moreau de Tours, describes Tante's *crises* alternately as hysterical, epileptic, and cataleptic. In the greatest literary undertaking in France during the early Third Republic, then, which maintained a national readership for over two decades, hysteria operates as one of two primal pathologies that could generate other vices in offspring, including alcoholism, prostitution, sexual perversion, criminality, and suicide.[37] Tracing these congenital neuroses through the full cycle of novels, Carter

[34] Ibid., 62–68.

[35] Ibid., 70.

[36] Carter, *Idea of Decadence*, 69–79.

[37] Protopathologies, that is, of female hysteria. On the male sides of the Rougon and Macquart families, the generative neuroses were imbecility and alcoholism.

implies that Zola gave increasing prominence to female characters who were hysterics.[38]

Carter also brings to light a novel by a disciple of Zola's, Henri Céard.[39] Published in 1906, Céard's *Terrains à vendre au bord de la mer* is most likely a literary rendition of a text by a Breton physician that appeared earlier that year, Dr. Firmin Terrien's *Hystérie et neurasthénie chez les paysans*. Céard's book relates the story of an entire province in Brittany in which the inhabitants, due to chronic drunkenness and consanguineous marriage, succumb to "hereditary hysteria." The novel was intended as a critique of the Zolan notion that the source of regeneration for the French people was interbreeding with healthy peasant stock. It is one of the few literary documents to deal with hysteria in a provincial setting.

In the writings of Joris-Karl Huysmans from the 1880s and 1890s, hysteria adapted once again to the changing cultural scene, as Carter shows us. In each stage of his career, Huysmans's novels are populated with nervous types. But in Huysmans, the day-to-day descriptive realism of Flaubert and the naturalistic degenerationism of Zola give way to a highly self-conscious cult of sensual and aesthetic decadence. Huysmans's characters, exemplified notoriously by Des Esseintes in *À rebours* (*Against Nature*) (1884), are men and women of the arts and the aristocracy who morbidly cultivate their tainted heredities as sources of social eccentricity and sensory gratification.[40]

In 1982, Carter's work was extended in an outstanding study by the French clinical psychologist and literary critic Jacqueline Carroy.[41] Carroy, whose work deserves to be better known among Anglophonic scholars, takes as her subject "the literary appropriation of hysteria" in modern French culture. In this endeavor, she assembles a splendid collection of texts—novels, poems, plays, works of literary criticism, and pri-

---

[38] He mentions in particular Marthe Mouret in *La conquête de Plassans* (1874), Nana in the novel by that name (1879), and Angélique in *Le rêve* (1888). For more on Zola, hysteria, and degenerationism, refer to Jean Borie, *Mythologies de l'hérédité au XIXe siècle* (Paris: Galilée, 1981); Yves Malinas, *Zola et les hérédités imaginaires* (Paris: Expansion scientifique française, 1985); and Daniel Pick, *Faces of Degeneration: A European Disorder, c. 1848—c. 1918* (Cambridge: Cambridge University Press, 1989), chap. 3.

[39] Carter, *Idea of Decadence*, 79–80.

[40] Ibid., 80–87.

[41] Jacqueline Carroy-Thirard, "Hystérie, théâtre, littérature au dix-neuvième siècle," *Psychanalyse à l'université* 7, no. 26 (March 1982): 299–317. See also idem, "Figures de femmes hystériques dans la psychiatrie française du 19e siècle"; idem, *Le mal de Morzine: De la possession à l'hystérie* (Paris: Solin, 1981); idem, "Possession, extase, hystérie au XIXe siècle," *Psychanalyse à l'université* 5, no. 19 (June 1980): 499–515; and Jacqueline Carroy, *Hypnose, suggestion et psychologie: L'invention de sujets* (Paris: Presses universitaires de France, 1991).

vate correspondence—that span from the writings of Charles Sainte-Beuve in the 1830s to the surrealist manifestos of the late 1920s. Like Carter, she pinpoints the 1850s as a watershed period in the modern cultural history of hysteria. Carroy defines as originative texts *Madame Bovary* and a well-known review of Flaubert's novel by Baudelaire. As the son and brother of physicians, a serious if unsystematic reader of the medical literature of his time, and a personal sufferer from idiopathic epileptiform seizures, Flaubert had good reasons to be interested in hysteria. To these biographical factors should be added his search for a literary style of material and psychological realism. In an often-quoted phrase, Sainte-Beuve observed that Flaubert "tient la plume comme d'autres le scapel," "wielded the pen as others do the knife," while other contemporaries commented on the writer's verisimilitudinous descriptions of sickness and death.[42]

In his masterpiece, Flaubert does not call Emma Bovary a hysteric as such. However, hysteria-like symptoms—dizziness, weak spells, heart palpitations, and bouts of nerves—abound in the novel.[43] At least once, after receiving her lover Rodolphe's letter of abandonment and watching his carriage speed by the house, Emma experiences generalized convulsions.[44] Moreover, critics past and present have agreed that *Madame Bovary* is preeminently a study in temperament, and it is above all Emma's character, rather than her physical symptoms, that distinguishes her as one of the most unforgettable figures in modern prose fiction. Her unfulfilled longings and elaborate fantasy life, her alternating moods of torpor and exaltation, her attraction to racy, sentimental novels, her frivolous, spendthrift ways, and her reckless amorous escapades at the expense of husband and child have earned her a reputation as the archetypal literary hysteric.

As Carroy indicates, it was the poet Baudelaire who first emphatically labeled Emma a hysteric. In a remarkable review of Flaubert's novel appearing in *L'artiste* on October 18, 1857, a review which Flaubert praised for its excellent understanding of his book, Baudelaire enumerated the features of Emma's personality.[45] He then makes a plea:

[42] Eugene F. Gray, "The Clinical View of Life: Gustave Flaubert's *Madame Bovary*," in Enid Rhodes Peschel, ed., *Medicine and Literature* (New York: Neale Watson, 1980), 81–87.

[43] English-language translators have often rendered Emma's nervous states as "hysterics." Compare Gustave Flaubert, *Madame Bovary: Moeurs de province*, in *Oeuvres complètes de Gustave Flaubert*, 16 vols. (Paris: Club de l'Honnête Homme, 1971), 1: 294 and 300 with *Madame Bovary: Patterns of Provincial Life*, trans. Francis Steegmuller (New York: Modern Library, 1957), 312, 319.

[44] *Madame Bovary*, in *Oeuvres complètes*, 233ff; *Madame Bovary*, Steegmuller trans., 233ff.

[45] Charles Baudelaire, "*Madame Bovary* par Gustave Flaubert," readily available in Bau-

Hysteria! Why couldn't this physiological mystery be made the sum and sub-stance of a literary work, this mystery which the Academy of Medicine has not yet solved and which, manifesting itself in women by the sensation of a stifling ball rising in the body (I mention only the chief symptoms), expresses itself in excitable men by every kind of impotence as well as by a tendency toward every type of excess?[46]

It is an important passage. Baudelaire's remarks establish that a major figure in the nineteenth-century Parisian literary avant garde followed ac-ademic medical debates about hysteria.[47] They reveal that Baudelaire considered hysteria a physiological, rather than psychological, malady and that (two years before Briquet and two decades before Charcot) he believed the disorder afflicted men as well as women. It is clear too that he regarded the disorder as desirable subject matter for a major work of art, although he does not tell us what such a work might look like. We will return to Baudelaire's review; but it will suffice at this point to note that two generations of creative writers in France accepted Baudelaire's anal-ysis, or rather diagnosis, of 1857 and drew inspiration from the image of Emma Bovary as hysterical heroine.

Building further on Carter, Carroy also shows that several years after the publication of *Madame Bovary* Flaubert provided a second memora-ble literary hysteric in *Salammbô*. In this work, Flaubert freely combined the themes of exoticism, hysteria, and nymphomania, which again re-mained ineradicably associated for the next two generations of writers and readers. Similarly, in 1864 the Goncourt brothers featured the las-civious, novel-reading Germinie—interestingly, a house servant—in the story *Germinie Lacerteux*. (Carroy observes that Germinie's story reads like a fictional rendition of the cases in the *Iconographie photographique de la Salpêtrière* from a decade and a half later.) The effect of these three novels, Carroy writes, was to establish hysteria less as a disease entity than "an erotic and an aesthetic."[48] In the following decades, a spate of

---

delaire's collection of art and literary criticism *L'art romantique*, in *Oeuvres complètes de Charles Baudelaire*, ed. Jacques Crépet, 17 vols. (Paris: Louis Conard, 1925), 3: 393–408.

   [46] Ibid., 404.

   [47] Baudelaire's comment about the Académie de Médecine most likely refers to a contro-versy that raged within the Parisian medical community during the 1830s and 1840s over the exact anatomical site of hysteria, a battle in which gynecological, neurological, and cerebral interpretations clashed. In 1845, the Academy posed the question of the nature and origins of hysteria in a formal academic *concours*. Unable to decide among the contestants, the academicians awarded the prize jointly to Brachet and Landouzy, adherents respectively of the neurological and uterine theories. Baudelaire's citation of the *boule* as "the chief symptom" of female hysteria probably refers to Brachet's winning essay, later expanded into *Traité de l'hystérie* (1847), in which the sensation of the esophageal ball appears as the defining mark of the disorder.

   [48] Carroy, "Hystérie, théâtre, littérature au dix-neuvième siècle," 316.

popular sensationalistic novels appeared in which hysteria figured variously as a cause of adulterous treacheries, the result of unrequited love, and a complication of sexual hyperactivity. Two texts that Carroy highlights are *Possession* (1887) and *Soeur Marthe* (1889) by Charles Richet. Better known as a psychologist, physiologist, and collateral member of the Salpêtrière circle, Richet, according to Ellenberger, was the person who first aroused in Charcot an interest in hypnosis.[49] Richet subsequently was a winner of the Nobel Prize in physiology and medicine for his research on the concept of anaphylaxis; he also wrote poetry and novels under the pen name of Charles Epheyre. These two novels of Richet, written at the peak of the Nancy/Salpêtrière controversy, interweave the themes of love, hysteria, hypnotism, and somnambulism.[50]

Yet another pertinent work from this period that extended the metaphorization of hysteria into new areas—and one not discussed by Carroy—is Augustin Galopin's *Les hystériques des couvents, des églises, des temples, des théâtres, des synagogues et de l'amour* (1886).[51] Galopin's is a weird and whimsical book. Partly novelistic in form, the book recounts in farcical terms the story of an outbreak of hysteria in the imaginary Convent of the Repentant Women in northeastern France while also presenting the author's rambling but quite pungent observations about hysteria as it currently gripped the big cities. The fifteenth chapter of the work details the different categories of "love hysteria," including "l'hystérique érotique," "l'hystérique de jalousie," "l'hystérique tendre," "l'hystérique ovarienne," and "l'hystérique de l'envie."[52]

A decade later, even Galopin's book was surpassed by Armand Dubarry's *Les déséquilibrés de l'amour*, which joined the literary representation of hysteria with the emergent medical sexology of the late nineteenth century. *Les déséquilibrés de l'amour* was projected to run to twenty novels, and the frontispiece of each volume announces it as "une série de romans passionnels psychopathologiques." A kind of lowbrow blend of Zola and Krafft-Ebing, each novel explores unblushingly some perceived excess or perversion of emotional and sexual life in contemporary French society. At least eleven volumes of Dubarry's series titillated Francophone readers, including books on sadism, incest, fetishism, flagellation, and hermaphroditism. The fourth novel in the set was titled *Hystérique*.[53] In it, Dubarry presents the hysteric as a universal character type. He inter-

[49] Ellenberger, *The Discovery of the Unconscious*, 90.

[50] Carroy, "Hystérie, théâtre, littérature au dix-neuvième siècle," 311–12.

[51] Augustin Galopin, *Les hystériques des couvents, des églises, des temples, des théâtres, des synagogues et de l'amour* (Paris: E. Dentu, 1886).

[52] Ibid., 141–53.

[53] Armand Dubarry, *Hystérique*, vol. 4 of *Les déséquilibrés de l'amour*, 11 vols. (Paris: Chamuel, 1897).

prets the disease as a variant of "erotic insanity" and a manifestation of female degeneracy. After a series of increasingly tragic *chagrins d'amour*, and a final fall into craven nymphomania, each character in the tale ends up either dying of disease, being committed to an asylum, or killing herself. By 1900, Dubarry's novels had gone through over twenty printings. The popularity of the books suggests that by the close of the century, the language of hysteria had taken over from earlier nonmedical vocabularies as a generic terminology for the vagaries of human sexual and emotional life.

Carroy reflects finally on Huysmans's *À rebours*. Huysmans's book provided the literary manifesto for the late nineteenth-century cult of decadence. Like *Madame Bovary*, the story of the debauched antihero Des Esseintes spawned a literary subgenre of its own. A cast of what might be called aspiring, borderline hysterics, whose nervous degeneration accompanies a morbid quest for sexual and aesthetic intensities, people the pages of French fiction during the final decade and a half of the century. In Huysmans's novel, we read that Des Esseintes craves artistic novelties, including "a few suggestive books . . . to shake up his nervous system with erudite hysterias." From the musical world he seeks new harmonies that will leave him "choked by the suffocating *boule* of hysteria."[54] Not surprisingly, the American cultural historian Debora Silverman has discovered that Huysmans drew directly on two medical texts—the *Traité des névroses* of Axenfeld and Huchard and Camille Bouchut's *Nouveaux éléments de pathologie générale*, both recently out in new editions—as guides to the depiction of Des Esseintes's nervous accidents.[55] Nor were these literary-medical linkages lost on readers at the time. In a review of *À rebours*, the critic Barbey d'Aurevilly lamented the main character of the novel: "The hero of Monsieur Huysmans . . . is sick, like all the heros of the novel of this sick era. . . . He is prey to the neurosis of the age [*la névrose du siècle*]. . . . He is from the *Hôpital Charcot*."[56]

Carter's and Carroy's splendid researches have opened up the literary history of hysteria in modern France to present-day scholars. Within the new hysteria studies, a full-scale account of the topic is currently in progress by the American literary historian Janet Beizer.[57] Like Carroy, Beizer is struck by "the hysterization of aesthetics and culture" during the

---

[54] Cited in Carter, *Idea of Decadence*, 83.

[55] Debora Leah Silverman, *Art Nouveau in Fin-de-Siècle France: Politics, Psychology, and Style* (Los Angeles: University of California Press, 1989), 78: 332, n. 15.

[56] Cited in Carter, *Idea of Decadence*, 86: Barbey d'Aurevilly's emphasis.

[57] Janet Beizer, *Ventriloquized Bodies: Narratives of Hysteria in Nineteenth-Century France* (Ithaca, N.Y.: Cornell University Press, 1994). See also Leslie E. Camhi, "Prisoners of Gender: Hysteria, Psychoanalysis, and Literature in *fin-de-siècle* Culture" (Ph.D. diss., Yale University, 1991).

latter half of the nineteenth century. She specifically takes as her subject "the hystericized novel," the novel in which hysteria functions as the central organizing figure. In an artistic manifesto published in 1928 in the avant-garde journal *La révolution surréaliste*, Beizer observes, Louis Aragon and André Breton, both of whom had attended medical school as young men, branded hysteria "the greatest poetic discovery of the end of the nineteenth century."[58] In their memorialization, Aragon and Breton reject present-day medical definitions and attempt to claim the disorder for the world of aesthetics: "Hysteria is not a pathological phenomenon," the poets conclude, "and can in every way be considered as a supreme mode of expression."[59] Like their Romantic predecessors, the surrealists sought the extrarational sources of artistic inspiration and believed that hysteria was too important to be left to the physicians. In these assertions by Aragon and Breton, Beizer finds a challenge to critics and historians and formulates a number of questions for her study: Why was hysteria deemed "metaphorically appropriate" to the expressive tasks of two generations of French literary intellectuals? By what means was contemporary medical information about the disorder turned into a series of literary tropes, or, to put it another way, how was the "narrative conversion" of hysteria achieved? And how did hysteria go on to operate as "a communicable metaphor" within a half century's literary history? Like Carter and Carroy, Beizer intends to probe these questions through readings of a series of texts, including *Madame Bovary*, the verse narrative *La servante* (1853) by Louise Colet, *Germinie Lacerteux* of the Goncourts, Maxime du Camp's *Les convulsions de Paris*, the Rougon-Macquart cycle of Zola, and *Monsieur Vénus* (1884) by Rachilde.[60]

In the 1950s, Jacques Chastenet, the historian of Third Republic France, referred to hysteria as one of the "*fin-de-siècle* neuroses."[61] By and large, social and cultural historians have been willing to endorse Chastenet's characterization.[62] However, as Barbey d'Aurevilly's comment, cited

[58] [Louis] Aragon and [André] Breton, "Le cinquantenaire de l'hystérie (1878–1928)," most accessible in Maurice Nadeau, ed., *Histoire du surréalisme: Documents surréalistes* (Paris: Seuil, 1948), 125.

[59] Ibid., 127.

[60] Summary based on a "Project Description" provided by Professor Beizer to the author.

[61] Jacques Chastenet, *Histoire de la troisième république*, 7 vols. (Paris: Hachette, 1955), vol. 3, *La république triomphante, 1893–1906*, chap. 1.

[62] See, for instance, the remarks in Raymond Rudorff, *Belle Époque: Paris in the Nineties* (London: Hamish Hamilton, 1972), 194–95; Eugen Weber, *France Fin de Siècle* (Cambridge, Mass.: Belknap Press, 1986), 20–21; Perrot, *A History of Private Life*, 4: 629–33; Frederic Morton, *A Nervous Splendor: Vienna 1888/1889* (Boston: Little, Brown, 1979), 203–4, 282–85; Allan Janik and Stephen Toulmin, *Wittgenstein's Vienna* (New York: Simon and Schuster, 1973), 76–77.

above, about Huysmans suggests, even hysteria's cultural history during the *belle époque* centered less on a literary text or author than on Charcot and the Paris hospitals. To a degree that has been surpassed by no other figure in the history of the disease, Charcot inspired paintings, novels, and plays as well as extensive commentary in the popular press.

As we have seen before, easily the best-known artistic conceptualization of the fin-de-siècle hysteric is Brouillet's *Une leçon clinique à la Salpêtrière*. Brouillet was an established painter who specialized in epic historical, military, and scientific scenes. His famous painting hung in the Paris Salon of 1887, where it was viewed by *le tout Paris*. Artistically rather undistinguished, the painting is remarkable for its dimensions, the figures being nearly life-size. The artist obviously deemed hysteria a suitable subject for monumental presentation. In 1983, Jean Louis Signoret, formerly a neurologist at the Salpêtrière, identified all twenty-five figures in the painting.[63] With nearly every young doctor and medical student from the Charcot Clinic finding his place in the work, the painting is truly a collective portrait of the school of the Salpêtrière. Contemporary reviews of the work, Signoret finds, reveal that the painting rapidly became a familiar popular icon.

The incursion of the hysteria metaphor into the visual arts took other forms, too. Silverman has put forward the original interpretation that Charcot's work on hysteria and hypnosis contributed to the formation of the art nouveau movement in France.[64] The "new psychology" of the 1880s and 1890s elaborated by Charcot, Bernheim, Binet, and Féré, explains Silverman, was derived from the study of hypnosis, hysteria, somnambulism, and the unconscious and placed a new emphasis on the interiority of psychological experience. In the stylistic realm, this development influenced the turning inward of interior design at the same time. Furthermore, Charcot's visual mode of pedagogy, his distinctive medical visualization of the hysteric, and his activities as personal collector and connoisseur of art provided additional correspondences with the aesthetic culture of the time.

Novelistic representations of Charcot-style hysteria were also common during the closing decades of the 1800s. Charcot personally was closely acquainted with many figures in the Parisian literary world who were as likely to appear at his formal hospital lectures as at his famous Tuesday soirées.[65] Not inaccurately, in her 1992 fictionalized historical account of the life of Charcot, Wanda Bannour includes a chapter titled "Le roman

[63] Jean Louis Signoret, "Variété historique: Une leçon clinique à la Salpêtrière (1887) par André Brouillet," *Revue neurologique* 139, no. 12 (1983): 687–701. See also *La leçon de Charcot*.
[64] Silverman, *Art Nouveau in Fin-de-Siècle France*, 83–91.
[65] Roudinesco, *La bataille de cents ans*, 76–84.

des grands hystériques." In these pages, Charcot conducts an imaginary conversation with Alphonse Daudet, Barbey d'Aurevilly, and Edmond de Goncourt in which he wryly observes the abundant nervous pathology in both the characters in these authors' novels and the authors themselves.[66]

French literary intellectuals seem simultaneously to have been attracted to and repelled by Charcot, often using their novels as a means to settle personal and professional disputes with the great man. Jules Claretie's *Les amours d'un interne*, published in 1881, relates the story of the young Salpêtrière interne Vilandry and his secret nocturnal *liaisons amoureuses* with hysterical patients in the wards of the hospital.[67] Claretie's irresistible tale circulated widely the belief that sexual escapades were common on the medical wards. Along the same lines, a year after Charcot's death, Léon Daudet (son of the novelist Alphonse Daudet, a former medical student, and later cofounder of the right-wing royalist Catholic organization Action française) published *Les morticoles*.[68] Daudet's novel conjures up a kind of medical antiutopia in which authoritarian physician-scientists rule over an oppressed patient-citizenry. Daudet provides acidulous caricatures of the senior medical personalities on the Paris Faculty, including Dr. Foutange (Charcot), described as "the doctor of hysterics and somnambulists," demonstrating on the patient "Rosalie" in a doomed amphitheatre of the "Hôpital Typhus." As Toby Gelfand has recently noted, the book became a national bestseller.[69] Similarly, in 1929 the Swedish physician Axel Munthe recorded his own observations of the fashionable Parisian medical world, including detailed accounts of life at the Salpêtrière during the 1880s.[70] Munthe's *The Story of San Michele* became one of the most popular novels in French publishing history. Bits of Charcotiana cropped up in many other pieces of imaginative writing too.[71]

Other works of fin-de-siècle fiction drew less on the personal image of Charcot and his hospital than on aspects of his teachings. In an essay appearing in 1987, Emily Apter, like Hunter and Shorter, studies the past figural representation of a single hysterical symptom.[72] Specifically, Apter

---

[66] Bannour, *Jean-Martin Charcot et l'hystérie*, chap. 11.

[67] Jules Claretie, *Les amours d'un interne* (Paris: E. Dentu, 1881).

[68] Léon Daudet, *Les morticoles* (Paris: Charpentier, 1894).

[69] Toby Gelfand, "Medical Nemesis, Paris, 1894: Léon Daudet's *Les morticoles*," *Bulletin of the History of Medicine* 60, no. 2 (Summer 1986): 155–76.

[70] Axel Munthe, *The Story of San Michele* (London: John Murray, 1929), chap. 18.

[71] Leo Tolstoy, *The Kreutzer Sonata* [1889], trans. Aylmer Maude in *The Death of Ivan Ilych and Other Stories* (New York: New American Library, 1960), 189, 200; Bram Stoker, *Dracula* [1897] (New York: Oxford University Press, 1983), 191. L.-F. Céline, *Mort à crédit* [1936], in *Romans*, ed. Henri Godard, 3 vols. (Paris: Gallimard, 1981), 1: 525.

[72] Emily S. Apter, "Blind Spots: Hysterical Vision from Charcot to Mirbeau" (Paper delivered at the Thirteenth Annual Meeting of the Colloquium in Nineteenth-Century French Studies, Northwestern University, Evanston, Ill., October 22–24, 1987, subse-

examines Charcot's clinical writings on hysterical disorders of vision, including hysterical scotomas, or visual defects in which perception is absent or impaired in an isolated area of the visual field. She then reconstructs the history of a medical-symptom-as-cultural-symbol. In one nonmedical field after another in the late nineteenth century, she finds that the idea of hysterical blind spots functioned metaphorically as a way of describing dulled or disordered or destroyed perception in the social, moral, and aesthetic worlds. Apter traces these usages through a diversity of French sources, including colonialist propaganda, anti-Semitic posters, literary presentations of the Dreyfus trial, and art criticism of the impressionists. She focuses on the novel *Le jardin des supplices* (1889), published by one of the leading younger naturalist writers, Octave Mirbeau. Mirbeau's novel concocts a fantastical botanical allegory in which a Chinese torture garden doubles as both an erotic floral paradise, modeled on Monet's Giverny, and a medical microcosm along the lines of the Salpêtrière. At the center of the story, Apter discovers, is a detailed description, with almost textbook fidelity, of a hysterical attack *à la Charcot*.[73]

Nor was Charcot the only medical figure to inspire literary intellectuals during this period. In 1966, Ellenberger brought to notice Marcel Prévost's *L'automne d'une femme*, published in 1893.[74] Prévost's novel, too, is set at the Salpêtrière. It tells the story of one Dr. Daumier, a gifted young physician who conducts long and sensitive psychological analyses with several neurotic patients beset by depression, lovesickness, and various hysterical stigmata. Ellenberger believes that Daumier is a portrait of Pierre Janet. Prévost was one of the major originators of psychological literary modernism in France, and, artistically speaking, *L'automne d'une femme* is arguably the finest *roman à l'hystérie* of its generation.

Prévost's novel may also have been part of a larger cultural development. As critics and historians have noted, European and American writers around the beginning of the twentieth century began to explore the genesis and structure of the human personality, the duality of consciousness, and the relation of the Self to the objective world, as can be seen in works by Henry James, Franz Kafka, James Joyce, Marcel Proust, Robert Musil, Virginia Woolf, and others. The origins of the modern psychological novel are multiple; but it is certainly conceivable that the work of the nineteenth-century French psychological school contributed.[75]

---

quently published with revisions as "The Garden of Scopic Perversion from Monet to Mirbeau," *October* 47 [Winter 1988]: 91–115).

[73] Octave Mirbeau, *Le jardin des supplices* (Paris: E. Fasquelle, 1899), 239ff.

[74] Ellenberger, "The Pathogenic Secret and Its Therapeutics," *Journal of the History of the Behavioral Sciences* 2, no. 1 (January 1966): 33–34.

[75] I owe this general idea to Judith Ryan's *The Vanishing Subject: Early Psychology and*

During the centennial celebrations of Charcot's birth in 1925, the minister of public instruction cited over a dozen authors, including Zola, the Goncourts, Maupassant, Huysmans, Mirbeau, Paul Bourget, and Proust, who were indebted to Charcot. With a quarter century's perspective, he proposed, it was clear that Charcot's teachings had inspired an entire generation of "littérateurs-psychiatres" who ushered in a new, more psychologically oriented literary sensibility.[76]

Of all the arts, theater proved most amenable to the representation of hysteria. The late nineteenth century witnessed a flowering of European drama, featuring many memorable female characters and bringing fame to numerous stage actresses. As Gail Finney has shown, the hysterical heroine flourished.[77] It is easy to see why. The theater is a public and highly performative artistic medium while hysteria is the most extroverted of psychopathologies, its own act and audience.[78] In the contemporary popular press, an analogy was commonly drawn between the amphitheater of the Salpêtrière and the theater proper. In his weekly demonstrations, Charcot hypnotically induced localized hysterias which were then literally "acted out" by patients before an audience, while his pedagogical techniques employing posters, photographs, and illuminated projections were based on "the theatricalization of symptoms."[79] It was not altogether inappropriate, then, that a decade after its appearance in book form Richet's novel *Soeur Marthe* was recast and performed in Paris as a lyrical drama. Similarly, when in 1884 Sarah Bernhardt, the most celebrated stage actress of her age, wished to perfect a performance of an attack of hysterical insanity in the play *Adrienne Lecouvreur*, she repaired for practice to a cell in the *quartiers des aliénées* at the Salpêtrière.[80]

The most entertaining source unearthed thus far by scholars pertaining to the theatrical history of hysteria is *Une leçon à la Salpêtrière*. This is a two-act play written by André de Lorde and performed in the spring of 1908 at the Théâtre du Grand-Guignol in Paris.[81] The play is a mishmash of ideas and themes from Brouillet's canvas, Claretie's *Les amours d'un*

Literary Modernism (Chicago: University of Chicago Press, 1991), which stresses the contributions of German and American psychologists.

[76] M. A. de Monzie, "Discours," *Revue neurologique* 41 (1925): 1159–62.

[77] Gail Finney, *Women in Modern Drama: Freud, Feminism, and European Theater at the Turn of the Century* (Ithaca, N.Y.: Cornell University Press, 1989). The sixth chapter of Finney's book discusses hysteria and maternity in Ibsen's *A Doll's House* (1879) and *Hedda Gabler* (1890).

[78] P. C. Racamier, "Hystérie et théâtre," *L'évolution psychiatrique* 2 (1952): 257–89.

[79] Roudinesco, *La bataille de cent ans*, 1: 35.

[80] This story is mentioned in Jules Claretie, *La vie à Paris: 1884*, 5e année (Paris: Victor-Havard, 1885), 450–51 and enlarged upon by S. Veyrac in "Une heure chez Sarah Bernhardt," *La chronique médicale*, 4e année, 19 (October 1, 1897): 614.

[81] Carroy, "Hystérie, théâtre, littérature au dix-neuvième siècle," 303–4.

interne, and Daudet's *Les morticoles*. Again, viewers get a pastiche of the bygone medical world of Paris, with fictionalized caricatures—Professor Marbois as Charcot; Suzanne as Blanche Wittmann; and a coterie of obsequious medical students—situated in an amphitheater.[82] Lorde, the son of a physician, dedicated the piece, one hopes ironically, to the Sorbonne psychologist Alfred Binet. Interestingly, the new hysteria studies have taken up Lorde's project in a different context. Since the late 1980s, American feminist drama historians and literary critics have been creatively restaging the nineteenth-century theatrical tradition of hysteria, which they believe captures vividly the combination of science, sexuality, and feminine pathology inherent in the history of hysteria and in patriarchal cultures generally.[83]

Finally, the hysteria motif a hundred years ago was by no means confined to the rarefied regions of high culture. In 1894, a Catholic critic of Charcot observed ruefully that "around 1878, the name of the Salpêtrière invaded even the popular magazines and newspapers."[84] In the one study to date of hysteria and the popular medical press, Robert Hillman, a former student of Veith, discovers that local physicians and educated readers in Alsace-Lorraine followed the Salpêtrière-Nancy wars with great interest.[85] In the same vein, Ruth Harris has found that popular Parisian newspapers of the 1880s and 1890s covered in loving and lurid detail several sensationalistic cases of adulterous acts and bloodcurdling crimes allegedly committed by hysterical women under posthypnotic suggestion.[86] An exhibition today at the Forum des Halles in central Paris gives fur-

[82] The text of the play may be found in André de Lorde, *Théâtre d'épouvante* (Paris: Charpentier et Fasquelle, 1909), 1–81.

[83] Jane Moss, "Le corps spectaculaire: le théâtre au féminin," *Modern Language Studies* 16, no. 4 (Fall 1986): 54–60; Dianne Hunter with Judy Dworin and Lenora Champagne, *Dr. Charcot's Hysteria Shows*, performed for the first time on the evenings of October 13–14, 1988 as part of "Theater of the Female Body," a conference at Trinity College, Connecticut; Coral Houtman, *Augustine* (Unpublished television play, London, 1989); Elin Diamond, "Staging Hysteria" (Lecture delivered at the Berkshire Conference on Women's History, June 10, 1990); Ann McFerran, "Acting Out with More. (Anna Furze Talks about her New Play 'Augustine,'" *New Statesman & Society* 4, no. 153 (May 31, 1991): 29; and Dianne Hunter, "Theory and Performance: The Creation of *Dr. Charcot's Hysteria Shows*," *Proceedings of the Seventh International Conference on Psychology and Literature* (forthcoming).

[84] G. Hahn, "Charcot et son influence sur l'opinion publique," *Revue des questions scientifiques*, 2d. ser., 6 (1894): 369.

[85] Robert G. Hillman, "A Scientific Study of Mystery: The Role of the Medical and Popular Press in the Nancy-Salpêtrière Controversy on Hypnotism," *Bulletin of the History of Medicine* 39, no. 2 (1965): 163–83.

[86] Ruth Harris, "Murder Under Hypnosis in the Case of Gabrielle Bompard: Psychiatry in the Courtroom in Belle Époque Paris," in W. F. Bynum, Roy Porter, and Michael Shepherd, eds., *The Anatomy of Madness: Essays in the History of Psychiatry* (London: Tavistock, 1985), 2: 197–241.

ther evidence that Charcot's ideas about hysteria became *vulgarisées*, in both the French and English senses of the word. The show is called "L'actualité à Paris à la Belle Époque" and features waxen figures arranged in twenty scenes representing the popular and cultural life of the capital during the fin de siècle. Music and voice recordings, available for tourists on cassettes in seven languages, accompany the show. Between the sixth and seventh scenes, showing respectively an evening at the Opéra and life on the *grands boulevards*, the figure of a woman seated at a chartreuse kiosk sells copies of *Le journal illustré*, *Le Gaulois*, and *Rire*. Holding in her hand a newspaper dated August 30, 1898, the woman shouts out the day's news of Charcot claiming to have cured a hysterical patient with hypnosis at the Salpêtrière.[87]

For historical accuracy, the tableau leaves something to be desired. (Charcot had been dead for five years by 1898, and he had little faith in hypnosis as a therapeutic, as opposed to experimental, procedure.) But the scene—visited, one imagines, by tens of thousands of people annually—indicates the place that Charcot and hysteria continue to occupy in the French sense of history and in French popular culture. The work of French physicians on the great neurosis a century ago produced articles in the daily tabloids, lay hypnotists in the Tuileries, and posters along the Boulevard de l'Hôpital announcing the day's public lectures. In late nineteenth-century travel guides to Paris, the Salpêtrière was even cited regularly as a site to visit, along with the musical performances at the Folies-Bergères, the giraffes at the Jardin des Plantes, and the newly completed Eiffel Tower.[88] Plainly, hysteria occupied a prominent and vivid place in the imagination of turn-of-the-century France, making its way up and down the cultural scale and percolating into a remarkable number of areas of artistic life.

POLITICS, HISTORY, SOCIETY

Hysteria's metaphorical history has by no means been confined to the world of the cultural arts. During the 1800s, the disorder also furnished a set of popular and highly serviceable images to many areas of social and political criticism. The use of the hysteria concept in these extrascientific

---

[87] The exhibition is sponsored by the Musée Grévin, the Paris wax museum, and costs twenty francs for admission.

[88] Alexandre Guérin, "Une visite à la Salpêtrière," *La revue illustrée* 4, no. 40 (August 1887): 97–103, 171–77; Maurice Guillemot, "À la Salpêtrière," *Paris illustré*, nos. 22 and 23 (September 24, 1887 and October 1, 1887): 354–65, 370–74; Ignotus [pseudo. Félix Platel], *Paris Secret* (Paris, 1889), 22–33; Henry S. Edwards, *Old and New Paris*, 2 vols. (London: Cassell, 1893–94), vol. 2, chap. 29.

domains was caught up with the larger phenomenon of "medicalization," the process by which medical assumptions, practices, values, and vocabularies penetrate traditional, prescientific attitudes, institutions, and practices. In late nineteenth-century Europe, medicalization was proceeding apace and included among its facets the application of descriptive disease imagery to the social and political world. The use of the language of nervous and mental pathology in particular became a common feature of French social, cultural, and political commentary between 1870 and 1914.

The historical context for these charged socioscientific rhetorics is complex. The *belle époque* of hysteria occurred at a distinctive, and difficult, moment in French social, political, and intellectual history. Among the educated middle classes, older religious mental habits were decisively on the decline. With the advent of the Third Republic in 1870, the waning of superstitious and religious worldviews was accelerated by a policy of programmatic anticlericalism on the part of the new republican government. The secularization of French thought and society greatly enhanced the intellectual prestige of medicine and science in this self-consciously positivist and progressivist period. At the same time, technical medical knowledge accumulated, and the medical profession was specializing. As mentioned above, the expansion of knowledge concerning the structure and function of the central nervous system led to the rapid growth of the mental sciences and the emergence of neurology as a clinical specialty. Correspondingly, new academic "sciences of society," such as sociology and anthropology, which sought to study society as a natural organism with its own laws of operation, were emerging. By the turn of the century, these factors had conspired to elevate physicians and the new "social scientists" into the arbiters of normality and abnormality for both individual and social behavior.[89]

These internal developments were accompanied by a tremendous growth of interest in medicine among the laity. Across the nineteenth century, general rates of literacy rose steadily, and a large popular medical and scientific press developed to bring the expanding medical knowledge to a new reading public. For the first time, the reading of medical books by lay people became a pastime. Included in this medical writing was a large and largely alarmist literature on the nervous disorders: their nature, causes, course, prognosis, and prevention. As Gérard Jacquemet has shown, entire new "popular maladies" came into existence.[90] The popu-

[89] Harry Paul, *From Knowledge to Power: The Rise of the Science Empire in France, 1860–1939* (Cambridge: Cambridge University Press, 1989); Jack D. Ellis, *The Physician-Legislators of France: Medicine and Politics in the Early Third Republic, 1870–1914* (Cambridge: Cambridge University Press, 1990).

[90] Gérard Jacquemet, "Médecine et 'maladies populaires' dans le Paris de la fin du XIXe siècle," *L'haleine des faubourgs: Recherches* 29 (December 1977): 349–64.

larization of medical knowledge added a new dimension to bourgeois consciousness, as people increasingly worried less about the fates of their souls in the afterlife and more about their physical and mental health in the here-and-now.[91]

Other medical events also informed the cultural history of hysteria. The later decades of the nineteenth century witnessed two major, interrelated developments within the history of epidemic disease. On the one hand, Paris experienced cholera epidemics in 1873, 1884, and 1892, and typhoid fever returned annually during the 1880s. In the 1890s, tuberculosis became a growing concern. Above all, syphilitic infections surged during the late nineteenth and early twentieth centuries, reaching truly epidemic proportions in many European cities. The French venereologist Alfred Fournier estimated that no fewer than 15 percent of the adult male population of Paris may have been infected with syphilis, while in certain municipal mental hospitals across Europe, general paretics composed 35 percent of the patient population.[92] The French social historian Alain Corbin has shown that intense fear of "the venereal peril" became a powerful presence in the mentality of middle-class Parisians during the fin de siècle, including many artists and intellectuals.[93]

On the other hand, the age of Charcot corresponded with dramatic scientific breakthroughs in the understanding of disease etiology, with French medical science contributing centrally to these advancements. During the late 1870s and 1880s, Louis Pasteur published his seminal essays on the germ theory of disease, which were debated hotly in the European medical community. According to the Pasteurian paradigm, many diseases were the result of specific microbial agents that were communicated from one environment to another and that followed specific, ascertainable laws of behavior. Pasteur's work in Paris inspired an energetic search for the pathogenic microorganisms of all diseases. In the closing decades of the century, the new visibility of epidemic diseases with strong social dimensions combined with the new knowledge about disease causation. Pasteur became the exemplary French medical scientist of the day, whose teachings were applied, and misapplied, far beyond the

[91] Theodore Zeldin has some interesting things to say about the impact of the popular medical press on sensibilities in *France 1848–1945: Anxiety and Hypocrisy* (Oxford: Oxford University Press, 1981), 59–64.

[92] Roger L. Williams, *The Horror of Life* (Chicago: University of Chicago Press, 1980), 49; Claude Quétel, *History of Syphilis*, trans. Judith Braddock and Brian Pike (Baltimore: Johns Hopkins University Press, 1990), 161.

[93] Alain Corbin, "Le péril vénérien au début du siècle: Prophylaxie sanitaire et prophylaxie morale," *L'haleine des faubourgs: Recherches* 29 (December 1979): 245–83; idem, "La grande peur de la syphilis," in Jean-Pierre Bardet et al., eds., *Peurs et terreurs face à la contagion: choléra, tuberculose, syphilis, XIXe–XXe siècles* (Paris: Fayard, 1988), 328–48.

boundaries of pathophysiology.[94] A widespread fear of, fascination with, and fixation on questions of disease, contagion, and epidemicity developed. In such an atmosphere, disease imagery of all sorts became culturally available to many public discourses of the day.

Finally, circumstances in French social, political, and military history contributed mightily to the cultures of hysteria that formed in France during the final third of the last century. The concept of the *belle époque* is of course a postbellum idealization, a retrospective creation that emerged only after the First World War. The early Third Republic was in fact fraught with military threats and social and political upheavals. After a half-century of peace, the French suffered a swift, humiliating defeat in the Franco-Prussian War of 1870–71. The war was followed by the territorial annexation of the eastern provinces of Alsace and Lorraine and the unification of the German states. The threat from a militantly nationalistic Germany, which many French people believed would eventuate in another war, loomed large throughout this period.

Paralleling the persistent external threat to France were deeply unsettling domestic events. The Franco-Prussian War had been punctuated, many people believed ignominiously, by what amounted to a civil war: the brief, abortive, and extremely bloody Paris Commune of the spring of 1871. Moreover, during the last three decades of the century, France underwent sudden and profound internal changes associated with the processes of industrialization, urbanization, and democratization. The concentration of workers in the cities led to organized and raucous socialist and syndicalist movements. An active and voluble feminist movement emerged in Paris. Violent anarchist acts terrorized politicians and the public. And the Boulanger Affair of 1886–89, followed by the Dreyfus Affair during the second half of the 1890s, convulsed the nation. New social problems arose and old problems were magnified in the expanding urban centers, which for the first time concentrated menacing subpopulations in one place for observation and analysis. Many French people a century ago found these transformations to be enormously anxiety-producing.[95]

Robert Nye, the American social and intellectual historian, has shown

---

[94] Bruno Latour, *The Pasteurization of Society*, trans. Alan Sheridan and John Law (Cambridge: Harvard University Press, 1988). On the concept of "the metaphorical microbe," see Andrew Robert Aisenberg, "Contagious Disease and the Government of Paris in the Age of Pasteur" (Ph.D. diss., Yale University, 1993), chap. 2.

[95] For more on the historical setting, consult the early chapters of David Thomson's classic *Democracy in France Since 1870*, 5th ed. (New York: Oxford University Press, 1969), as well as Jean-Marie Mayeur, *Les débuts de la troisième république, 1871–1898* (Paris: Éditions du Seuil, 1973); Jean-Pierre Azéma and Michel Winock, *La IIIe république (1870–1940)* (Paris: Calmann-Lévy, 1976); and Robert D. Anderson, *France 1870–1914: Politics and Society* (London: Routledge and Kegan Paul, 1984).

that this concatenation of occurrences in France during the post-Commune decades gave rise to the distinctive notion of "the social pathologies." In an important study that appeared in 1984, Nye investigates "the medical model of national decline" that pervaded French culture between 1870 and 1900.[96] He establishes that one area of social and political thought after another was medicalized during this period, a process that included the use of images of neuropathology and psychopathology to account for many of the most disturbing changes of the day. New clinical entities linking disease to urban and industrial life appeared while older, stigmatized behaviors were morbidified for the first time. According to Nye, the main projected social pathologies in the late nineteenth century were alcoholism, prostitution, homosexuality, criminality, venereal disease, and suicide.[97]

The new hysteria studies directly confirm Nye's historical findings. In addition, they suggest that the hysteria concept played an important role in the social pathologizing impulse of the period. Hysteria's heyday, it should be recalled, was precisely coincident with the commencement and early years of the Third Republic. Also, like a number of the pathologies listed above, hysteria in pre-Freudian European medicine was believed to be an affliction of the nervous system, acquired either through heredity or bad living habits and communicated by means of suggestion and imitation. Accordingly, in an array of social, political, and cultural texts from the post-Commune era, the ideas and languages of Charcot, Bernheim, Luys, Dumontpallier, Grasset, and Lasègue mixed readily with the other major scientific and pseudoscientific rhetorics of the time, including Morelian degenerationism, Le Bonian crowd psychology, and Lombrosian criminal anthropology. Furthermore, in the troubled, traumatized sociopolitical world of the early Third Republic, hysteria joined in turns with the discourses of national decline, alcoholism, prostitution, criminality, sexual perversion, and venereal disease. In these social commentaries, hysteria alternately subsumed and was subsumed by other pathologies. Moreover, whereas interest in hysteria within the medical community was associated, as Jan Goldstein has demonstrated, with liberal, republican causes, the subject in society and politics was habitually pressed into the service of conservative, if not reactionary, programs and points of view.

Since 1980, degenerationism has become a topic of lively interest among historical scholars, and a secondary literature of high quality has now

---

[96] Robert A. Nye, *Crime, Madness, and Politics in Modern France: The Medical Concept of Decline* (Princeton: Princeton University Press, 1984), 136. Particularly relevant is Nye's fifth chapter, "Metaphors of Pathology in the Belle Époque: The Rise of the Medical Model of Cultural Crisis."

[97] Ibid., 132–70. See also Pick, "The Empire of Pathologies" in *Faces of Degeneration*, 50–59.

appeared.[98] The most influential and extravagant integration of the hysteria and degeneration paradigms in nineteenth-century European culture was Max Simon Nordau's bestselling *Entartung* (*Degeneration*), a reprint of which was issued in 1993.[99] By birth a Hungarian Jew, Nordau earned a medical degree in Germany, and for most of his adulthood practiced medicine in Paris. In addition, he found time to write voluminously as a cultural critic and medical journalist. Later in life he emerged as a major figure in the Zionist movement. Nordau's book appeared in German in 1892–93 and was translated with fanfare into French soon thereafter.[100] The work makes for fascinating reading today, not least of all because by late twentieth-century standards its cultural judgments are so consistently perverse.

The framework of *Degeneration* is explicitly medical. The long opening part presents a chapter-by-chapter presentation of the "Symptoms," "Diagnosis," and "Etiology" of Europe's current cultural malaise, while the concluding section offers disquisitions on "Prognosis" and "Therapeutics." Throughout the work, Nordau's main diagnostic categories are hysteria and degeneration, which run in close, if completely confused, relation to one another. Nordau takes as established fact "the enormous increase of hysteria in our day" as well as the correspondence between individual hysteria and the features of fin-de-siècle Europe as a whole.[101] References to the publications of Charcot, Richer, Binet, Axenfeld, Huchard, and Gilles de la Tourette litter the bottom of his pages.

The book is essentially an extended antimodernist diatribe, in which hysteria serves as the metaphor of choice for cultural innovation and experimentation of all sorts. The bulk of the argument consists of an exam-

---

[98] On the general cultural history of degenerationism in France, Italy, and Britain, see Pick, *Faces of Degeneration*. For the psychiatric origins and history of the concept, there is Dowbiggin's *Inheriting Madness*. And Jean Borie examines the literary history of the subject in *Mythologie de l'hérédité au XIXe siècle*. On the theme in individual disciplines, consult the collection edited by J. Edward Chamberlin and Sander L. Gilman, *Degeneration: The Dark Side of Progress* (New York: Columbia University Press, 1985).

[99] Max Nordau, *Degeneration* (Lincoln, Nebr.: University of Nebraska Press, 1993). This is a reprint of the 1968 edition published by Howard Fertig, which includes the excellent introduction "Max Nordau and His *Degeneration*," by George Mosse. See also Chamberlin and Gilman, *Degeneration*, passim; Pick, *Faces of Degeneration*, 24–25; P. M. Baldwin, "Liberalism, Naturalism and Degeneration: The Case of Max Nordau," *Central European History* 13 (1980): 99–120; George L. Mosse, "Max Nordau, Liberalism, and the New Jew," *Journal of Contemporary History* 27, no. 4 (October 1992): 565–82; and William Greenslade, *Degeneration, Culture and the Novel, 1880–1940* (New York: Cambridge University Press, 1994).

[100] Nordau, *Entartung*, 2 vols. (Berlin: C. Dunker, 1892–93); *Dégénérescence*, trans. Auguste Kietrich, 2 vols. (Paris: Alcan, 1894). In the following discussion, I cite from Nordau, *Degeneration*, translated from the second German edition, with an introduction by George L. Mosse (New York: Howard Fertig, 1968).

[101] Nordau, *Degeneration*, 36.

ination of figures and movements from recent decades that Nordau sees as indications of a despicable cultural decay. Artists as diverse as Ibsen, Zola, Wilde, Tolstoy, and Nietzsche and movements such as Pre-Raphaelitism, naturalism, impressionism, and symbolism receive the author's disapprobation. Nordau applies the term "hysteria" to the artists themselves, the works they produce, and the cultural styles they manifest. The tendency of contemporary culture to fragment into schools and "isms," the dizzying succession of artistic movements and aesthetic ideologies that mark the birth of modernism, and the short attention span of the gallery-going public are all to him so many symptom-formations.

The medical literalness of Nordau's analyses is bracing. In one passage that nicely illustrates Emily Apter's article, the author discusses the latest medical literature on hysterical amblyopia (dullness of vision) and dyschromatopsia (distorted color perception) and applies it to the impressionist painting of the day. Artists in this camp, Nordau declares flatly, are "hysterical painters." They misperceive color, and their vision breaks up from an integrated field into isolated spots over the retina. How else to explain "the whitewash of a Puvis de Chavannes," "the screaming yellow, blue, and red of a Besnard," and "the violet pictures of Manet and his school"? The canvases of avant-garde artists, Nordau adds, "spring from no actually observable aspect of nature, but from a subjective view due to the condition of the nerves." They become "at once intelligible to us if we keep in view the researches of the Charcot school into the visual derangements in degeneration and hysteria."[102] No less did Nordau excoriate literary modernism. Huysmans, he charged, was "the classical type of the hysterical mind without originality who is the predestined victim of every suggestion."[103]

Most of the cultural activity deplored by Nordau was centered in Paris, that cauldron of cultural modernism. In France, Nordau contended, degeneration typically assumed aesthetical forms. In Germany, he believed, people had been increasingly predisposed to nervous illness since the wars of unification. However, since the Germans had little native artistic sense, German hysteria was expressing itself through other channels, most notably rampant anti-Semitism and "the Wagner-fashion."[104] The latter in particular exercised Nordau. The emotional intemperance of Wagner's music, with its strident cultural nationalism and breast-beating eroticism,

---

[102] Ibid., 27–29. Criticism of impressionism as optical disease seems to have been common during the eighties and nineties. Huysmans, for instance, wrote of one exhibition that "most of the paintings corroborate Dr. Charcot's experiments on changes in color perception which he noted in many of his hysterics at the Salpêtrière. . . . They had a malady of the retina" (quoted in Apter, "Hysterical Vision," 19).

[103] Nordau, *Degeneration*, 302.

[104] Ibid., 171–213.

and the cultist gatherings of the Bayreuth festivals were again, to Nordau's thinking, signs of "the hysteria of the age." "Wagner's hysteria assumed the collective form of German hysteria."[105] In the conclusion of the book, Nordau's rhetoric achieves almost apocalyptic proportions: "We stand now in the midst of a severe mental epidemic, of a sort of black death of degeneration and hysteria, and it is natural that we should ask anxiously on all sides: 'What is to come next?'"[106] Despite its hyperbole and breathlessness, Nordau's *Degeneration* was easily the most widely-read piece of cultural criticism in central Europe between Nietzsche's *Thus Spoke Zarathustra* (1883–84) and Oswald Spengler's *The Decline of the West* (1918).

Hysteria also made its way during these years into French political and historical criticism. Since the late eighteenth century, French alienists had commented upon catastrophic political events as potential causes of mental disturbance. However, beginning in the 1870s, this line of reasoning reversed, and a descriptive psychopathology of the Right emerged in which violent political activity was interpreted as the manifestation of a prior latent state of individual or collective insanity. This new counter-revolutionary historiography focused on the French Revolution of the 1790s and the Paris Commune of 1871. In his monumental account of modern French history, Hippolyte Taine trotted out the vocabulary of "collective madness," "group hysteria," "mass suicide," and "political paroxysm" to describe the actions of the *sans culottes* and the events of the Revolutionary Terror.[107] As Susanna Barrows, Daniel Pick, and Jaap van Ginnekin have shown, Taine conceptualized the history of the French nation as a study in the social and political psychology of a people, a sort of pre-Freudian psychohistory.[108] And like Zola's Rougon-Marquart series in the literary sphere, Taine's *Les origines de la France contemporaine* was the most ambitious historical project of its age.

In a parallel development, the nightmare of *l'année terrible* of 1870–71 had barely passed before conservative political critics formulated a theory of "morbid psychology" to account for the gruesome events. Some au-

---

[105] Ibid., 209. This statement recalls Nietzsche in a well-known passage of *The Wagner Case* (1888): "Wagner's art is sick. The problems he brings onto the stage—nothing but the problems of the hysterics—the convulsive nature of his emotion, his overexcited sensibility, his taste for sharper and sharper spices. . . . *Wagner est une névrose*" (*Nietzsche Reader*, ed. R. J. Hollingdale [Harmondsworth, Middlesex: Viking, 1981], 142–43).

[106] Nordau, *Degeneration*, 537.

[107] Hippolyte Taine, *Les origines de la France contemporaine* [1876–93], 6 vols. (Paris: Hachette et Cie, 1877), vol. 2, *La révolution—L'anarchie*, book 1.

[108] Susanna Barrows, *Distorting Mirrors: Visions of the Crowd in Late Nineteenth-Century France* (New Haven: Yale University Press, 1981), chap. 3; Pick, *Faces of Degeneration*, 67–73; Jaap van Ginneken, *Crowds, Psychology, and Politics 1871–1899* (Cambridge: Cambridge University Press, 1992), chap. 1.

thors specifically presented their political critiques as applications of contemporary medico-psychological theories.[109] In 1882, the writer Guy de Maupassant characterized the Commune as "pas autre chose qu'une crise d'hystérie de Paris," "nothing else than Paris having an attack of hysteria."[110] Similarly, Claretie and the conservative belletrist Maxime du Camp brought Taine's Dantesque terminology to descriptions of the Commune in multivolume histories of their own.[111] And Zola, in the next to the last volume of the Rougon-Macquart series, La débâcle (1892), which deals with the Commune, comments of the event twenty years after the fact that it was "an outbreak of a morbid nervous condition, a contagious fever."[112]

A second wave of historical writing in this genre appeared around the turn of the century. Spurred by the Dreyfus Affair, this work fused reactionary political conservatism with Nancean ideas about hypnotic suggestibility and the new pseudoscience of crowd psychology. The most conspicuous author in this camp was one Lucien Nass. A practicing physician, Nass was struck by the periodicity of political upheavals in France during the preceding one hundred years. With this pattern in mind, the good doctor developed a theory of the "national revolutionary neurosis." According to Nass's scheme, the sorry sequence of events in 1789, 1792, 1830, 1834, 1848, and 1871 represented the political spasms of an incipiently and inherently hysterical people who, like an epileptic or hysterical patient, was prone to convulsions at regular intervals. To Nass's thinking, not only individuals and families but collectivities—Paris, the working classes, the French nation—could suffer from bad heredity, and with the appropriate agent provocateur, lapse into violent attacks of hysteria.[113] Latter-day historians have generally eschewed the politics of Taine and Nass, but they have often accepted the medicalized vocabularies of these critics in their accounts of events. In recent historical studies, the hysteria label has been used to describe the outpouring of emotion during the public funeral of Victor Hugo in the spring of 1885, idolatrous demon-

---

[109] J.B.V. Laborde, Les hommes et les actes de l'insurrection de Paris devant la psychologie morbide: Lettres à M. le Dr. Moreau (Paris: G. Baillière, 1872).

[110] Guy de Maupassant, Chroniques, ed. Hubert Juin, 3 vols. (Paris: Union générale d'éditions, 1980), 2: 112.

[111] Jules Claretie, Histoire de la révolution de 1870–71, 6 vols. (Paris: George Decaux, 1875–76); Maxime du Camp, Les convulsions de Paris [1878–79], 4 vols. (Paris: Hachette et Cie, 1889). See especially the account of the burning of the Hôtel de Ville in the fourth volume of Du Camp.

[112] Émile Zola, La débâcle (1892), in Armand Lanoux and Henri Mitterand, eds., Les Rougon-Macquart (Paris: Gallimard, 1960–67), 5: 449.

[113] Drs. Cabanès and L. Nass, La névrose révolutionnaire, preface by Jules Claretie (Paris: Société française d'imprimerie de librairie, 1906); Nass, Le siège de Paris et la Commune: Essai de pathologie historique (Paris: Plon-Nourrit et Cie, 1914).

strations among royalists and army officers in support of General Boulanger in 1889, reactions to the stabbing death in 1894 of President Sadi Carnot, right-wing newspaper attacks on Alfred Dreyfus, and xenophobic outbursts against the Germans during the Fashoda incident of 1898.[114]

Hysteria also figured metaphorically in the emergent social sciences of the fin de siècle, including social psychology and criminology. The concept of crowd psychology was a disciplinary novelty of late nineteenth-century France and Italy. Analytical interest in crowds as a political phenomenon was sparked by the riots of the Commune, which displayed the frightening capacity of large gatherings of people to engage in acts of spontaneous destruction. Then with the coming of democratic, parliamentarian government in 1870, the authority of traditional ruling elites in France began to dwindle, and the political place of the masses increased further. Mass political parties formed, and in 1884 France became the first European nation to introduce universal (male) suffrage. The late 1880s and 1890s also witnessed the organization of large workers' movements across Europe. As the workers of the world united, hundreds of strikes and marches occurred during the 1890s. Many conservative intellectuals regarded these developments with horror, and in response the nascent academic disciplines of psychology and sociology generated ponderous tracts, written by aspiring scientists of society such as Scipio Sighele, Henri Fournial, Gustave Le Bon, and Gabriel Tarde, that studied the crowd as a destructive political force.[115]

The most influential of these publications were a trio of texts written by Le Bon in the five years following Charcot's death: *La psychologie des peuples* (1894), *La psychologie des foules* (1895), and *La psychologie du socialisme* (1898). Like Nordau and Nass, Le Bon was trained in medicine but made his career in social commentary. While a young man, he worked as a military doctor during the Commune revolt, an experience that affected him deeply. Le Bon was strongly nationalistic, fearful of the

---

[114] Rudorff, *Belle Époque*, 23; Nicholas Halasz, *Captain Dreyfus: The Story of a Mass Hysteria* (New York: Simon and Schuster, 1955); J. Kim Munholland, *Origins of Contemporary Europe, 1890–1914* (New York: Harcourt, Brace and World, 1970), 51; Roger Shattuck, *The Banquet Years: The Origins of the Avant Garde in France, 1885 to World War I*, rev. ed. (New York: Vintage Books, 1968), 14–15; Anderson, *France, 1870–1914*, 142.

[115] R. L. Geiger, "Democracy and the Crowd: The Social History of an Idea in France and Italy, 1890–1914," *Societas: A Review of Social History* 7, no. 1 (1977): 47–71; D. Cochart, "Les foules et la Commune: Analyse des premiers écrits de psychologie des foules," *Recherches de psychologie sociale* 4 (1982): 49–60; Alexandre Métraux, "French Crowd Psychology: Between Theory and Ideology," in William R. Woodward and Mitchell G. Ash, eds., *The Problematic Science: Psychology in Nineteenth-Century Thought* (New York: Praeger, 1982), 276–99; Y. Thiec and J. R. Théanton, "La foule comme objet de 'science,'" *Revue française de sociologie* 24, no. 1 (1983): 119–36.

new social egalitarianism, and rabidly antisocialist. He was also highly impressed by recent scientific research on animal magnetism, somnambulism, hysteria, hypnotic phenomena, and alternate states of consciousness.

In "The Mind of Crowds," the opening section of *La psychologie des foules*, Le Bon asserts that collectivities lose the faculties of will and ratiocination possessed by individuals. The mental mechanism operating between the crowd and its demagogic leader, he reasons, has been elucidated by medical research. He likens the excitability of crowds to a spreading disease infection, to electrical and magnetic radiation, and to outbursts of hysteria and somnambulism and characterizes modern mass activities as epidemic contagions and mental illnesses. He claims too that the psychological features of the individual in the crowd are those of the constitutional hysteric: immorality, impulsiveness, susceptibility to suggestion, and emotional excitability. As Barrows, Thiec, Théanton, and Jaap van Ginnekin have shown, Le Bon drew the primary building blocks for his psychology of crowds from Lamarck's evolutionary biology, Charcot's theory of hysterical pathology, and Bernheim's ideas about hypnotic suggestion.[116] According to Ginneken, Le Bon maintained personal friendships with Richet, Paul Régnard (the coauthor of the *Iconographie photographique de la Salpêtrière*), and Luys. Nye states that Le Bon had also attended Charcot's lectures.[117]

The fledgling field of criminology was yet another discipline that appropriated the fin-de-siècle idea of hysteria. The acknowledged expert in this field, if that is the word, was Cesare Lombroso, whose hugely influential *Criminal Man* appeared in the original Italian in 1893. Lombroso here attempted to found the discipline of criminal anthropology, which studied the physical and mental typologies of criminality.[118] For his new science, Lombroso too drew on the most up-to-date medical ideas, images, and terminologies. In his elaborate characterology of criminality there appears the ludicrous category of "the hysterical criminal."[119] Unlike the individuals in his other classifications, however, Lombroso's hysterical criminals were all women. The salient features of the hysterical criminal in the Lombrosian system were again behavioral. She was willful, deceitful, egoistical, and often sexually promiscuous. Moreover, she combined an illegal act of some sort with social and sexual insubordination, especially in her relations with male authority figures, such as employers,

---

[116] Barrows, *Distorting Mirrors*, chap. 7; Ginneken, *Crowds, Psychology, and Politics 1871–1899*, 138–49; Thiec and Théanton, "La foule comme objet de 'science.'"

[117] Ginneken, *Crowds, Psychology, and Politics*, 143, 146; Nye, *Origins of Crowd Psychology*, 30.

[118] César Lombroso, *L'homme criminel: Étude anthropologique et psychiatrique*, 2d French ed., 2 vols. (Paris: Félix Alcan, 1895).

[119] Ibid., vol. 2, Part 3, chap. 6, esp. 412–17.

doctors, or policemen. In Lombroso's mind, the most common crimes involving hysteria were theft and slander, but the disorder could also accompany arson, assault, false accusation, infanticide, and murder.

In Le Bon's crowd psychology and Lombroso's criminal anthropology, hysteria was deployed, in ways that are fairly transparent, to characterize and control groups deemed threatening to the bourgeois professional classes. A study published in 1988 by the American social historian Ruth Harris, however, demonstrates just how subtle and complicated the social and legal applications of the diagnosis could be at this time.[120] Harris discovers that between 1880 and 1910 hundreds of women were brought to trial in the Paris Cour d'assises for committing violent crimes against their husbands and lovers and that the diagnosis of hysteria played a key part in the court proceedings. These cases, she finds, were strikingly stylized. Defendants, invariably middle- or lower-middle-class women, had been abandoned by their fiancés, left pregnant and unprotected by lovers, or subjected to infidelities by their husbands. Desperate pleadings, love letters, and suicidal threats to their partner had proven ineffective, and so, frustrated by official social and legal channels, these women acted. Most commonly, the *criminelle passionnelle* sought out her victim/lover in public—in a café, for example, on the street—and then threw vitriol in his face or shot at him with a pocket revolver. In a majority of cases, the men survived unscathed or suffered only superficial wounds. After the deed, the perpetrators were usually horrified by the violence of their actions and oftentimes gave themselves up to the police. However, in almost every instance, they were acquitted.

Plumbing the pretrial judicial dossiers compiled by the magistrates and physicians who interviewed these women, Harris finds that the hysteria diagnosis appears routinely. A few defendants experienced sensory stigmata or minor hysterical fits, but by and large the conception of the disorder was again attitudinal. In the French forensic context, hysteria was a medical metaphor for willfulness, erraticism, and a lack of emotional self-control. Harris speculates further that *crimes passionnels* became an "accepted" form of female criminality in the late nineteenth century because they involved syntheses of prescribed gender roles. According to the judicial mentality of the time, these crimes merely carried normal female behavior to an unacceptable extreme. Constitutionally volatile, women were unable to control their emotions and lashed out in this childish manner when their matrimonial and sexual lives were threatened.[121] As a

---

[120] Ruth Harris, "Melodrama, Hysteria and Feminine Crimes of Passion in the Fin-de-Siècle," *History Workshop* 15 (Spring 1988): 31–63, repr. with revisions in Harris, *Murders and Madness: Medicine, Law, and Society in the Fin-de-Siècle* (Oxford: Oxford University Press, 1989), chap. 6.

[121] Harris, "Melodrama, Hysteria and Feminine Crimes of Passion," 56.

result, the courts responded protectively, while the press reacted with sympathetic sensationalism. Harris also implies that there was an unspoken collusion between all the parties involved. The ritualized crime of passion was a means for male professionals to administer justice, for bourgeois women to maneuver through patriarchal society, and for the two sexes to negotiate tensions.[122]

Harris's study deals with women in the legal system. A related attempt at maintaining the sexual status quo during these years appeared in the first generation of writings directed against the women's movement. Steven Hause and Anne Kenney have explained that an organized and militant movement for women's rights in France, led by Hubertine Auclert, made its first significant legislative gains in the late 1870s and early 1880s.[123] The issue of female suffrage was for the first time brought to the floor of the national parliament, and a network of secondary schools for girls was mandated by law. The initial entrance of women into the French legal and medical professions also occurred at this time.[124] Numerically, the women's movement during the early Third Republic remained small, and the suffrage for French women did not come until 1944. But the idea of female emancipation now became sufficiently prominent to enter the social and political consciousness of bourgeois Parisians and to arouse a sharp and defensive counterresponse.[125]

And once again, "hysteria" was invoked to oppose and stigmatize the forces of change. We might take as an example Daniel Lesueur's novel *Névrosée*, published in 1884.[126] An antifeminist yarn with a hysterical heroine, *Névrosée* offers a latter-day version of *Madame Bovary* set, somewhat improbably, in the world of Parisian academe. Maxime Dulaure is a brilliant professor at the Collège de France and Étiennette an exceptionally intelligent young woman who at the age of eighteen advances to the study of the biological sciences. A notorious misogynist, Dulaure nonetheless falls in love with Étiennette, who, unlike the other masculine Amazonian women attending his lectures, is slight, blond, and

---

[122] For male crimes of passion, consult Harris, *Murders and Madness*, chap. 8.

[123] Steven C. Hause with Anne R. Kenney, *Women's Suffrage and Social Politics in the French Third Republic* (Princeton: Princeton University Press, 1984), 3–27.

[124] The first French woman to receive a doctorate in medicine was granted her degree by the Paris Faculty of Medicine in 1875; women went on to compete for positions as medical *externes* in 1881 and *internes* in 1885.

[125] Brian H. Harrison, *Separate Spheres: The Opposition to Women's Suffrage in Britain* (London: Cromm Helm, 1978); Peter Gay, *The Bourgeois Experience: Victoria to Freud*, vol. 1, *Education of the Senses* (New York: Oxford University Press, 1984), 169–97; Annelise Maugue, *L'identité masculine en crise au tournant du siècle, 1871–1914* (Paris: Éditions rivages, 1987).

[126] Daniel Lesueur, *Névrosée* (Paris: Alphonse Lemerre, 1890[?]). I was led to Lesueur's book by a reference in Barrows, *Distorting Mirrors*, 178, n. 48.

beautiful. Maxime and Étiennette court and marry, and the union is hailed by the Parisian intellectual community. However, things begin to go awry almost immediately. Étiennette gets pregnant; but she soon becomes frail, sickens, and miscarries. Later, depressed and bored by her life with Maxime, she is increasingly thrilled at the idea of an extramarital affair. She devours questionable literature and eventually gives herself over to a lecherous cousin. (In one scene, Maxime discovers his wife reading *Autour de l'adultère: Psychologie d'une névrosée* and then lectures her about the treatment of sex-obsessed, novel-reading women at the Salpêtrière!)[127] In the end, desperate at having destroyed her beautiful marriage, Étiennette swallows an overdose of morphine and drifts melodramatically to an early death. For its compression of contemporary cultural anxieties into one text, *Névrosée* is unsurpassed. In Lesueur's novel, we have hysteria linked to the national concern over depopulation (described by Nye as the "master pathology" of the time) and, through this, to sin, suicide, sexual perversion, and the new idea of the *femme savante*.[128] The interest of the book heightens when we learn that Daniel Lesueur was a nom de plume of Madame Jeanne Loiseau Lapauze, a popular novelist and playwright who in 1910 was the first woman to be awarded the Légion d'honneur for literature.[129]

During the later nineteenth century, the hysteria diagnosis also made its way into French medical commentaries on specialized sociological problems. The overwhelming majority of cases of hysteria published in France during these years were set in the modern metropolis. Paris in particular was the usual mise en scène, conveying the idea that the pathology was a kind of natural outgrowth of the noxious urban environment. A choice document on this score is Henri Legrand du Saulle's *Les hystériques* (1893).[130] Legrand du Saulle was trained at the Salpêtrière during the 1850s and began his career in the 1860s as a degeneration theorist. During the 1870s and 1880s, he worked as senior admitting psychiatrist at the central police prefecture of Paris. As such, every criminal case brought into city police headquarters, day or night, that was suspected of psychiatric complications passed under his scrutiny. Legrand du Saulle was an important and powerful man, the official interface between the French psychiatric profession and daily Parisian street life.

The most heavily prescriptive commentary about hysteria from the nineteenth century comes from French and German legal psychiatry, and

---

[127] Lesueur, *Névrosée*, 191–92.

[128] Nye, *Crime, Madness, and Politics in Modern France*, 140.

[129] For more on this general subject, refer to Jennifer R. Waelti-Walters, *Feminist Novelists of the Belle Époque: Love as a Lifestyle* (Bloomington: Indiana University Press, 1990).

[130] [Henri] Legrand du Saulle, *Les hystériques: État physique et état mental: Actes insolites, délictueux et criminels* (Paris: J.-B. Baillière, 1883).

in this mold Legrand du Saulle's *Les hystériques* does not dissapoint. His four-hundred-page exposé offers a compendium of urban criminality, including thefts, slanders, arsons, poisonings, abductions, infanticide, sexual crimes, and murders.[131] Of the hundreds of cases discussed in the book, nearly all involve women, and in each case Legrand du Saulle argued that they reveal an underlying hysterical neuropathology. While the purely medical aspects of hysteria were currently being studied exhaustively, Legrand du Saulle comments, "the medico-legal study of hysteria" remained to explore. He urges his professional colleagues to study the disease sociologically, in its "thousand relations with civic life." Furthermore, based on his unique institutional placement, he estimated that at present there were "around 50,000" hysterics in Paris, including 10,000 suffering from convulsions.[132]

In Legrand du Saulle's book, the hysteria diagnosis is applied to some of the most *au courant* social problems in Paris. As Michael Miller and Patricia O'Brien have shown, the final quarter of the 1800s saw the construction of the *grands magasins*, the first generation of department stores such as the Bon Marché, Le Printemps, and La Samaritaine. However, along with the stores came a wave of shoplifting, often on the part of respectable, middle-class women who proved unable to resist the material luxuries in these new emporia. From the age-old moral and legal category of theft there now emerged the clinical entity "kleptomania."[133] In keeping with the times, Legrand du Saulle includes in *Les hystériques* a chapter on "department store thefts" as a new variant of hysteria.[134] He reports that, between 1868 and 1881, he encountered 109 cases of kleptomania at the Paris police prefecture. Forty-one of these women exhibited mild hysterical symptoms while nine suffered from full-fledged "hysterical insanity."[135]

Similarly, since the time of Esquirol the study of suicide was a specialty within French mental medicine. In the face of a national crisis of population, physicians and social scientists during the early Third Republic grew alarmed by the growing number of self-destructions, a concern that culminated in Émile Durkheim's *Suicide* of 1897. Sure enough, Legrand du

---

[131] Ibid., 329–513. For the historical background, consult Pierre Darmon, *Médecins et assassins à la belle époque: La médicalisation du crime* (Paris: Seuil, 1989).

[132] Ibid., 2, 5, 3. Legrand du Saulle's ideas were later elaborated upon in Théodor Andrev, "De l'irresponsabilité des hystériques en matière criminelle" (Ph.D. diss., University of Toulouse, 1905).

[133] Michael B. Miller, *The Bon Marché: Bourgeois Culture and the Department Store, 1869–1920* (Princeton: Princeton University Press, 1981), 197–206; Patricia O'Brien, "The Kleptomania Diagnosis: Bourgeois Women and Theft in Late Nineteenth-Century France," *Journal of Social History* 17 (Fall 1983): 65–77.

[134] Legrand du Saulle, *Les hystériques*, 435–56.

[135] Ibid., 449–50.

Saulle's *Les hystériques* discusses many instances of attempted and completed suicides.[136] His book also includes two chapters devoted to hysteria and marital relations, particularly legal separation and divorce. Not coincidentally, during the very time he was writing, a national parliamentary commission was investigating these issues, which led to the Naquet Law of 1884 relegalizing divorce in France.[137]

Finally, hysteria during these years merged with what were regarded as the most destructive and deadly of social and medical pathologies. As mentioned above, syphilis became a grave threat in many European cities during the late nineteenth and early twentieth centuries. Since syphilis and hysteria were both regarded as neurodegenerative in nature, neurologists, alienists, and venereologists pondered the etiological links between the two diseases.[138] Did syphilitic infections provoke hysterical attacks? Was hysteria an incipient form of venereal disease? Or was syphilis the result of hysterically promiscuous behavior? One physician even warned of a new and virulent hybrid pathology, "hystero-syphilis."[139] The hysteria diagnosis associated similarly with alcoholism.[140]

Along these same lines, Alain Corbin has demonstrated that the conservative medical press of the late nineteenth century posited connections between hysteria, degeneration, and prostitution.[141] Lombroso, for instance, reviewing the data in Legrand du Saulle's book, calculated that 12 percent of the hysterical female population of Paris were prostitutes.[142] Corbin, Charles Bernheimer, and Jann Matlock have also shown that the image of "the hysterical prostitute," often afflicted simultaneously with syphilis or alcoholism, appeared recurrently in French novels and short

[136] Ibid., 360–76.

[137] Ibid., 493–513.

[138] Georges Gilles de la Tourette, "Hystérie et syphilis," *Le progrès médical*, 2d ser., 6, no. 51 (December 17, 1887): 511–12; Alfred Fournier, "Influence de la syphilis sur les névroses et notamment sur l'hystérie," *Gazette des hôpitaux* 61, no. 96 (August 23, 1888): 892–93; Lucien Bertrand, "Contribution à l'étude de l'hystérie dans ses rapports avec la syphilis secondaire" (Ph.D. diss., Medical Faculty, University of Lyon, 1892); Nicolas Kirkoff, "Contribution à l'étude de l'hystérie dans ses rapports avec la syphilis acquise et héréditaire" (Ph.D. diss., University of Paris, 1898).

[139] M. Hudeyo, "Hystéro-syphilis," *Annales de dermatologie et de syphiligraphie*, 3d ser., 3 (1892): 839–42.

[140] Ferdinand Dreyfous, *De l'hystérie alcoolique* (Paris: Delahaye et E. Lecrosnier, 1888); Michel Guillemin, "Contribution à l'étude de l'hystérie alcoolique," *Annales médico-psychologiques*, 7th ser., 7 (March 1888): 230–35; Francisco Salmeron, "De l'hystérie alcoolique" (Ph.D. diss., University of Paris, 1890); Louis Camuzet, "Contribution à l'étude de l'hystérie d'origine hérédo-alcoolique" (Ph.D. diss., University of Paris, 1891).

[141] Alain Corbin, *Les filles de noce: Misère sexuelle et prostitution aux 19e et 20e siècles* (Paris: Aubier Montaigne, 1978), 439–40.

[142] Lombroso, *L'homme criminel* 2: 416.

stories of the second half of the century.[143] Hysteria even made its way into the new academic discipline of French ethnography, where it proved useful, during an era of expansionist colonialism, in the comparative description of European, African, and South Pacific peoples.[144]

The cumulative impression from this summary of sources is that hysteria was nearly ubiquitous in French culture and society a century ago. Many contemporaries shared the impression: in 1880, the physician/novelist Charles Richet observed that "as for mild hysteria [*hystérie légère*] one finds it everywhere,"[145] while two years later, a bemused Guy de Maupassant confirmed that "we are all hysterics."[146] Writing in his diary at the end of the 1880s, Edmond de Goncourt could exclaim: "It is truly a bit unsettling—Léon Daudet would say stupefying—how society women are carrying on right now. They all seem like the *hystériques* of the Salpêtrière, let loose by Charcot upon the world."[147] The clearest statement, however, came from the journalist Jules Claretie, who, in addition to his novel writing, published popular yearly chronicles of social and cultural life in the French capital. In March 1881, Claretie devoted half a chapter to his favorite disease:

> The illness of our age is hysteria. One encounters it everywhere. Everywhere one rubs elbows with it. . . . Studying hysteria, Monsieur Lassegue [*sic*], the illustrious master, and Monsieur Charcot have put their finger on the wound of the day. It is not only enclosed within the gray walls of the Salpêtrière; this singular neurosis with its astonishing effects; it travels the streets and the world.

At the close of the chapter, as he reflects on his Parisian contemporaries, with their extravagant, feverish, and self-absorbed lives, Claretie could only proclaim in exasperation, "Hystériques! Hystériques! Tous hystériques!" "Hysterics, hysterics, all hysterics."[148]

[143] Corbin, *Les filles de noce*, 440, n. 201; Charles Bernheimer, *Figures of Ill Repute: Representing Prostitution in Nineteenth-Century France* (Cambridge: Harvard University Press, 1989), chap. 8; Jann Matlock, *Scenes of Seduction: Prostitution, Hysteria, and Reading Difference in Nineteenth-Century France* (New York: Colombia University Press, 1993).

[144] Dr. Collineau, "Les inférieurs: L'hystérique: Point de vue ethnographique," *L'homme: Journal illustré des sciences anthropologiques*, 4e année, no. 22 (November 25, 1887): 673–87; Philip S. Ray, "L'hystérie chez le nègre," *L'encéphale* 8 (1888): 563–66; Dr. Audry, "Les névroses au point de vue démographique," *Archives d'anthropologie criminelle* 7 (1892): 88–99.

[145] Charles Richet, "Les démoniaques d'aujourd'hui," *Revue des deux mondes* 37, no. 1 (January 15, 1880): 342.

[146] Maupassant, *Chroniques*, 2: 111.

[147] Diary entry of April 17, 1889, in Goncourt, *Journal*, 16: 62.

[148] Jules Claretie, *La vie à Paris: 1881* (Paris: Victor Havard, n.d.), 126, 135. In the prefatory notice to his *Les amours d'un interne* of 1881, Claretie observed similarly that "rien de plus fréquent, dans notre société moderne que ces névroses bizarres qui produisent soit les affolées du monde ou du théâtre, soit les exaltées de la politique et des réunions

A full cultural history of hysteria in turn-of-the-century Europe would be a fascinating enterprise. From the rapid overview above, several points emerge about the metaphorics of hysteria in fin-de-siècle French culture. There is, first, the almost endless extension of the arena of application. From its origins in medicine, hysteria—the word, image, theory, and diagnosis—penetrated one cultural area after another, including fiction, poetry, dramaturgy, historical writing, social and political criticism, sociology, criminology, and anthropology. Indeed, during the height of the French fascination with the subject in the late eighties and early nineties, there seems scarcely to have been an area of activity (cuisine, perhaps?) that was not at one time or another described as hysterical.

Second, the linkages between scientific knowledge and social, political, and cultural ideology during this episode in the history of the disorder were manifest and extensive. In large measure, hysteria's great metaphoric appeal lay in the fact that it helped to make sense of the new conditions of modern urban life emerging suddenly and uncontrollably in later nineteenth-century Europe. To this effect, the stigmatizing functions of the concept are unmistakable. Time and again, the application of the diagnosis centered on the dominant and most threatening social problems of the day. Hypothetical disease etiologies served to project and to rationalize widely held social values and moral attitudes. Moreover, by cloaking normative social and moral judgments in the terminology of contemporary neuropathology and psychopathology, authors sought to increase their explanatory power and cultural authority. The representational power of hysteria was further enhanced by the antiquity and elasticity of the concept: because the disorder had meant so many different things in the past, it was exceptionally easy to apply it to a spectrum of social, political, and cultural phenomena in the present. Ironically, the most stigmatizing of these commentaries about hysteria were frequently delivered in rhetorical tones that were themselves hysterical.

Third, the high degree of interconnectedness between the authors and texts in hysteria's cultural history a hundred years ago is striking. During *les années Charcot*, it is indeed accurate to speak of "a culture of hysteria." In 1894, Nordau, a physician who wrote cultural criticism, lavishly dedicated his *Degeneration* to the criminal anthropologist Lombroso. Lombroso in return dedicated *Le crime: Causes et remèdes* of 1899 to Nordau. Richet, scientist and Salpêtrian, wrote novels about hysteria and nymphomania and penned the preface to the French edition of Lombroso's *L'homme de génie*. Madame Jeanne Loiseau Lesueur was a close companion and perhaps lover of Gustave Le Bon, who reputedly

---

populaires: les déséquilibrées du foyer ou de la place publique. L'hystérie est un peu partout à l'heure où nous sommes."

took their relationship as the model for the plot of *Névrosée*. Claretie, who wrote a six-volume history of the Commune as well as the preface to the book by Cabanes and Nass on "revolutionary neuroses," also attended Charcot's lectures, authored *Les amours d'un interne*, and directed the Théâtre français. And Brouillet's canvas of the school of the Salpêtrière features two novelists (Claretie and Paul Arène), a politician (Alfred Naquet), and an impressionist art critic (Philippe Burty). The teachings of Charcot and his colleagues were picked up by and refracted through the works of all of these authors.

I say refracted through, rather than reflected in, because a fourth point emerging from this study concerns what Debora Silverman has described as "the artistic community's *selective* assimilation of the lessons of the Salpêtrière."[149] The definitions of hysteria advanced by Briquet, Charcot, Bernheim, Freud, and Janet were tolerably precise. Occasionally, as in Mirbeau's *Le jardin des supplices*, a depiction of the malady captured with as much accuracy as possible a specific medical model. However, most creative writers were rarely constrained in this way. Charcot, for example, argued repeatedly against the notions that hysteria was a peculiarly French affliction and that it was on the rise in modern times. Yet Nordau, Zola, and Durkheim interpreted hysteria self-evidently as a "pathology of hypercivilization" and a sign of national decline. Most obvious in this regard were the enduring sexual associations of the disorder. Despite rigorous polemicizing by Briquet, Charcot, and Bernheim, the notion that hysteria in women bred lubricity survived throughout this period in one piece of fiction after another. Generalizing, then, we can say that artists, social scientists, and cultural critics played regular lip service to the medical men of their time, on whom they relied for many of their initial ideas and vocabularies and for the cultural and intellectual prestige that had by then accrued to the medical sciences. However, they did not adhere to medical doctrine of any sort, and much of what they wrote in fact flew in the face of the most important medical teachings of the time.[150] Nonphysicians felt free to employ contemporary medical theory in the service of their own personal, aesthetic, and ideological agendas.

Fifth and finally, the sheer accumulation of meanings of hysteria a hundred years ago is nothing short of extraordinary. During the later 1800s alone, hysteria was employed as a metaphor for artistic experimentation, collective political violence, radical social reformism, foreign nationalism, and a host of other new and unsettling developments. It became shorthand for the irrational, the willess, the incomprehensible, the er-

[149] Silverman, *Art Nouveau in Fin-de-Siècle France*, 334; my italics.

[150] Carroy perceives this point in commenting that imaginative writers created "une esthétique de l'hystérie qui s'appuie sur les descriptions médicales en les subvertissant" ("Hystérie, théâtre, littérature au dix-neuvième siècle," 304).

ratic, the convulsive, the sexual, the female, "the Other." It was a synonym for everything that seemed extreme or frivolous or excessive or absurd about the age. In the arts, where its metaphorical status was acknowledged more openly than in the medical or social sciences, it was employed by establishment and avant-garde writers alike. It was integrated into realist, naturalist, decadent, and symbolist aesthetics. And it was used by writers across the political spectrum. In sociologically oriented narratives, it was applied equally to the individual body and the body politic, and up and down the social scale. It was used to characterize women, socialists, workers, alcoholics, prostitutes, syphilitics, crowds, *les classes dangeureuses*, city life, the French people. It served sometimes as a primary pathology, at other times as a complicating secondary reaction, a behavioral gloss, or a rhetoric. On the eve of psychoanalysis, hysteria was as likely to appear in novels, social science textbooks, and newspaper editorials as in the sickroom, the medical lecture hall, or the physician's study, and with a spectrum of meanings that was every bit as multifarious.

One result of the promiscuous application of the hysteria concept was metaphorical usages that were contradictory or indiscriminate. Zola cited hysteria, epilepsy, and catalepsy interchangeably throughout his novels, except in *Nana*, where he equated it with nymphomania, as did Dubarry. Nordau used hysteria and degeneration synonymously; Taine employed the word to denote a type of collective violence; Galopin construed it as a form of lovesickness; and LeBon saw it as a sign of mass impressionability. The disease's social and cultural symptomatology ranged from Wagner's operas and Manet's choice of pigmentation to rising rates of suicide and the latest wave of shoplifting. Flaubert's entry in his posthumously published *Dictionnaire des idées reçues*—"Hysteria: confuse with nymphomania"—captures both the popular misconceptions of the 1860s and 1870s and the corresponding attempt of post-Briquetian physicians to define the term more rigorously.[151]

Their efforts, of course, were entirely futile. By the penultimate decade of the century, hysteria had become little more than popular phraseology—a quasi-medical *façon de parler*, akin to the Freudian and Jungian jibberish of our own time, *une maladie à la mode*. "In effect," comments Roudinesco, "if *everybody* is hysterical, from Napoleon to the city of Paris, then hysteria is no longer a 'disease' in the classical sense of the word but a neurosis that can strike anyone."[152] As early as the summer of 1882, in the popular newspaper *Gil Blas*, Maupassant playfully protested against just such an eventuality:

[151] Flaubert, *Dictionary of Received Ideas*, in *Bouvard and Pécuchet*, trans. A. J. Krailsheimer (Hammondsworth, Middlesex: Penguin, 1976), 311.
[152] Roudinesco, *Histoire de la psychanalyse*, 1: 77; Roudinesco's italics.

Hysteria, madame, now there is the word of the day. Are you in love? You are a hysteric. Are you indifferent to the passions that arouse other people? You are a hysteric, but a chaste hysteric. Do you cheat on your husband? You're a hysteric, but a sensual hysteric. Do you steal pieces of silk in a shop? Hysterical. You lie at every occasion? Hysterical! (Lying is even the distinguishing characteristic of hysteria.) Are you a glutton? Hysterical! Are you prone to nervousness? Hysterical! You are this, you are that, you are finally what all women have been since the world began? Hysterical! Hysterical, I tell you![153]

By this point, it should be abundantly evident that what the British cultural historian Daniel Pick has written of degenerationism, that its languages eventually became massively overdetermined, holds true for hysteria, too.[154] No less than its history from Briquet to Janet, the story of hysteria from Baudelaire to Mallarmé, from Taine to Tarde, is one of relentless expansion. As in the medical field, hysteria became the wastebasket term of social, political, and cultural commentary. For a half generation, this uninhibited application generated the glorious Age of Hysteria that we associate today with Paris during the *belle époque*. But such a situation could hardly last, and what the French philosopher Gaston Bachelard called "interpretive overload" in time led to the end of this phase in the cultural history of the disease.[155] Hysteria during the European fin de siècle came to mean so many different things that by around 1900 it ceased to mean anything at all. It no longer performed the basic designative function of language. This, I believe, is the final parallel between hysteria's two primary histories. As we saw above, the classic nineteenth-century medical diagnosis "disappeared" in the early twentieth century due in part to extreme clinical overextension. During the same period, hysteria in the arts and in the social and political arenas also exhausted its metaphorical potential and, as a result, receded rapidly from the scene.

[153] Guy de Maupassant, "Une femme," in *Gil Blas* (August 16, 1882), repr. in Maupassant, *Chroniques*, 2: 111.

[154] Pick, *Faces of Degeneration*, 49.

[155] Gaston Bachelard, *Le nouvel esprit scientifique* [1934] (Paris: Presses universitaires de France, 1983), Introduction.

Chapter 4

CULTURES OF HYSTERIA: FUTURE ORIENTATIONS

Conceptualizing Cultural Influence

I N THE preceding chapter, I reviewed descriptively the role of the hysteria metaphor, with particular attention to a single segment of its history. In this final portion of my study, I would like to reflect in rather more interpretive terms on the disorder and its metaphorical traditions. I propose to do so by considering in detail three issues relating to the general project of writing the cultural history of disease. By and large, I will retain my previous focus on the French experience in the 1800s. As stated above, hysteria in France during these decades became part of the general cultural vocabulary of the age. Furthermore, moving in this final quarter of the book from a synchronic to a diachronic approach provides an opportunity to explore comparatively the ways in which a single nosographical concept has operated as a "cultural signifier" in a range of contemporaneous media within a single culture. Finally, this concentration on one nation and century is intended to illustrate my earlier methodological recommendation for studying past disease entities in their intricate, defining contexts of place and time.

Thus far in this study, I have presented the medical and cultural histories of hysteria separately and have considered the actual relations between the two historical categories only implicitly and in fairly broad abstractions. However, the interaction of the two sets of representations is at the heart of hysteria's cultural history, and it is time to examine it squarely. What, for example, is the connection between Shakespeare's *King Lear* of 1606 and Jorden's *Briefe Discourse of a Disease Called the Suffocation of the Mother* of 1603? How was Pope's *Rape of the Lock* influenced by the writings of Robert Burton, Thomas Willis, and Thomas Sydenham? What is the relation between André Brouillet's painting and the writings of Charcot? Or between D. M. Thomas's *The White Hotel* of 1981 and Breuer and Freud's *Studies on Hysteria* from a century earlier?

In 1944, the great medical historian Henry Sigerist noted the intimate interconnections between disease and literature, poetry, painting, and drama and called for their close investigation.[1] During the following generation, studies appeared devoted to medical themes in the lives and

---

[1] Henry Sigerist, *Civilization and Disease* (Ithaca, N.Y.: Cornell University Press, 1944), esp. 184–85, 191–94.

works of individual literary figures;[2] but the general historical study of medicine and literature failed to attract much scholarly attention. Then in 1981, the American literary historian George Rousseau published a highly suggestive and analytically sophisticated study in the history of science journal *Isis*.[3] Picking up on Sigerist's call, Rousseau appealed to literary historians, science historians, and cultural historians alike to pursue this subject in depth. In the past few years, a flurry of far-ranging essay collections by European and North American scholars has done precisely that.[4] The journal *Literature and Medicine* was established in 1982, and the Society for Literature and Science, which produces an annual newsletter and bibliography, was founded in 1985. Most recently, the University of Wisconsin Press has announced a new book series, Science and Literature. In the early 1990s, the exploration of the disciplinary interface between the sciences and creative literature has become a major, cross-disciplinary concern.

Collectively, this recent scholarship explores the ways in which men and women of letters and the arts have acquired knowledge of medical science and practice. A surprising number of writers—Rabelais, Smollett, Keats, Chekhov, Breton, Céline, William Carlos Williams—were personally trained in medicine and later drew on this education in their artistic productions. Other authors, such as Flaubert, Proust, Hemingway, and Auden, had family members who were physicians and whose work they observed closely. Some literary intellectuals had close medical acquaintances (for instance, the Goncourt brothers, and Alphonse and Léon

[2] Majorie Hope Nicolson, *Newton Demands the Muse* (Princeton: Princeton University Press, 1946); L. Binet and P. Vallery-Radot, *Médecine et littérature* (Paris: Expansion scientifique française, 1963); Marjorie Hope Nicolson and George Rousseau, *This Long Disease My Life: Alexander Pope and the Sciences* (Princeton: Princeton University Press, 1968); John B. Lyons *James Joyce and Medicine* (Dublin, Dolmen Press, 1973); Roland Antonioli, *Rabelais et la médecine* (Geneva: Dvos, 1976); Kenneth Dewhurst and Nigel Reeves, *Friedrich Schiller: Medicine, Psychology, and Literature* (Berkeley: Univ. of California Press, 1978); Bernard Straus, *Maladies of Marcel Proust: Doctors and Disease in His Life and Work* (New York: Holmes and Meier, 1980).

[3] G. S. Rousseau, "Literature and Medicine: The State of the Field," *Isis* 72, no. 263 (September 1981): 406–24. See also idem, "Medicine and the Muses: An Approach to Literature and Medicine," in Marie Roberts and Roy Porter, eds., *Medicine and Literature* (London: Routledge, 1992), 23–57.

[4] Joanne Trautmann, ed., *Healing Arts in Dialogue: Medicine and Literature* (Carbondale: Southern Illinois University Press, 1981); George Levine, ed., *One Culture: Essays in Science and Literature* (Madison: University of Wisconsin Press, 1987); idem, ed., *Realism and Representation: Essays on the Problem of Realism in Relation to Science, Literature, and Culture* (Madison: University of Wisconsin, 1992); Frederick Amrine, ed., *Literature and Science as Modes of Expression* (Dordrecht: Kluwer Academic Publishers, 1989); Stuart Peterfreund, ed., *Literature and Science: Theory and Practice* (Boston: Northeastern University Press, 1990); Roberts and Porter, *Literature and Medicine during the Eighteenth Century*.

Daudet) while others, like Sterne and Zola, researched systematically in the medical writings of their day. Still others—Flaubert and Dostoevsky come to mind—suffered personally from diseases they sought to depict fictionally. In a similar vein, the ways in which medicine has figured in the artistic work of writers have been diverse. Most commonly, this has involved the inclusion of medical characters (i.e., doctors and nurses) in a novel or short story or descriptions of disease and death. In certain texts, such as Thomas Mann's *The Magic Mountain*, Albert Camus's *The Plague*, Céline's *Nord*, and Alexander Solzhenitsyn's *Cancer Ward*, an author has created a medical institution or environment that serves as a microcosm of a larger "sick" world.[5]

In recent writings on literature and medicine, scholars have had comparatively little to say about literature and *psychological* medicine, which is particularly surprising given the striking affinities between the two. The links between imaginative literature and psychiatry are arguably richer and more complex than between literature and any other branch of the medical sciences. Literature, psychiatry, and psychology share the subject matter of the human emotions and the private life of the mind. They are all centrally concerned with the portrayal of the human personality as it evolves over time and the representation of states of mind through the medium of language. Psychiatrists, psychologists, and psychoanalysts often rely more on intuition and introspection in their role as therapists than do other medical specialists—again like poets and novelists. And the stylistic similarities between a psychiatric case history and fictional narrative have been widely commented upon. Moreover, because psychiatry is among the so-called soft medical sciences, it is open to other areas of medical and nonmedical influence. In other words, in its subject matter, methodologies, and epistemological status, psychology and psychiatry bridge the worlds of medical science and human science. As a consequence, the possibilities of cultural interaction between literature and this branch of medicine are particularly great.

To date, scholarship in this emergent field has dealt with literary descriptions of psychiatrists and patients; representations of madness in literary texts; the portrayal of life in mental institutions; the writings of so-called mad persons; and the extreme mental states of the imaginative writer.[6] Occasionally, a psychological theorist provides a model of per-

---

[5] For a selection of writings in these categories, see *The Physician in Literature*, ed. Norman Cousins (Philadelphia: Saunders Press, 1982).

[6] Bergen Evans, *The Psychiatry of Robert Burton* (New York: Columbia University Press, 1944); Irving I. Edgar, *Shakespeare, Medicine and Psychiatry* (New York: Philosophical Library, 1970); Shoshana Felman, *La folie et la chose littéraire* (Paris: Éditions du Seuil, 1978); Lillian Feder, *Madness in Literature* (Princeton: Princeton University Press, 1980); Stephen Trombley, *"All that Summer She Was Mad": Virginia Woolf and Her Doctors*

sonality or of consciousness bearing a strong resemblance to the style of self-consciousness developed in a work of art. (Examples here are the relations between Freud and D. H. Lawrence, Janet and Proust, or Lacan and a number of contemporary French writers). In a few cases, a medical theory of hysteria has determined the actual structure of a novel, as in Thomas's *The White Hotel.*

Each of these modes of cultural interaction will no doubt repay investigation by the historian of hysteria. However, I believe that what would be most valuable at this point is to examine more thoroughly the dynamics of cultural influence themselves in the medicine-literature relation. As Rousseau has pointed out, nearly all existing scholarship on medicine and literature traffics in vague biographical "parallels" between writers and doctors or descriptive similarities between the two types of text. Moreover, the direction of cultural influence projected in these studies (as well, incidentally, as in earlier sections of this book) is always the same: it has invariably been assumed that, at least since the seventeenth century, ideas have originated in the realm of the sciences and then spread out concentrically to various nonscientific arenas. "The arrows of influence in this body of scholarship are always drawn in one direction," Rousseau observes, "*from* medicine *to* literature. . . . Although literary scholars may probe medical texts for their influence on literature, they do not probe medical texts for the influence of literature; at least they have not as yet. They have not presumed that the sources of medical hypotheses may have derived from plays, novels, and poems."[7] Furthermore, existing scholarly work has been conducted chiefly by literary critics and literary historians whose aim, naturally enough, has been to elucidate literary texts.

The need to modify this approach, not least in the historical study of literature and psychiatry, is now being realized. Rousseau has demonstrated elsewhere the interaction of medical and literary writings about

---

(London: Junction Books, 1981); D. A. Peterson, ed., *A Mad People's History of Madness* (Pittsburgh: University of Pittsburgh Press, 1982); Peter Graham, ed., *Literature and Medicine* (1985), vol. 4, *Psychiatry and Literature*; Roy Porter, "Bedlam and Parnassus: Mad People's Writing in Georgian England," in Levine, *One Culture*, 258–86; Ekbert Fass, *Retreat into the Mind: Victorian Poetry and the Rise of Psychiatry* (Princeton: Princeton University Press, 1988); John M. MacGregor, *The Discovery of the Art of the Insane* (Princeton: Princeton University Press, 1991); Judith Ryan, *Vanishing Subject: Early Psychology and Literary Modernism* (Chicago: University of Chicago Press, 1991); George MacLennon, *Lucid Interval: Subjective Writing and Madness in History* (Rutherford, N.J.: Fairleigh Dickinson University Press, 1992); Allan Ingram, *The Madhouse of Language: Writing and Reading Madness in the Eighteenth Century* (London: Routledge, 1992); Michael Neve, "Medicine and Literature," in W. F. Bynum and Roy Porter, eds., *Companion Encyclopedia of the History of Medicine*, vol. 2 (London: Routledge, 1994), 1520–35.

[7] Rousseau, "Literature and Medicine," 409, 410; Rousseau's italics.

the nervous distempers in eighteenth-century Britain.[8] The French literary historian Jacques Borel has studied the interplay of literary and psychiatric themes and vocabularies in the writings of Esquirol and Honoré de Balzac.[9] And Freud scholars have long been sensitive to the mutual influences between Freud and the literary culture of his time.[10] With nineteenth-century France in mind, Carroy insisted in 1982 that relations between the arts and the medical sciences are "far from being a popularization of concepts pure and simple." The chronicle of these relations is "the story of encounters, but also one of misunderstandings, between doctors and literati. Psychiatric and novelistic narratives follow parallel trajectories, but also observe lines of development running askew in which men of letters go in other directions, and farther even, than the 'men of science.'"[11] In the same vein, Janet Beizer has insisted that "the literary proliferation of a disease cannot be explained as a mere reflection of a medical reality." "Such an approach presupposes . . . that there is a hierarchic relationship between medical and literary discourses and that the medical definition is the founding concept, the 'proper' sense from which literary representations of hysteria depart." In place of this view, Beizer proclaims the urgent need "to re-read the relationship between the medical and literary discourses of hysteria."[12]

In an attempt to develop the project of a fuller, multidimensional cultural history of hysteria, as set out by Rousseau, Carroy, and Beizer, I would like now to consider in some detail an instance in the history of hysteria in which the "arrows of influence" ran in the opposite direction, *from* literature *to* medicine. This is a case in which fictional literature exerted an influence through a powerful model of characterization and in which a work of imaginative fiction affected—I believe, decisively—the formulation of professional diagnostic theory.

[8] George Rousseau, "The Discourses of the Psyche," in *Enlightenment Crossings: Pre- and Post-Modern Discourses: Anthropological* (Manchester: Manchester University Press, 1991), 61–121.

[9] Jacques Borel, *Médecine et psychiatrie balzaciennes: La science dans le roman* (Paris: J. Corti, 1971).

[10] From recent book-length studies, consider Sabine Prokhoris, *La cuisine de la sorcière* (Paris: Aubier, 1988); Barry Richards, *Images of Freud: Cultural Responses to Psychoanalysis* (New York: St. Martin's Press, 1989); and Alexander Grinstein, *Freud at the Crossroads* (Madison, Conn.: International Universities Press, 1990). On the theme of hysteria in particular: Bernd Urban, "Schnitzler and Freud as Doubles: Poetic Intuition and Early Research on Hysteria," *Psychoanalytic Review* 65, no. 1 (Spring 1978): 131–65.

[11] Carroy, "Hystérie, théâtre, littérature," 300.

[12] Beizer, "Project Description" for *Ventriloquized Bodies* and abstract of "Doctors and Writers: The Narrative Conversion of Hysteria" (Paper delivered at the Thirteenth Annual Meeting of the Colloquium in Nineteenth-Century French Studies, Northwestern University, October 22–24, 1987).

In chapter 3, I discussed the analyses by Carter and Carroy of Gustave Flaubert's *Madame Bovary*. Emma Bovary, I noted there, was most memorable as a study in temperament. Furthermore, I pointed out that Baudelaire was the first person to declare Emma hysterical, that contemporary critics found the label compelling, and that subsequent readers have largely adopted it. Here is a lengthy excerpt, combined from a number of passages in the first half of *Madame Bovary*, that provides a sense of Emma's distinctive *caractère*:

> Emma was becoming capricious, hard to please. She would order special dishes for herself and then not touch them; one day she would drink nothing but fresh milk; the next, cups of tea by the dozen. Often she refused absolutely to go out; then she would feel stifled, open the windows, change to a light dress. . . . She no longer hid her scorn for anything or anyone; and she was beginning now and then to express peculiar opinions, condemning what everyone else approved and approving things that were perverse and immoral—a way of talking that made her husband stare at her wide-eyed. . . . She grew pale and developed palpitations. . . . Some days she chattered endlessly, almost feverishly; and such a period of overexcitement would suddenly be followed by a torpor in which she neither spoke nor moved. . . . Her carnal desires, her cravings for money, and the fits of depression engendered by her love gradually merged into a single torment. . . . She reacted to the drabness of her home by indulging in daydreams of luxury and to matrimonial caresses by adulterous desires. . . . Such a crisis always left her shattered, gasping, prostrate, sobbing to herself, tears streaming down her face. . . . A woman who had assumed such a burden of sacrifice was certainly entitled to indulge herself a little. She bought herself a Gothic *prie-dieu* and in a month spent fourteen francs on lemons to blanch her fingernails; she wrote to Rouen for a blue cashmere dress; and at Lheureux's she chose the finest of his scarves. . . . She decided to learn Italian; she bought dictionaries, a grammar, a supply of paper. She went in for serious reading—history and philosophy. . . . But her books were like her many pieces of needlepoint: barely begun, they were tossed into the cupboard; she started them, abandoned them, discarded them in favor of new ones. . . . "I have a lover! I have a lover!" she kept repeating to herself, reveling in the thought as though she were beginning a second puberty. At last she was going to know the joys of love, the fever of the happiness she had despaired of. She was entering a marvelous realm where all would be passion, ectasy, rapture. . . . She remembered the heroines of novels she had read, and the lyrical legion of those adulterous women began to sing in her memory with sisterly voices that enchanted her. Now she saw herself as one of those *amoureuses* whom she had so envied: she was becoming, in reality, one of that gallery of fictional figures; the long dream of her youth was coming true.[13]

[13] *Madame Bovary*, in *Oeuvres complètes de Flaubert*, 1: 105, 145, 146, 161, 194, 195; *Madame Bovary*, trans. Steegmuller, 74, 75, 122, 123, 141, 183.

With this background of Flaubert's nimble, descriptive prose, let us now pull back from *Madame Bovary* and turn to the medical culture of the time, including contemporary scientific writing about hysteria. Specifically, I want to investigate, not what medical authors were writing about hysteria *before* Flaubert wrote *Madame Bovary* (i.e., how medical texts "influenced" the novel) but what they wrote *after* the publication of Flaubert's book in 1857.

In the intellectual history of hysteria, the salient development in French medicine between Pierre Briquet's treatise of 1859 and Charcot's first case histories was the emergence of the interconnected concepts of "hysterical insanity" and "the hysterical constitution." Individual traits composing these categories had been present in medical writings since the 1600s, but in earlier works they were ancillary and fragmentary features of the diagnosis. During the third quarter of the nineteenth century, however, the alleged behavioral aspects of hysteria came to the fore and for the first time were granted central, at times pathognomonic, status. The notion of hysterical character pathology, as an independent nosological concept, emerged. Veith notes this development and cites as the beginnings of the idea in France a speech delivered by Dr. Jules Falret in 1866.[14] In a more recent study, Chris Alam and Harold Merskey emphasize the contributions of Parisian alienists later in the century.[15]

In truth, the doctrine of the hysterical disposition appeared in French psychiatric discourse in two sets of nineteenth-century texts: a series of chapters in psychiatric textbooks published during the 1860s and a cluster of journal articles from the early 1880s. The first explicit enunciation of the concept of hysterical temperamentality appeared in 1860 in B. A. Morel's *Traité des maladies mentales*.[16] His classic study of degeneration three years behind him, Morel turned to compiling a psychiatric textbook intended to supplant the earlier treatise of Esquirol. In a chapter of the book, Morel introduced the category of "folie hystérique," hysterical madness. In this context, Morel was primarily concerned with hysteria as a precursory form of insanity. He claimed, however, that hysterical insanity in this incipient form manifested itself in exaggerated nervousness and peculiarities of behavior. Of one recent hysterical patient, Morel commented that "her character has always been sulky, capricious, and fantastical. . . . She cried and laughed for no reason and yielded early on to all kinds of bizarreries and eccentricities." Other "irregularities of character" that accompanied the "hysteropathic state," according to Morel's

[14] Veith, *Hysteria*, 210–12.

[15] Chris N. Alam and H. Merskey, "The Development of the Hysterical Personality," *History of Psychiatry* 3, no. 10 (June 1992): 135–65.

[16] B[énédict] A[uguste] Morel, *Traité des maladies mentales* (Paris: Victor Masson, 1860), book 4, chap. 3, esp. 672–91.

definition, were "transitory ideas," "fantastical schemes," "a childish naiveté," and "a tendency to suicide."[17]

In the wake of Briquet's authoritative study published the preceding year, Morel was at pains officially to deemphasize the role of sexuality in the disorder. Nevertheless, he interpreted hysteria as overwhelmingly female, and he related it to gynecological, especially menstrual, problems. He also observed that the hysterical temperament was accompanied in many cases by an unfocused nongenital eroticism. The causes of the erotic forms of the condition, he projected, included "betrayed love," "a vicious education," and "exaggeration of the religious sentiment."[18] Morel mentioned in addition that hysterical women often proved insupportable to those near to them, including parents, friends, husband, and children.

In Morel's 1860 textbook, the theory of hysterical personality is nascent, but no more. Other physicians, however, including several of his own students, followed in Morel's footsteps and elaborated on his novel concept. In 1862, Louis-Victor Marcé, an alienist at the Bicêtre hospital on the outskirts of Paris, published his own *Traité pratique des maladies mentales*. Marcé endorsed the Morelian concept of hysterical insanity; but he placed greater emphasis on the "erotico-religious" component of the disorder.[19] He also observed "the tendency on the part of hysterics to invent fanciful and extravagant stories," "their fleeting and irresistible desires which stop at nothing," and "the erotic ideas which complicate the original illness and become the point of departure for inexplicable passions."[20]

Two years later, in 1864, Alexandre Axenfeld, in his encyclopedic treatise on the neuroses, followed Briquet in ascribing to hysteria a mixed neurological and psychological symptomatology. But within the composite province of hysteria, Axenfeld maintained, one could isolate a distinct condition that he proposed to label "hystericism" ("hystéricisme"). The signs of hystericism were manifold, but foremost were egocentricity, a vivid imagination, emotional lability, and chronic nervousness. Axenfeld also asserted that in contrast to pure hysteria, the diffuse neurotic state of hystericism was nearly universal in the female sex.[21]

As Veith determined, the most detailed formulation of the idea of hysterical characterology came in 1866 with a lecture by Jules Falret to the

---

[17] Ibid., 676, 679, 682, 681.

[18] Ibid., 681.

[19] L.-V. Marcé, "De l'hystérie," in *Traité pratique des maladies mentales* (Paris: J.-B. Baillière, 1862), 553–576, esp. 562–63 and 567–68.

[20] Ibid., 563.

[21] [Alexandre] Axenfeld, *Des névroses* (Paris: Germer Baillière, 1864), 474–94 and 604–72, esp. 479–85.

Paris Société médico-psychologique.[22] The son of the alienist Jean-Pierre Falret, Jules Falret was then emerging as a leading member in his own right of the French psychiatric community. Primarily known up to that point for his work on epilepsy and general paralysis, Falret *fils* now began to branch out into more general psychiatric subjects. At a meeting of the Society on January 8, 1866, he spoke on "moral madness" and devoted a portion of the address to his own new theory of "hysterical insanity."[23] Falret criticized Morel and his adherents for defining the concept too broadly. Independent of full-fledged hysterical insanity, he contended, there occurred a milder, nonpsychotic form of the disorder: "la folie raisonnante des hystériques," "the reasoning madness of hysterics." "To study clinically this variety of mental illness," Falret continued, "it is necessary to begin by distinguishing carefully what one might call the hysterical character from hysterical insanity in the true sense of the word."[24] Following Axenfeld, Falret proposed that "the special intellectual and moral symptoms relating to hysterical neurosis" be separated from both the well-known physical manifestations of the disease, such as convulsions, as well as from the psychotic forms requiring institutionalization. In other words, Falret was the first physician to decouple clinically the physical from the affective aspects of hysteria and to elevate the latter into an autonomous diagnostic entity.

In his 1866 presentation, Falret described his vision of the hysterical character in detail:

> All doctors who have observed many women afflicted with hysteria, all those who have had the misfortune to share their lives with them, know perfectly that they have, as part of their character and intelligence, a moral physiognomy which is peculiar to them and which allows one to recognize in them the existence of this illness, even before observing the physical symptoms. . . . The primary character trait belonging to hysterics is first the great mobility of their psychological temperament at the time one is observing them. They pass alternately and at very frequent intervals from excitation to depression, just as, on a physical level, they shift erratically from an outburst of laughter to one of tears. They become enthusiastic with ardor and passion for a person or object they want to possess at any cost; they stop at nothing, at no sacrifice to achieve their goal. . . . This is their character in all things: fantastical and capricious, with an extreme mobility of ideas and sentiments. . . . Another equally important characteristic of hysterics is their love of contradiction and argument. . . . Ob-

---

[22] Jules Falret, "Folie raisonnante ou folie morale" [1866], repr. in *Études cliniques sur les maladies mentales et nerveuses* (Paris: J.-B. Baillière, 1890), 475–525.

[23] Ibid., 499–507.

[24] Ibid., 500.

stinacy and passive resistance assume in them a truly sickly quality. . . . Another important fact . . . is their spirit of duplicity and lying. . . . They make up veritable novels in which they intercalate, often cleverly and in an inextricable manner, the true and the false in a way so as to fool even the most perceptive person. . . . They affect airs of piety and devotion and succeed in passing themselves off for saints while in secret abandoning themselves to the most shameful actions and at home making the most violent scenes with their husbands and children, scenes in which they make crude and sometimes obscene remarks and engage in the most disruptive acts. . . . Finally, hysterical women are generally dreamy and romantic [romanesque], disposed to allow the fantasies of their imagination to predominate over the needs and necessities of real life. They also frequently have pronounced erotic tendencies, although this typical disposition has often been exaggerated, for they are usually coquettes and braggarts rather than truly ardent and sexual.[25]

In the years following Falret's lecture, the clinical portrait of the hysterical temperament was further embroidered within French mental medicine. In 1869, J.-J. Moreau de Tours published his own monograph on hysteria.[26] For him, too, hysteria was a variety of "neuropathic insanity." However, Moreau de Tours proposed that hysterical insanity did not affect the intellectual faculties of the patient, which Falret had implicated, but solely the "moral" sphere. Its symptoms included a high degree of impressionability, "irresistibility of penchants," exaggerated erotic impulses, sexual insatiability, and a tendency to suicidal threats or actions.[27] Along the same lines, the internist, pathologist, and former dean of the Paris Medical Faculty, Ambroise Tardieu, proposed in 1872 that hysterical insanity was strictly limited to adult and adolescent females.[28] The victim of hysterical madness, Tardieu held, was not genuinely insane but suffered from "the perversion of the affective faculties." He also dissented strongly from Briquet: the hysteric nearly always manifested a certain sexual restlessness, "the caresses of her husband having failed to satisfy her," and could collapse at any time into wanton nymphomania.[29]

Following Tardieu's book, Charcot blazed onto the European medical scene with his comprehensive neurologization of the hysteria diagnosis.

[25] Ibid., 500–503.

[26] Jacques-Joseph Moreau (de Tours), *Traité pratique de la folie névropathique (vulgo hystérique)* (Paris: Germer Baillière, 1869). This was an expansion of Moreau de Tours's earlier "De la folie hystérique, et de quelques phénomènes nerveux propres à l'hystérie (convulsive), à l'hystéro-épilepsie et à l'épilepsie," *L'union médicale* 27 (June–July, 1865). See esp. 178–84.

[27] Moreau de Tours, *Traité pratique de la folie*, 163–70.

[28] Ambroise Tardieu, *Étude médico-légale sur la folie* (Paris: J.-B. Baillière, 1872), 159–74.

[29] Ibid., 163.

During the remainder of the 1870s, the theory of hysterical character pathology receded.[30] However, in the early 1880s, the psychiatric community re-asserted itself, and several medical authors returned to the subject. Shorn of its earlier association with the insanities, and more manifest in its misogyny, the concept of the hysterical constitution now received a number of influential restatements.

In 1881, Charles Lasègue, abandoning his earlier study of the hysterias based on individual bodily symptoms, argued that the central feature of the disease was a pathological tendency to lying.[31] A year later, Henri Huchard repeated Falret's formulation almost verbatim in a widely cited article in the *Archives de neurologie*. In a section devoted to "the spirit of duplicity, lying, and simulation," Huchard cited approvingly Morel's earlier statements about the treachery of female hysterics in the face of masculine authority: "they . . . deceive their husbands and their parents as well as their doctors."[32] In 1880, Charles Richet again took up the topic and attempted to universalize the theory of hysterical character. "This mild hysteria is not a real disease," Richet pronounced. "It is one of the varieties of the female character. One could even say that hysterics are more woman than other women [*On peut même dire que les hystériques sont femmes plus que les autres femmes*]."[33] Typical of the biographies of hysterical women, Richet professed further, are "shattered dreams, lost illusions, [and] chimerical hopes." "In Paris, for example, and in the large towns," he added, "where the young women of the lower classes and the *petite bourgeoisie* receive an education superior to their social station, hysteria is very frequent. Indeed, it is often very difficult to find the ideal husband of their dreams."[34] From the writings of Morel, Axenfeld, Marcé, Falret, Lasègue, Huchard, and Richet, the idea of the female hysterical character entered the emerging social sciences, including Legrand du Saulle's medical-legal *Les hystériques* and the criminological writings of Lombroso.

Such are the medical-historical origins and early development of the idea of hysterical temperamentality in brief. Two questions now immediately present themselves: after centuries of medical theorizing, why did a specifically characterological conceptualization of hysteria appear on

---

[30] The one explicit statement of the concept I have found during the later seventies is Henri Taguet, "Du suicide dans l'hystérie," *Annales médico-psychologiques*, 5th ser., 17 (May 1877): 346–59.

[31] Charles Lasègue, "Les hystériques, leur perversité, leurs mensonges," *Annales médico-psychologiques*, 6th ser., 6 (July 1881): 111–18.

[32] Henri Huchard, "Caractère, moeurs, état mental des hystériques," *Archives de neurologie* 3, no. 8 (March 1882): 194. The essay was slightly recast later that year in Axenfeld and Huchard, *Traité des névroses*, 2d ed., rev. and enl. (Paris: Germer Baillière, 1882).

[33] Richet, "Les démoniaques d'aujourd'hui," 346.

[34] Ibid., 345–46.

the French medical scene during the third quarter of the nineteenth century? And why did this theory assume the particular form that it did? Unquestionably, several factors contributed to this strand of thinking about the disease;[35] but, as readers will doubtless have divined, I want to suggest that a significant influence on the formation of the concept was what Hippolyte Bernheim in 1907 called "l'hystérique de roman," "the hysteric of the novel," and in particular Flaubert's Emma Bovary.[36]

The historical circumstances for such an interpretation are in fact powerfully suggestive: *Madame Bovary* was published in expurgated and serialized form in the *Revue de Paris* during the autumn and early winter of 1856 and in a full and uncensored version during the spring of 1857—in other words, just two to three years prior to the initiation of this line of medical theorization. The well-known post-Enlightenment bifurcation of the arts and the sciences was slow and partial, and in the cultural hothouse of nineteenth-century Paris in particular, the traffic in ideas and images between the arts and the sciences remained heavy and constant. French literary, medical, and scientific elites of the time interacted far more extensively than their counterparts do today. Furthermore, a much-publicized censorship trial conducted by the government of Louis Napoleon made of Flaubert's novel an immediate *succès de scandale* throughout the French capital. Doctors in the Parisian medical establishment of the 1860s almost certainly would have been familiar with the book.[37]

Most conspicuous, however, are the overwhelming descriptive congruences between the image of the hysteric as recorded in the two sets of representations, the literary and the medical. Both Flaubert in *Madame Bovary* and French physicians writing in the fifteen years following the publication of the novel placed egoism, vanity, self-indulgence, emotional volatility, and self-dramatization at the center of their depictions. Moreover, readers with a fresh memory of the novel will likely have noticed many more detailed correspondences: both Flaubert's protagonist and the hysterical patients discussed by Morel, Marcé, Falret, and Moreau de

[35] They include a counterresponse to Briquet's treatise of 1859, with its desexualized model of hysteria; the translation of the second edition of Wilhelm Griesinger's psychiatric textbook, *Die Pathologie und Therapie der psychischen Krankheiten* (1861) into French in 1865; the transition from physical to mental typologies within the European mental sciences during the mid-nineteenth century; a negative reaction to the assertive political role of French women during the revolutionary upheaval of 1848; and the general social and moral conservatism of the Second Empire.

[36] Hippolyte Bernheim, "Définition et nature de l'hystérie," in *Comptes rendus du congrès des médecins aliénistes et neurologistes de France et des pays de langue française* (Geneva and Lausanne, August 1–7, 1907), 2 vols. (Paris: Masson, 1907), 2: 388.

[37] Dominick LaCapra, *Madame Bovary on Trial* (Ithaca, N.Y.: Cornell University Press, 1982).

Tours exhibited selfish and whimsical behaviors, a cycle of erotic and religious enthusiasms, frivolity in financial matters, a superficial and abortive seductiveness, threats of suicide, irresponsibility toward domestic duties, an attraction to orgiastic literature, and a tendency to lie to their husbands. Like Emma Bovary, the patients were often lost in a life of dreams and were greatly frustrated in their amorous aspirations. Like her also, they experienced a progressive worsening of their moral and psychological condition, degenerating into disease and death. In short, the doctrine of the hysterical character, as it emerged in French psychiatric thought during the 1860s, reads remarkably like a codification into diagnostic theory of the fictional character of Emma Bovary.

And why, we ask next, should a work of fiction produced by a previously little-known author have generated such a potent response from the medical community of the time? In part, no doubt, because of the power of Flaubert's characterization; in part because of the aforementioned public trial; and in part because of the presence of medical personalities in the novel. However, I would venture that the response may also have reflected a more negative reaction to the controversial contents of the book itself. As is well known, the judicial establishment of the Second Empire responded to Flaubert's novel, and in particular to its neutral, noncondemnatory presentation of Emma's adulterous actions, as an intolerable moral offense and an attack on the contemporary establishment. As a consequence, it attempted to censor the book. In a parallel way, it is likely that Morel, Falret, Marcé, and others of their kind, as nineteenth-century male bourgeois physicians, found the book at least as inflammatory as did their professional counterparts in the courts.

It might be recalled that Flaubert's novel is set in the world of French provincial medicine, and the depiction of that world is largely unflattering. Emma's husband, Charles Bovary, is a lowly country doctor, an *officier de santé*. Flaubert establishes Charles's boorishness and incompetence with merciless clarity, the scene of the bungled clubfoot operation being only the most graphic example of this characterization. Throughout the story, Emma demeans her husband and his work, with Flaubert conveying the sense that Charles's poor performance in the eyes of his wife is both professional and sexual. The figure of Homais, the pompous village pharmacist endlessly spouting positivist clichés, is a memorable secondary figure.

The social and professional world of Parisian alienists was remote from that of Charles Bovary; nevertheless, as physician-husbands themselves, ministering to intractable female patients, at a time when their own medical specialty was in precarious professional repute, French psychiatrists in the later 1850s and 1860s might well respond sympathetically and defensively to the plight of the hapless Charles Bovary at the hands of his habitually and destructively hysterical wife. We can speculate further that this initial unease was reinforced over the next decade and a half by a raft of sensationalistic popularizations of Flaubert's story—beginning with Ernest Feydeau's *Fanny* of 1858—that featured their own cast of hysterical femmes fatales. The second wave of medical writings on the hysterical character dating from the early 1880s may have been further provoked in part by early organized feminist challenges to the structures of professional Parisian authority, including to the medical faculties, which occurred during these same years. Physicians in 1857, of course, could not literally censor Flaubert's book as had their brethren in the legal profession. However, they could respond in the same way as the British physician Robert Brudenell Carter had when confronted several years earlier with unmanageable hysterical patients, or as Freud later would when grappling with Dora: with derogatory medical theorization. The two most important and powerful professions in Second Empire France, then, took notice of Flaubert's female protagonist, and interestingly, both of their reactions took the form of remoralizations. Like their contemporaries in the law, Parisian psychiatrists found the character of Emma Bovary all too believable, and they responded through pathologization: they elevated, or rather degraded, Emma into a psychiatric category, a "personality type."

And did nineteenth-century medical writers acknowledge this literary influence on their thinking? By and large, no, and for obvious reasons. The 1800s witnessed the coming of a new "scientific medicine" based on laboratory research in pathology and physiology. Enmeshed in the professionalizing process of the later nineteenth century, physicians were then acutely conscious of their scientific credentials. Officially speaking, the sole source of their knowledge was the empirical findings of the clinic. In the rhetoric of disciplinary self-presentation, nonclinical sources of insight into the world of human pathology—and certainly literary inspiration—were beyond acknowledgment. There was, however, a significant exception to this rule.

Richet, it will be recalled, was both a physician and a novelist, who during the 1880s wrote about hysteria concurrently in the scientific/empirical and literary/subjective modes. Perhaps because of his dual professional activities and sensibilities, he was able momentarily to break through the official silence on this matter.[38] In 1880, Richet published in the *Revue des deux mondes*, a prominent literary and cultural journal, a two-part article on "demoniacs past and present" in which he discussed the latest medical findings about hysteria, hypnosis, and somnambulism.[39] In this

---

[38] Richet, however, was by no means the only hysteria doctor who applied himself seriously in the arts. Both Alfred Binet and H.-E. Beaunis wrote novels under pseudonyms.

[39] Richet, "Les démoniaques d'aujourd'hui"; idem, "Les démoniaques d'autrefois."

context, Richet lamented the myriad popular misconceptions about these subjects and traced many of the erroneous beliefs in circulation to the deleterious influence of contemporary fiction. However, he goes on to note how closely recent clinical and fictional representations of hysteria had come to resemble each other. "Novelists have understood the benefit to be drawn from the study of this character type. In recent times especially, since the descriptive style has become fashionable, and since writers have undertaken to combine art and pathology, there have been numerous portraits of attacks of hysteria or of hysterical figures."[40] Richet proceeds to specify five characters from contemporary French fiction whom he believes exemplify the hysterical temperament as defined medically, including figures from works by the Goncourt brothers, Octave Feuillet, Anatole France, Albert Delpit, and an unidentified fifth author. He then closes with this:

> But of all the hysterics whose story the novelists have told, the most lifelike, the truest, the most passionate, is Madame Bovary. . . . In a few lines, Monsieur Flaubert characterizes hysteria, and in his precise and seductive description one does not know whether to admire more the talent of the artist or the science of the observer.[41]

Richet in this passage cites *Madame Bovary* as ex post facto evidence of the medical observation of hysterical temperamentality. But, given the comparative chronology of composition of the relevant medical and literary texts, I wonder in this instance whether it is not science that imitated art.[42]

There is, finally, a postscript to my analysis. As stated before, characterological theories of hysteria went into eclipse during the Charcot era, and the psychological sciences during the early twentieth century were dominated by the theories of Freud, Kraepelin, and Skinner, which eschewed this approach. During the interwar period, however, psychiatric characterology, including the concept of hysterical constitution, reemerged. Ernst Kretschmer placed the idea on a more sophisticated theoretical foundation in the 1920s;[43] during the early 1930s, Fritz Wittels and Wilhelm Reich provided psychoanalytic formulations;[44] and elements of

[40] Richet, "Démoniaques d'aujourd'hui," 346.

[41] Ibid., 348.

[42] Later in the decade Richet published one of his own novels of hysteria in this same journal. See Charles Ephèyre, "Soeur Marthe," année 49, 93 (May 15, 1889): 384–431.

[43] Ernst Kretschmer, *Über Hysterie* (Leipzig: Thieme, 1923); idem, *Physique and Character: An Investigation of the Nature of Constitution and of the Theory of Temperament*, trans. W.J.H. Sprott (New York: Harcourt, Brace, 1925).

[44] Fritz Wittels, "The Hysterical Character," *Medical Review of Reviews* 36, no. 3 (March 1930): 186–90; and Wilhelm Reich, *Character Analysis* [1933], 3d ed., enl. (New York: Farrar, Strauss and Giroux, 1949), 189–93.

the concept appeared in selected French psychiatric texts during the second quarter of the twentieth century.[45]

From these sources, the theory was integrated into the first edition of the *Diagnostic and Statistical Manual of Mental Disorders* (1952) under the guise of "hysterical personality type." With minor changes in classification and terminology from edition to edition, the idea has retained a place in European and American psychiatric manuals ever since. To be sure, it has been a long and convoluted evolution, but the concept has traveled better than one might expect. To the long quotations above from *Madame Bovary* and Falret's lecture, juxtapose the following passage from a more recent but scarcely less influential source:

> 301.50 Histrionic Personality Disorder:
>
> Individuals with this disorder are lively and dramatic and are always drawing attention to themselves. They are prone to exaggeration and often act out a role, such as the "victim" or "princess," without being aware of it.
>
> Behavior is overly reactive and intensely expressed. Minor stimuli give rise to emotional excitability, such as irrational, angry outbursts or tantrums. Individuals with this disorder crave novelty, stimulation, and excitement and quickly become bored with normal routines.
>
> Interpersonal relationships show characteristic disturbances. Initially, people with this disorder are frequently perceived as shallow and lacking genuineness, though superficially charming and appealing. . . . Once a relationship is established they can become demanding, egocentric, and inconsiderate. Manipulative suicidal threats, gestures, or attempts may be made. . . .
>
> Such individuals are typically attractive and seductive. They attempt to control the opposite sex or enter into a dependent relationship. Flights into romantic fantasy are common; in both sexes overt behavior often is a caricature of femininity. . . .
>
> The disorder is apparently common, and diagnosed far more frequently in females than in males.[46]

As a point of historical fact, this conception of hysteria is not Briquetian, Charcotian, Janetian, Freudian, or Lacanian. It is Flaubertian.

If I am correct in this surmise that at a particular moment in the past hysteria doctors learned in important ways from contemporary men and women of letters—that the subtext of nineteenth-century French medical writing on hysterical character is in fact a *literary* text—then what does this say about the dynamics of the historical interaction between litera-

---

[45] Ernest Dupré, *Pathologie de l'imagination et de l'émotivité* (Paris: Payot, 1925); Henri Codet, "Le problème actuel de l'hystérie," *L'évolution psychiatrique* 4 (1935): 3–44; Julian Ajuriaguerra, "Le problème de l'hystérie," *L'encéphale* 1 (1951): 50–87.

[46] American Psychiatric Association, *Diagnostic and Statistical Manual of Mental Disorders*, 3d ed. (Washington, D.C.: American Psychiatric Association, 1980), 313–14.

ture and medicine? Surely it establishes at once the point made by Rousseau, Carroy, and Beizer: a basic popularization model of cultural influence, running one-directionally from the putatively originative realm of medicine to literature and the arts, is insufficient to account for the range of historical relations between the two sets of representational categories. Novels did not simply and secondarily voice a language of pathology created elsewhere. Rather, doctors were as influenced by literary representations and popular stereotypes as novelists and poets were knowledgeable about the findings of medical science. Indeed, in the present instance, a fictional text, far from representing a self-conscious literary reworking of existing medical theory, offered an independently created discourse of disease that later quietly influenced medical theorists.

A number of other facts, too, become apparent from this analysis and may help us to theorize the medicine-literature relation. First, cultural "influence," we see here, entails a complex of effects that may be both positive *and* negative. Literary and scientific intellectuals may be *provoked* as well as inspired into their work by ideas and images outside their field. Second, in conceptualizing medical-literary studies, it is important to consider the particular scientific epistemology and artistic ideology in operation. Like other mid-century French poets, novelists, and painters, Flaubert in the 1850s worked within a "realist" aesthetic that attempted to describe the social world—especially its extreme, pathological aspects —as accurately, objectively, and impersonally as possible. Thus we have the novel's graphic scenes of the scrofulous infection of the blind beggar, the operation on a hotel servant for clubfoot, and Emma's death from arsenical poisoning. With a naturalistic observational style and a quasi-scientific artistic program, his works were particularly accessible to physicians during this period of high and self-conscious scientific positivism. And third, we learn from this example that influences within the medicine-literature relation often entail fundamental changes in evaluative context. One hundred thirty years ago, I have proposed, doctors responded to a novelist's creation of an individual character by extrapolating from it to a "personality type." But in *Madame Bovary*, Flaubert sympathetically created a believable and individualized character in what is judged today as a supreme work of art, a masterpiece of early modernist prose fiction. Meanwhile, Flaubert's medical counterparts formulated a crude and reductive portrait, one that is currently being dismantled as a sexist diagnostic caricature.[47] In short, in their common chosen task of human characterization, a literary intellectual was in a real sense more successful than

[47] Bart and Scully, "The Politics of Hysteria: The Case of the Wandering Womb," in Gomberg and Franks, *Gender and Disordered Behavior*, 366–78; Lerner, "The Hysterical Personality," 157–64; and Kaplan, "A Woman's View of DSM-III," 786–92.

his scientific counterparts. Ironically, it was Flaubert's novel, with its ethos of ethical neutrality, that offered the most "objective" and value-free account—precisely the amoral presentation that Second Empire magistrates found so objectionable—while medical textbooks gave themselves over to a highly prescriptive, mid-Victorian mode.

Finally, this line of analysis leads to yet another consideration. In its inception, the concept of hysterical character pathology owed as much to the work of an imaginative writer as to any medical author. Yet, if doctors were not impermeable to external influence, neither were novelists, and it would be foolish for me to attempt merely to replace an old, one-directional model of cultural influence with another, newer one. Flaubert was the son of a successful Norman doctor. He grew up on the grounds of the Hôtel-Dieu in Rouen. He read sporadically in the medical writing of his time, including the literature of hysteria, and he suffered personally from strange convulsive episodes. Consequently, the question of where Flaubert may have gotten *his* inspiration in creating Emma, including possible medical sources, is directly relevant to our inquiry.[48] Moreover, Flaubert published *Madame Bovary* in 1856–57. Soon thereafter, Baudelaire dubbed Emma "hysterical." Baudelaire's interpretation was then reinforced by Flaubert's *Salammbô* and by the literary vulgarizations of the 1860s, which themselves appeared in tandem with the works of Morel, Marcé, and Falret. In the early 1880s, another spate of psychiatric writings appeared which drew on all of the available textual precedents. At least one figure from this second wave of authors, a physician-litterateur as well as an associate of Charcot, acknowledged the similarities and influences between the two categories of characterization. A decade later still, sociologists, criminologists, and anthropologists extrapolated from all of these sources in their formulation of new social scientific theories.

The conclusion, it seems to me, is that once a disease concept enters the domain of public discussion, it effectively becomes impossible to chart its lines of cultural origin, influence, and evolution with any accuracy. Rather, visual, dramatic, and medical theories and images become inextricably caught up with one another. Eventually, this criss-cross of ideas, information, and associations forms a single sociocultural milieu from which all authors—professional and popular, scientific and literary—may draw. Ultimately, in writing the cultural history of medicine, I believe it will prove most appropriate and productive to work toward a model of influence that is neither one- nor two-directional but *circular*. In France during the nineteenth century in particular, the three primary cultures of

[48] The best study of this subject remains Claudine Gothot-Mersch, *La genèse de Madame Bovary* (Paris: José Corti, 1966).

hysteria were medical, literary, and religious. To stress the isolation and exclusion of these cultures in the public sphere is to ignore deeper, underlying cultural and discursive continuities among them. As the case of Flaubert's *Madame Bovary* and the theory of the hysterical constitution establishes, these textual traditions continually fertilized one another. In pursuing the emergent, interdisciplinary project of medicine and literature, we need to avoid erecting artificial barriers between these converging and diverging discourses and instead to explore the intermixture of imaginations in past cultural systems.

HYSTERIA, GENDER, CULTURE

The information presented thus far about the cultural history of hysteria doubles back at many points on the medical history of the disorder and illuminates the relation between the two categories. But, in today's academic climate, one area of contact between past medical and cultural representations of hysteria is particularly noteworthy and that is gender. As we have seen, within the past decade and a half historians and critics working within the feminist tradition have transformed historical studies with an avalanche of writing about gender. Until recently, feminist scholarship about hysteria centered on the historical experience of women and the ways in which stigmatizing diagnostic labels have operated within hegemonic male cultures. Correspondingly, the cultural history of the subject has dealt either with fictional texts by male authors who wrote disparagingly about female hysterical characters or with the autobiographical writings of women who gave voice to the emotional anguish of their lives in closed, patriarchal worlds.

However, in writing about hysteria culturally no less than medically, it is unacceptable to exclude half of the human population from the historical account. In fact, the study of hysteria, culture, and *male* gender unexpectedly proves one of the richest and most revelatory aspects of the history of the disorder. As readers may have noticed, a significant share of the individuals labeled hysterical in the cultural, particularly literary, history of hysteria have been males. From Shakespeare's Lear to Cervantes' Don Quixote, from the nervous degenerates filling the novels of the Second Empire to the psychologically maimed soldiers of interwar British fiction, the male hysteric has appeared prominently in Western literature. As George Rousseau has indicated, the figure of the literary hypochondriac of Georgian times was almost invariably male. Nearly all of the people discussed in Nordau's *Degeneration* were men, and the political radicals animating the historical narratives of Taine and Du Camp were mostly males. What's more, from the eighteenth century onward, a second and psychologically more complex phenomenon has appeared: the tendency of male poets, novelists, essayists, and critics to characterize themselves, and to be characterized by other men of letters, as hysterical. Since around 1990, scholars, led by literary critics and literary historians, have begun to discover the history of male literary hysteria, and with the most promising results.

Once again, this topic was first opened up by Carroy. In her 1982 landmark article in *Psychanalyse à l'université*, Carroy includes a short, fascinating excursus on the hysteria of literary men in nineteenth-century France.[49] She observes there that the writings of key figures in the literary avant-garde anticipated by a full generation Charcot's better-known medical researches on masculine hysteria. She locates some twenty male-authored works, including poems, novels, letters, and works of literary criticism, that appeared between the late Romantic and symbolist eras and that apply the hysteria metaphor either to fictional male characters, to other male writers, or to the author himself.[50] In these works, the diagnosis is applied alternately with humor, irritation, and desperation and for a wide range of expressive purposes. Not least remarkably, these textual references appeared at a time when the malady of hysteria was almost universally considered by European physicians to be the exclusive preserve of women.

"From 1825 to 1857," wrote the conservative political critic Charles Maurras, "that is to say from Sainte-Beuve and Vigny to Baudelaire, and from 1857 to 1895, or from Baudelaire to Huysmans and Mallarmé, important subgroups of literary intellectuals withdrew from the world of consumers and readers and cast into obscurity the culture which they had come to call *their hysteria*."[51] Not surprisingly, precisely what "their hysteria" meant to nineteenth-century male creative writers differed substantially from individual to individual.

Consider Baudelaire. In "Le mauvais vitrier" ("the Bad Glazier"), among the best-known prose-poems in his collection *Le spleen de Paris*, Baudelaire talks, in the first person, of the strange demoniacal *élans* that may suddenly seize an otherwise calm and contemplative nature and impel him to cruel, dangerous, and unconscionable actions. These "nervous pranks," he writes, are momentary madnesses caused by "that humor called hysterical by the doctors, satanic by those with more insight than

---

[49] Carroy, "Hystérie, théâtre, littérature au dix-neuvième siècle," esp. "Portrait de l'artiste en hystérique" (312–16).

[50] See the chronology of texts, ibid., 317.

[51] Charles Maurras, *L'avenir de l'intelligence* (Paris: A. Fontemoing, 1905), 49; Maurras's emphasis.

doctors."[52] Later in *Le spleen de Paris*, Baudelaire returned to this image with a different purpose in mind. In "Le vieux saltimbanque" ("the Old Acrobat"), he narrates a visit to a popular outdoor fair with its kaleidoscope of colors, sounds, and sensations. Amidst the tawdry splendor, he encounters an old and broken-down clown draped in a tattered costume who is unable any longer to attract an audience. The poet's response to the pathetic scene is strong and immediate: "With what a profound and unforgettable expression his [the clown's] eyes wandered over the crowds and the lights, the moving flood that stopped just short of his repulsive misery! I felt the terrible hand of hysteria grip my throat. I felt rebellious tears that would not fall blurring my sight."[53]

Several years later, ruminating in his private journal, Baudelaire again drew on hysteria for its unique expressive resources. In one of the few dated entries, Baudelaire monitors, as he was wont to do, his own mercurial nervous condition. In a well-known passage from his *Fusées*, he notes that:

> In the realm of the moral, as in that of the physical, I have always had a feeling of the abyss, not only the abyss of sleep but also the abyss of action, of dreams, of memory, of desire, of regret, of remorse, of the beautiful, of the many, etc. I have cultivated my hysteria with pleasure and terror. Now, I always experience dizziness, and today, the 23d of January, 1862, I have received an unusual warning: I have felt pass over me *the wind from the wings of imbecility*.[54]

It is a difficult passage. But, as with Wordsworth's early poetry, hysteria appears here to be an experience both desired and feared—cultivated "avec jouissance et terreur"—for its mystery and emotional intensity. Moreover, we find here that the nineteenth-century poet, no less than the nineteenth-century physician, was uncertain if hysteria represented a mental malady expressed bodily or a physical ailment with emotional manifestations.

[52] "Cette humeur, hystérique selon les médecins, satanique selon ceux qui pensent un peu mieux que les médecins," in "Le mauvais vitrier," in *Le spleen de Paris*, in *Oeuvres complètes de Charles Baudelaire*, vol. 4, *Petits poèmes en prose*, 23.

[53] "Mais quel regard profond, inoubliable, il promenait sur la foule et les lumières, dont le flot mouvant s'arrêtait à quelques pas de sa répulsive misère! Je sentis ma gorge serrée par la main terrible de l'hystérie, et il me sembla que mes regards étaient offusqués par ces larmes rebelles qui ne veulent pas tomber" ("Le vieux saltimbanque," in *Le spleen de Paris*, 43; Eng. trans. by Louise Varèse.) My thanks to Fernando Vidal of the University of Geneva for bringing this passage to my attention.

[54] Within Baudelaire's *Journaux intimes*, this entry is classed differently from edition to edition. In *Oeuvres complètes*, ed. Claude Pichois (Paris: Gallimard, 1975), see "Hygiène," vol. 1, entry 86; 668. Baudelaire's highlights.

Nor is this quite all. In the closing year of his life, "la main terrible de l'hystérie" struck Baudelaire again, but this time under tragically altered circumstances. Early in January 1866, Baudelaire was on a lecture tour in Brussels when he suffered a sudden onrush of symptoms. It was the beginning of the illness that a year and a half later would lead to his death, the result of a stroke, exacerbated by anxiety, drugs, and alcohol, and accelerated almost certainly by cerebral syphilis.[55] Baudelaire immediately called in a number of local physicians; but he came away angry and dissatisfied with the consultations. Writing on January 15 to his fellow critic and lifelong friend Sainte-Beuve, he summarizes the endless medications prescribed for him as well as each doctor's diagnosis: "Another told me for my only consolation that I am *hysterical*," he reported wryly. He then asks Sainte-Beuve sardonically, "Do you admire as I do the flexible usage of these big words well chosen to conceal our ignorance of everything?"[56] Two weeks later, Baudelaire wrote along the same lines to his mother, who was living back in France and was all too familiar with her son's sufferings. Disillusioned, destitute, and deeply anxious about his health, Baudelaire rambles back and forth between his own condition and his mother's health. To the body of the letter he appends a list of the strange and intensifying symptoms he had endured over the past twelve months: weakness, vertigo, headaches, neuralgias, vomiting, cold sweats, and an ominous incoordination in movement. "The doctor mentioned the word: hysteria," he notes disconsolately. "That means: I give up [*je jette ma langue aux chiens*]."[57]

Evidently, Baudelaire disapproved of the verdict of hysteria when applied to himself in these contexts, and in other letters too he indignantly repeated the story of his doctor's diagnosis, as if trying to laugh the matter off.[58] But in truth his reaction was more complicated. A week later still, on February 12, 1866, he again wrote to his mother, reporting his latest frustrations about getting his work published and talking once more about his dilapidated nervous system. This time, however, he closed the letter with a new idea: "There is in Paris a man who could have been of service to me. I shall see him on my next trip. It is Charles Lassègue [*sic*], my former preceptor of philosophy, when I was a young man. He

[55] Claude Pichois, *Baudelaire*, trans. Graham Robb (London: Hamish Hamilton, 1989), part 7.

[56] Letter from Baudelaire to Sainte-Beuve, January 15, 1866, in *Baudelaire: Correspondance*, ed. Claude Pichois and Jean Ziegler, 2 vols. (Paris: Gallimard, 1973), 2: 583; Baudelaire's emphasis.

[57] Letter from Baudelaire to Madame Aupick, February 6, 1866, in *Correspondance*, 2: 589.

[58] Letter from Baudelaire to Charles Asselineau, February 5, 1866, in *Correspondance*, 2: 587; Letter to Madame Aupick, February 10, 1866, in *Correspondance*, 2: 594.

has abandoned philosophy. He has become a doctor, and . . . a famous one. His specialty is *madmen* and *hysterics*."[59]

We discover in these letters that Baudelaire was irritated by the invocation of hysteria when he was genuinely ill. It might cause people to think that he was merely the victim of *une maladie imaginaire*. Yet, privately, he took the diagnosis seriously enough to plan consultation with one of the foremost specialists in Paris, whom, coincidentally, he had known from his schooldays.[60] Perhaps also, as his symptoms failed to remit, and much direr eventualities loomed, Baudelaire was less agitated than consoled by the thought that this latest *mal baudelairien* was "only hysteria." Whatever the case, six weeks later Baudelaire suffered the massive apoplectic attack that left him aphasiac and paralyzed on the right side of his body. By March of the following year, he was permanently bedridden, his existence increasingly vegetative, until, late in August 1867, at age forty-six, he died.[61] From these passages, scattered through ten years of artistic and epistolary writings, we find that Baudelaire's hysteria was shifting, idiosyncratic, and highly personalized. For the finest French poet of the nineteenth century, the condition could figure now as an impulse to irrational actions, now as a cover for professional medical ignorance, now as a source of emotional exotica. Near the end of his life, it also served as a metaphor for the subjective experience of the dreaded descent into disease and death.

Flaubert too figures in the literary history of *hystérie virile*. Flaubert's personal letters are among the most fascinating literary correspondences in history, and from them Carroy ferrets out over a dozen passages in which the novelist styles his own mental and physical vicissitudes as hysterical. These mainly involve letters from Flaubert to Louise Colet, a noted poet, novelist, and playwright who for several years was Flaubert's occasional lover, and to George Sand, the famous heroine of the French literary scene.

On April 8, 1852, Flaubert wrote to Colet. Deeply absorbed in the composition of *Madame Bovary* and saturated with his own psychological situation, he complained bitterly of "les hystéries d'ennui," "hysterias of boredom." "In body and mind, I am broken and annihilated."[62] Sim-

[59] Letter from Baudelaire to Madame Aupick, February 12, 1866, in *Correspondance*, 2: 597 and 961; Baudelaire's emphasis.

[60] Lasègue in fact later paid a visit to Baudelaire during the poet's illness. See the letter from Dr. Charles Lasègue to Madame Aupick, June 22, 1866, repr. in Jacques Crépet, "Derniers jours de Charles Baudelaire," *La nouvelle revue française* 39, no. 230 (November 1, 1932): 671.

[61] Baudelaire's 1862 reference to "le vent de l'aile de l'imbécilité" first passing over him may presage the onset of this organic mental deterioration.

[62] Letter from Flaubert to Louise Colet, April 8, 1852, in *Correspondance, 1850–1859*, in *Oeuvres complètes de Flaubert*, 13: 179.

ilarly, writing years later to Sand from the town of Croisset in western France, Flaubert complained characteristically of the crushing boredom of life in the provinces. "I have palpitations for no reason (something comprehensible moreover in an old hysteric like me). For I maintain that men can be hysterics just like women and that I am one." Flaubert went on to confess to Sand that nervous symptoms often supervened as he struggled to do his literary work: "When I was writing *Salammbô*, I read 'the best authors' on the subject, and I recognized all of my symptoms. I have the *boule* and the *clou* sensation in the back of the head. All of this is the result of our happy occupation. That is what it means to torment oneself in body and soul."[63]

In the spring of 1874, writing once more to Sand, Flaubert complained yet again, this time of the stinging reception accorded his latest novel, *The Temptation of St. Anthony*. His nerves had been so bad of late, he confessed, that he consulted a certain Dr. Hardy, "who calls me 'a hysterical woman'—an observation I find profound."[64] Flaubert agreed with the diagnosis. Some years later, the symptoms came on again, including the classic *clou* sensation in the center of his forehead. This time, too, Flaubert accepted a friend's offhand comment: he was only "une grosse fille hystérique," "an old hysterical woman."[65]

Clearly, Flaubert was less disturbed by the application of this medical terminology to himself than was Baudelaire. His declarations of his own hysterical pathology, including some of its most stylized symptoms, are at times little more than passing, playful self-denigrations. In other places, they come off as the rather conscious self-dramatizations of the sensitive literary intellectual, akin to the endless self-dissections of Rousseau in the *Confessions* or the cultivated *Weltschmerz* of Goethe, Musset, and Vigny. However, at still other times, Flaubert's autodiagnoses were something more. As Carroy points out, in these statements "hysteria becomes a point of identification and designates the impasses and the delights of lived experiences and of literary creation, a necessary symptom, but one cultivated in ambivalence."[66] Hysteria, in short, became a symbolic means of registering, to the writer himself and to other sympathetic mem-

[63] Letter from Flaubert to George Sand, January 12–13, 1867, in *Correspondance, 1859–1871*, 14: 323.

[64] Letter from Flaubert to George Sand, May 1, 1874, in *Correspondance, 1871–1877*, vol. 15 of *Oeuvres complètes de Flaubert*, 298.

[65] Letter from Flaubert to his niece Caroline, April 25, 1879, in *Correspondance, 1877–1880*, in: *Oeuvres complètes*, 16: 198. In the same volume, see also the letter of November 1879 to Madame Brainne on page 271.

[66] Carroy, "Hystérie, théâtre, littérature," 312–13.

bers of the guild, the effort and agony unavoidably associated with the production of a great work of art.[67]

These self-descriptions by French men of letters, at a time when the idea of masculine hysteria was beyond the official medical knowledge of the day, are striking. Yet, it is well to keep in mind that they occurred in private, epistolary contexts, as exchanges between lovers, close friends, fellow writers, and family members, in which it was safe to apply such a potentially radical label to oneself. They owe much to French literary Romanticism, with its rich tradition of the autobiographical display of psychological suffering.[68] For the image of the male hysterical artist to enter fully into public discourse seems to have required the work of Charcot. While Baudelaire, Flaubert, Mallarmé, Verlaine, and Valéry each alluded briefly in half a dozen passages or so to what they perceived as their own neuroses, Charcot put male hysterical patients on display to large, public audiences throughout the 1880s and published studies of over six dozen cases of the masculine form of the disease for all the world to read.

Interestingly, following the medical legitimation of the concept, a genre of literary criticism flourished in France, freely engaged in by medical and literary authors alike, that diagnosed retrospectively the nervous and mental diseases of past writers, artists, and philosophers. This body of writing, which presaged our own psychobiography and psychoanalytic criticism, provided "pathographies" of Rousseau, the Marquis de Sade, Byron, Poe, Dostoevsky, and Nietzsche, as well as medico-psychological analyses of cultural movements like Romanticism and decadence.[69]

As Roger Williams has shown, Flaubert in particular became the subject of a debate of this sort during the early twentieth century.[70] Since Flaubert's death in 1880, doctors had assumed that the novelist suffered from periodic grand mal seizures. But when, after Flaubert's death, Maxime du Camp revealed that his seizures had been accompanied by depressions, neuralgias, crying spells, and sexual frigidity, speculation arose that

[67] For similar remarks by the symbolist poets Mallarmé, Verlaine, and Valéry, see ibid., 314, 315.

[68] Paul de Man, *The Rhetoric of Romanticism* (New York: Columbia University Press, 1984), chap. 4.

[69] Ernest Seillière's *Le mal romantique: Essai sur l'impérialisme irrationnel* (Paris: Plon, Nourrit et Cie, 1908) is probably the most substantial work in this mold by a literary scholar. From the medical literature, see Raoul Odinot, "Étude médico-psychologique sur Alfred de Musset" (Ph.D. diss., University of Lyon, 1906); Zacharie Lacassagne, "La folie de Maupassant" (Ph.D. diss., University of Toulouse, 1907); B. Carrère, "Dégénérescence et dipsomanie d'Edgar Poe" (Ph.D. diss., University of Toulouse, 1907); and G. Lavalée, "Essai sur la psychologie morbide de Huysmans" (Ph.D. diss., University of Paris, 1917).

[70] Williams, *The Horror of Life*, 190–215.

the writer's nervous attacks had been hysterical.[71] The culmination of the controversy was reached with René Dumesnil's medical thesis "Flaubert et la médecine" in 1905. Dumesnil, who subsequently became a professional Flaubert scholar, exhaustively reviews the available documentation about the writer's life, alongside the latest medical research on the differential diagnosis of convulsive disorders, and confidently pronounces Flaubert's a case of "hystero-neurasthenia."[72]

One point that emerges unmistakably from literary and cultural critics such as Dumesnil is the difference in valuation between literary and medical representations of the male hysteric. In my own work, I have tried to show that for centuries the idea of attributing hysterical disorders to members of the male sex, for theoretical and psychological reasons, was profoundly unpalatable to male physicians. They therefore resourcefully overlooked the phenomenon for centuries. Even Charcot, as I have shown, felt the need to desexualize and deemotionalize the diagnosis while his followers adopted alternative strategies of resistance. These evasive manoeuvres, however, proved unnecessary in dealing with the male hysterical artist. Despite the fact that the symptoms of the disorder cited by literary savants were the same as in contemporaneous medical cases, hysteria in artistic and literary men was construed positively, as a desirable, impressive, even ennobling attribute. The difference in valuation is almost certainly due to the fact that the cultural context for understanding nervous disease in the independent, avant-garde man of arts and letters was wholly different from that for the working-class male hysterical types treated by Charcot and his medical colleagues.

This point becomes unmistakably clear in a number of texts from the period. Throughout his outlandish *Les hystériques des couvents*, which appeared at the peak of medical interest in male hysteria in 1886, Augustin Galopin pontificates about hysteria in both its masculine and feminine forms. Male hysterics in particular, Galopin comments, have become "les fous courants," "the fashionable insane." Then in the thirteenth chapter of his book, Galopin rails against the old and apparently indestructible gynecological view of the disease and speculates that in certain social groups there is actually *more* hysteria among men than women.

[71] Interestingly, one of the first medical writers to postulate a hysterical component in Flaubert's case was a former student of Charcot who had contributed to the Salpêtrian literature on male hysteria. Compare Paul Michaut, "La mort de Flaubert" and "Un livre à écrire sur Gustave Flaubert," both in *La chronique médicale* 7 (1900): 703–4, 771–76 with idem, "Contribution à l'étude des manifestations de l'hystérie chez l'homme" (Ph.D. diss., University of Paris, 1890).

[72] René Dumesnil, *Flaubert et la médecine* (Ph.D. diss., University of Paris; Paris: Société française d'imprimerie et de librairie, 1905), 86–112. See as well Philibert de Lastic's *La pathologie mentale dans les oeuvres de Gustave Flaubert* (Paris: J. B. Baillière, 1906), 100–108.

This is especially true, he continues, of poets, writers, musicians, actors, and (not to exclude his own profession) journalists: "It is there that one finds the largest number of men who are victims of the contemporary neuroses."[73] The cause of these elevated rates, Galopin imagines, is the innate heightened sensitivity, the relentless use of the imagination, and the stress of continual creative struggle. Later, Galopin explicitly contrasts "l'hystérie vulgaire," common hysteria, and "l'hystérie de l'artiste," the hysteria of the artist, concluding that the first form is undesirable while the second is a necessary function of creativity.[74] He even applauds "l'homme hystérique" in the name of cultural nationalism: "The great hysterics of the arts and literature have never dishonored their country. We salute and venerate the sweet and harmonious melancholy of these sublime and privileged madmen."[75]

In 1911, these same attitudes were expressed, a bit more responsibly, in the short biographical and literary-critical study *Chateaubriand et l'hystérie*, written by Henri Albert Potiquet.[76] Like Dumesnil and Galopin, Potiquet, a physician, nonchalantly declared his subject hysterical. Following a discussion of the medical writings of Ribot, Huchard, and Hartenberg, Potiquet reviews the biographical facts of Chateaubriand's life and the contents of his novels, memoirs, and letters. The point of the essay is to establish that hysteria defines and unites Chateaubriand's character. To this end, Potiquet makes much of Chateaubriand's well-known tendency to break out into tears in public places over minor sentimentalities and contends that "this flood of tears in a man of his age . . . by itself makes us suspect hysteria."[77] According to Potiquet, Chateaubriand's other hysterical features include pride, egoism, restlessness, exuberance, theatricality, seductiveness, and emotional mobility—traits, we can't help but notice, that might as easily have been identified in Emma Bovary. But to these qualities Potiquet adds Chateaubriand's charisma and brilliance and then interprets the lot as signs of a high level of creativity combined with a passionate, Romantic individuality. "Does it diminish Chateaubriand to attach to his name the label of hysteric?" Potiquet asks rhetorically in his concluding paragraph. "Not at all. . . . Nor is it by any means to place him in bad company. . . . How many great writers, how many artists, were touched by this psychosis in its multiple modalities!"[78]

[73] Galopin, *L'hystérie des couvents*, 125.

[74] Ibid., 133.

[75] Ibid., 134–35.

[76] Dr. [Henri Albert] Potiquet, *Chateaubriand et l'hystérie: Essai de psychologie* (Paris: Laisney, 1911).

[77] Ibid., 11.

[78] Ibid., 29.

What Potiquet did for Chateaubriand other commentators attempted with other historical personages. During 1884–86, the *Gazette des hôpitaux*, one of the most widely read publications in the French medical profession, ran a seven-part series by one Lanoaille de Lachèse. In "Tarassis: Troubles de l'âme et du corps chez l'homme dans les temps modernes et dans l'histoire," Lanoaille de Lachèse coins the term "tarassis" as a substitute for "male hysteria."[79] After a review of cases currently in the Paris hospital wards, he ransacks the historical record for more eminent specimens. Socrates, Caesar, Mohammed, and Rousseau, he judges, were all, so to speak, closet "tarrassics." At roughly the same time, Maupassant generalized that "all great men were [hysterical]," adding that "Napoleon I was (but not the other one), [and] Marat, Robespierre, and Danton were." Lanoaille de Lachèse added that "the doctors also teach us that talent is a type of hysteria, and that it comes from a cerebral lesion. Therefore, genius must come from two neighboring lesions; it is double hysteria [*c'est de l'hystérie double*]."[80] Later in the 1880s, Lombroso, who viewed the female hysteric with such contempt, elaborated on Maupassant's association between hysteria, epilepsy, and male genius;[81] and a decade later, the American psychologist Frederic Myers speculated on the psychological continuities between cultural creativity and hysterical neurosis.[82]

In sum, the male hysteria concept, unlike its female counterpart, evolved substantially independent discursive traditions within the medical and the cultural arenas. Writing in the Rousseauvian autobiographical mode, French literary elites, for a variety of purposes, dramatized their personal emotional situations as hysterical. But in the self-application of the disease category hysteria they were placing themselves within a lineage of cultural figures that extended from the degenerate genius of the fin de siècle, back to the tubercular Romantic poet, thence through the melancholic writer of eighteenth-century England, and all the way back to Plato's image of the mad, divine poet. Their autodiagnoses were intended to signalize superior sensibility; they were conceived as certificates of artistic and intellectual individualism. As a consequence, while the psychological states they designated were subjectively real and powerful, the hysterical poet and novelist escaped the stigmatizing connotations of the diagnosis so salient in nineteenth-century medical settings.

[79] Subsequently repr. as Lanoaille de Lachèse, *Tarassis: Troubles de l'âme et du corps chez l'homme dans les temps modernes et dans l'histoire* (Paris: J.-B. Baillière, 1886).
[80] Maupassant, *Chroniques*, 2: 112.
[81] Cesare Lombroso, *L'homme de génie* (Paris: Félix Alcan, 1889), 465–85.
[82] Frederic Myers, "Hysteria and Genius," *Journal of the Society for Psychical Research* 8, no. 138 (April–May 1897): 50–59, 69–71

Exploring "their hysteria," to return to Maurras's phrase, has meant something else, too, for imaginative writers in the past. Throughout its history, hysteria has operated as a favorite metaphor for professional male observers attempting to portray the essence of the opposite sex. However, if adult men as well as women could be hysterics, then the disease was theoretically not sex-dependent. From the perspective of the disorder as a centuries-old male-authored commentary on the female, the implications of the idea of hysteria in the male are at least twofold: first, it implies a masculinization of women, that is, a realization that the pathologies of hyperfemininity ascribed medically to women in the past represented gross gender caricatures; and second, it implies an exploration of the "feminine" (i.e., the vulnerable and emotional) component in the male psyche. In both instances, the potential of the male hysteria concept for what I have called "gender relativization" is very considerable.[83] In conservative, patriarchal cultures, these issues are exceptionally delicate, and the social and psychological resistance to anything that blurs gender boundaries has been great. Moreover, it is not only doctors who have realized the revolutionary potential latent in the idea of masculine hysterical neurosis but figures in many areas of culture.

Today, the historical study of these themes within the history of male literary hysteria is emerging as one of the hottest topics within the new hysteria studies. Predicated theoretically on the Lacanian concept of "hysterical narrativity" and pioneered by Showalter's literary-historical studies, the recent swell of interest in male hysterical narratives provides a kind of cultural counterpart to my own work on the medical history of the subject.[84] The initial findings of this scholarship are already mutually illuminating. Both the number of literary artifacts that may be read from this perspective and the variety of stylistic and psychological strategies that writers have employed to explore these themes is great.

In Marie Addyman's analysis of hysteria in Shakespearean England, the two main dramatic characters are Lear and Leontes, both males. In *King Lear*, among Shakespeare's finest creations and perhaps the greatest tragedy in any language, the old and once-great king is driven mad by the actions of Goneril and Regan. Shakespeare in a real sense reverses Jane Gallop's formulation to give us hysteria, not as "the daughter's disease" provoked by an overbearing Victorian paterfamilias, but "the father's disease," caused by treacherous and rebellious daughters. Moreover, Shake-

[83] Micale, "Diagnostic Discriminations," part 3; idem, "Charcot and the Idea of Hysteria in the Male," 409–10; idem, "Hysteria Male/Hysteria Female," 211–14.

[84] Showalter, *Female Malady*, chap. 7; idem, *Sexual Anarchy: Gender and Culture at the Fin de Siècle* (New York: Viking, 1990), chap. 6; idem, "Hysteria, Feminism, and Gender," in Gilman et al., *Hysteria Beyond Freud*, 286–344; and idem, *Hystories* (work in progress).

speare, as we learned above, employed the most graphically anatomical language of the female—"O! how this mother swells up toward my heart"—to convey the scene of male emotional anguish. In other words, Shakespeare has Lear experience his suffering specifically as a feminization which must be repressed, beaten back down, in order to regain control over his kingdom, his family, and himself.[85]

Similar themes were played out two centuries later in English Romantic poetry. While Alan Bewell has highlighted Wordsworth's fascination with the figure of the female hysteric, Susan Wolfson is studying the hysteria motif applied by Wordsworth to the male poet generically and to himself.[86] Concentrating on the first edition of the *Lyrical Ballads* of 1800, a key Romantic text, Wolfson has located "the voices and figures of feeling men."[87] She looks closely at passages in which Wordsworth experiences strong elemental states of emotion—joy, love, passion, tenderness, grief— and then communicates these sentiments either by assuming the role of a female narrator or by presenting "feminized" states of feeling in his own voice. These sentiments contrast starkly, Wolfson maintains, with the self-control and rationality that conventionally defines the masculine Self. But for Wordsworth, as for Baudelaire, this experience was to be sought after. Fused with the all-important faculty of "Imagination," the hysterical passions enhanced the poet's expressive powers. In the end, Wolfson interprets Wordsworth's poetry, and the Romantic aesthetic of intersubjectivity generally, as a subversion of "the traditions of opposition and difference" found in Enlightenment discourses on the sexes.[88]

Baudelaire and Flaubert are relevant here again too. Carroy has observed that the self-representation of literary Frenchmen as hysterics was closely caught up with the theme of the androgyne, inherited from Romantic culture,[89] and the image of the hysterical writer and poet as "man-woman." Announcing their identities as hysterics, Carroy observes, became for artists a means of exposing, exploring, and extending the androgynous element in their own natures, their psychological bisexuality.[90] In his review of *Madame Bovary*, for instance, Baudelaire did

---

[85] A reading along these same lines with a feminist psychoanalytic gloss may be found in Coppélia Kahn, "The Absent Mother in *King Lear*," in Margaret W. Ferguson, Maureen Quilligan, and Nancy J. Vickers eds., *Rewriting the Renaissance: The Discourses of Sexual Difference in Early Modern Europe* (Chicago: University of Chicago Press, 1986), 33–49.

[86] Susan Wolfson, "*Lyrical Ballads* and the Language of (Men) Feeling: Writing Women's Voices," in *Figures on the Margin: The Language of Gender in English Romanticism* (work in progress).

[87] Ibid., 2 (cited from the typescript).

[88] Ibid., esp. 45–46.

[89] Diane L. Hoeveler, *Romantic Androgyny: The Woman Within* (University Park, Pa.: Pennsylvania State University Press, 1990), esp. 1–23.

[90] Carroy, "Hystérie, théâtre, littérature au dix-neuvième siècle," 309–10, 314. For a restatement of Carroy's interpretation, see Jan Goldstein, "The Uses of Male Hysteria: Medical and Literary Discourse in Nineteenth-Century France," *Representations* 34 (Spring

more than just designate as hysterical one of Flaubert's characters. After his diagnosis of Emma, the poet examined the more sensitive and elusive issue of the novelist's intense, intimate identification with his literary creation. In the process, Baudelaire probed what today would be called the gender identities of both artist and protagonist. Most significantly, Baudelaire perceived a subtle but deep psychological and sexual symbiosis between Flaubert and Emma, and he implied that the immense artistic success of the novel was the result of this relationship.

A striking feature of *Madame Bovary*, reflected Baudelaire, was that the author communicates in the novel through a female character. The sympathetic creation by a male artist of a complex and convincing female figure—that is, the achievement of genuine cross-genderal knowledge—was in Baudelaire's mind an extraordinary feat:

> To accomplish this *tour de force* in its entirety the author had only to divest himself (as much as possible) of his sex and to make himself into a woman. The result is a marvel; in spite of all his zeal as an actor, he could not keep from infusing a virile blood into the veins of his creation, and Madame Bovary, in what is most forceful, most ambitious, and also most dreamy in her nature, has remained a man. Just as Pallas Athena sprang armed from the head of Zeus, so this strange androgynous creature has kept all the attraction of a virile soul in a charming feminine body.[91]

I believe that this is an exciting textual moment within the cultural history of hysteria. Attempting to portray eternally the human reality of hysteria, Flaubert, in Baudelaire's analysis, struggled first to feminize himself and, failing in this task, unwittingly masculinized his female protagonist. We find laid bare in this passage, for perhaps the first time, the central theoretical possibility of the idea of male hysteria: namely, its capacity for a deep relativizing of gender norms. Furthermore, we have here a powerful instance in which the metaphorics of hysteria were employed, not to depict pejoratively and stereotypically female sexuality and female human nature, but to explore constructively the gender identities and indeterminacies of both sexes.

There is much in Flaubert's life and work to support this line of interpretation. It is a commonplace that all fiction writing is in some measure autobiographical, especially an author's first work. Emma and Flaubert suffered equally from convulsions and lifelong nervous complaints. And a fact frequently cited by late nineteenth-century critics who diagnosed Flaubert as hysterical was the psychological affinities between the novelist

---

1991): 134–65, esp. 145–46, 149–50, 156–57.

[91] Baudelaire, "*Madame Bovary* par Gustave Flaubert," 400–401. In later paragraphs of the review, Baudelaire continues to underscore that Emma is fundamentally endowed with male characteristics. Her character is "almost male"; certain of her actions are executed "in an almost masculine way"; and Flaubert's image of the female is "so near to the ideal man."

and his celebrated heroine. We also know that many of Flaubert's contemporaries called attention to his feminine nature while biographers have hinted at a latent homosexuality or a tendency to transsexuality. Also interesting in this light is the author's own much-quoted account of the gestation of his novel. Later in his career, Flaubert was repeatedly asked on whom in real life he had patterned Emma's character. At least once, he is reported to have quipped, "Madame Bovary, c'est moi; d'après moi."[92] Margaret Gilman has suggested that Flaubert's identification with his protagonist may have been unconscious and that it was only after reading Baudelaire's review that he uttered this bon mot.[93] Moreover, Baudelaire's review, with its emphasis on the integrated androgynous and autobiographical elements in the novel, was, to repeat, the one commentary on his book of which Flaubert is said to have approved.[94] In this, then, his first novel, Flaubert gave us Emma, "a virile soul in a charming feminine body," instead presumably of the obverse, what he himself was: a charming feminine soul inside a virile body. Working syncretistically, Flaubert and Baudelaire used hysteria as a vehicle to explore at once the feminine component in the male psyche and the masculine component in the female psyche and this simultaneously on the personal and artistic levels.[95]

The exploration of masculine hysterical states as an interrogation of traditional sex/gender systems occurred in literary works later in the nineteenth century too. Significantly, two of the most important texts in this regard appeared in the mid-1880s, again in tandem with the height of

[92] The origins of this remark are unfortunately rather murky. Flaubert is supposed to have made the comment in a conversation with his close friend Madame Amelie Bosquet, who then repeated it to others, including eventually to Flaubert's early biographer, René Descharmes. The statement seems first to have been set down in print by Descharmes in *Flaubert: Sa vie, son caractère et ses idées avant 1857* (Paris: Librairie des amateurs, 1909), 103, n. 3.

[93] Margaret Gilman, *Baudelaire the Critic* (New York: Columbia University Press, 1943), 99.

[94] See letter from Flaubert to Baudelaire, October 21, 1857, in *Correspondance, 1850–1859*, in *Oeuvres complètes de Flaubert*, 13: 610.

[95] Another commentator who registered the potential of the hysteria theme for a powerful questioning of gender paradigms (as well as for superficial popularization) was George Sand. Responding on January 12–13, 1867 to Flaubert's letter in which he declares his hysterical symptomatology, Sand muses "Qu'est-ce au fond d'être hystérique? Je l'ai peut-être été aussi, je le suis peut-être; mais je n'en sais rien, n'ayant jamais approfondi la chose et en ayant ouï parler sans l'étudier. N'est-ce pas un malaise, une angoisse causée par le désir d'un impossible quelconque? En ce cas, nous en sommes tous atteints, de ce mal étrange, quand nous avons de l'imagination; *et pourquoi une telle maladie aurait-elle un sexe? Il n'y a qu'un sexe. Un homme et une femme, c'est si bien la même chose que l'on ne comprend guère les tas de distinctions et de raisonnements subtils dont se sont nourries les sociétés sur ce chapitre-là*" (Letter from Sand to Flaubert, January 15, 1867, cited in Carroy, 314; my italics.)

debate about male hysteria within the medical world. Claire Kahane has addressed this theme in Henry James's *The Bostonians*.[96] James's novel, published in 1885, is a powerful study in personal and cultural contrasts: the chivalrous manliness of the antebellum South represented in the character of Basil Ransom clashes throughout the story with the new and hostile feminism of New England, embodied in the cold, crypto-lesbian Olive Chancellor.

In a well-known passage that here takes on added meaning, Ransom explains to the young Verena Tarrant that it is his intention to save his sex from "the most damnable feminization" of the present time. James then has Ransom, in a desperate outburst, equate hysteria and the women's movement and experience the two, again both personally and culturally, as a demasculinization:

> The whole generation is womanized; the masculine tone is passing out of the world; it's a feminine, a nervous, hysterical, chattering, canting age, an age of hollow phrases and false delicacy and exaggerated and coddled sensibilities, which, if we don't soon look out, will usher in the reign of mediocrity, of the feeblest and flattest and the most pretentious that has ever been. The masculine character, the ability to dare and endure, to know and yet not fear reality, to look the world in the face and take it for what it is . . . that is what I want to preserve, or rather, as I may say, to recover.[97]

In ways we have seen before, James's character uses hysteria as an epithet to signify a number of contemptible social modernizations. But, as Kahane points out, Ransom (like Nordau, LeBon, and Taine) undercuts the very dichotomy between the masculine and the feminine that he seeks to reaffirm by crying out in language that is itself hystericized.[98]

In a similarly provocative analysis, Elaine Showalter highlights these issues in a literary text that was contemporaneous with James's.[99] Robert Louis Stevenson's *The Strange Case of Dr. Jekyll and Mr. Hyde*, Showalter proposes, may meaningfully be read as "a fable of *fin-de-siècle* homosexual panic" and "a case study of male hysteria."[100] Stevenson seems to have experienced strong homoerotic impulses but was trapped in a repressive social world and an unhappy marriage. Showalter points out that the novel, which is devoid of female characters, operates as a veiled story of

[96] Claire Kahane, "Hysteria, Feminism, and the Case of *The Bostonians*," in Richard Feldstein and Judith Roof, eds., *Feminism and Psychoanalysis* (Ithaca, N.Y.: Cornell University Press, 1989), 280–97.

[97] Henry James, *The Bostonians* (New York: Modern Library, 1956), 343. For the context of the passage, see chap. 34 of the novel.

[98] Kahane, "Hysteria, Feminism, and *The Bostonians*, 289–90.

[99] Showalter, *Sexual Anarchy*, chap. 6.

[100] Ibid., 104.

emotional bonding and erotic desire among men. Stevenson's work, she argues, offers a masked exploration of the-feminine-in-the-masculine that allowed for an expression of the author's unspeakable sexuality. But here the theme is explored, not by attributing a hysterical physiology to a male character as in *King Lear* or by fashioning a female character and then "identifying" with it as Flaubert did, but rather by exploring it through the distancing device of a male protagonist, Henry Jekyll, who has a secret double self that includes "feminine," "hysterical" tendencies and that engages in criminal acts. Stevenson's novel appeared in 1886. Showalter conjectures that an influence on its composition was the case of "Louis V.," the most publicized of male hysterics in the French medical literature, which was popularized in Britain by Stevenson's friend and doctor Frederic Myers.[101]

I have come to believe, however, that the single most instructive figure to consider in the cultural history of male hysteria was neither poet, novelist, playwright nor critic. He was a physician, a very exceptional physician. Commenting on the case of his patient Elisabeth von R., he writes:

> It still strikes me myself as strange that the case histories I write should read like short stories and that, as one might say, they lack the serious stamp of science. I must console myself with the reflection that the nature of the subject is evidently responsible for this, rather than any preference of my own. The fact is that local diagnosis and electrical reactions lead nowhere in the study of hysteria, whereas a detailed description of mental processes *such as we are accustomed to find in the works of imaginative writers* enables me, with the use of a few psychological formulas, to obtain at least some kind of insight into the course of that affection.[102]

In this passage written in 1895 in *Studies on Hysteria*, Freud contrasts directly, and a bit defensively, the literary and scientific modes of inquiry into the mind.[103] He acknowledges that the two approaches normally remain separate, but suggests that in the study of psychology, and in particular hysteria, the technique of the novelist may be the more productive of the two. As a physician who was uncommonly well-read in the ancient classics and modern German literature, he was in a good position to know.

In her 1982 study, Carroy throws out an idea that appears to reinforce the thrust of Freud's comment from a historical perspective. Reflecting on

[101] Ibid., 102–14. See also Stephen Heath, "Psychopathia Sexualis: Stevenson's Strange Case," *Critical Quarterly* 28 (Spring–Summer 1986): 93–108.

[102] Freud, *Studies on Hysteria*, in *Standard Edition*, 2: 160–61; my italics.

[103] Later, in writing about Dora, Freud expressed the fear that his case history might be received by readers "not as a contribution to the psychopathology of the neuroses, but as a *roman à clef* designed for their private delectation" (*Standard Edition*, 7: 9).

the literary-medical relation generally, she suggests that the exploration of a category as delicate and potentially subversive as masculine hysteria could only have been accomplished outside of the scientific field. The medical sciences employ an objectifying language and methodology, which by design distances the theorist from the object of study, while literature and the arts operate subjectively, drawing freely on both self-knowledge and observation of the external, human world. "The hysteric is and will remain, in official medical theories, the Other, generally female, either likable or hateful, but always alien." In contrast, she adds, in the speculations of Baudelaire, Flaubert, Mallarmé, Gide, and Valéry, "hysteria becomes the index of an interrogation of the Self, of the condition of a creativity of which it is at once the inspiration and the inhibition."[104]

Carroy's (and Freud's) observation is intensely interesting. For the post-Enlightenment period generally, which witnessed the beginning of the bifurcation of the cultural and medical histories of disease, their generalization may well hold true. However, I wish to contend that the outstanding example of Freud himself ultimately undermines the distinction between the scientific and artistic idioms of inquiry and unites the two representational traditions of hysteria in a single historical moment.

The 1890s were exceptionally eventful years in Freud's intellectual biography. It was the founding decade of psychoanalysis, during which Freud broke away from the strict medical organicism of his scientific training and worked toward a new psychological theory of the mind. This accomplishment, which entailed years of sustained intellectual exertion, required the rejection of the hereditarian model of mental illness, the construction of a theory of the psychosexual origins of neurosis, the elaboration of ideas of repression and defense, the adoption and then abandonment of the seduction theory, and the formulation of the concept of the Oedipus complex. Throughout the later 1880s and the 1890s, a basic source of Freud's clinical data for this work was his private practice, which consisted mainly of well-to-do adult and adolescent women suffering from nervous disorders.

Strikingly, as William McGrath has emphasized, the same period was also one of great personal turmoil for Freud.[105] He was deeply frustrated by the lack of professional respect accorded his new ideas and by his continual inability to secure a prominent academic appointment at the University of Vienna. With the election of the actively anti-Semitic Karl Lueger as mayor in 1897, he also felt increasingly uncomfortable in

---

[104] Carroy-Thirard, "Hystérie, théâtre, littérature," 314, 315. Again, compare Goldstein in "Uses of Male Hysteria," 137–38, 150–56.

[105] McGrath, *Freud's Discovery of Psychoanalysis*, chaps. 4 and 5.

Vienna. Most importantly, the death of his father in October 1896 initiated in Freud a psychological crisis in which a flood of repressed and conflicted feelings about his family, friends, and colleagues came to the fore and at times nearly incapacitated him. As is well known, Freud's unique experience of systematic psychological self-analysis, running from 1897 to 1900, played a key role in his return to equilibrium. Freud's intense, unprecedented self-analysis, which has attained almost mythological status in traditional accounts of his life, became both a therapeutic activity for Freud and an adjunct to his search for knowledge about human psychic processes.[106]

In addition to his theoretical labors, clinical activities, and personal predicaments during the 1890s, Freud during these years also conducted an extraordinary correspondence with his friend and colleague Wilhelm Fliess, a Berlin physician specializing in diseases of the ear, nose, and throat. Taking Breuer's earlier place, Fliess in the later nineties became Freud's intimate intellectual and emotional confidant. Their correspondence, which became available in a reliable, complete, and unexpurgated form in 1985, consists of roughly three hundred letters from Freud to Fliess.[107] Freud used Fliess as a sounding board for his emerging psychological theories. His letters brim with ideas, schemes, diagrams, and formulations about the etiology and structure of the neuroses, the nature of unconscious mentation, the motives and mechanisms of symptom formation, and the place of repression and fantasy in psychic life. They are intellectual progress reports, in which Freud formulates working hypotheses, then evaluates, rejects, revises, and adopts them. Throughout, he shares generously with Fliess the range of thought processes—the epiphanic moments of insight as well as the dark periods of intellectual paralysis—involved in the creation of a fundamentally new field of human knowledge. For their driving intellectual curiosity and sheer theoretical fertility, the letters are unmatched in the history of the psychological sciences.

However, along with reports on his intellectual work, Freud intersperses comments of a much more personal nature. Pertinent to our purposes, and much more evident in the recent, complete edition of the letters, Freud spends much time in these letters complaining about his physical and nervous ill health. In particular, during the two years following his father's death, he reports in himself a host of psychosomatic symp-

[106] Jones, *Life and Work of Sigmund Freud*, 1: 319–27; Max Schur, *Freud: Living and Dying* (New York: International Universities Press, 1972), chap. 4; Gay, *Freud*, 87–100; Didier Anzieu, *Freud's Self-Analysis* [1959], trans. Peter Graham (London: Hogarth Press and the Institute of Psycho-analysis, 1986).

[107] *The Complete Letters of Sigmund Freud to Wilhelm Fliess 1887–1904*, trans. and ed. Jeffrey Moussaieff Masson (Cambridge: Harvard University Press, 1985).

toms, including fear of death, a mild travel phobia, migraines, digestive disturbances, a nasal infection, sudden changes of mood, and bouts of depression. Throughout these letters, Freud refers without inhibition to his "neurosis," "neurasthenia," and "hypochondria." Three times he speaks of himself as a victim of hysteria.

On August 14, 1897, Freud wrote to Fliess from Aussee, Italy, where he was vacationing with his family. He confesses to Fliess that he was in "a period of bad humor." His Mediterranean holiday was not preventing him from being "tormented by grave doubts about my theory of the neuroses" nor "diminishing the agitation in my head and feelings." He observes further that "my little hysteria, though greatly accentuated by my work, has resolved itself a bit further." Referring to his self-analysis, which he decided to continue while on vacation, he concludes that "the chief patient I am preoccupied with is myself."[108] Similarly, in the fall of that same year, Freud, now back in Vienna, in one of his liveliest letters to Fliess, remarks: "There is still very little happening to me externally, but internally something very interesting. For the last four days my self-analysis, which I consider indispensable for the clarification of the whole problem [of the neuroses], has continued in dreams and has presented me with the most valuable elucidation and clues." Freud then relates a rush of images from his recent dream life and expresses the hope that his analysis of these images will "succeed in resolving my own hysteria."[109] And once more, on August 31, 1898, before departing Vienna with his wife for another trip to the Adriatic coast of his beloved Italy, Freud returned to the same theme. Bleakly, he complains to Fliess of his lack of motivation, of a period of depression and disorientation, and of the slow pace of his work. "The secret of this restlessness," he concludes, "is hysteria."[110]

The significance of the Freud/Fliess correspondence for the intellectual origins of psychoanalysis is well established. From the present perspective, however, these letters may also be read as a most remarkable group of documents in the history of male hysteria. What is significant about the passages above, I believe, is not that Freud should have affixed the hysteria label to himself but that his protracted neurotic episodes were so intimately bound up with his prodigious intellectual activities during the same period. During the later half of the 1890s, Freud was engaged sys-

---

[108] Letter from Freud to Fliess, August 14, 1897, in *Complete Letters of Sigmund Freud to Wilhelm Fliess*, 261.

[109] Letter from Freud to Fliess, October 3, 1897, in *Complete Letters of Sigmund Freud to Wilhelm Fliess*, 268–69.

[110] Letter from Freud to Fliess, August 31, 1898, in *Complete Letters of Sigmund Freud to Wilhelm Fliess*, 325. See also the letter from Freud to Fliess, October 15, 1897, in *Complete Letters*, 272, in which Freud, reflecting on ancient Greek theater and Shakespeare, refers to "Hamlet the hysteric."

tematically and simultaneously in treating a female hysterical clientele, writing books and articles about the psychoneuroses, conducting his analysis of himself, and writing to Fliess. Each activity contributed to the making of psychoanalysis. While biographers and historians have traditionally focused on the formative roles of the first two experiences, they have recently begun equally to explore the private, emotional sources of psychoanalysis.[111] In a detailed chronological way, McGrath has reconstructed the changing personal psychic conflicts that accompanied Freud's theoretical shifts in 1896–97.[112] During these years, by means of analyzing his own unconscious mental life, including his wishes, fears, frustrations, anxieties, and depressions, Freud was led to crucial insights about human psychic life generally. *The Interpretation of Dreams*, by Freud's own estimation the most important book he wrote, includes abundant autobiographical material. And in one letter to Fliess after another, Freud's drives for self-knowledge and for systematized psychological theory intermesh.[113]

To underscore the role that Freud's personal psychological conflicts played in the constitution of psychoanalytic theory is by no means to diminish his achievement but rather to clarify its complex origins. In light of the preceding discussion, it may in fact enhance that achievement. In the creation of psychoanalysis, Freud drew openly on the case-historical data that subsequently appeared in his printed works as well as on his own case. As McGrath writes, "his own mental disturbance opened up to him the possibility of understanding hysteria directly through internal perception as well as external observation."[114] Stated otherwise, the burst of intellectual activity in the 1890s that produced the core of classic psychoanalytic thought derived from a combination of clinical knowledge and self-knowledge, from a study of both "the Self" and "the Other." Freud's complete writings from this period—read as the simultaneous productions of a single mind—overcome the gulf between the natural sciences and the humanities, obliterate the dichotomy between the literary/subjective/introspective and the scientific/objective/analytical modes of inquiry, and combine the medical and cultural discourses of hysteria.[115]

I would like to pursue this line of thinking one step further by suggest-

---

[111] John E. Toews offers an intelligent account of this historiographical development in "Historicizing Psychoanalysis: Freud in His Time and for Our Time," *Journal of Modern History* 63 (September 1991): 516–24.

[112] McGrath, *Freud's Discovery of Psychoanalysis*, 152–229.

[113] For a particularly clear example of this union, consider his letter to Fliess, July 7, 1987, in *Complete Letters of Sigmund Freud to Wilhelm Fliess*, 254–56.

[114] McGrath, *The Discovery of Psychoanalysis*, 173.

[115] The same point has been made about psychoanalysis as a whole. See, for instance, Gedo and Pollock, *Freud: The Fusion of Science and Humanism*.

ing finally that Freud's writings dealing with hysteria—both his own and his patients'—may very profitably be set alongside the literary texts discussed above. In particular, the parallels between the Freud/Fliess correspondence and the letters of Flaubert to Colet, Baudelaire, and Sand are richly suggestive. Both sets of documents offered intimate, daily accounts of their authors' work in progress. Both Flaubert in the 1850s and Freud in the 1890s were gifted young men striving to achieve professional recognition and to create their first masterpieces. Diagnosing themselves as hysterical, both men registered the pain, loneliness, and uncertainty of creation of a high order. The novelist who depicted fictional characters "like a surgeon wielding a knife" and the doctor whose "case histories . . . read more like short stories" than science made themselves into two of the most profound commentators on human nature in history. In addition, Freud and Flaubert, during the most intellectually and artistically creative decades of their lives, sought to explore the human condition specifically through the representation of hysteria. But in the process, both men, in ways they doubtless did not suspect at the outset, found it necessary first to confront the hysterical element within themselves. This in turn required an exploration—half conscious, half unconscious—of the "feminine" component in their own psyches. Through this self-confrontation, both men captured, and then camouflaged, their own femininity. Flaubert accomplished this by crafting a work of fiction that offered one of the strongest female characters in modern fictional literature while Freud produced the most influential sexual science of our time.[116]

At the same time, what Freud and Flaubert concealed in their formal artistic and scientific writings, they displayed, openly and neurotically, in private epistolary formats. Furthermore, the impressive self-interrogations found in their personal correspondences were almost certainly made possible by the unique characters of those to whom these letters were addressed. Flaubert explored his own hysteria, his mental and emotional femininity, in conversations with three exceptional individuals: a male poet, a female poet and playwright with whom he had a protracted sexual relationship, and an exceptionally intelligent and intellectual woman who assumed a male authorial identity. As for Freud, he confided the most private details of his self-analysis to Fliess, in an intense and idealized friendship that contained a self-avowedly homoerotic component.[117]

[116] Pertinent here is Camille Paglia's thesis in *Sexual Personae: Art and Decadence from Nefertiti to Emily Dickinson* (New Haven: Yale University Press, 1990) that the inner dynamics of artistic creation in the Western tradition have often involved a fleeting union between male and female components of the psyche.

[117] For an account of the relationship, including its homoerotic ingredient, see Gay, *Freud*, 55–59, 86–87, 274–77. Writing to Fliess late in their friendship, Freud commented nostalgically, "No one can replace for me the relationship with the friend which a special—

In post-medieval Western literature, the figure of the male hysteric appears with surprising frequency. But the cultural history of male hysteria is altogether different from both the medical history of masculine hysteria and the cultural history of female hysteria. Throughout the ages, hysteria in women has been conceptualized almost without exception in controlling, pathologizing, and stigmatizing images. In contrast, with male hysteria in the cultural realm a range of nonpejorative implications, applications, and explorations has been achieved. Representations and self-representations of male hysteria have been employed by male artists and writers to strike fashionable literary poses, to advance the cause of cultural modernism, to register the *Sturm und Drang* of artistic creativity, and to probe and problematize dominant gender definitions. Additionally, the hysteria concept, construed metaphorically, has allowed male literary intellectuals to explore the feminine element within the masculine Self. While in medical contexts the label has carried highly undesirable, unmanning implications for male patients, artists and writers who were men largely avoided, or welcomed, these effeminizing connotations. As a result, they were able to use the category to develop new modes of sensibility and thereby to expand the scope of the emotional, intellectual, and aesthetic resources at their command.

In the near future, it is likely that the historiography of hysteria, culture, and male gender will grow rapidly.[118] That history, I have tried to show here, is a varied, eventful, and exciting one.

HYSTERIA AND RELIGION RECONSIDERED

Finally, we cannot conclude this study of the cultural histories of hysteria without considering the primary counterculture of hysteria in nineteenth-

---

possibly feminine—side demands." (Letter to Fliess, May 7, 1900, in *Complete Letters of Sigmund Freud and Wilhelm Fliess*, 412.)

[118] At the annual conference of the Modern Language Association held in Washington, D.C. in 1992, a section devoted to "Male Hysterical Narratives" elicited forty-five applicants. Topics for prospective presentations included Sander Gilman, "Mark Twain and Hysteria in the Holy Land"; Frederick A. Lubich, "Mann's *Magic Mountain*: Decadence's Master Narrative of 'Hysteria Passio'"; Sarah Blake, "The Literal Hysteria of Frankenstein: Narrators as Wandering Wombs"; Earl G. Ingersoll, "*The Rime of the Ancient Mariner*: Coleridge's Mariner as Male Hysteric"; Phillip McCaffrey, "Eluding the Story: Hysterical Rhetoric in E.T.A. Hoffmann's 'The Sandman'"; Helen McNeil, "The Insistence of the Letter *A*: Hawthorne and Male Hysteria"; Stephanie Moss, "Bram Stroker's H(is)teria"; Robert Ponterio, "Male Hysteria in Guy de Maupassant's 'La Nuit de Noël'"; Debrah Raschke, "Conrad's Marlow as Reluctant Hysteric"; Ellen Rosenberg, "Male Hysterical Narrative: The Case of Henry James"; Nancy I. Rubino, "Figures of Male Hysteria: Effeminate Artists in Decadent Literature"; Margot Sempreora, "Editing His Hysteria: Three Stories by Ernest Hemingway"; Diana Stevenson, "David Lynch's Male Hysterics"; and Priscilla L. Walton, "Writing Other: Anthony Trollope as Male Hysteric."

century France: Catholicism. In nearly all historical writing about psychiatry, the religious and psychiatric worldviews are presented at sharp variance with one another. In the 1800s, introductory historical chapters to psychiatric textbooks and dissertations often pointedly contrasted the current state of enlightened medical knowledge with past religious obscurantism and philosophical mysticism. During the 1930s and 1940s, the first full narrative histories of psychiatry retailed similar scenarios. In his influential *A History of Medical Psychology* (1941), Gregory Zilboorg presented psychiatric history in almost Manichean terms, as the world-historical clash of the religious/supernatural and medical/naturalistic models of mind. This view was then subsequently bolstered by the biographical literature on Freud. With his outspoken and uncompromising personal atheism, his interpretations of piety as psychopathology, and his polemical antireligious statements *The Future of an Illusion* and *Moses and Monotheism*, the founder of psychoanalysis seemed to exemplify the opposition between institutional religion and psychiatry that has existed throughout history.

This same interpretation is inscribed in the historical scholarship about hysteria. Nineteenth-century French physicians, from Calmeil to Charcot, working self-consciously within an anticlerical Enlightenment tradition, produced authoritative-sounding commentaries that diagnosed past religious behaviors as signs of hysterical pathology. Similarly, Veith's *Hysteria: The History of a Disease*, which draws heavily on Zilboorg, highlights the struggle of modern science to free itself from mystical, spiritistic, or demonological readings of the disease. Most recently, Goldstein, we learned above, has written extensively about the relation between hysteria doctors and clericalism during the age of Charcot.[119] In France during the final quarter of the nineteenth century, the long-running conflict between the Catholic Church and political republicanism entered a particularly antagonistic phase. The school of the Salpêtrière, Goldstein has established, played a significant part in this confrontation, laicizing hospital nursing staffs, establishing new chairs on the Paris Medical Faculty, and publishing the *Bibliothèque Diabolique*, comprised of texts that reinterpreted neuropathologically past religious events and personalities. In the theoretical realm, Charcot integrated into his work elements of demonological hysteria, reformulated in the terms of positivist medicine. Charcot's newly scientized theory of the disease, Goldstein has contended, was a classic episode in the historical clash of the religious and the scientific mentalities, with the latter emerging triumphant.

Methodologically and interpretively, the historical researches of Zilboorg, Veith, Goldstein, and the nineteenth-century positivist doctors

---

[119] See the discussion of her work above, 98–100, 103.

pursue very different approaches. But present latently in each of them is the view that the religious and psychiatric conceptualizations of mental illness generally, and of hysteria specifically, have been inherently antagonistic and irreconcilable. Each of these writings conceptualize science and religion oppositionally. I have no doubt whatsoever that there is a great deal of truth in this perspective. However, I want to suggest here that the extant scholarship on this topic does not exhaust the story of the relations between psychiatry and religion in the history of hysteria but rather only opens the subject up for additional investigation. My point is that past relations between the theological and scientific models of the disease have been much more diverse, complicated, and at times accommodative than previously realized and that this aspect of the subject uncovers an equally rich vein for historical analysis. This is especially true, I believe, for the Catholic Mediterranean countries of Europe, where the interactions between the two representations of hysteria have been extensive. This fact becomes apparent if we move beyond the loud public rhetorics of the officialdoms of each camp to other, less conspicuous constituencies and beyond avant-garde ideas and writings to everyday beliefs and practices. It comes further into focus if we venture beyond medical and religious texts to types of writings that are less ideologically invested, such as fictional literature.[120]

The case for continuity between the religious and medical cultures of hysteria in France is in fact comparatively easy to make. During the fin-de-siècle years, the most heated topic of controversy in France between the medical and the clerical professions was not the makeup of the Paris medical faculty, or medical interpretations of past religious events and personalities, or governmental hospital policy in the cities. It was Lourdes.

---

[120] I believe that on this point hysteria studies may profit from the example of Darwin studies. For decades, historians of Darwinism generalized from the most dramatic and confrontational episodes, such as the Huxley/Wilberforce debate and the Scopes trial, to highlight "the warfare between science and religion." A generation of scholarship, however, has established that religious responses to Darwinian evolutionary science were vastly more varied than previously pictured, and not least of all in France. Contrast, for example, Andrew Dickson White's well-known *A History of the Warfare of Science with Theology in Christendom* (1896) to Frank Miller Turner, *Between Science and Religion: Religious Faith and Scientific Naturalism in Late Victorian England* (New Haven: Yale University Press, 1974); James R. Moore, *The Post-Darwinian Controversies: A Study of the Protestant Struggle to Come to Terms with Darwin in Great Britain and America, 1870–1900* (New York: Cambridge University Press, 1979); Harry W. Paul, *The Edge of Contingency: French Catholic Reaction to Scientific Change from Darwin to Duhem* (Gainesville: University Presses of Florida, 1979); John Durant, ed., *Darwinism and Divinity: Essays on Evolution and Religious Belief* (Oxford: Basil Blackwell, 1985); and Jon H. Roberts, *Darwinism and the Divine in America: Protestant Intellectuals and Organic Evolution, 1859–1900* (Madison: University of Wisconsin Press, 1988).

Notre-Dame de Lourdes, in the Department of the Hautes-Pyrénées in southwestern France, was founded on the alleged apparitions of the Virgin Mother to a fourteen-year-old peasant girl named Bernadette Soubirous in 1858. Several years later, word of Bernadette's experiences had spread, and local bishops declared her visions authentic. Soon thereafter a basilica was built upon the rock of Massabielle, where the Virgin Mother had supposedly appeared, and by 1873 annual national pilgrimages to the site began. The sanctuary expanded rapidly, and by the early 1890s tens of thousands of pilgrims from across Europe were converging on it each year. Lourdes was the most popular pilgrimage site in the nineteenth-century Catholic world and the prime religious sensation of its time. In this final section, I want to suggest that the Catholic cult of Lourdes, Charcot's school of the Salpêtrière, and Bernheim's school of Nancy, as the three developed during the 1880s and 1890s, may be viewed as alternative psychotherapeutic cultures, that a complex of similarities and differences exist between these contemporaneous institutional worlds, and that the theory and practice of hysteria played a critical part in all three settings.

To the best of my knowledge, the appearance of the miraculous in the final quarter of the nineteenth century, during the years that are supposed to have represented the heyday of atheistic scientism, has not yet been adequately explained by historians. It is probably not coincidental that Lourdes was founded and flourished during the highpoint of what William James called "medical materialism."[121] The late nineteenth century was a period of assertive positivist ideology—led in philosophy by Émile Littré and Ernest Renan and in the medical, biological, and chemical sciences by Claude Bernard, P.-E.-M. Berthelot, Charles Robin, and Charcot —in which science was believed by many people to provide self-sufficient explanations for all natural as well as social phenomena. In this light, Lourdes, to many members of the scientific intelligentsia, represented an affront to the spirit of the age, a perverse throwback to a superstitious, prescientific past. Not surprisingly, many physicians commented on the Catholic shrine with hostility and incredulity.

In his 1869 article introducing the idea of "retrospective medicine," Littré reflected skeptically on a series of miraculous cures of paralyzed pilgrims at the tomb of Saint-Denis during the thirteenth century.[122] Several years later, Auguste Voisin, an alienist at the Salpêtrière, argued that Bernadette's ecstasies had only been hallucinatory deliria that presaged an acute psychiatric deterioration. The celebrated inspiratress of Lourdes,

[121] William James, *The Varieties of Religious Experience: A Study in Human Nature* [1902] (New York: Modern Library, 1936), 14.

[122] Émile Littré, "Un fragment de médecine rétrospective," *La philosophie positive: Revue 5*, no. 1 (July–August 1869): 103–20.

added Voisin, was in fact currently being cared for at the Ursuline convent of Nevers, where she was now quite insane—a charge that Catholic commentators denied vociferously.[123] At roughly the same time, Dr. Paul Diday (later known for his work in venereology) applied Voisin's pathologizing line of analysis to the pilgrims of Lourdes as a whole.[124]

During the mid-1880s, a second major critique of the shrine emerged, this one from doctors in Nancy who interpreted the goings-on at Lourdes according to their own psychological doctrines. In *De la suggestion et de ses applications à la thérapeutique* of 1886, Bernheim posited a parallel between the hypnotic psychotherapeutics pioneered in his clinic and what he called the "miraculous therapeutics" of Lourdes. Both phenomena, contended Bernheim, were fully explicable as the result of exaggerated impressionability in susceptible individuals.[125] Piety and hysterical psychopathology resulted equally from excessive autosuggestion. During the following decades, several works by physicians repeated with minor variations the Bernheimian analysis.[126]

The most controversial statement about Lourdes from this period, however, issued not from a physician or scientist but a man of letters. By 1893, Émile Zola had completed his multivolume Rougon-Macquart series. But France's most famous and energetic living author would scarcely stop writing. During the middle years of the 1890s, Zola was occupied with *Les trois villes*, a trilogy of novels set in three major European locations. The first of the three novels dealt with Lourdes.

During the summers of 1891 and 1892, Zola visited the Marian shrine to gather information for a major fictional work. Throughout 1893, he worked steadily on the novel, and in August of 1894, during that year's Assumptionist pilgrimage, *Lourdes* hit the Paris newsstands.[127] Not surprisingly, the novel was anti-Catholic through and through. Zola structured his story around the experiences of one Pierre Froment, a well-intentioned priest who travels to Lourdes but becomes increasingly skeptical about what he sees. The novel consists of five main sections, with the parts

[123] Auguste Voisin, "Conférences cliniques sur les maladies mentales et les affections nerveuses (1870): Folie du jeune âge," *L'union médicale* 13, no. 76 (June 27, 1872): 927.

[124] Dr. Paul Diday, *Examen médical des miracles de Lourdes* (Paris, 1873).

[125] Hippolyte Bernheim, *De la suggestion et de ses applications à la thérapeutique* (Paris: Octave Doin, 1886), 214–18.

[126] Medicus, *Lourdes et le surnaturel* (Paris, 1894); Dr. M. Gaud, *De certains processus psychiques de guérisons* (Lyons: A. Rey, 1907); Dr. Hippolyte Baraduc, *La force curatrice à Lourdes et la psychologie du miracle* (Paris: Bloud et Cie, 1907); Dr. Hubert Lavrand, *La suggestion et les guérisons de Lourdes* (Paris: Bloud et Cie, 1908). See also P. Saintyves, *La simulation du merveilleux*, preface by Pierre Janet (Paris: Ernest Flammarion, 1912), esp. 52–90; and Auguste Aumaitre, "Contribution à l'étude de l'hystérie religieuse" (Ph.D. diss., University of Paris, 1935).

[127] Émile Zola, *Lourdes* (Paris: G. Charpentier et E. Fasquelle, 1894).

corresponding to the successive days in Froment's visit. In the course of the book, Zola narrates in depth the fortunes of many minor characters who had come to the sanctuary in search of a cure. He describes the powerful image of the pilgrim trains—"véritables hôpitaux ambulants," he calls them—transporting crowds of people to the town; he records the appalling sight of hundreds of people suffering from leprosy, elephantiasis, and every other imaginable disease; and he discusses the many dramatic daily scenes at Lourdes, including the gathering of stretchers and wheelchairs in front of the Grotto, submersions in the fountain of holy waters, and the nighttime processions by torchlight. Zola sympathized on the human level with what he saw at Lourdes; but the much-touted cures, he insisted, were bogus, the result either of errors of diagnosis or nervous disorders relieved psychologically. In the end, he presents a picture of human deception, pathetic credulity, and religious mania—"he catches the general hysteria of the place," one biographer has written[128]— and voices Bernheim's view that the whole thing is the result of "autosuggestion."

While not particularly noteworthy artistically, and infrequently read today, Zola's book was an immense popular success at the time. Not unexpectedly, the reception in the Catholic world was furiously negative. In addition to being placed promptly on the Index, *Lourdes* gave rise almost overnight to a number of lively countercritiques.[129] Moreover, by the late 1880s the conflict in France between old religion and the new rationalism had grown acute, and a full-scale reaction against positivist atheism, organizing under Fernand Brunetière's banner of "the bankruptcy of science," was gathering strength. A serious Catholic revival was underway, and the growing cult of Lourdes and the attack on Zola's novel were expressions of it.

On the specific issue of religion and retrospective medical diagnostics, the clerical press now began to regain its confidence and fight back. Joseph de Bonniot, senior science editor for the Jesuit publication *Études*, led the way. In a series of articles entitled "Hysteria and Saintliness" that appeared in a journal of popular science, Bonniot offered a defense of hagiographical history.[130] Citing the work of Tardieu, Huchard, Richet,

---

[128] Joanna Richardson, *Zola* (New York: St. Martin's Press, 1978), 167.

[129] P. Raffaele Ballerini, *Lourdes: Le miracle et la critique d'Émile Zola* (1894); Abbé Paulin Moniquet, *Un mot à M. Émile Zola et aux détracteurs de Lourdes* (Paris: Tolra, 1895); Abbé E. Henry Duplessy, *Zola et Lourdes* (Paris, 1895); Abbé Joseph Crestey, *Critique d'un roman historique* (Paris: Chamuel, 1896).

[130] Joseph de Bonniot, "Hystérie et sainteté," *Le cosmos: Revue des sciences et de leurs applications*, new ser., 3, nos. 57–60 (March 1886): 343–48, 369–72, 397–400, 426–29, combined and enlarged as *Opposition entre l'hystérie et la sainteté* (Paris: Letowzey et Ané, 1886). See also R. P. Grégoire de Saint-Joseph, *La prétendue hystérie de Sainte Thérèse* (Lyon: E. Vitte, 1895).

and Lasègue (but not Charcot), Bonniot cleverly defined hysteria according to the dominant psychiatric, rather than neurological, theories of the day. In the eyes of French alienists, he maintained, hysteria was characterized by a loss of personal will and self-control, leading to vain, selfish, sexually indulgent, and emotionally frivolous behaviors. In contrast, Bonniot went on, the great saints of the Church possessed, often to a superhuman degree, the typically Christian qualities of austerity, control of the will, and self-sacrifice. Despite the demystifying recensions of the doctors, the Catholic saints had been sturdy, wholly unhysterical characters. Furthermore, Bonniot reviewed the much-publicized stages of Richer's hystero-epileptic attack and then juxtaposed these to the recorded visions and ecstasies of the best-known saints—a kind of clerical reworking of the *Démoniaques dans l'art* of Richer and Charcot.[131] The two phenomena, insisted Bonniot, were radically different. Past experiences of the Catholic saints, he asserted, were authentic divine inspirations, not manifestations of nervous disease. In conclusion, he insisted on the incompetence of medical men to pass judgment on these matters and condemned their arrogant trespass into the spiritual realm.

Two years later, writing in *Études*, Bonniot and his coreligionists not only rejected the "rationalist thesis" of the physicians about these matters but went on the offensive. This time they assailed Charcot and his clan directly for their all-consuming "hystérologie," accusing them of unconscionably abandoning their therapeutic duties and claiming that the occasional quasi-miraculous cures occurring in hospital clinics were the work of the Almighty.[132] At roughly the same time, Élie Méric, professor of theology at the Sorbonne, sermonized against Charcot and Bernheim for the reckless and immoral use of hypnosis with hysterical subjects.[133] Charcot's unexpected death several years later encouraged additional critiques. One writer, the Jesuit G. Hahn, attacked what he regarded as vulgar misapplications of Salpêtrian doctrine and cast doubt on the scientific integrity of the demonstrations of Charcot, Luys, and Dumontpallier. Shorn of its sober-sounding, pseudoscientific vocabulary, Hahn argued, the experimentation taking place in the Paris hospitals with metals and hypnosis bore suspicious resemblance to the earlier charlatanry of phre-

---

[131] Bonniot, "Hystérie et sainteté," *Cosmos*, 343–48, 371–72, 399–400.

[132] Bonniot, review of *Démoniaques dans l'art* in "Iconographie des possessions," 2 parts, *Études: Religieuses, philosophiques, historiques et littéraires*, 43–44 (April–May 1888): 480–99, 23–41; idem, "Les miracles de l'Évangile: La crédulité des médecins: La foi chrétienne," 2 parts, *Études*, 43 (January–February 1888): 23–52, 199–211; Joseph Brucker, "Les miracles de l'histoire sainte devant la critique," 2 parts, *Études* 48–49 (December 1889, March 1890): 564–75, 457–69.

[133] Élie Méric, *Le merveilleux et la science: Étude sur l'hypnotisme* (Paris: Letouzey et Ané, 1887), esp. Book 3.

nology and animal magnetism: "If Gall and Mesmer had not existed," Hahn concluded in mock imitation of Voltaire, "one would probably not speak of Charcot."[134] In sum, the campaign of Charcot and the Salpêtrians to appropriate ideas, texts, and figures from the theological past did not silence the opposition but rather inspired a spirited Catholic countercritique in an ongoing confrontation that extended well into the twentieth century. Indeed, in the Catholic press of the 1880s and 1890s, no scientific subject, with the exception of Darwinian evolutionism, aroused a stronger or longer critical response than the medical literature about Lourdes.

Confronted with Zola's novel and the writings of scientific skeptics, Lourdes found a particularly indefatigable apologist in Abbé Georges Bertrin. Briefly trained in medicine during his youth, Bertrin served for many years as the official keeper of medical records at Lourdes and later held a professorship at the Institut Catholique in Paris. Bertrin's *Histoire critique des événements de Lourdes*, which first appeared in 1905, became a standard source of information about the shrine for a generation of sympathetic readers.[135] In loving detail, Bertrin's *Histoire critique* relates the story of Bernadette's visions, the papal recognition of their authenticity, the founding of the basilica, and the growth of the pilgrimages. Bertrin also took on Lourdes's two major enemies, "the professors of the Paris School" and "the suggestionists," that is to say Charcot, Bernheim, and their followers. Not failing to note Bernheim's personal religious affiliation, Bertrin argued against Bernheim's authority to speak on matters pertaining to Christian faith and defended the Lourdes cures as genuine supernatural occurrences. In an appendix to the English translation of his book, Bertrin recorded the number and category of diseases cured at Lourdes in recent years and pointed out that the nervous diseases Charcot diagnosed as hysteria contributed only fractionally to the sum.[136]

The Catholic Church fought back against its scientific critics most effectively, however, through the sheer popular success of Lourdes. Whatever scientific urbanites might think or say about it, Lourdes throughout the late nineteenth century attracted tens, and eventually hundreds, of thousands of people yearly.[137] Furthermore, Catholic countercritics assailed medical professionals at their weakest point—namely, their inability to provide a cure, or often even consolation, for many patients, includ-

---

[134] Hahn, "Charcot et son influence sur l'opinion publique," 379.

[135] Georges Bertrin, *Histoire critique des événements de Lourdes: Apparitions et guérisons* [1905], 2d ed. (Lourdes: Bureaux de la Grotte; Paris: Librairie Gabalda, 1913).

[136] Georges Bertrin, *Lourdes: A History of Its Apparitions and Cures*, trans. Mrs. Philip Gibbs (London: Kegan Paul, Trench, Trubner, 1928), appendix 4, 293–96.

[137] By 1908, Bertrin had tallied 4,919,000 pilgrims since the opening of the facility. Many more visited as curious onlookers.

ing a large percentage of those suffering from nervous and neurological ailments. Throughout the 1880s and 1890s, Lourdes generated an enormous clerical literature, modeled on Henri Lasserre's bestselling *Notre-Dame de Lourdes* (1886), that was designed to give the shrine worldwide publicity. Interestingly, many of the authors of these tracts set up an opposition between the Catholic sanctuary and the modern lay hospital. Moreover, pro-Catholic writers explicitly presented those cases that found relief at Lourdes as examples of success *where the world of urban professional medicine had failed.*[138] In a word, "la foi qui guérit" was also "la médecine qui ne guérit pas."

Viewed in medical-historical and social-historical context, this juxtaposition is hardly surprising. For people of affluent backgrounds suffering from nervous, psychological, and neurological ailments, there were spas, medical holidays, hydropathic institutes, and private nerve clinics. But sick people with these same infirmities from lower socioeconomic backgrounds, whether in the cities or the countryside, were much more likely to be subjected to impersonal, municipal medical institutions, painful physical procedures, and denigratory diagnostic labels. Even more to the point, therapeutic practice for nervous and mental disorders at this time was still constrained by degenerationist thinking. At best, it offered hydrotherapy and electricity, with little optimism about prognosis and almost no sense of the psychological component in many of these cases. The clinics of Charcot, Bernheim, Luys, and Dumontpallier were above all sites for medical observation and experimentation. Generally speaking, the second half of the nineteenth century, while a major period of advancement in the etiological understanding of disease, was not a great age of healing.

In direct contrast, Lourdes, in popular Catholic literature, was presented preeminently as a recuperative site. In a manner of speaking, it offered a type of group psychotherapy on a massive scale. As a consequence, thousands of people throughout this period, and especially French men and women from rural backgrounds, found far greater solace at Lourdes, where they discovered a spirit of hope, equality, and communal suffering, and where powerful (if unacknowledged) psychological forces were at work, than in the so-called best medical facilities of the day. Chronologically, the rise of Lourdes is precisely synchronous with the emergence of the schools of Nancy and the Salpêtrière, and with the "age of hysteria" in the cities. Moreover, both Lourdes and the Salpêtrière were large, closed institutional environments, with professionally trained

---

[138] Bertrin, *Histoire critique des événements de Lourdes*, 180, 196–98, 324–25; H. Martin, "Zola à Lourdes," *Études* 57 (November 1892): 421–41; idem, "Le miracle au dix-neuvième siècle: Lourdes devant la science," 3 parts, *Études* 51 (November–December 1890): 355–70, 602–20; 52 (January 1891): 5–27; Gustave Boissarie, *Les grandes guérisons de Lourdes* (Paris: Charles Douniol, 1900), passim. Also, in Zola's *Lourdes*, see 1–21 and 138–60.

staffs and highly suggestive atmospheres, with great numbers of people from similar educational and socioeconomic backgrounds, who suffered not only from incurable organic ailments but also malleable nervous disorders. Considered culturally and psychologically, then, Lourdes functioned as a kind of popular nonmedical counterculture of hysteria in late nineteenth-century Europe. Or, viewed from a somewhat different historical perspective, the Lourdes cult, the neuropsychiatry of Charcot, and the suggestive therapeutics of Bernheim may be seen as different but contemporaneous manifestations of the possiblity of a therapeutics of mind in the immediate pre-Freudian era.

The opportunities today for exploring the idea of Lourdes as a counterculture of hysteria are outstanding. It is not simply that there exists an abundance of primary sources about the shrine. It is also that a large amount of this material recounts in detail the alleged cures that transpired at Lourdes and that much of this writing takes the form of what to the late twentieth-century historian may properly be called case histories. The story of Bernadette, for instance, was copiously documented.[139] From 1868 to 1890, authorities at Lourdes published an official yearly bulletin, the *Annales de Notre-Dame de Lourdes*, that included a substantial section on cures that took place at the shrine. Moreover, as medical statistician of Lourdes, Bertrin assembled quantities of information about the sickness and health of the pilgrims. The final third of his *Histoire critique de Lourdes* presents at length the personal and medical biographies of seven patients.[140] Bertrin kept expanding his study until it eventually comprised four bulky volumes, titled *Lourdes et les miracles*. Volume 3, *Un miracle d'aujourd'hui*, relates in 160 pages the story of a single case of Pott's disease which was miraculously "cured" at Lourdes.[141] "This remarkable study of Pott's disease," reads the publisher's advertisement for the book, "recalls . . . the most beautiful and erudite lessons of the Andrals, the Velpeaus, the Potains and all the great master clinicians who have illustriously characterized the French medicine of the past sixty years."[142]

No less valuable is Gustave Boissarie's *Lourdes: Histoire médicale: 1858–1891*.[143] From 1891 to 1917, Boissarie, who had trained in the

[139] R. Laurentin, *Lourdes: Dossier des documents authentiques*, 7 vols. (Paris: P. Lethielleux, 1957–66).

[140] Bertrin, *Histoire critique de Lourdes*, 240–403. See in particular 267–348, where Bertrin locates the medical records of four of the individuals discussed pseudonymously in Zola's novel and reinterprets their cases!

[141] Bertrin, *Un miracle d'aujourd'hui* (Paris: Lecoffre, 1908).

[142] Bertrin, *Histoire critique de Lourdes*, publisher's note on the inside front cover.

[143] Dr. [Propser-Gustave] Boissarie, *Lourdes: Histoire médicale: 1858–1891* (Paris: Librairie Victor Lecoffre, 1891), esp. books 2 and 3.

Parisian medical system, worked as chief physician-in-residence at Lourdes. His book, which was intended to serve as the official medical history of Lourdes, is chock full of cases of sick pilgrims. It includes as well excerpts from the *Annales de Notre-Dame de Lourdes* and two chapters titled "Hysteria at Lourdes."[144] *Lourdes: Histoire médicale*, published in 1891, became enormously popular, and under separate cover Boissarie published a collection of the shrine's most dramatic medical stories, heavily illustrated with photographs, that was widely disseminated.[145]

Above all, there are the available archival sources. Ideologically, the Catholic Church shunned the modern medical worldview; but, ironically, in attempting to authenticate its own cures, it inadvertently adopted the methods of modern medical record-keeping. On the grounds of Lourdes, near the main shrine, a Bureau des constatations médicales was established in 1883.[146] Here, all manner of documents pertaining to cases that resulted in recoveries, whether partial or complete, were carefully preserved. As Zola explained, "Each patient who accompanied the pilgrimage arrived with a dossier, in which there was almost always a certificate of the doctor who had been attending the case. At times, there were even certificates from several doctors, hospital reports, an entire history of the illness."[147] Once at Lourdes, Bertrin, Boissarie, and the other physician/priests in attendance added their own materials to the dossiers, including, when appropriate, *certificats de guérisons*. All in all, these documents usually record the full name of the individual, his or her place of origin, the physician in charge of the case beforehand, the diagnosed disease, the symptoms and course of the sickness, and the date of the cure. After returning to their homes, some individuals were treated again by local doctors and then sent additional information (i.e., "follow-up data") back to the bureau. Boissarie states that in the 1880s approximately fifty cures were recorded each year during the August pilgrimages alone and that by the late 1890s the number had risen to over two hundred annual recoveries.[148] By 1908, the fiftieth anniversary of the shrine, Bertrin claimed to have documented 3,962 cures attributable to its sacred influence.[149]

[144] Ibid., 147–262, 388–423. For a skeptical reading of the book from within the medical camp, take a look at Dr. Verrier, "Les miracles de Lourdes et le livre de Dr. Boissarie," *Revue de l'hypnotisme et de la psychologie physiologique* 9, no. 9 (March 1895): 275–78.

[145] Boissarie, *Les grandes guérisons de Lourdes*, édition illustrée de 140 semiligravures (Paris: P. Tequi, 1900).

[146] The history of the facility is related in Boissarie, *Lourdes*, 263–79 as well as in Françoise Boissarie de l'Épine, "Études sur la clinique de Lourdes: Son évolution de 1858 jusqu'à nos jours" (Ph.D. diss., 1952).

[147] Zola, *Lourdes*, 187.

[148] Boissarie, *Grandes guérisons de Lourdes*, 10, 11; idem, *Lourdes*, 277. Boissarie estimates that a quarter of the cured cases involved males.

[149] Georges Bertrin, "Lourdes," in *The Catholic Encyclopedia*, 15 vols. (New York: Robert Appleton, 1910), 9: 390.

The records of the medical certification office at Lourdes were compiled by clerical authorities in order to establish the veracity of miracles and the superiority of religious to medical ministration. But the student of the history of hysteria may respond differently to these sources. If we are willing (on the basis of *our* faith in scientific naturalism) to accept a secular reading of what occurred at Lourdes, then these documents record an immense pool of severe psychogenic somatic ailments, especially gross motor conversions in adult and adolescent women, from a century ago. In form and content, the "case histories" of Bertrin and Boissarie read remarkably like the contemporaneous clinical narratives of Charcot, Bernheim, Luys, and Dumontpallier. In their accounts of patients' personal and medical biographies and subjective psychological worlds, these religious records, in fact, are frequently more informative than their medical counterparts. Bertrin's account of the individual who recovered miraculously from Pott's Disease may be the single lengthiest case history of a hysterical patient from the period.[150] Taken together, the printed books and articles about Lourdes, the *Annales de Notre-Dame de Lourdes*, and the manuscript materials at the Bureau des constations médicales offer an entire archive for the historian of hysteria and suggest that the most popular and populous setting for the treatment of the disorder in late nineteenth-century Europe was not Paris, Nancy, or Vienna, but this small, isolated, Pyrenean village.[151]

While Lourdes may be viewed as a nonmedical counterculture of hysteria, a second and more complicated set of relations between Catholicism and medicine emerged during the fin de siècle. At this point, it is well to recall the repeated admonition of Theodore Zeldin that beneath the neat, black-and-white division of French political and intellectual history into atheistic, scientific intellectuals and uncritical and reactionary defenders of the faith there often ran deeper continuities.[152] Zeldin's insight is highly apt in regard to the history of hysteria.

We are again first put in mind of this fact by the literature on Lourdes: among the earliest and angriest critics of Zola's novel *Lourdes*, it turns out, were Catholic physicians who produced books and pamphlets in profusion defending what transpired at the sanctuary.[153] In fact an in-

---

[150] Compare Bertrin's *Un miracle d'aujourd'hui* with Charcot, "Simulation hystérique du mal de Pott chez un garçon âgé 24 ans," *Leçons du mardi à la Salpêtrière: Policlinique: 1888–1889* (Paris: Bureaux du Progrès Médical, Lecrosnier et Babé, 1889), lesson 9, 189–98.

[151] The records at the Lourdes medical certification office are open today, without restriction, to all physicians of any nationality and religious orientation.

[152] Theodore Zeldin, *France 1848–1945*, vol. 1, *Ambition, Love, and Politics* (Oxford: Clarendon Press, 1973), 37; vol. 2, *Intellect, Taste, and Anxiety* (Oxford: Clarendon Press, 1977), 982, 1024–39.

[153] Dr. D. Moncoq, *Réponse complète au Lourdes de M. Zola* (Caen: Le Boyteux,

creasing number of people writing sympathetically about Lourdes in the decade and a half following Zola's work were medical professionals.[154] Bertrin and Boissarie stated that large numbers of French and foreign physicians—during the 1890s, over 200 per year—visited Lourdes, and in 1906 a petition circulated with some 350 signatures of physicians attesting to the legitimacy of the miracles that occurred there.[155] Boissarie offered a detailed defense of Bernadette, cast in medical terms, in the face of charges by Voisin and Diday.[156] A prominent medical professor from Clermont-Ferrand produced a sympathetic, book-length tome about Louise Lateau in the face of repeated disparagements of her in Bourneville's *Bibliothèque Diabolique* series.[157] Several years later, the most thoroughgoing critique of the practice of rediagnosing religious phenomena in neuropathological terms came from the pen of an American physician-philosopher who had observed both Charcot's lectures at the Salpêtrière and events at Lourdes.[158] Other British and American psychiatrists and psychologists expressed strong interest in Lourdes as well.[159]

Among the medical professionals who attentively and appreciatively followed developments at Lourdes were also major medical theorists of hysteria. A case in point is Janet, whose career bridges the medical and religious cultures of hysteria nicely. After a youthful training in philosophy during the early 1880s, partly undertaken in pursuit of a strong personal interest in the philosophy and psychology of religion, Janet turned to the clinical study of the nervous and mental disorders. While at the Salpêtrière, he maintained a lively interest in and respect for miraculous cures and the occult sciences.[160] Also, during the late 1890s and early 1900s, Janet treated an extraordinary young woman named "Mad-

---

1894); Dr. L. Rascoul, *Étude critique sur "Lourdes" de M. Émile Zola* (1894). See also Boissarie, *Grandes guérisons de Lourdes*, chap. 17.

[154] Boissarie, *Lourdes depuis 1858 jusqu'à nos jours* (Paris: Sanard et Derangeon, 1894); idem, *Lourdes*; idem, *Grandes guérisons*; Dr. Berteaux, "Lourdes et la science," *Revue de l'hypnotisme et de la psychologie physiologique* 9, no. 7 (January 1895): 210–17; Dr. Félix de Backer, *Lourdes et les médecins* (Paris: Maloine, 1905); Dr. Hyppolyte Baraduc, *La force curatrice à Lourdes et la psychologie du miracle* (1907); Dr. Hubert Lavrand, *La suggestion et les guérisons de Lourdes* (Paris: Bloud et Cie, 1908); and idem, *Hystérie et sainteté* (Paris: Bloud et Cie, 1911).

[155] Bertrin, *Histoire critique de Lourdes*, 231–39; Boissarie, *Grandes guérisons de Lourdes*, 11, 12.

[156] Boissarie, *Lourdes*, 45–96.

[157] Dr. Antoine Imbert-Gourbeyre, *La stigmatisation, l'extase divine et les miracles de Lourdes: Réponse aux libres-penseurs*, 2 vols. (Clermont-Ferrand: Librairie catholique, L. Bellet, 1894), vol. 2, chaps. 25–28, esp. 457–80.

[158] I am referring to William James, whose *Varieties of Religious Experience* of 1902 opens with a now famous chapter on "Religion and Neurology."

[159] See, for instance, A. T. Myers and F.W.H. Myers, "Mind, Faith-Cure and the Miracles of Lourdes," *Proceedings of the Society for Psychical Research* (1893–94): 160–209.

[160] Pierre Janet, "Le spiritisme contemporain," *Revue philosophique* 33, no. 1 (1892): 413–42.

eleine," whose symptoms included mystical hallucinations, a peculiar contracture of the leg muscles that permitted her to walk only on tiptoe, and bleeding spots on the backs of her hands and feet that resembled the stigmati of Christ. Janet served as Madeleine's private psychotherapist for many years, during which time the patient also had a regular spiritual advisor. Janet respected Madeleine greatly, and years later, in one of his richest and most detailed clinical reports, presented her case as a mixture of psychopathology and genuine religious sentiment.[161] After the 1920s, Janet returned increasingly to his youthful interest in religious psychology, including the psychology of spiritism and the occult sciences.[162] Nor was he the only hysteria doctor during this period who found no difficulty in balancing strong scientific and religious interests.[163]

From the other side of the issue, the Catholic church at times listened to, and learned from, medical professionals in the nineteenth century. We have already seen that Lourdes, with its medical bureau, in-house doctors, and elaborate keeping of records, embraced select contemporary medical practices. In a similar vein, the contagions of hysteria that occasionally seized French villages and convents, and that Galopin and others satirized, were genuine problems for the Church. In severe situations, clerical authorities turned to doctors for assistance. As Catherine-Laurence Maire and Carroy have shown, one particularly severe outbreak occurred early in the 1860s in the French Alpine town of Morzine. The Bishop of Annecy called for help from the government in Paris, which sent in first a team of psychiatrists and eventually the national army. Headed by L.J.J. Constans, the inspecteur-général of French national asylums, and the alienist Louis-Florentin Calmeil, physicians worked amicably with ecclesiastical and governmental officials to clean up the mess.[164] In their official reports, Constans and Calmeil employed a mixed religious and medical vocabulary of "hystero-demonopathy" to account for the popular outburst.[165] Along the same lines, a certain Abbé Touroude in 1894 published *L'hystérie: Sa nature, sa fréquence, ses causes, ses symptômes et ses effets*.[166] Touroude's book in effect offers a detailed guide, approved by

[161] Janet, *De l'angoisse à l'extase: Études sur les croyances et les sentiments*, 2 vols. (Paris: Alcan, 1926–28), 1: 9–200.

[162] Janet, "La psychologie de la croyance et le mysticisme," *Revue de métaphysique et de morale* 43 (1936): 327–58, 507–32; 44 (1937): 369–410.

[163] See, for example, Joseph Grasset, *Le spiritisme devant la science*, preface by Pierre Janet (Montpellier and Paris: Coulet et fils, 1904).

[164] The story is told in Catherine-Laurence Maire, *Les possédées de Morzine, 1857–1873* (Lyons: Presses universitaires de Lyons, 1981) and Carroy, "Possession, extase, hystérie au 19e siècle," 502–9.

[165] This point is brought out in Jacqueline Carroy-Thirard, *Le mal de Morzine: De la possession à l'hystérie, 1857–1877* (Paris: Colin, 1981).

[166] Abbé P.-P.-A. Touroude, *L'hystérie: Sa nature, sa fréquence, ses causes, ses symptômes et ses effets* (La Chapelle-Montligeon: Imprimerie de l'oeuvre expiatoire, 1894).

Church authorities, that outlines the medical teachings of the day for use by convent administrators in the event of an outbreak of hysteria. As Carroy comments of Touroude's book and similar texts, "If the doctor becomes an exorcist and spiritual director, the enlightened priest becomes a bit of the alienist and therapist."[167]

Another significant intermediate statement between the worlds of medicine and religious was Félix Lacaze's *Pour le vrai: À Lourdes avec Zola* (1894).[168] Lacaze was close friends with Charcot and Bernheim, as well as a devout Catholic, and he sought to reconcile the leaders of France's two leading medical schools and to accommodate the religious and scientific perspectives on Lourdes. Lacaze's book, which is dedicated to Pope Leo XIII, offers a compendium of contemporary lay, clerical, and medical opinion on the shrine. It was intended to include prefaces by Charcot and Bernheim; but Charcot's death when the volume was nearing completion compelled Lacaze to write the second preface himself and imparted a poignancy to the volume.[169] For his part, Bernheim repeated his view that "medical faith acts like religious faith" and that all sudden remissions, in the hospital and the temple alike, were fully comprehensible in secular, psychological terms. However, Bernheim goes on to acknowledge undogmatically that Lourdes often delivered very effective psychotherapy. Being "no materialist *à outrance*," he advises his professional colleagues to refrain from dredging too deeply in these waters. Mystification was a crucial part of the special curative psychology of Lourdes and should be respected as such.[170]

Most importantly, I believe that these ideas, texts, and occurrences furnish the indispensable historical context for understanding one of Charcot's most interesting pieces of writing, his late essay "La foi qui guérit." At the height of the controversy over Lourdes, *The New Review*, a British journal, invited Charcot to share his thoughts on the matter with the public. Charcot's response was the article "The Faith-Cure," printed simultaneously in Britain and France, in both popular and medical formats and with minor variations, between December 1892 and January 1893.[171] The immediate context of the essay is important to keep in

[167] Carroy-Thirard, "Possession, extase, hystérie au XIXe siècle," 508.

[168] Félix Lacaze, *Pour le vrai: À Lourdes avec Zola: Parallèle au roman de Zola*, double préface: par l'auteur, en mémoire du Professeur Docteur Charcot, pour l'École de la Salpêtrière; par le Professeur Docteur Bernheim, pour l'École de Nancy (Paris: E. Dentu, 1894).

[169] Ibid., ix–x.

[170] Ibid., xi–xiv.

[171] Charcot, "La foi qui guérit," *Revue hebdomadaire* (December 3, 1892): 112–32; idem, "The Faith-Cure," *The New Review* 8 (January 1893): 18–31; idem, "La foi qui guérit," *Archives de neurologie* 25, no. 73 (January 1893): 72–87. The essay has recently been reprinted in Didi-Huberman, *Les démoniaques dans l'art*, 125–82.

mind: the preceding year, Boissarie had come out with his *Histoire médicale*; Lombroso had recently provided a stinging restatement of the positivist analysis of miraculous cures;[172] and Zola, it was widely known, was deep in the composition of his novel about Lourdes. "La foi qui guérit" was published eight months before Charcot's death. It is in many ways his most personal statement on hysteria and one of his few publications to address the therapeutics of the disorder. The essay is a document of considerable significance not only in Charcot's intellectual biography but in the cultural history of hysteria and in the prehistory of twentieth-century psychosomatic medicine.[173]

Attempting to divorce himself from the current mêlée about miracle cures, Charcot does not at first discuss Lourdes directly in "La foi qui guérit" but refers only to "the shrines now in vogue."[174] He considers the general historical phenomenon of sanctuaries and pilgrimages in different lay and religious settings from classical and early Christian times to the present. To be sure, his interpretation of the happenings at these sites is firmly naturalistic. In his opinion, both the visions experienced by St. Francis of Assisi and St. Theresa and the cures effected by St. Ignatius and St. Martin remain "undeniably hysterical."[175] In a like manner, he provides a perceptive assessment of the common psychological components involved in so-called faith cures: a background of desperation on the part of the individual, the long and physically exhausting journey to the shrine, an atmosphere of collective enthusiasm and expectation, and so on.[176]

However, the tone of Charcot's late essay is altogether different from that found in the *Démoniaques dans l'art* and the writings in the *Bibliothèque Diabolique*. While comparative positivist valuations of science and religion persist, the piece is uncharacteristically concessive in tone, and not at all combative or anticlerical. Charcot acknowledges that cer-

---

[172] Cesar Lombroso, "Les faits spiritiques et leur explication psychiatrique," *Revue de l'hypnotisme et de la psychologie physiologique* 6, no. 9 (September 1892): 289–98.

[173] See the discussions in Guillain, *Charcot*, chap. 16; A.R.G. Owen, *Hysteria, Hypnosis and Healing in the Work of J.-M. Charcot*, chap. 5; Goldstein, *Console and Classify*, 380–83; J. and M. Postel, "J.-M. Charcot et 'La foi qui guérit,'" *Histoire des sciences médicales* 20, no. 2 (1986): 153–56; and Bannour, *Jean-Martin Charcot et l'hystérie*, chap. 20.

[174] Charcot, "La foi qui guérit," *Archives de neurologie*, 87; idem, "Faith-Cure," 31. See, however, his earlier skeptical reference to Lourdes and miraculous cures in *Leçons sur les maladies du système nerveux faites à la Salpêtrière*, recueillies et publiées par Bourneville (Paris: Delahaye, 1872–73), 314–15.

[175] Charcot, "La foi qui guérit," *Archives de neurologie*, 76, 80; "Faith-Cure," 21, 24.

[176] Charcot, "La foi qui guérit," *Archives de neurologie*, 76–78; "Faith-Cure," 21–23. Among the respondents to this portion of Charcot's analysis were two medical men: Imbert-Gourbeyre, *La stigmatisation*, chap. 27; and Dr. A. Vourch, *La foi qui guérit: Étude médicale sur quelques cas de guérisons de Lourdes* (Bordeaux: Féret et fils, 1911).

tain of the cures at Lourdes are "well authenticated"; he announces that
he is currently gathering materials for a statement about the institution—
a reference perhaps to the planned Lacaze preface; and he insists on the
need for physicians to tap "the great resources of the faith-cure."[177] Despite recent advances in the scientific understanding of disease, a great
many medical phenomena, Charcot concedes, remain unexplained, and
he ends his article with a favorite citation from Shakespeare's *Hamlet*:
"There are more things in heaven and earth, Horatio,/Than are dreamt of
in your philosophy."[178]

Above all, toward the close of the essay, in a single half-sentence, Charcot makes a critical admission: he states that he himself has at times sent
his own patients, intractable cases of nervous illness, from the Salpêtrière
to Lourdes for treatment![179] Many sources from the time confirm that
Charcot in fact did this.[180] Boissarie even quotes from a personal letter of
Charcot addressed to a fellow physician in which Charcot states that he
was in the habit of referring "50 or 60 patients" from the Salpêtrière to
the shrine each year.[181] In its list of official cures, the *Annales de Notre-
Dame* periodically devoted a section to "Malades de la Salpêtrière,"[182]
and the registries of the Medical Office at the Grotto in Lourdes today
record many instances from the 1880s and 1890s of cured or ameliorated
patients referred to the shrine from the *Clinique Charcot*.[183] In other
words, despite Charcot's widely publicized atheism and materialism as
well as the official rhetorics of opposition generally between the religious
and medical camps at this time, there appears in late nineteenth-century
France to have been a small but steady flow of human traffic between the
institutional environments of medicine and Catholicism.[184]

In addition to providing an element in his therapeutic arsenal, Lourdes
also, I believe, had an significant influence on Charcot's etiological thinking about hysteria. Given his previous anticlerical stance, to say nothing

---

[177] "Foi qui guérit," *Archives de neurologie*, 73; "Faith-Cure," 19.

[178] "Foi qui guérit," *Archives de neurologie*, 87; "Faith-Cure," 31.

[179] "Foi qui guérit," *Archives de neurologie*, 87; "Faith-Cure," 31.

[180] From the texts cited in this chapter alone, Zola, *Lourdes*, 190; Martin, "Le miracle
au dix-neuvième siècle," 367; and Boissarie, *Lourdes*, 258 refer to pilgrims at Lourdes who
had previously been cared for at the Clinique Charcot.

[181] Boissarie, *Lourdes*, 18–19.

[182] See, for instance, the annual report for 1889, vol. 22, 35–42.

[183] Personal conversation between Henri F. Ellenberger and the author.

[184] Typical of this movement from the life of pilgrim to patient and back again was the
experience of "D . . . ", cited by Dr. Verrier in 1895. After passing six years at the
Salpêtrière in the 1880s, where he was diagnosed as a hopeless and progressive case of
locomotor ataxia, "D . . . " went to Lourdes and was "cured." A number of years after his
recovery, the patient, back in Paris, suffered a relapse. This time, he spent a week at the
Sainte-Anne asylum, from which he was discharged as a simulator, and then returned to
Lourdes where he again found solace. (See Verrier, "Les miracles de Lourdes," 277).

of his personal unbelief, Charcot might well have dismissed the occurrences at Lourdes as the product of pious gullibility. But the fact that Lourdes, if you will, healed some people, including some of his own most recalcitrant cases, compelled Charcot and other doctors to inquire seriously into the precise nature of *l'effet Lourdes*. Pondering these unexpected recoveries, physicians at first considered that an unknown material agent might be responsible, such as the chemical composition of the water in the basins of the grotto, which they likened to medical hydrotherapy. But it quickly became apparent to them that these dramatic remissions could not be explained as the result of any known physiological mechanism.

Now, in his research on hysteria during the preceding two decades, Charcot had been deeply engaged in the differential diagnosis of organic and hysterical disorders and the comparative range of the two categories of causality. To this end, he discovered that paralyses, contractures, and convulsions, as well as many neurological diseases like tabes dorsalis, Pott's Disease, and syringomyelia, could be simulated hysterically. Often, the hysterical nature of a case could only be established by its evolution and outcome, so closely did the initial symptoms resemble those of organic disease. In late nineteenth-century medical theory, hysteria, like the other *névroses*, was presumed to involve the nervous system; but, unique among the functional and nonfunctional neuroses, it could also ape other disorders and remit suddenly, dramatically, or erratically. Among the Lourdes cases, then, a sudden or lengthy remission or a full and permanent recovery in Charcot's view confirmed the status of a case as hysterical rather than as a genuine neurodegenerative disease with a fixed and irrevocable course. Not unexpectedly, Charcot found large numbers of pseudoneurological infirmities among the cures returning from Lourdes and had no difficulty in explaining them.

However, if we return to "La foi qui guérit," we find that a large portion of the essay is devoted to a quite technical discussion of fevers, tumors, muscular atrophy accompanying paralyses, and skin ulcerations leading to edemas and cutaneous gangrene.[185] Previously, Charcot had not considered these maladies as being potentially hysterogenic. However, he was now witnessing with his own eyes the ostensible cure at Lourdes of cases that he previously believed to be irreversibly and organically degenerate. Moreover, it was precisely cases of this nature, involving ulcers and cancerous tumors, that Boissarie had cited the year before as irrefragable evidence of the miraculous in the cures at Lourdes.[186]

Rejecting supernatural agency as an explanation of such cures, Charcot

---

[185] "La foi qui guérit," *Archives de neurologie*, 80–86; "Faith-Cure," 24–31.

[186] Boissarie, *Lourdes*, 277. Note also the prominent inclusion of these types of cases in Bertrin's catalogue of cures (Bertrin, *Lourdes*, appendix 4, 293–96).

in the 1890s began to realize that these medical infirmities too could be the object of hysterical causation. This in turn allowed him in "La foi qui guérit" to begin to reconceptualize hysteria as a problem in mind/body relations, rather than as a neuropathic entity with a missing lesion. Further, it caused him to pose to himself for the first time a question that the young Freud was addressing in print at precisely the same time: namely, what is "the *psychical* mechanism of hysterical phenomena"?[187] In two technical case histories written during this same period, Charcot explored in greater depth the potentially neuromimetic origins of one of these new symptom categories, tissue edemas.[188] But his untimely demise soon thereafter prevented him from proceeding further. In short, the miracle cult of Lourdes, as it developed during the final decades of the nineteenth century, may well have caused Charcot to broaden—from the outside, as it were, and under the stimulus of a most unexpected source—the projected scope of psychological causation in his study of nervous disease. I would also venture to suggest that it was the experience of observing cases returning from Lourdes (in addition to the Nancean critique of his work) that motivated Charcot in his final years to question the sufficiency of the strict somaticist paradigm of hysteria and to inch his way toward a more ideogenic model of the mind. Finally, the Lourdes phenomenon may further have contributed to the general movement of the late nineteenth century toward the psychologization of the neuroses. Among the nonclinical, cultural determinants of the medical history of hysteria, it appears that religion, in addition to art and literature, must be included.[189]

[187] The essays of Charcot and Freud on this matter, both of which appeared in January 1893, make rewarding comparative reading. Along with Charcot's "La foi qui guérit," see Sigmund Freud, "On the Psychical Mechanism of Hysterical Phenomena," in *Standard Edition*, 3: 27–39, a coauthored reformulation of which later became the opening chapter, or "Preliminary Communication," of *Studies on Hysteria*.

[188] Charcot, "L'oedème bleu des hystériques" and "Hystéro-traumatique chez deux soeurs: Oedème bleu hystérique chez la cadette; coxalgie hystérique chez l'aînée," both in *Clinique des maladies du système nerveux: M. le Professeur Charcot: Leçons du Professeur: Mémoires, Notes et Observations, 1889–1890 et 1890–1891*, 2 vols. (Paris: Bureaux du progrès médical, Babé et Cie, 1892–93), 1: 95–126.

[189] Nor is this the only instance in which Catholic doctrine contributed to the constitution of modern psychiatric theory. Morel, for instance, studied theology as a young man and initially planned a career in the Catholic Church. The Belgian psychiatric historian Axel Liégeois has shown that Morel's nosological concept of degeneration drew extensively on Thomist beliefs about the role of free will and the passions and the relation between body and soul. See "La théologie et l'éthique sous-jacentes à la psychiatrie de B.-A. Morel," *Ephemerides Theologicae Lovanienses* 65, no. 4 (December 1989): 330–57, which is derived from Liégeois's more extensive, but unfortunately untranslated, study, "Verholen theologie en ethiek in de psychiatrie: Een relectuur van de degeneratietheorie en de noslogie van Bénédict-Augustin Morel (1809–1873)" (Ph.D. diss., University of Leuven, 1988). Similarly, Peter Swales has argued that an important intellectual influence on Freud's abandonment of the theory of actual seduction as the etiology of the neuroses and his adoption of a

Finally, these same intricate lines of continuity between the medical and religious cultures of hysteria can be detected in other areas too, including in French diagnostic theory, in the biographies of Charcot's hysterical patients, and in the creative literature of the era. As scholars have noted, key features of Charcotian theory are Catholic in content. The sensory stigmata, those anesthetic or hyperaesthesic patches Charcot believed to be the most dependable diagnostic indicators of the disease, derived directly from the Christian *stigmata diaboli* used by Renaissance inquisitors to identify witches. As Ruth Harris has written, "It is no exaggeration to say that the specific symptoms and dramatic stages [of the hysterical fit] were molded to some degree by . . . religious iconography. The *attitudes passionnelles* in particular showed the kinship between religious symbolism and female pathology, with women poised in positions of religious supplication, ecstasy, and even crucifixion."[190] Charcot's practice of ovarian compression in cases of hysteria originated with the demonological procedure of pressing on the stomach of a religious convulsionary, while one of the most dramatic stages of the classic Salpêtrian fit was labeled "the crucifix stage." Numerous other remnants of theological thinking about the disease, which prevailed in France for over a thousand years, also run through the medical discourses of the nineteenth century. Do these features represent the positivization of Catholic theological teaching or the Catholicization of French psychiatric theory?

Still other continuities may be found in the lives of the hysterical patients themselves. A recent study by Mary James attempts to reconstruct the personal and medical biographies of the *grandes hystériques* of the Salpêtrière.[191] In a chapter titled "The Divine and the Pathological," James discovers that many of the women discussed in the *Iconographie photographique de la Salpêtrière* were brought up in convent schools and went through periods of deep religious inspiration. Two had previously been nuns. Geneviève, James points out further, was born and raised in the town of Loudon, with its rich religious folklore of hysteria, while Blanche Wittmann consciously fashioned herself on Louise Lateau with her intense spirituality.[192] In short, the "illness behaviors" of these indi-

---

theory of fantasized seduction was a reading of Weyer and sixteenth-century Catholic manuals of witchcraft. According to Swales, Freud then deemphasized these nonscientific sources of his thinking because of the positivist climate of the time. See Swales, "Freud, Johann Weier, and the Status of Seduction: The Role of the Witch in the Conception of Fantasy" (1982), privately printed by the author; and idem, "A Fascination with Witches," *The Sciences* 22 (1982): 21–25.

[190] Harris, *Murders and Madness*, 205. See also Carroy-Thirard, "Possession, extase, hystérie," 509.

[191] Mary James, "The Therapeutic Practices of Jean-Martin Charcot (1825–1893) in Their Historical and Social Context," (Ph.D. diss., University of Essex, 1989).

[192] Ibid., chap. 6.

viduals, which served as a crucially important field of observation and theorization for hysteria doctors in the late nineteenth century, may well have been learned from their youthful Catholic heritage. Extending James's findings, Cristina Mazzoni, in a recent, fascinating study, has documented in sympathetic detail the cultural and psychological continuities between nineteenth-century hysterical pregnancies and the imagery of the Virgin Birth.[193]

The same interweaving of representations of hysterical pathology, religious euphoria, and sexual exaltation on display in the *Iconographie photographique* is embodied in nineteenth-century imaginative literature. As McGrath has emphasized, Catholicism to those outside the faith, such as Freud, was typically experienced as a source of political and cultural oppression.[194] However (as readers with a Catholic upbringing will know), Catholic culture for members of the church combines stringent moral and sexual repression with a high degree of sensory stimulation: the passions of the body, the torture of Christ, the martyrdom of the saints, and other horrifying or alluring subjects are often dramatized extravagantly in the arts. It was these associations that recurred in French novels about hysteria a century ago.

Like the young women in the *Iconographie photographique*, Emma Bovary had received a convent education. To Baudelaire, with his superb reading of Flaubert's novel, this fact was not biographical trivia but the essence of Emma's character, of her hysteria. It was in the convent, he stressed, that Emma began to develop her yearning for spiritual and emotional intensities and became infatuated with the smell of the incense, the secrecy of the confessional, and the image of Christ as otherworldly lover. Later in life, Emma sought gratification of this impulse in the secular, sensory world. In a passage that remains partially opaque, Baudelaire wrote: "By a paradox which may be credited to nerves, she replaced the real God in her heart by the God of her imagination, the God of the future and of chance, a picture-book God with spurs and mustache; and there you have the hysterical poet!"[195] Emma's subsequent emotional career was in fact marked by a cycle of frenetic engagements with fictional literature, religious mysticism, and romantic sexuality, with each stage manifesting her hysteria. In his well-known study of Emma's temperament in 1902, Jules de Gaultier observed aptly that "Bovaryism," that mixture of dreamy dissatisfaction and a drive toward the unattainable, might well have been channeled in other directions: "Mme. Bovary could have been

[193] Cristina Maria Mazzoni, "Hysterical Pregnancies and Virgin Births: Neurosis and Mysticism in French and Italian Literature at the Turn of the Century" (Ph.D. diss., Yale University, 1991).

[194] McGrath, *Freud's Discovery of Psychoanalysis*, chap. 4.

[195] Baudelaire, "*Madame Bovary* par Gustave Flaubert," in *Oeuvres complètes*, 404.

some great mystic, along the lines of Saint Theresa, or, with a gift for achievement, an artist."[196]

This same intermixture of imaginative worlds may be found through two generations of French fiction writing from Baudelaire to Proust. When Barbey d'Aurevilly's conservative novel, *Un prêtre marié*, extolling the virtues of a life of priestly celibacy, appeared in 1865, the young Zola went into action. He headed his acerbically critical review of the book "Le catholique hystérique." Barbey d'Aurevilly earned this epithet, Zola explained, because of "the abuse of mysticism and abuse of passion" throughout the book.[197] In 1883, Alphonse Daudet published his novel *L'évangéliste*, featuring the theme of "religious hysteria." The dedication of Daudet's volume: "A l'éloquent et savant professeur J.-M. Charcot, Médecin de la Salpêtrière."[198] The following year, Galopin devoted one of the more outré chapters of *Les hystériques des couvents* to the question of the comparative rates of hysteria among Catholics, Protestants, and Jews. Catholics, Galopin decided, were most prone to the malady, and he canonized St. Augustine as "our patron hysteric."[199] And in *Chateaubriand et l'hystérie*, Potiquet conveys the idea that Chateaubriand's neurosis was part of his religious as well as artistic sensibility. However, as with Emma Bovary, the attraction for Chateaubriand was less to Catholicism's theological doctrines than its romantic paraphernalia: "Guided in all things by sentiment and imagination more than by reason, *like every hysteric, a little bit of a woman in this way*, he [Chateaubriand] was more touched by the external trappings of Catholicism, by the pomp of ceremonies, by the poetry of the legends, than by the reality of its doctrines and the wisdom of its teachings."[200] In the style and substance of his work, Potiquet seems to say, Chateaubriand produced a more profound piece of writing in *Génie du christianisme* because of a feminine tendency to hysteria. Given the repeated interactions between these themes in fin-de-siècle French culture, it is perhaps not surprising that the one study of a literary figure written by Bertrin, the leading theologian of hysteria at Lourdes, took Chateaubriand as its subject.[201]

The most instructive example, however—and I will end with this—was Huysmans. During a period that corresponds directly with hysteria's heyday, Huysmans managed to traverse in turns hysteria's three major sub-

[196] Jules de Gaultier, *Le Bovarysme* (Paris: Société de Mercure de France, 1902), 31–32.

[197] Émile Zola, "Le catholique hystérique" [1865], in *Mes haines: Causeries littéraires et artistiques* (Geneva: Collection ressources, 1979), 41.

[198] Alphonse Daudet, *L'évangéliste: Roman parisien* (Paris: E. Dentu, 1883). A popular imitation of Daudet's book appeared two years later in Camille Lemonnier's *L'hystérique* (Paris: G. Charpentier, 1885).

[199] Galopin, *Les hystériques des couvent*, chap. 21, 146.

[200] Potiquet, *Chateaubriand et l'hystérie*, 25; my italics.

[201] Georges Bertrin, *La sincérité religieuse de Chateaubriand* (Paris: V. Lecoffre, 1900).

cultures of medicine, literature, and religion. Huysmans followed this itinerary simultaneously in his personal emotional development, his aesthetic style, and the lives of his fictional male characters. Huysmans began his literary career as a member of the so-called Médan group, strongly under the sway of Zolan naturalism. In his early novels of the 1870s, he strove to represent modern urban society, including its representative characters and their degenerate nervous traits, as realistically as possible. But this was only the beginning of a lifelong artistic evolution. In the early 1880s, Huysmans rejected the naturalistic aesthetic and moved in À rebours to his cult of decadent aestheticism. This was typified by Des Esseintes—the most important male hysteric in French literature of the decadence—who, incidentally, in his youth had been educated as a Jesuit. As with Flaubert and Madame Bovary, there was more than a touch of autobiography in À rebours. Like Des Esseintes, Huysmans was no stranger to nervous hypochondria.[202]

At the conclusion of À rebours, however, Huysmans has Des Esseintes abandon his self-conscious agnosticism and material and sexual debauchery and adopt a life of religious faith. Correspondingly, in the 1890s Huysmans began to find the philosophy of decadence lacking, and, like Oscar Wilde, his English counterpart whom he influenced so deeply, he turned slowly toward the Roman Catholic Church. And there he remained until the end of his life. Again, it was a style of Catholicism laced with mysticism and exoticism. Huysmans recorded his hysterical conversion first in Là-bas of 1891, a transitional work exploring the theme of satanism in modern Paris, and then more explicitly in En route of 1895. Among his later titles are La cathédrale (1898), dealing with medieval Christian art and architecture; L'oblat (1903), set in a Benedictine monastery; Sainte Lydwine de Schiedam (1901), a study in Catholic hagiography; and Le quartier Notre-Dame (1905).[203]

Not inappropriately, Huysmans's final novel was Les foules de Lourdes.[204] Following the precedent of Zola, his former teacher, Huysmans travelled personally to Lourdes to research this book. He was appalled by the place architecturally but deeply respectful of its spirituality. In September 1904, his biographer reports, Huysmans spent three weeks at the sanctuary,

[202] Recall that it was with À rebours and Des Esseintes in mind that Nordau berated Huysmans as "the classical type of the hysterical mind without originality."

[203] The standard biography of Huysmans remains Robert Baldick, The Life of J.-K. Huysmans (Oxford: Clarendon Press, 1955). A discussion of Huysmans's turn to Catholicism may be found in Madeleine y Ortoleva, Joris-Karl Huysmans: Romancier du salut (Quebec: Éditions Naaman, 1981), chap. 1, while the changing representation of nervous disease in his work is analyzed in François Livi, J.-K. Huysmans: À rebours et l'esprit décadent (Brussels: A. G. Nizet, La renaissance du livre, 1976), chaps. 4 and 7. Also relevant is Oswald Wirth's Huysmans et la médecine (Paris: Belles lettres, 1950).

[204] Huysmans, Les foules de Lourdes (Paris: Plon-Nourrit, 1906).

"mingling with the crowds, watching the sick being dipped in the baths, sitting in the Medical Bureau with Dr. Boissarie as he examined possible cures, and paying daily visits to the hospital of Notre-Dame-des-Sept-Douleurs."[205] Huysmans was in physical pain during the visit, suffering from the advanced stages of palate and throat cancer. He came away from Lourdes convinced of the superiority of liturgical to medical treatments of disease; but, alas, he was not himself among the *miraculés*. *Les foules de Lourdes* appeared in September 1906, and half a year later its author was dead.[206]

From the rationalist/scientific to the aesthetic/decadent and then to the mystico-religious: on the individual and collective levels, was this a characteristic evolution within nineteenth-century French culture? If, as Israël has posited, hysteria in Protestant and Jewish cultures has often been sublimated into social good works in secular situations, did it channel in Catholic cultures into piety? There is considerable evidence to suggest that a century ago hysteria, creative writing, Romantic/decadent sexuality, and Catholic mysticism did exist on a kind of cultural and psychological continuum. Of course, the worlds of nineteenth-century medicine, literature, and religion each possessed a rhetoric to account officially and publically for their relations with each other. But, in reality, a network of cultural criss-crossings formed among them. Avant-garde poets and novelists read the medical literature of the day and then diagnosed their characters, and themselves, as hysterical. Physicians incorporated motifs from contemporary fictional writings into their diagnostic theories. The artistic beau monde attended Charcot's soirées; convent directors consulted medical manuals to quell outbreaks of hysteria in their establishments; and Charcot quietly sent his patients to Lourdes. The historical image once again is of a circle of influences.

Needless to say, the goal and appeal and power of hysteria's three primary subcultures a century ago differed greatly. Catholicism, the most long-lived of the three but in the late 1800s increasingly on the defensive, aimed at spiritual loyalty through emotional consolation of the masses. The medical profession, then in the ascent, desired descriptive knowledge and intellectual authority. Artists and writers sought in hysteria heightened expressive power and self-knowledge. Furthermore, individual French men and women in the nineteenth century navigated through these three domains along substantially separate pathways. Charcot constructed a model of hysteria that was singularly brilliant as scientific system. But, despite the smooth and objective rhetorical surfaces that com-

---

[205] Baldick, *The Life of J.-K. Huysmans*, 332.

[206] For a text by another of our authors who wrote in turn on hysteria and Lourdes, see Armand Dubarry, *Lourdes amoureuse et religieuse* (Paris: Chamuel, 1900), one of the later volumes in *Les déséquilibrés de l'amour*.

pose his clinical writings, he was influenced, far more than he was willing to acknowledge, by forces outside the clinic, including contemporary literature and religion. In contrast, Huysmans, an independent man of letters, had the leisure to experiment alternately with art, medicine, and religion, settling eventually on an aestheticized and hystericized Catholicism. Finally, there was Emma—poor Emma—who had to make her way in an isolated and inhospitable environment created and controlled by men. In successive crises, Emma too spent time in the worlds of love, literature, medicine, and religion; but in the end she found solace and satisfaction in none of them, and killed herself. In the comparative study of the cultures of hysteria, the oppositions and interpenetrations appear endless.[207]

[207] My exposition of the cultural history of hysteria has centered on the French experience in the nineteenth century. While this setting proves exceptionally congenial to such study, the same could almost certainly be done for other periods, including eighteenth-century Britain, fin-de-siècle Germany and Austria, and the final decades of the twentieth century. For "cultures of madness" in Georgian England, consult Porter, *Mind-Forg'd Manacles*, chap. 2; and Rousseau, " 'A Strange Pathology.' " Information about nineteenth-century Germany is available in Johann Bresler, "Kulturhistorischer Beitrag zur Hysterie," *Allgemeine Zeitschrift für Psychiatrie* 53 (1896–97): 333–76. For turn-of-the-century Viennese society, see Madeline L. Feingold, "Hysteria as a Modality of Adjustment in *Fin-de-Siècle* Vienna" (Ph.D. diss., California School of Professional Psychology, Berkeley, 1963); and Manfred Schneider, "Hysterie als Gesamtkunstwerk," in Alfred Pfabigan, ed., *Ornament und Askese im Zeitgeist des Wien der Jahrhundertwende* (Vienna: Brandstätter, 1985), 212–29. For a recent and ambitious attempt to portray another nosographical concept from this perspective (i.e., "cultures of schizophrenia"), consider Louis A. Sass's *Madness and Modernism: Insanity in the Light of Modern Art, Literature, and Thought* (1992).

CONCLUSION: REMEMBERING HYSTERIA

I HAVE TRIED in this book to provide a kind of historical phenomenology of a disease. Using intellectual history and the history of science and medicine as my disciplinary bases, I have attempted to survey as encyclopedically as possible a single historical object, the disease category hysteria, and the host of interpretations that it has given rise to in the past and the present.

Scanning the history of hysteria now in its entirety, we are perhaps struck above all by its extreme, almost obscene, interpretability. In a multitude of historical settings from ancient Greece to the present, through every style of disease reasoning, inside professional medicine and out, hysteria has elicited commentary. Throughout its long career, the disorder has been viewed as a manifestation of everything from divine poetic inspiration and satanic possession to female unreason, racial degeneration, and unconscious psychosexual conflict. It has inspired gynecological, humoral, neurological, psychological, and sociological formulations, and it has been situated in the womb, the abdomen, the nerves, the ovaries, the mind, the brain, the psyche, and the soul. It has been construed as a physical disease, a mental disorder, a spiritual malady, a behavioral maladjustment, a sociological communication, and as no illness at all. Individual symptoms—the stigmata, the *boule*, the fit—have given rise to entire medical and popular folklores of their own. As Gérard Wajeman has observed, "There doesn't seem to be anything that medicine hasn't said about hysteria."[1]

Hysteria's galaxy of meanings is mirrored in its recent historiography. In 1965, Ilza Veith observed at the opening of *Hysteria: The History of a Disease* that "apart from a small number of articles and of brief references in general histories of psychiatry, the only books devoted to this subject were written in French and are no longer readily available."[2] I trust it will now be apparent to readers that this situation is no longer true. Once the narrow province of a few physicians and medical historians, the history of hysteria at present attracts attention from neurologists, psychoanalysts, psychiatrists, psychologists, intellectual and cultural historians, social historians, historians of science and medicine, women's studies specialists, feminist theorists, Freud scholars, literary critics, and art historians. By the early 1990s, the history of the disease had been conceptualized as a scientific, clinical, social, economic, politi-

---

[1] Wajeman, "The Hysteric's Discourse," 1.
[2] Veith, *Hysteria*, vii.

cal, sexual, cultural, and aesthetic construction. It has been interpreted as a chapter in the history of medical thought, an episode in the discovery of the unconscious, a study in mind/body relations, and an example of the misdiagnosis of organic disease. It has been written about as a repressed cry for sexual release, an exhibitionistic erotic performance, and a passive, pathological escape from social oppression; as a caricature of femininity, an exploration of masculinity, and a codification of misogynistic male science; as an exercise in scientific pornography and a program for gender normalization. It has been studied as a social metaphor, a literary topos, a visual icon, and a surrogate form of religious experience; as a morbid manifestation of Victorian civilization, a secret strategy for professional expansion, a modern middle-class substitute for primitive carnival practices,[3] and a sinister act of protopathologization. It has even been discussed as an actual psychiatric disorder. There doesn't seem to be anything that historians haven't said about hysteria.

This striking heterogeneity of writings results in part from individual and disciplinary differences among authors. But, as I have attempted to show in the foregoing pages, it also reflects the elastic clinical content of the disorder itself and the exceptionally rich textual inheritance the disease has generated through the centuries. Clearly, it would be foolish, and impossible, to attempt to synthesize, or even reconcile, these many approaches. Nonetheless, as I hope readers will agree at this point, each of the major interpretive traditions canvassed here has yielded valuable insights. Narrative intellectual histories provide the indispensable service of marshaling pertinent primary texts and establishing a longitudinal medical-historical context for the subject. Social and cultural historians uncover new printed and archival materials that place the diagnosis in its defining contexts of place and time. Physicians remain most fluent with the technical aspects of the topic and most attuned to its crucial clinical dimensions. Women's historians and feminist critics are uniquely sensitive to the key cross-genderal aspects of the disease. And literary critics and literary historians are most adept at decoding hysteria's multitudinous metaphors. Taken together, these scholarly literatures have fabulously enhanced our understanding of the subject over the past decade and a half.

In my judgment, the single greatest strength of the new hysteria studies rests in the large number of interpretive strategies being brought to bear on the topic. Surveying this research as a whole, drawn as it is from a wide spectrum of disciplines and traditions, proves an immensely enlightening exercise. Despite a considerable amount of mutual suspicion and incomprehension among the researchers, the scholarship of one field is

[3] Peter Stallybrass and Allon White, "Bourgeois Hysteria and the Carnivalesque" in *The Politics and Poetics of Transgression* (London: Methuen, 1986), 171–90.

often replete with ideas and information relevant to the others. Writing the history of disease, it should now be evident, is necessarily a multidisciplinary enterprise. By gathering together in one place texts, ideas, methodologies, and interpretations from regions of study that have previously remained separate, I have attempted to encourage that enterprise.

And what might a comprehensive conceptualization of disease history look like? This will obviously vary from disease to disease, and without further empirical studies it is probably still premature to say with any certainty. However, based on the present study of a single clinical entity, we can provisionally conclude a number of things. In the future, we need at the outset to acknowledge and to confront the methodological difficulties and epistemological indeterminacies involved in writing the history of a disease. We should initially define the disease concept in clear, contextualist terms as well as pay close attention to its local, linguistic identities. In our selection of subject matters, we should include, but creatively venture beyond, the best known theorists, patients, texts, and periods. With regard to the history of psychodiagnostic categories, we desperately need to extend our range of research beyond the Victorian era and beyond Freud's case histories.

Along similarly lines, we ought to continue to develop a strong awareness of an increasingly wide array of intersecting external variables, including class, race, and gender. This pertains equally to the patients and the doctors involved. At the same time, medical history, like medical science, seems to require the notion of multiple etiology. We should resist the temptation, for the sake of either interpretive convenience or ideological gratification, to reduce the historical meaning of a disease to a single preconceived analytical category. I have been at pains in this book to establish that we need to bridge the difficult gap between the medical and humanistic perspectives by developing an informed, integrated, and nondogmatic sociosomatic model that combines extrinsic factors with clinical and medical-scientific perspectives. Furthermore, analytical coverage should extend to both genders as well as to medical populations up and down the socioeconomic scale. In the face of the flood of feminist scholarship from the past two decades, I have laid particular emphasis on the need to add issues of masculinity to our historiographical models of gender, disease, and history.

Last but hardly least, we should, in so far as possible, study concurrently the "realist" and the representational histories of disease. There has never been a time when men and women have not suffered from sickness, and for the artist, social scientist, and cultural critic no less than for the physician, diseases through the ages have provided important, popular, and powerful images and concepts. Segregating the medical and cultural stories of disease primarily reflects the disciplinary compartmentalizations of the late twentieth-century academy rather than any historical reality. In the future, we would do well to reconstruct the range of representations of diseases and their many horizontal connections with the world from which they came and in which they operated. Regarding hysteria in particular, these guidelines for "how to write the history of disease" may prove difficult, if not impossible, to fulfill.[4] Over the years, hysteria has spanned nearly the entire field of medical pathology. The subject sprawls across twenty centuries of medical history and includes texts from as many cultures and in as many languages. It encompasses a range of historical personalities from the pilgrims of the Aesculapian temples in the fourth century B.C. to the defendants in seventeenth-century witchcraft trials, from Freud's bourgeois neurotic patients on the couch to shell-shocked soldiers in the trenches of the First World War. The topic appears to entail a daunting historical eclecticism: psycho-medico-socio-cultural scholarship. Given the primacy of the disease experience in human history, however, it is my hope that this challenge will inspire, not discourage, research.

There remains finally the question of the *reasons* for the new hysteria studies. In a word, why in the past decade and a half has writing about the history of this disorder evolved from a scholarly backwater into one of the most active and dynamic research sites within the humanities? A number of factors are clearly intraacademic. The historiography of science and medicine in recent years has enlarged its boundaries to encompass collateral disciplines and methodologies. Interdisciplinary history and the new cultural studies encourage the study of new, cross-disciplinary topics. For many Anglo-American academic intellectuals, the influence of the French philosopher-critic Michel Foucault in writing "the history of madness" has been enormous. And, in a generation during which the ideology of the avant garde, for better or worse, has penetrated the university, the study of the history of hysteria has proven irresistibly fashionable.

However, given the volume and variety of historical writing involved, it is likely that something more is taking place than simply the investigation of a new corner of medical history by academic specialists. When people doing intellectual work from widely divergent disciplines converge spontaneously on a single subject in large numbers and at the same time, deeper forces are almost certainly at work. So these questions arise: What social and intellectual conditions of the late twentieth century does this convergence of professional interests reflect? What is the cultural meaning

---

[4] I allude to Arnold I. Davidson's "How to Do the History of Psychoanalysis: A Reading of Freud's *Three Essays on the Theory of Sexuality*," in Françoise Meltzer, ed., *The Trial(s) of Psychoanalysis* (Chicago: University of Chicago Press, 1987), 39–64.

of the proliferation of studies of disease history? And what are the new hysteria studies symptomatic of? What are *they* a metaphor for? In my concluding pages, I would like to suggest four cultural contexts for understanding the newly constituted field of hysteria studies.

The first and most obvious context is the gender revolution of the final third of the twentieth century. While the lineage of feminist theory traces back two hundred years or more, and the suffrage movements of Europe and North America are over a century old, the pervasive cultural and sociological ramifications of the emancipation of women have been (and are being) worked out largely since the 1960s. One cultural aspect of this far-reaching transformation involves the critical evaluation of those historical structures that have undergirded patriarchal systems and rationalized female subordination. Given the intellectual authority of science and medicine in the modern West, and the prominent place of hysteria in the mythology of women through the ages, it is not surprising that women's historians have fastened their attention on the historical study of the disease. The historiography of hysteria has contributed to this revolution in two ways: as part of a largely deconstructive analysis of past male-dominated beliefs, practices, and institutions; and as part of a more constructive effort to formulate new, more accurate, and less skewed psychologies of the sexes. In both cases, the study of hysteria may be viewed as an element in the great metacritique of gender that in retrospect is certain to be regarded as one of the defining features of the thought, culture, and society of the late twentieth century.

A second, and somewhat more speculative, context for the fascination with hysteria in the academic world today is the AIDS epidemic. The new hysteria studies emerged early in the 1980s, at the same time as the first recorded cases of AIDS, and they have both developed unabated up to the present. I suspect that this is more than happenstance. The large majority of scholars in hysteria studies are at the beginning or middle point of their careers. They were born in the 1940s or 1950s, went to school during the 1960s and 1970s (with their greater social and sexual freedoms), and began their publishing careers in the 1980s. Moreover, this generation has undergone a distinctive historical experience. Until the late 1950s, men and women, from childhood on, lived with the apprehension, at times the outright terror, of pandemic diseases: the bubonic plague, smallpox, diphtheria, cholera, syphilis, typhoid, typhus, yellow fever, tuberculosis, influenza, poliomyelitis, and so on. The possibility that deadly infectious disease could strike without notice and effect large numbers of people was a basic part of the human worldview. However, the new hysteria studies have been produced by the first generational cohort to grow up in the era of antibiotics, through which these age-old threats seemed to have been contained or conquered. In the 1980s, however, this changed very abruptly with the emergence of a new disease—a disease, furthermore, that was transmitted sexually, that had a long latency period, that could be carried by individuals with no evident signs of infection, and that could lead to a protracted, agonizing death.

The impact of AIDS on the existential sensibilities of members of this generation has not, to my knowledge, been explored. However, I believe that the recent vigorous scholarly interest in the history of diseases (of which the new hysteria studies are a part) may well reflect the rapid and traumatizing reintroduction of the reality of epidemic disease into the mental life of this group. From this perspective, the study of disease history, the driving desire to "explain epidemics," is born of a combination of fascination and fear;[5] it becomes a means of recapturing a lost historical experience that has suddenly become imperatively important. This historical recovery in turn functions as a form of intellectual (and therefore psychological) mastery of the situation. The fact that individual and collective reactions to AIDS have themselves at times been hysterical may add to the attractions of the topic.

A third cultural context may help to explain why so much attention has been focused of late on hysteria specifically. AIDS of course is by no means the only "new" disease of our time. Within psychological medicine, the incidences of at least three other illnesses have risen dramatically since the late 1970s, today taking on epidemical appearances; and, unlike AIDS, these ailments are to varying degrees gender-related. I am referring to the functional eating disorders, such as anorexia nervosa and bulimia, multiple personality disorder and its related dissociative states, and the chronic fatigue syndromes.

The cultural and historical homologies between hysteria in earlier times, particularly in its late nineteenth-century incarnations, and these present-day diseases are detailed and undeniable. Just as the history of hysteria reached a high point in France during the penultimate decades of the nineteenth century, so anorexia nervosa, multiple personality, and chronic fatigue syndrome are experiencing their golden ages during the 1980s and 1990s. Anorexia and bulimia are overwhelmingly "female" pathologies, afflicting especially young and adolescent women (although the number of cases involving males is on the rise), while in the United States, multiple personality is diagnosed up to ten times more frequently in females than males.[6] In a like manner, the eating disorders, dissociative disorders, and fatigue syndromes—again, like hysteria—are heavily context-dependent. They are perceived as social and cultural diseases re-

---

[5] Charles E. Rosenberg, *Explaining Epidemics and Other Studies in the History of Medicine* (New York: Cambridge University Press, 1992).

[6] Ian Hacking, "Multiple Personality and Gender," in Mary V. Seeman, ed., *Gender and Psychopathology* (Washington, D.C.: American Psychiatric Association Press, forthcoming).

flective in some direct, if undetermined, way of social and cultural conditions unique to the present. Moreover, although the etiologies of all three ailments remain uncertain, sexual factors are believed to play an important part, whether in the form of childhood sexual abuse or fear of adult sexuality and pregnancy. Furthermore, these contemporary disorders, like hysteria, are easily spread by suggestion and imitation, and the models for imitation are provided in individual cases that have been widely publicized in novels, films, and journalism. The role of medical suggestion is also very strong in all three diseases. Lastly, entire therapeutic cultures have developed in recent years to cater to the specialized needs of the more financially secure victims of these disorders, not unlike the nerve doctors and nerve clinics of a century ago.[7]

In a classic formulation, the cultural critic and Freud scholar Philip Rieff once reflected on the emergence of "Psychological Man" in the twentieth century. In the same mold, French medical critics have declared that we live today in "an advanced psychiatric society," in which the operative ideas and vocabularies for understanding ourselves and our society originate within the psychosciences.[8] In our psychological century, new or emergent forms of psychopathology are not limited to technical medical discussion but rather develop strong social and cultural resonances. As Susie Orbach has proposed, these behaviors may be read as metaphors for the age itself.[9] With the rise to prominence of anorexia nervosa, the multiple personality disorders, and the fatigue syndromes, scholars have developed an intense interest in the phenomenon of "new" and "fashionable" mass psychogenic disorders. As with anorexia, MPD,

---

[7] The historical links between hysteria and its late twentieth-century counterparts become tighter still when we realize that in earlier medical systems these conditions were often subclassifications of the hysterias. On the nineteenth- and early twentieth-century concept of "hysterical anorexia," see Edward Shorter, "The First Great Increase in Anorexia Nervosa," *Journal of Social History* 21 (Fall 1987): 69–96; and Elisabeth Young-Bruehl and Sarah Cummins, "What Happened to 'Anorexie Hystérique'?" *The Annual of Psychoanalysis* 21 (1993): 179–98. In "Psychiatric Misadventures," *American Scholar* (Autumn 1992): 504–9, Paul R. McHugh argues that what is now called multiple personality disorder would previously have been labeled hysteria and should be reclassified under the older diagnosis, and Simon Wesseley convincingly demonstrates the clinical continuities between the viral fatigue syndromes of our day and nineteenth-century neurasthenia in "Old Wine in New Bottles: Neurasthenia and 'ME,'" *Psychological Medicine* 20, no. 1 (February 1990): 35–53.

[8] Philip Rieff, *Freud: The Mind of the Moralist* (Garden City, N.Y.: Doubleday, 1959), chap. 10; Françoise Castel, Robert Castel, and Anne Lovell, *La société psychiatrique avancée* (Paris: Grasset, 1979). See also Martin L. Gross, *The Psychological Society: A Critical Analysis of Psychiatry, Psychotherapy, Psychoanalysis, and the Psychological Revolution* (New York: Simon and Schuster, 1978).

[9] Susie Orbach, *Hunger Strike: The Anorectic's Struggle as a Metaphor for Our Age* (Boston: Faber, 1986).

and CFS today, hysterical neurosis was the primary gendered functional psychopathology of its time. Like all historical study, then, writing and rewriting the history of hysteria becomes a way of achieving an understanding of, and perspective on, ourselves and our social world.

Finally, I believe there exists at least one other cultural framework for the new hysteria studies. Near the opening of this book, I ended my capsule history of hysteria with the mysterious disappearance of the disorder in the present century. In a later section, I attempted to establish that the alleged demise of the disease to a large extent involves a process of clinical redefinition and reclassification. In the post-Charcotian years, I argued, French and German physicians, in Joseph Babinski's memorable phrase, "dismembered" the diagnosis out of all recognition, using its component parts to construct new clinical categories.

Well, during the past half century, North American and European psychiatrists have continued the clinical and terminological dismemberment of the former hysterias. In successive editions of the *International Classification of Diseases* and the *Diagnostic and Statistical Manual of Mental Disorders*, hysteria has been suppressed and replaced by more scientific-sounding diagnoses. What had remained of classic conversion hysteria when these psychiatric manuals first appeared, in the 1930s and 1950s respectively, has now been divided into "factitious illness behavior," "dissociative disorder—conversion type," "histrionic personality type," "psychogenic pain disorder," and "undifferentiated somatoform disorder." Despite the efforts of select physicians to retain earlier concepts of hysteria, there currently exist no plans in either *ICD-10* or the forthcoming *DSM-IV* to resuscitate the diagnosis.[10] In the minds of many North American psychiatrists today, hysteria remains inextricably linked to psychoanalysis, and its removal has become part of a wider de-Freudianization of psychiatric science in an age of ascendant biological psychiatry. To be sure, some psychiatrists, especially in France, will no doubt cling to the category out of nationalistic nostalgia, and individual practitioners throughout the world may still employ it in specialized diagnostic contexts. But these local and sporadic uses pale by comparison with the programmatic interest in hysteria we find in earlier generations of physicians. For all intents and purposes, the ongoing attempt to exorcise hysteria from the psychiatric textbooks has been successful.

Nor has the progressive delimitation of the hysteria concept been confined to physicians hostile to psychoanalysis. Outside of psychiatric medicine, the second half of the century has brought four fundamental reconceptualizations of hysterical neurosis: the Szaszian social-communicative critique, the Slaterian organic reinterpretation, the Anglo-American femi-

---

[10] Letter from Robert L. Spitzer to the author, February 6, 1992.

nist rereading, and the Lacanian discursive and narratological model. In their origins and aims, these models are drastically dissimilar; however, all four are alike in that they take the form of *depathologizations*. That is, they represent attempts to strip hysteria of its ancient and privileged status as medical disease, thereby reinforcing independent developments within psychiatric medicine.

I should make it clear that I am not contending that the behaviors formerly constitutive of hysteria no longer exist. Many of them probably do. But the past synthesis of knowledge and ignorance that allowed these wide-ranging behaviors to be defined as a single, unitary disease entity called hysteria has been lost, and it is difficult to conceive of any circumstances that would ever allow for their clinical reconstitution. As a result, *hysteria as medical diagnosis* is almost certainly vanishing irretrievably.

As I hinted in my introduction, I have come to see a connection between the retreat of hysteria from the medical realm and the emergence of the new hysteria studies. I want to suggest in closing that, rather than discouraging the study of the disease historically, the medical dismemberment of hysteria has provided the indispensable intellectual preconditions for its definitive historicization. When the diagnosis was alive and well, writing hysteria's histories mainly served the partisan purposes of illustrating contemporary medical doctrine. In contrast, it is only when a subject is securely in the past that it can fully and successfully be studied historically. The achievement of modern historicism is the realization that we can properly comprehend the relation of what has been to what is only when we have recognized the independence of the past from the present and acknowledge that the two may be divided from each other. In the late twentieth century, as we distance ourselves increasingly from the psychodynamic paradigms that dominated the past few generations of mental medicine, and from the diagnostic categories that composed those paradigms, we have discovered the ability to produce a newly enriched history of hysteria.

If my interpretation of the recent broad interest in this topic is correct, then a striking historical irony is at play. The terminal decades of the past three centuries have brought outbursts of medical interest in hysterical disease accompanied by paradigm shifts in its scientific conceptualization. In the 1680s, Willis and Sydenham rejected centuries of classical and medieval thinking to develop a fundamentally new neurological model of the disorder. In the late eighteenth century, Bossier de Sauvages, Cullen, and Pinel reeroticized the diagnosis as part of a far-ranging reorientation of attitudes toward the psyche and the body. And during the *belle époque*, Freud used hysteria to create psychoanalysis. Today, we find ourselves at another century's end; yet, this time, the *fin de siècle*—which is also a *fin de millénaire*—has brought the *fin d'hystérie* itself. However, in place of a surge of medical theorization, we have the new hysteria studies. Far from declining or dying, *historical* discourses of hysteria are now experiencing *their* golden age. In 1995 we reach the centenary of the publication of the *Studies on Hysteria*, and once again hysteria is in the news; but, this time around, it is historians, rather than physicians, who are covering the story. Today, the great neurosis is being "re-membered" through the work of scholars, critics, and historians.

"The word 'hysteria' should be preserved, although its primitive meaning has much changed," advised a young Pierre Janet in 1894. "It would be very difficult to modify it nowadays, and, truly, it has so grand and so beautiful a history that it would be painful to give it up. But since every epoch has given it a different meaning, let us try to find out what meaning it has today."[11] I have attempted in this study to describe in detail the great number and diversity of the meanings of hysteria in the past. More tentatively, I have also pointed out several ways in which hysteria is meaningful still for our own time. Almost assuredly, the corpus of texts that compose the new hysteria studies, including the present one, reflect other "deep structures" of our age too, but we are too close to the spectacle to perceive these meanings. At best, we can only record the phenomenon as accurately as possible and speculate dimly on its larger implications—leaving these to be discovered, perhaps, by some enterprising historian of the late twenty-first century.

[11] Janet, *État mental des hystériques*, 300.

BIBLIOGRAPHY

THIS BIBLIOGRAPHY is restricted to scholarly writings dealing with the history of hysteria. It records secondary sources and recently reprinted primary texts. For a recital of medical texts from centuries past dealing with hysteria, readers should consult the bibliographies appended to Henri Cesbron, *Histoire critique de l'hystérie* (Paris: Asselin et Houzeau, 1909); and Ilza Veith, *Hysteria: The History of a Disease* (Chicago: University of Chicago Press, 1965). Guides to the contemporary medical literature in English can be found in Harold Merskey, *The Analysis of Hysteria* (London: Baillière Tindall, 1979), 277–300; and Phillip R. Slavney, *Perspectives on "Hysteria"* (Baltimore: Johns Hopkins University Press, 1990), 191–211. For detailed reviews of recent French-language writings, see Augustin Jeanneau, "L'hystérie: Unité et diversité," *Revue française de psychanalyse* 49, no. 2, special issue (January–February 1985): 107–326; and Martha Noel Evans, *Fits and Starts: A Genealogy of Hysteria in Modern France* (Ithaca, N.Y.: Cornell University Press, 1991), 243–59.

Abbott, E. Carl. "The Wicked Womb." *Canadian Medical Association Journal* 148, no. 3 (1993): 381–82.

Abricossoff, Glafira. *L'hystérie aux XVIIe et XVIIIe siècles: Étude historique.* Paris: G. Steinheil, 1897.

Abse, D. Wilfred. *Hysteria and Related Mental Disorders.* 2d ed. Bristol: Wright, 1987.

Acker, S. "Comment aujourd'hui peut-on comprendre les manifestations hystériques à la lumière de l'évolution du concept d'hystérie au cours de l'histoire de la médecine." Ph.D. diss., University of Paris, 1973.

Addyman, Marie E. "The Character of Hysteria in Shakespeare's England." Ph.D. diss., University of York, 1988.

Aguayo, Joseph. "Charcot and Freud: Some Implications of Late 19th-Century French Psychiatry and Politics for the Origins of Psychoanalysis." *Psychoanalysis and Contemporary Thought* 9, no. 2 (1986): 223–60.

Amselle, Gaston. *Conception de l'hystérie: Étude historique et clinique.* Paris: Doin, 1907.

Andersson, Ola. Chaps. 2, 3, and 4 in *Studies in the Prehistory of Psychoanalysis.* Stockholm: Svenska Bokförlaget, 1962.

———. "A Supplement to Freud's Case History of 'Frau Emmy v. N.' in Studies on Hysteria 1895." *Scandinavian Psychoanalytic Review* 2, no. 1 (1979): 5–16.

Appignanesi, Lisa, and John Forrester. Part 2 in *Freud's Women: Family, Patients, Followers.* New York: Basic Books, 1992.

Apter, Emily S. "The Garden of Scopic Perversion from Monet to Mirbeau." *October* 47 (Winter 1988): 91–115.

Auvray-Escalard, Béatrice. "Un méconnu de l'hystérie: Jules Bernard Luys (1828–1897)." Ph.D. diss., University of Caen, 1984.

Axenfeld, Alexandre, and Henri Huchard. *Traité des névroses*. 2d enl. ed. Paris: Germer Baillière, 1883.

Bart, Pauline B. "Social Structure and Vocabularies of Discomfort: What Happened to Female Hysteria?" *Journal of Health and Social Behavior* 9 (September 1968): 188–93.

Bart, Pauline B., and Diana H. Scully. "The Politics of Hysteria: The Case of the Wandering Womb." In Edith S. Gomberg and Violet Franks, eds., *Gender and Disordered Behavior: Sex Differences in Psychopathology*. New York: Brunner/Mazel, 1979.

Beizer, Janet. *Ventriloquized Bodies: Narratives of Hysteria in Nineteenth-Century France*. Ithaca, N.Y.: Cornell University Press, 1994.

Bercherie, Paul. "Le concept de la folie hystérique avant Charcot." *Revue internationale d'histoire de psychiatrie* 1, no. 1 (1983): 47–58.

———. *Genèse des concepts freudiens: Les fondements de la clinique*. Paris: Navarin, 1983.

Berg, Jan Hendrik van den. Chap. 3 in *The Changing Nature of Man: Introduction to a Historical Psychology (Metabletica)*. Translated by H. F. Croes. New York: Norton, 1961.

Bernheimer, Charles. Chap 8 in *Figures of Ill Repute: Representing Prostitution in Nineteenth-Century France*. Cambridge: Harvard University Press, 1989.

Bernheimer, Charles, and Claire Kahane, eds., *In Dora's Case: Freud—Hysteria—Feminism*. New York: Columbia University Press, 1985; 2d ed., 1990.

Bewell, Alan J. "A 'Word Scarce Said': Hysteria and Witchcraft in Wordsworth's 'Experimental' Poetry of 1797–1798." *ELH* [*English Literary History*], 53, no. 2 (Summer 1986): 357–90.

Biéder, J. "La 'communication préliminaire' de 1893." *Annales médico-psychologiques*, 130, no.3 (March 1972): 401–6.

Biéder, J., and D. Bohn. "À propos de l'ouvrage de Pomme sur les 'affections vaporeuses': théorie et clinique, histoire naturelle des maladies." *Annales médico-psychologiques* 146 (1988): 664–76.

Bitter, Wilhelm. "Die Hysterieforschung der 'Französischen Schule' und die Neurosenlehre von Breuer und Freud." In *Psychotherapie und Seelsorge: Eine Einführung in die Tiefenpsychologie, Gesammelte Vorträge*. Stuttgart: Gemeinschaft "Arzt und Seelsorger," 1954.

Blais, Joline Jeannine. "Plotting Against Oedipus: Narrative Alternatives to Hysteria in the Novels of Jean Rhys and Marguerite Duras." Ph.D. diss., University of Pennsylvania, 1991.

Bonnet, G. "Regards sur les revues: De l'hystérie à la production artistique." *Psychanalyse à l'université* 14, no. 53 (1989): 141–47.

Boss, Jeffrey M. N. "The Seventeenth-Century Transformation of the Hysteric Affection, and Sydenham's Baconian Medicine." *Psychological Medicine* 9, no. 2 (May 1979): 221–34.

Brain, W. Russell. "The Concept of Hysteria in the Time of William Harvey." *Proceedings of the Royal Society of Medicine* 56, no. 4 (April 1963): 317–24.

Bresler, Johann. "Kulturhistorischer Beitrag zur Hysterie." *Allegemeine Zeitschrift für Psychiatrie* 53 (1896–97): 333–76.

Briole, G., and B. Lafont. "La bataille de l'hystérie pendant la guerre de 1914–1918." *Synapse* 31, no. 31 (March 1987): 48–52.

Bruttin, Jean-Marie. *Différentes théories sur l'hystérie dans la première moitié du XIXe siècle.* Zurich: Juris Druck, 1969.

Bynum, W. F., Roy Porter, and Michael Shepherd, eds. *The Anatomy of Madness: Essays in the History of Psychiatry.* 3 vols. London: Tavistock, 1989.

Camhi, Leslie E. "Prisoners of Gender: Hysteria, Psychoanalysis, and Literature in *fin-de-siècle* Culture." Ph.D. diss., Yale University, 1991.

Cappello, Mary. "Alice James: 'Neither Dead nor Recovered.'" *American Imago* 45, no. 2 (Summer 1988): 127–162.

Carroy, Jacqueline. "Le noviciat de l'hystérie selon Georgette Dega." *Psychanalyse à l'université* 12, no. 45 (January 1987): 141–52.

———. Chap. 2 in *Les personnalités doubles et multiples: Entre science et fiction.* Paris: Presses universitaires de France, 1993.

Carroy-Thirard, Jacqueline. "Figures de femmes hystériques dans la psychiatrie française du 19e siècle." *Psychanalyse à l'université* 4, no. 14 (March 1979): 313–24.

———. "Hystérie, théâtre, littérature au dix-neuvième siècle." *Psychanalyse à l'université* 7, no. 26 (March 1982): 299–317.

———. *Le mal de Morzine: De la possession à l'hystérie.* Paris: Solin, 1981.

———. "Possession, extase, hystérie au XIXe siècle." *Psychanalyse à l'université* 5, no. 19 (June 1980): 499–515.

Carter, A. E. Chap. 3 in *The Idea of Decadence in French Literature, 1830–1900.* Toronto: University of Toronto Press, 1958.

Carter, K. Codell. "Germ Theory, Hysteria, Freud's Early Work in Psychopathology." *Medical History* 24, no. 3 (July 1980): 259–74.

———. "Infantile Hysteria and Infantile Sexuality in Late Nineteenth-Century German-Language Medical Literature." *Medical History* 27, no. 2 (April 1983): 186–96.

Catonné, Jean-Philippe. "Femmes et hystérie au XIXe siècle." *Synapse* 88 (September 1992): 33–43.

———. "L'hystérie Hippocratique." *Annales médico-psychologiques* 150, no. 10 (December 1992): 705–19.

Cazali, Joelle. "Histoire de l'hystérie: Ses variations sémiologiques et thérapeutiques à travers les siècles." Ph.D. diss., University of Paris V, 1985.

Certeau, Michel de. "Ce que Freud fait de l'histoire: À propos de 'Une névrose démoniaque au XVIIe siècle.'" *Annales: Économies, sociétés, civilisations* 25, no. 3 (May–June 1970): 654–67.

Cesbron, Henri. *Histoire critique de l'hystérie.* Paris: Asselin et Houzeau, 1909.

Chaillou, Marie-Elisabeth. "Évolution des conceptions étiologiques de l'hystérie." Ph.D., diss., University of Paris XIII, 1985.

Charbonneau, Christine M. "À partir d'un traité des vapeurs du XVIIIe siècle: Éternelle hystérie. . . ." Ph.D. diss., University of Paris V, 1984.

Charcot, Jean-Martin. *À propos de six cas d'hystérie chez l'homme.* Paris: Théraplix, 1969.

———. Lesson 5 in *Charcot the Clinician: The Tuesday Lessons.* Translated by Christopher G. Goetz. New York: Raven Press, 1987.

————. *Clinical Lectures on Diseases of the Nervous System*. Translated by Thomas Savill (1889). Introduction by Ruth Harris. Tavistock Classics in the History of Psychiatry, edited by W. F. Bynum and Roy Porter. London: Routledge, 1991.

————. *L'hystérie*. Edited by É. Trillat. Toulouse: Privat, 1971.

————. *Leçons sur l'hystérie virile*. Introduction by Michèle Ouerd. Paris: S.F.I.E.D., 1984.

Charcot, Jean-Martin and Paul Richer. *Les démoniaques dans l'art*. Introduction by Pierre Fédida. Postscript by Georges Didi-Huberman. Paris: Macula, 1984.

Chertok, Léon. "À l'occasion d'un centenaire Charcot: L'hystérie et l'hypnose." *Perspectives psychiatriques* 21, no. 2 (1983): 81–89.

————. "Hysteria, Hypnosis, and Psychopathology: History and Perspectives." *Journal of Nervous and Mental Disease* 161, no. 6 (December 1975): 367–78.

————. *Hystérie: Langage du corps*. Sciencefilm, 1967. Film; versions in French, German, English, and Dutch.

Cixous, Hélène. "Castration or Decapitation?" *Signs* 7, no. 1 (Autumn 1981): 36–55.

————. *Portrait de Dora*. Paris: Éditions des femmes, 1976. Translated by Anita Barrows as *Portrait of Dora*. London: John Calder, 1979.

Cixous, Hélène and Catherine Clément. *La jeune née*. (Paris: Union générale d'édition, 1975). Translated by Betsy Wing as *The Newly Born Woman*. Introduction by Sandra M. Gilbert. Manchester: Manchester University Press, 1986.

Clark, Michael J. "'Morbid Introspection,' Unsoundness of Mind, and British Psychological Medicine, c. 1830–1900." In vol. 3 of W. F. Bynum, Roy Porter, and Michael Shepherd, eds., *The Anatomy of Madness: Essays in the History of Psychiatry*. 3 vols. London: Tavistock, 1989.

————. "The Rejection of Psychological Approaches to Mental Disorder in Late Nineteenth-Century British Psychiatry." In Andrew Scull, ed., *Madhouses, Mad-Doctors, and Madmen: The Social History of Psychiatry in the Victorian Era*. Philadelphia: University of Pennsylvania Press, 1981.

Clavreul, Jean. Chap. 11 in *L'ordre médical*. Paris: Seuil, 1978.

Clément, Catherine. "Enclave/Esclave." In Isabelle de Courtivron and Elaine Marks, eds., *New French Feminisms: An Anthology*. Amherst: University of Massachusetts Press, 1981.

Coriat, Isador H. *The Hysteria of Lady Macbeth*. New York: Moffat, Yard and Company, 1912.

Corraze, Jacques. "La question de l'hystérie." In Jacques Postel and Claude Quétel, eds., *Nouvelle histoire de la psychiatrie*. Toulouse: Privat, 1983.

Critchley, E.M.R., and H. E. Cantor. "Charcot's Hysteria Renaissant." *British Medical Journal* 289, no. 6460 (December 22–24, 1984): 1785–88.

Cummings, Katherine. *Telling Tales: The Hysteric's Seduction in Fiction and Theory*. Stanford, Calif.: Stanford University Press, 1991.

Cumston, Charles G. "A Note on Dr. Charles Lepois' Writings on Hysteria." London: Wellcome Institute for the History of Medicine, Reprints Collection, n.d.

David-Ménard, Monique. *L'hystérique entre Freud et Lacan: Corps et langage en psychanalyse*. Paris: Éditions universitaires, 1983. Translated by Catherine Porter as *Hysteria from Freud to Lacan: Body and Language in Psychoanalysis.* Foreword by Ned Lukacher. Ithaca, N.Y.: Cornell University Press, 1989.

De Boor, Clemens, and Emma Moersch. "Emmy von N.—eine Hysterie?" *Psyche* 34, no. 3 (March 1980): 265–79.

Debru, A. "La suffocation hystérique chez Galien et Aetius: Réécriture et emprunt de 'je.'" in A. Garzya, ed., *Tradizione e ecdotica dei testi medici tardoantichi e bizantini.* Naples: M. D'auria, 1992.

Decker, Hannah S. *Freud, Dora, and Vienna 1900.* New York: Free Press, 1991.

———. Chap. 2 in *Freud in Germany: Revolution and Reaction in Science, 1893–1907.* Monograph 41 of *Psychological Issues* (11, no. 1). New York: International Universities Press, 1977.

Decottignies, Jean, ed. *Physiologie et mythologie du "féminin."* Lille: Presses universitaires de Lille, 1989.

"De la névrose d'angoisse à l'hystérie." Proceedings of the Forty-Fourth Congrès des psychanalystes de langue française, Lisbon, 1984. *Revue française de psychanalyse* 49. Paris: Presses universitaires de France, 1984.

Delmas-Marsalet, P. "L'évolution des idées sur l'hystérie." *Journal médical de Bordeaux* 113 (1936): 195–202.

Didi-Huberman, Georges. "Ästhetik und Experiment bei Charcot." In Jean Clair, Cathrin Pichler, and Wolfgang Pircher, eds., *Wunderblock: Eine Geschichte der modernen Seele.* Vienna: Locker, 1989.

———. *Invention de l'hystérie: Charcot et l'Iconographie photographique de la Salpêtrière.* Paris: Macula, 1982.

Doerner, Klaus. *Madmen and the Bourgeoisie: A Social History of Psychiatry.* Translated by J. Neugroschel and J. Steinberg. Oxford: Basil Blackwell, 1981.

Dottin-Orsini, M. *Cette femme qu'ils disent fatale: Textes et images de la misogynie fin de siècle.* Paris: Grasset, 1993.

Drinka, George F. Chap. 4 in *The Birth of Neurosis: Myth, Malady and the Victorians.* New York: Simon and Schuster, 1984.

Edmunds, Susan. "'I Read the Writing When He Seized My Throat': Hysteria and Revolution in H.D.'s (Hilda Doolittle's) 'Helen in Egypt.'" *Contemporary Literature* 32, no. 4 (Winter 1981): 471–96.

Ehrenreich, Barbara, and Deirdre English. *Complaints and Disorders: The Sexual Politics of Sickness.* Glass Mountain Pamphlets, no. 2. Old Westbury, N.Y.: Feminist Press, 1973.

Ellenberger, Henri F. "A propos du *Malleus Maleficarum.*" *Schweizerische Zeitschrift für Psychologie* 10 (1951): 136–48.

———. "Aspects ethno-psychiatriques de l'hystérie." *Confrontations psychiatriques* 1, no. 1 (1968): 131–45.

———. Chaps. 3, 4, 8, 9, and 10 in *Beyond the Unconscious: Essays of Henri F. Ellenberger in the History of Psychiatry.* Introduction by Mark S. Micale. Princeton: Princeton University Press, 1993.

———. "La conférence de Freud sur l'hystérie masculine (15 octobre 1886): Étude critique." *L'information psychiatrique* 44, no. 10 (1968): 921–29.

———. *The Discovery of the Unconscious: The History and Evolution of Dynamic Psychiatry.* New York: Basic Books, 1970.

————. "L'histoire d'"Emmy von N.': Étude critique avec documents nouveaux." *L'évolution psychiatrique* 42, no. 3 (July–September 1977): 519–41.

————. "La psychiatrie et son histoire inconnue." *L'union médicale du Canada* 90, no. 3 (March 1961): 281–89.

————. "The Story of 'Anna O.': A Critical Review with New Data." *Journal of the History of the Behavioral Sciences* 8, no. 3 (July 1972): 267–79.

Ernoul, E. "Du mutisme hystérique: Étude historique, clinique et thérapeutique." Ph.D. diss., University of Paris, 1987.

Evans, Martha Noel. *Fits and Starts: A Genealogy of Hysteria in Modern France.* Ithaca, N.Y.: Cornell University Press, 1991.

————. "L'hystérie et la séduction de la théorie." *Frénésie: Histoire. psychiatrie. psychanalyse,* 4 (Autumn 1987): 50–61. Translated with minor alterations as "Hysteria and the Seduction of Theory." In Dianne Hunter, ed., *Seduction and Theory: Readings of Gender, Representation, and Rhetoric.* Chicago: University of Illinois Press, 1989.

Ey, Henri. "Introduction à l'étude actuelle de l'hystérie (Historique et analyse du concept)." *Revue du praticien* 14, no. 11 (1964): 1417–31. Translated as "Hysteria: History and Analysis of the Concept." in Roy, ed., *Hysteria.*

Falaise, C. "Le 'Tout Paris' des années 1880, à propos de la leçon clinique à la Salpêtrière (Brouillet, 1887)." Ph.D. diss., University of Caen, 1989.

Fancher, Raymond E. Chap. 2 in *Psychoanalytic Psychology: The Development of Freud's Thought.* New York: Norton, 1973.

Fedikew, Patricia. "Marguerite Duras: Feminine Field of Hysteria." *Enclitic* 6 (1982): 78–86.

Feingold, Madeline L. "Hysteria as a Modality of Adjustment in Fin-de-Siècle Vienna." Ph.D. diss., California School of Professional Psychology, Berkeley, 1983.

Feldman, Marie. "De Freud à Cixous: Une autre perspective sur Dora l'hystérique." Master's thesis, Florida Atlantic University, 1991.

Ferry, Susan J. "Lives Measured in Coffee Spoons? A Study of Hysteria, Class, and Women in Nineteenth-Century Britain." Master's thesis, Queen's University at Kingston, Canada, 1989.

Fichtner, Gerhard, and Albrecht Hirschmüller. "Freuds 'Katharina'—Hintergrund, Entstehungsgeschichte und Bedeutung einer frühen psychoanalytischen Krankengeschichte." *Psyche* 39, no.3 (March 1985): 220–40.

Findlay, Heather Ann. "Madwomen, Witches and Lady Writers: Hysteria in English Renaissance Texts." Ph.D. diss., Cornell Univeristy, 1993.

Finney, Gail. Chap. 6 in *Women in Modern Drama: Freud, Feminism, and European Theater at the Turn of the Century.* Ithaca, N.Y.: Cornell University Press, 1989.

Fischer-Homberger, Esther. "Hysterie und Misogynie: Ein Aspekt der Hysteriegeschichte." *Gesnerus* 26, nos.1/2 (1969): 117–27.

————. *Krankheit Frau und andere Arbeiten zur Medizingeschichte der Frau.* Bern: Hans Huber, 1979.

————. "On the Medical History of the Doctrine of the Imagination." *Psychological Medicine* 9, no. 4 (November 1979): 619–28.

Forrester, John. "The True Story of Anna O." Chap. 1 in *The Seductions of Psy-*

choanalysis: Freud, Lacan, Derrida. Cambridge: Cambridge University Press, 1990.

Fortineau, Elisabeth. "Bernheim face à Charcot et Freud: L'école de Nancy." *Information psychiatrique* 41, no. 3 (April 1985): 413–20.

Foucault, Michel. *Folie et déraison: Histoire de la folie à l'âge classique.* Paris: Plon, 1961. Translated by Richard Howard as *Madness and Civilization: A History of Insanity in the Age of Reason.* London: Tavistock, 1967.

———. *Histoire de la sexualité.* Vol. 1, *La volonté de savoir.* Paris: Gallimard, 1976. Translated by Robert Hurley as *The History of Sexuality.* Vol. 1, *An Introduction.* New York: Vintage, 1980.

———. *Michel Foucault: Résumé des cours 1970–1982.* Seminars, essays, and lectures delivered at the Collège de France. Paris: Julliard, 1989.

Fredriksen, Paula. "Hysteria and the Gnostic Myths of Creation." *Vigiliae Christianae* 33, no. 3 (September 1979): 287–90.

Freeman, Phyllis, Carley Rees Bogarad, and Diane E. Sholomskas. "Margery Kempe, A New Theory: The Inadequacy of Hysteria and Postpartum Psychosis as Diagnostic Categories." *History of Psychiatry* 1, no. 2 (June 1990): 169–90.

Gallop, Jane. *The Daughter's Seduction: Feminism and Psychoanalysis.* London: Macmillan, 1982.

Gasarian, Gérard. "La figure de poète hystérique ou l'allégorie chez Baudelaire." *Poétique* 86 (April 1991): 177–91.

Gasser, Jacques. "Jean-Martin Charcot (1825–1893) et le système nerveux: Étude de la motricité, du langage, de la mémoire et de l'hystérie à la fin du XIXième siècle." Ph.D. diss., École des hautes études en science sociales, 1990.

Gay, Peter. *Freud: A Life for Our Time.* New York: Basic Books, 1988.

———. *The Tender Passion.* vol. 2 of *The Bourgeois Experience: Victoria to Freud.* 2 vols. New York: Oxford University Press, 1986.

Gedo, John E. et al. "*Studies on Hysteria*: A Methodological Evaluation." In John E. Gedo and George H. Pollock, eds., *Freud: The Fusion of Science and Humanism*, monograph 34/35 of *Psychological Issues* 1976. (9, nos. 2/3). New York: International Universities Press, 1976.

Gelfand, Toby. "Becoming Patrimony: When, How, and Why Charcot Got into Hysteria." In C. G. Goetz, ed., *History of Neurology: Jean-Martin Charcot.* Minneapolis: American Academy of Neurology Publications, 1993.

Gilles de la Tourette, Georges. Chap. 1 in vol. 1 of *Traité clinique et thérapeutique de l'hystérie d'après l'enseignement de la Salpêtrière.* 3 vols. Paris: E. Plon, Nourrit et Cie, 1891.

Gilman, Sander L. "The Image of the Hysteric." In Sander Gilman, Helen King, Roy Porter, George Rousseau, and Elaine Showalter, *Hysteria beyond Freud.* Berkeley: University of California Press, 1993.

———. Chap. 16 in *Seeing the Insane: A Cultural History of Madness and Art in the Western World.* New York: John Wiley and Sons, 1982.

Gilman, Sander L., Helen King, Roy Porter, George Rousseau, and Elaine Showalter. *Hysteria beyond Freud.* Berkeley: University of California Press, 1993.

Girard, R. "Pierre Janet: Psychopathology and the Psychotherapy of Neurosis." *Confrontations psychiatriques* 6, no. 11 (1973): 55–82.

Glaser, Gilbert H. "Epilepsy, Hysteria and 'Possession': A Historical Essay." *Journal of Nervous and Mental Disease* 166, no. 4 (April 1978): 268–74.

Gobbi, Jean-Pierre. "Le retour à Briquet: Enquête sur la disparition de la notion d'hystérie dans le DSM III." Ph.D. diss., University of Paris VI, 1985.

Goblot, Jean-Jacques. "Extase, hystérie, possession: Les théories d'Alexandre Bertrand." *Romantisme* 24 (1979): 53–59.

Godet, J. A. "Lecture de Jean Wier: Réflexions sur l'histoire de la sorcière et de l'hystérique, de leurs maux et de leurs thérapeutes." Ph.D. diss., University of Paris, 1980.

Goetz, Christopher G., Michel Bonduelle, and Toby Gelfand. Chap. 6 in *Constructing Neurology: Jean-Martin Charcot 1825–1893*. New York: Oxford University Press, forthcoming.

Goldstein, Jan. Chap. 9 in *Console and Classify: The French Psychiatric Profession in the Nineteenth Century*. New York: Cambridge University Press, 1987.

———. "The Hysteria Diagnosis and the Politics of Anticlericalism in Late Nineteenth-Century France." *Journal of Modern History* 54, no. 2 (June 1982): 209–39.

———. "The Uses of Male Hysteria: Medical and Literary Discourse in Nineteenth-Century France." *Representations* 34, (Spring 1991): 134–65.

Gorceix, A., M. Gligseliger, and G. Koin. "Les cinquante ans du cinquantenaire." *Annales médico-psychologiques* 136, no. 4 (April 1978): 617–19.

Gordon, E. et al. "The Development of Hysteria as a Psychiatric Concept." *Comprehensive Psychiatry* 25, no. 5 (September–October 1984): 532–37.

Gorog, F., and F. Leguil. "Histoire de l'hystérie." *Soins-psychiatriques* 27 (January 1983): 3–6.

Goulemot, Jean Marie. "'Prêtons la main à la nature . . .': II. Fureurs utérines." *Dix-Huitième Siècle* 12, special number (*Représentations de la vie sensuelle*) (1980): 97–111.

Gourévitch, Danielle. Chap. 5 in *Le mal d'être femme: La femme et la médecine dans la Rome antique*. Paris: Société d'Édition "Les Belles Lettres," 1984.

Gourévitch, Michel, and Danielle Gourévitch. "Les cas Aelius-Aristide, ou mémoires d'un hystérique au IIe siècle." *Information psychiatrique* 44 (1968): 897–902.

Granier, Herve. "Folie et hystérie: Étude historique et clinique." Ph.D. diss., University of Montpellier I, 1984.

Green, Monica Helen. Chap. 1 in "The Transmission of Ancient Theories of Female Physiology and Disease through the Early Middle Ages." Ph.D. diss., Princeton University, 1985.

Greenslade, William. "Women and the Diseases of Civilization: George Gissing's 'The Whirlpool.'" *Victorian Studies* 32, no. 4 (Summer 1989): 507–34.

Guillain, Georges. "Il est injustifié et erroné d'oublier l'oeuvre de J.-M. Charcot sur l'hystérie et les névroses." *La semaine des hôpitaux de Paris* 25, no. 4 (January 14, 1949): 147–60.

———. Chaps. 13 and 14 in *J.-M. Charcot (1825–1893): Sa vie, son oeuvre*. Paris: Masson, 1955. Translated by Pearce Bailey as *J.-M. Charcot, 1825–1893: His Life—His Work*. New York: Paul B. Hoeber, 1959.

Guyotat, Jean. "Retour à l'hystérie gynécologique?" *Psychanalyse à l'université* 11, no. 41 (January 1986): 129–39.

Haberberg, Georges. "De Charcot à Babinski: Étude du rôle de l'hystérie dans la naissance de la neurologie moderne." Ph.D. diss., University of Paris, Créteil, 1979.

Hare, E. "The History of 'Nervous Disorders' from 1600 to 1840, and a Comparison with Modern Views." *British Journal of Psychiatry* 159, (1991): 37–45.

Harrington, Anne. "Hysteria, Hypnosis, and the Lure of the Invisible: The Rise of Neo-Mesmerism in *fin-de-siècle* French Psychiatry." In vol. 3 of Bynum, Porter, and Shepherd, *The Anatomy of Madness*.

———. "Metals and Magnets in Medicine: Hysteria, Hypnosis, and Medical Culture in *fin-de-siècle* Paris." *Psychological Medicine* 18, no. 1 (February 1988): 21–38.

Harris, Ruth. Introduction to *Clinical Lectures on Diseases of the Nervous System*, by J.-M. Charcot. London and New York: Tavistock/Routledge, 1991.

———. "Melodrama, Hysteria and Feminine Crimes of Passion in the fin-de-siècle." *History Workshop* 25, (Spring 1988): 31–63.

———. "Murder under Hypnosis in the Case of Gabrielle Bompard: Psychiatry in the Courtroom in Belle Époque Paris." In vol. 2 of Bynum, Porter, and Shepherd, *The Anatomy of Madness*.

———. Chaps. 5 and 6 in *Murders and Madness: Medicine, Law, and Society in the Fin de Siècle*. Oxford: Clarendon Press, 1989.

Havens, Leston L. "Charcot and Hysteria." *Journal of Nervous and Mental Disease* 141, no. 5 (1966): 505–16.

Hawkins, Ernest L. "The Raging Womb: An Archetypal Study of Hysteria and the Early Psychoanalytic Movement." Ph.D. diss., University of Dallas, 1978.

Herndl, Diane Price. "The Writing Cure: Charlotte Perkins Gilman, Anna O., and 'Hysterical' Writing." *NWSA Journal* 1 (1988): 52–74.

Hillman, Robert G. "A Scientific Study of Mystery: The Role of the Medical and Popular Press in the Nancy-Salpêtrière Controversy on Hypnotism." *Bulletin of the History of Medicine* 39, no. 2 (March–April 1965): 163–82.

Hirschmüller, Albrecht. "Eine bisher unbekannte Krankengeschichte Sigmund Freuds und Josef Breuers aus der Entstehungszeit der 'Studien über Hysterie.'" In *Jahrbuch der Psychoanalyse*, vol. 10. Bern: Hans Huber, 1978.

———. "Durch Leiden zur schöpferischen Kraft? Anna O. und Bertha Pappenheim." In *Dokumentation zum 50. Todestag von Bertha Pappenheim*. Neu-Isenberg, 1988.

———. *Physiologie und Psychoanalyse im Leben und Werk Josef Breuers*. Bern: Hans Huber, 1978. Translated as *The Life and Work of Josef Breuer: Physiology and Psychoanalysis*. New York: New York University Press, 1989.

———. "Die Wiener Psychiatrie der Meynert-Zeit: Untersuchungen zu Sigmund Freuds nervenärztlicher Ausbildung." Ph.D. diss., Eberhard-Karls Universität, Tübingen, 1989.

Hollender, Marc H. "The Case of Anna O.: A Reformulation." *American Journal of Psychiatry* 137, no. 7 (July 1980): 797–800.

———. "Conversion Hysteria: A Post-Freudian Reinterpretation of 19th-Century Psychosocial Data." *Archives of General Psychiatry* 26, (April 1972): 311–14.

Hunter, Dianne. "Hysteria, Psychoanalysis, and Feminism: The Case of Anna O." *Feminist Studies* 9, no. 3 (Fall 1983): 464–88. Chap. 4 in Shirley N. Garner,

Claire Kahane, and Madelon Sprengnether, eds. *The (M)other Tongue: Essays in Feminist Psychoanalytic Interpretation.* (Ithaca, N.Y.: Cornell University Press, 1985.

Hurst, Lindsay, C. "Freud and the Great Neurosis." *Journal of the Royal Society of Medicine* 76, no.1 (January 1983): 57–61.

———. "What was Wrong with Anna O.?" *Journal of the Royal Society of Medicine* 75, no. 2 (February 1982): 129–31.

Hutschemaekers, Giel. "Hysteria: The Historical and Contextual Approach." in *The Investigation of Culture.* Tilburng: Tilburng University Press. Forthcoming.

———. Chaps. 10 and 11 in *Neurosen in Nederland: Vijfentachtig jaar psychisch en maatschappelijk.* Nijmegen: S.U.N., 1990.

"Die Hysterie." *Ciba Zeitschrift* 10, no. 120 (January 1950): 4406–36.

Hystérie, cent ans après—résumés. Abstracts of papers delivered at the seventh annual conference of the Association française de psychiatrie, Paris, January 22–24, 1988. *Psychiatrie française* 19, special number (May 1988).

Hystérus, special number of *Frénésie: Histoire. psychiatrie. psychanalyse* 4 (Autumn 1987).

Imbert, P. "Le problème de l'hystérie dans le passé." Ph.D. diss., University of Nancy, 1931.

Irigaray, Luce. Part 3 of *Speculum de l'autre femme.* Paris: Éditions de minuit, 1974. Translated by Gillian C. Gill as *Speculum of the Other Woman.* Ithaca, N.Y.: Cornell University Press, 1985.

Israël, Lucien. "Le corps hystérique." *Soins-psychiatriques* 27 (January 1983): 15–19.

———. "L'école de Minne." *Confrontations psychiatriques* 25 (1985): 45–62.

———. *L'hystérique, le sexe et le médecin.* Paris: Masson, 1979.

Jacquart, Danielle, and Claude Thomasset. *Sexualité et savoir médical au moyen âge.* Paris: Presses universitaires de France, 1985.

James, Mary. "The Therapeutic Practices of Jean-Martin Charcot (1825–1893) in Their Historical and Social Context." Ph.D. diss., University of Essex, 1989.

Janet, Pierre. *The Mental State of Hystericals.* Translated by Caroline Rollin Corson. Preface by Daniel N. Robinson. Washington, D.C.: University Publications of America, 1977.

Jeanne des Anges, Soeur. *Autobiographie d'une hystérique possédée.* Preface by J.-M. Charcot. Paris: Jérome Millon, 1985.

Jennings, Jerry L. "The Revival of 'Dora': Advances in Psychoanalytic Theory and Technique." *Journal of the American Psychoanalytic Association* 34, no. 3 (1986): 607–35.

Jorden, Edward. *Briefe Discourse of a Disease called the Suffocation of the Mother.* 1603. New York: De Capo Press, 1971.

Kahane, Claire. "Hysteria, Feminism, and the Case of *The Bostonians.*" In Richard Feldstein and Judith Roof, eds., *Feminism and Psychoanalysis.* Ithaca, N.Y.: Cornell University Press, 1989.

Kane, Alison, and Eric T. Carlson. "A Different Drummer: Robert B. Carter and Nineteenth-Century Hysteria." *Bulletin of the New York Academy of Medicine* 58, no. 6 (September 1982): 519–34.

Kenyon, E. "Hysteria in the Wandering Womb." *Australian and New Zealand Journal of Psychiatry* 13 (1979): 3–6.

Khan, M. R. "Grudge and the Hysteric" [1974]. In *Hidden Selves: Between Theory and Practice in Psychoanalysis*. London: Hogarth Press, 1983.

Kiell, Norman. Chaps. 1, 3, and 7 in *Freud without Hindsight: Reviews of His Work (1893–1939)*. Translated by Vladimir Rus and Denise Boneau. Madison, Conn.: International Universities Press, 1988.

King, Helen. "From Parthenos to Gynē: The Dynamics of Category." Ph.D. diss., University College London, 1985.

———. "Once Upon a Text: Hysteria from Hippocrates." In Gilman et al, *Hysteria beyond Freud*.

Kloë, Elisabeth. *Hysterie im Kindesalter: Zur Entwicklung des kindlichen Hysteriebegriffes*. Vol. 9 of *Freiburger Forschungen zur Medizingeschichte*. Freiburg: Hans Ferdinand Schulz, 1979.

Kloë, Elisabeth, and Hildburg Kindt. "Zur Entstehung und Entwicklung des kindlichen Hysteriebegriffes." *Gesnerus* 38, nos. 3/4 (1981): 281–300.

Knibiehler, Yvonne. "Le discours médical sur la femme: Constats et Ruptures." *Romantisme* 13–14 (1976): 41–55.

Knight, Isabel F. "Freud's *Project*: A Theory for *Studies on Hysteria*." *Journal of the History of the Behavioral Sciences*. 20, no. 4 (October 1984): 340–58.

Knoff, William F. "Four Thousand Years of Hysteria." *Comprehensive Psychiatry* 12, no. 2 (March, 1971): 156–64.

Kraemer, R. *Der Wandel in den wissenschaftlichen Anschauungen über Hysterie unter besonderer Berücksichtigung der letzten Jahrzehnte*. Würzburg, 1932.

Kris, Ernst. Introduction to Marie Bonaparte, Anna Freud, and Ernst Kris, eds., *The Origins of Psychoanalysis: Letters to Wilhelm Fliess, Drafts and Notes: 1887–1902 by Sigmund Freud*. New York: Basic Books, 1954.

Kristeva, Julia. *Les nouvelles maladies de l'âme*. Paris: Fayard, 1994.

Krohn, Alan. *Hysteria: The Elusive Neurosis*. Monograph 45/46 of *Psychological Issues* (12, nos. 1/2). New York: International Universities Press, 1978.

Kubes, Ursula. "'Moderne Nervositäten' und die Anfänge der Psychoanalyse." In Franz Kadrnoska, ed., *Aufbruch und Untergang. Österreichische Kultur zwischen 1918 und 1938*. Vienna: Europa Verlag, 1981.

Lakoff, Robin Tolmach, and James C. Coyne. *Father Knows Best: The Use and Abuse of Power in Freud's Case of "Dora."* New York: Teachers College Press, 1993.

La Plante, Eve. *Seized: Temporal Lobe Epilepsy as a Medical, Historical, and Artistic Phenomenon*. New York: Harper Collins, 1993.

Laplassotte, François. "Sexualité et névrose avant Freud: Une mise au point." *Psychanalyse à l'université* 3, no. 10 (1978): 203–26.

Lasègue, Charles. *Du délire des persécutions; Le délire alcoolique; De l'anorexie hystérique; Les exhibitionistes*. Nendeln, Liechtenstein: Kraus Reprints, 1978.

———. Chaps. 7–9 in *Écrits psychiatriques*. Edited by J. Corraze. Toulouse: Édouard Privat, 1971.

Laxenaire, M., and A. Chanson. "Les vapeurs: Aperçu historique." *Annales médico-psychologiques* 146 (1988): 637–44.

Lechuga, Paul. "Introduction à une anatomie de la pensée médicale, à propos de l'hystérie au XIXe siècle." Ph.D. diss., University of Montpellier, 1978.

La leçon de Charcot: Voyage dans une toile. Exhibition catalogue. Musée de l'assistance publique, Paris, September 17–December 31, 1986. Paris: Tardy Quercy, 1986.

Leed, Eric J. Chap. 5 in No Man's Land: Combat and Identity in World War I. Cambridge: Cambridge University Press, 1979.

Lefkowitz, Mary R. Heroines and Hysterics. London: Duckworth, 1981.

Leibbrand, Annemarie, and Werner Leibbrand. "Die 'kopernikanische Wendung' des Hysteriebegriffes bei Paracelsus." In Sepp Domandl, ed., Paracelsus: Werk und Wirkung. Vol. 13 of Salzburger Beiträge zur Paracelsusforschung. Vienna: WGO, 1975.

Lellouch, Alain. "La méthode de J.-M. Charcot (1825–1893)." History and Philosophy of the Life Sciences 11, no. 1 (1989): 43–69.

Leroux-Hugon, Véronique, and Claude Quétel. "Charcot, le 'Napoléon de la névrose.'" L'histoire 103 (September 1987): 30–36.

Levin, Kenneth. Chaps. 3 and 4 in Freud's Early Psychology of the Neuroses: A Historical Perspective. Hassocks, Sussex: Harvester Press, 1978.

———. "Freud's Paper 'On Male Hysteria' and the Conflict between Anatomical and Physiological Models." Bulletin of the History of Medicine 48, no. 3 (Fall 1974): 377–97.

———. "Sigmund Freud's Early Studies of the Neuroses, 1886–1905." Ph.D. diss., Princeton University, 1974.

———. "S. Weir Mitchell: Investigations and Insights into Neurasthenia and Hysteria." Transactions and Studies of the College of Physicians of Philadelphia 38, no. 3 (January 1971): 168–73.

Leyne, P. "Évolution du concept de psychose hystérique." Ph.D. diss., University of Paris, 1978.

Libbrecht, Katrien. Hysterical Psychosis: An Historical Survey. New Brunswick, N.J.: Transaction Books, 1994.

Livi, Jocelyne. Vapeurs de femmes: Essai historique sur quelques fantasmes médicaux et philosophiques. Dijon: Collection du Studiola, Navarin, 1984.

Lloyd, Geoffrey G. "Hysteria: A Case for Conservation?" British Medical Journal, 293 (November 15, 1986): 1255–56.

Lorentz, Helmut-Johannes. "Si mulier obticuerit: Ein Hysterierezept des Pseudo-Apuleius." Sudhoffs Archiv, 38 (1954): 20–28.

Losserand, Jean. "Épilepsie et hystérie: Contribution à l'histoire des maladies." Revue française de psychanalyse 92, no. 3 (1978): 411–38.

Lowenberg, Peter. "Otto Bauer, Freud's 'Dora' Case, and the Crises of the First Austrian Republic." In Decoding the Past. New York: Knopf, 1983.

MacDonald, Michael. "Women and Madness in Tudor and Stuart England." Social Research 53, no. 2 (1986): 261–81.

———. Introduction to Witchcraft and Hysteria in Elizabethan London: Edward Jorden and the Mary Glover Case. Edited by Michael MacDonald. Tavistock Classics in the History of Psychiatry, edited by W. F. Bynum and Roy Porter. London and New York: Tavistock/Routledge, 1991.

Mace, C. J. "Hysterical Conversion I: A History." *British Journal of Psychiatry* 161 (1992): 369–77.

McGrath, William J. Chap. 4 in *Freud's Discovery of Psychoanalysis: The Politics of Hysteria*. Ithaca, N.Y.: Cornell University Press, 1986.

MacKenzie, Charlotte. "'The Life of a Human Football'? Women and Madness in the Era of the New Woman." *The Society for the Social History of Medicine— Bulletin* 36 (June 1985): 37–40.

Macmillan, Malcolm B. "Delboeuf and Janet as Influences on Freud's Treatment of Emmy von N." *Journal of the History of the Behavioral Sciences* 15, no. 4 (October 1979): 299–309.

———. "Freud and Janet on Organic and Hysterical Paralyses: A Mystery Solved?" In O. Zentner, ed., *Papers of the Freudian School of Melbourne: Australian Psychoanalytic Writings*. Melbourne: Freudian School of Melbourne, 1988. Reprinted in *International Review of Psycho-Analysis* 17, part 2 (1990): 189–203.

———. Chaps. 1–7 in *Freud Evaluated: The Completed Arc*. Amsterdam: Elsevier Science Publishers, 1990.

———. "Souvenir de la Salpêtrière: M. le Dr. Freud à Paris 1885." *Australian Psychologist* 21, no. 1 (March 1986): 3–29.

Mai, Francois M. "The Forgotten Avant Garde." *Trends in Neurosciences* 5, no. 3 (March 1982): 67–68.

———. "Pierre Briquet: 19th-Century Savant with 20th-Century Ideas." *Canadian Journal of Psychiatry* 28, no.6 (October 1983): 418–21.

Mai, Francois M., and Harold Merskey. "Briquet's Concept of Hysteria: An Historical Perspective." *Canadian Journal of Psychiatry* 26, no. 1 (February 1981): 57–63.

———. "Briquet's *Treatise on Hysteria*: A Synopsis and Commentary." *Archives of General Psychiatry* 37, no. 12 (December 1980): 1401–5.

Maître, Jacques. *Les stigmates hystériques et la peau de son évêque*. Paris: Anthropos, Economica, 1993.

Mangriotis-Caracosta, Hélène. "Note étymologique sur l'hystérie." *Revue française de psychanalyse* 50, no. 3 (May–June 1986): 993–97.

Marneffe, Daphne de. "Looking and Listening: The Construction of Clinical Knowledge in Charcot and Freud." *Signs* 17, no. 1 (Autumn 1991): 91–112.

Martini, Umberto de. "L'isterismo: Da Ippocrate a Charcot." *Pagine di Storia della Medicina* 12 (1968): 42–49.

Massey, E. Wayne, and Lawrence C. McHenry. "Hysteroepilepsy in the Nineteenth Century: Charcot and Gowers." *Neurology* 36, no. 1 (January 1986): 65–67.

Masson, Jeffrey M. *A Dark Science: Women, Sexuality and Psychiatry in the Nineteenth Century*. New York: Farrar, Straus and Giroux, 1986.

In materia di amore: Studi sul discorso isterico. Introduction by Armando Verdiglione. Milan: Spirali Edizioni, 1980.

Matlock, Jann. Part 2 of *Scenes of Seduction: Prostitution, Hysteria, and Reading Difference in Nineteenth-Century France*. New York: Columbia University Press, 1993.

Matus, Jill L. "St. Teresa, Hysteria, and *Middlemarch.*" *Journal of the History of Sexuality* 1 (1990): 215–40.

Mazzoni, Cristina Maria. "Hysterical Pregnancies and Virgin Births: Neurosis and Mysticism in French and Italian Literature at the Turn of the Century." Ph.D. diss., Yale University, 1991.

Meares, Russell et al. "Whose Hysteria: Briquet's, Janet's or Freud's?" *Australian and New Zealand Journal of Psychiatry* 19, no. 3 (1985): 256–63.

Meissner, W. W. "Studies on Hysteria—Frau Emmy von N." *Bulletin of the Menninger Clinic* 45, no. 1 (January 1981): 1–19.

———. "*Studies on Hysteria*: Katharina." *Psychoanalytic Quarterly* 48, no. 4 (October 1979): 587–600.

———. "A Study on Hysteria: Anna O. *Rediviva.*" In *The Annual of Psychoanalysis*, vol. 7. New York: International Universities Press, 1979.

Mensior, Marc. "De Duncan à Pilet de la Mesnardière: Le débat médical autour de la possession de Loudon, 1632–1637." Ph.D. diss., University of Paris, VI, 1986.

Menzaghi, Frédérique, Annie Millot, and Michèle Pillot. "Évolution de la conception de l'hystérie de 1870 à 1930 dans un service de l'asile de Maréville." 2 vols. Master's thesis, University of Nancy II, 1987.

Merskey, Harold. *The Analysis of Hysteria.* London: Baillière Tindall, 1979.

———. "Anna O. Had a Severe Depressive Illness." *British Journal of Psychiatry* 161, (August 1992): 185–94.

———. "Hysteria: The History of a Disease: Ilza Veith." *British Journal of Psychiatry* 148, (November 1985): 576–79.

———. "Hysteria: The History of an Idea." *Canadian Journal of Psychiatry* 28, no. 6 (October 1983): 428–33.

———. "Shell Shock." In German E. Berrios and Hugh L. Freeman, eds., *British Psychiatry's Strange Past: 150 Years of British Psychiatry, 1841–1991.* London: Gaskell, 1991.

Merskey, Harold and Susan Merskey. "Hysteria, or 'Suffocation of the Mother.'" *Canadian Medical Association Journal* 148, no. 3 (1993): 399–405.

Merskey, Harold, and Paul Potter. "The Womb Lay Still in Ancient Egypt." *British Journal of Psychiatry* 154 (June 1989): 751–53.

Meyer, Philippe. *Sommeils indiscrets.* Paris: Orban, 1990.

Micale, Mark S. "Charcot and *les névroses traumatiques*: Scientific and Historical Reflections." *Journal of the History of the Neurosciences.* Forthcoming.

———. "Charcot and the Idea of Hysteria in the Male: Gender, Mental Science, and Medical Diagnosis in Late Nineteenth-Century France." *Medical History* 34, no. 4 (October 1990): 363–411.

———. "Diagnostic Discriminations: Jean-Martin Charcot and the Nineteenth-Century Idea of Masculine Hysterical Neurosis." Ph.D. diss., Yale University, 1987.

———. "Hysteria and Its Historiography—A Review of Past and Present Writings." 2 parts. *History of Science* 27, no. 77 (September 1989): 223–61; no. 78 (December 1989): 317–51.

———. "Hysteria and Its Historiography: The Future Prespective." *History of Psychiatry* 1, no. 1 (March 1990): 33–124.

———. "Hysteria Male/Hysteria Female: Reflections on Comparative Gender Construction in Nineteenth-Century France and Britain." In Marina Benjamin, ed., *Science and Sensibility: Essays on Gender and Scientific Enquiry, 1780–1945*. London: Basil Blackwell, 1991.

———. "On the 'Disappearance' of Hysteria: A Study in the Clinical Deconstruction of a Diagnosis." *Isis* 84 (October 1993): 496–526.

———. "Psychiatry and Literature: The Case of Gustave Flaubert's *Madame Bovary*." In Elaine Showalter, ed., *Hysteria and Narrative*. New York: Rutgers University Press. Forthcoming.

———. "The Salpêtrière in the Age of Charcot: An Institutional Perspective on Medical History in the Late Nineteenth Century." *Journal of Contemporary History* 20, no. 4 (October 1985): 703–31.

Michalos, Peter. *Psyche: A Novel of the Young Freud*. New York: Doubleday, 1993.

Miller, Edgar. "Behaviour Modification Mid-19th-Century Style: Robert Brudenell Carter and the Treatment of Hysteria." *British Journal of Clinical Psychology* 27, no. 4 (November 1988): 297–30.

Millot, Catherine. *Nobodaddy: L'hystérie dans le siècle*. Paris: Point hors ligne, 1988.

Miloche, Philippe. "Un méconnu de l'hystérie: Victor Dumont Pallier (1826–1899)." Ph.D. diss., University of Caen, 1982.

Mirandol, Christian. "Contribution à une étude du concept d'hystérie au 19e siècle." Ph.D. diss., Aix et Marseille II, 1987.

Mitchell, Juliet. "From King Lear to Anna O. and Beyond: Some Speculative Theses on Hysteria and the Traditionless Self." *Yale Journal of Criticism* 5, no. 2 (Spring 1992): 91–108.

———. *Women: The Longest Revolution*. (London: Virago, 1984).

Mitchinson, Wendy. "Hysteria and Insanity in Women: A Nineteenth-Century Canadian Perspective." *Journal of Canadian Studies* 21, no.3 (Fall 1986): 87–105.

Morantz, Regina Markell. "The Perils of Feminist Hisory." *Journal of Interdisciplinary History* 4, no. 4 (Spring 1973): 649–60.

Morgan, Wesley G. "Freud's Lithograph of Charcot: A Historical Note." *Bulletin of the History of Medicine* 63 (1989): 268–72.

Morsier, Georges de. "La 'grande hystérie' de Charcot: Essai sur les causes d'une erreur médicale et judiciaire: Doctrine et perception." *Revue médicale de la Suisse Romande* 89, no. 3 (March 1969): 177–203.

———. "Jean-Martin Charcot, 1825–1893." In vol. 1 of Kurt Kolle, ed., *Grosse Nervenärzte*. 3 vols. Stuttgart: Georg Thieme, 1956.

Mullan, John. "Hypochondria and Hysteria: Sensibility and the Physicians." *The Eighteenth-Century: Theory and Interpretation* 25, no. 2 (Spring 1984): 141–74.

Muller, C. "Épilepsie et hystérie (problème historique et d'actualité)." *Revue médicale de la Suisse Romande* 82, no. 2 (February 1962): 98–102.

Muller, John P. "A Re-Reading of *Studies on Hysteria*: The Freud-Breuer Break Revisited." *Psychoanalytic Psychology* 9, no. 2 (Spring 1992): 129–56.

Nasio, J. D. *L'hystérie ou l'enfant magnifique de la psychanalyse*. Paris: Rivages, 1990.

Nassif, Jacques. Part 1 of *Freud: L'inconscient: Sur les commencements de la psychanalyse*. Paris: Galilée, 1977.

Ober, William B. "Margery Kempe: Hysteria and Mysticism Reconciled," in *Bottoms Up! A Pathologist's Essays on Medicine and the Humanities*. Carbondale Ill.: Southern Illinois University Press, 1987.

Oberkönig, Angelika. "Die Hysterie als Frauenkrankheit in den frühen Schriften von Freud und im Vergleich zum Hysteriebegriffe heute." Ph.D. diss., Institute for the History of Medicine, Münster, work in progress.

Oppenheim, Janet. "*'Shattered Nerves': Doctors, Patients, and Depression in Victorian England*. New York: Oxford University Press, 1991.

Orr-Andrawes, Alison. "The Case of Anna O.: A Neuropsychiatric Perspective." *Journal of the American Psychoanalytic Association* 35, no. 2 (1987): 387–419.

Owen, A[lan] R[obert] G[eorge]. *Hysteria, Hypnosis and Healing: The Work of J.-M. Charcot*. London: Dobson, 1971.

Palis, James, Evangelos Rossopoulos, and Lazaros Triarhou, "The Hippocratic Concept of Hysteria: A Translation of the Original Texts." *Integrative Psychiatry* 3, no. 3 (September 1985): 226–28.

Pappenheim, Else. "More on the Case of Anna O." *American Journal of Psychiatry* 137, no. 12 (December 1980): 1625–26.

Pélicier, Yves, ed. *Colloque sur l'hystérie*. Paris: C. Del. Duco, 1974.

Pierce, Jennifer L. "The Relation between Emotion Work and Hysteria: A Feminist Reintepretation of Freud's 'Studies on Hysteria.'" *Women's Studies* 16, nos. 3–4 (October 1989): 255–71.

Pioger, Thierry. "Réflexions sur l'histoire de l'hystérie." Ph.D. diss., University of Angers, 1985.

Pons Bartran, R. "La histeria clasica y su larga agonia." *Revista de Psiquiatria de la Facultad de Medicina de Barcelona* 16, no. 5 (September–October, 1989): 233–42.

Pontalis, Jean-Bernard. *Entre Freud et Charcot*. Paris: Gallimard, 1977.

Porter, Roy. "The Body and the Mind, the Doctor and the Patient: Negotiating Hysteria." In Gilman et al., *Hysteria Beyond Freud*.

———. *Mind-Forg'd Manacles: A History of Madness in England from the Restoration to the Regency*. London: Athlone, 1987.

———. *A Social History of Madness: Stories of the Insane*. London: Weidenfeld and Nicolson, 1987.

Powrie, Phil. "Configurations of Melodrama: Nostalgia and Hysteria in 'Jean de Florette' and 'Manon des Sources.'" *French Studies* 46, no. 3 (July 1992): 266–76.

Ramas, Maria. "Freud's Dora, Dora's Hysteria: The Negation of a Woman's Rebellion." *Feminist Studies* 6, no. 3 (Fall 1980): 472–510.

Rand, Richard. "Hysteron Proteron, or 'Woman First.'" *Oxford Literary Review* 8, nos. 1–2 (1986): 51–56.

Reeves, Christopher. "Breuer, Freud and the Case of Anna O.: A Reexamination." *Journal of Child Psychotherapy* 8 (1982): 203–14.

Reichard, Suzanne. "A Re-Examination of 'Studies in Hysteria.'" *Psychoanalytic Quarterly* 25, no. 2 (1956): 155–77.

Revue du praticien 32, no. 13 (March 1982). Special issue on hysteria.

Richer, Paul. *Étude descriptive de la grande attaque hystérique ou attaque hystéro-épileptique et de ses grandes variétés* [1879]. In vol. 27 of *The Origins of Psychiatry and Psychoanalysis*. Nendeln, Liechtenstein: Kraus Reprint, 1978.

Riefolo, Giuseppe, and Filippo M. Ferro. "Sguardo e metodo in Babinski: La concezione dell'isteria." *Giornale Storico de Psicologia Dinamica* 15, no. 29 (January 1991): 163–80.

Risse, Guenter. "'The Great Neurosis': The Clinical Construction of Hysteria, 1876–1895." Benjamin Rush Lecture, Annual Meeting of the American Psychiatric Association, San Francisco, May 10, 1989.

———. "Hysteria at the Edinburgh Infirmary: The Construction and Treatment of a Disease, 1770–1800." *Medical History* 32, no. 1 (January 1988): 1–22.

Robb, Dr. "Hippocrates on Hysteria." *Johns Hopkins Hospital Bulletin* 3, (June 1892): 78–79.

Roccatagliata, Giuseppe. *A History of Ancient Psychiatry*. Westport, Conn.: Greenwood Press, 1986.

———. *L'idea dell'isteria: Il mito della sessualità*. Pisa: ETS Editrice, 1990.

———. *Isteria*. Rome: Il Pensiero Scientifico Editore, 1990.

———. *Riflessioni sulla decadenza dell'isteria*. Naples: Liguori, 1992.

Rosenbaum, Max and Muroff, Melvin, eds., *Anna O.: Fourteen Contemporary Reinterpretations*. New York: Free Press, 1984.

Roudinesco, Elisabeth. Vol. 1, part 1, of *La bataille de cent ans: Histoire de la psychanalyse en France*. 2 vols. Paris: Ramsay, 1982.

Rousseau, George S. "'A Strange Pathology': Hysteria in the Early Modern World, 1500–1800." In Gilman et al, *Hysteria beyond Freud*.

———. "Discourses of the Nerve." in Frederick Amrine, ed., *Literature and Science as Modes of Expression*. Dordrecht: Kluwer Academic Publishers, 1989.

Rousselle, Aline. "Images médicales du corps: Observation féminine et idéologie masculine: Le corps de la femme d'après les médecins grecs." *Annales: Économies, Sociétés, Civilisations* 35, no. 5 (September–October 1980): 1089–1115.

———. Chap. 4 in *Porneia: On Desire and the Body in Antiquity*. Translated by Felicia Pheasant. (Oxford: Basil Blackwell, 1988).

Roy, Alec, ed., *Hysteria*. Chichester: John Wiley and Sons, 1982.

Rubinstein, Benjamin B. "Freud's Early Theories of Hysteria." in R. S. Cohen and Larry Laudan, eds., *Physics, Philosophy and Psychoanalysis: Essays in Honor of Adolf Grünbaum*. Dordrecht: D. Reidel, 1983.

Safouan, Moustapha. "In Praise of Hysteria." In Stuart Schneiderman, ed., *Returning to Freud: Clinical Psychoanalysis in the School of Lacan*. New Haven: Yale University Press, 1980.

Satow, Roberta. "Where Has All the Hysteria Gone?" *Psychoanalytic Review* 66, no. 4 (1979): 463–77.

Sauri, Jorge. "La concepcion Hipocratica de la histeria." *Actas Luso-Espanolas de Neurologia Psiquitria y Ciencias Afinas* 1, no. 4 (July–August 1973): 539–46.

———. ed. *Las histerias*. Buenos Aires: Ediciones nueva visión, 1975.

Schaps, Regina. *Hysterie und Weiblichkeit: Wissenschaftsmythen über die Frau*. Frankfurt: Campus, 1982.

Schiller, Francis. *A Möbius Strip: Fin-de-Siècle Neuropsychiatry and Paul Möbius*. Berkeley: University of California Press, 1982.

Schneider, Manfred. "Hysterie als Gesamtkunstwerk." In Alfred Pfabigan, ed. *Ornament und Askese im Zeitgeist des Wien der Jahrhundertwende*. Vienna: Brandstätter, 1985.

Schneider, Monique. *De l'exorcisme à la psychanalyse: Le féminin expurgé*. Paris: Retz, 1979.

Schoenberg, P. J. "A Dialogue with Mandeville." *British Journal of Psychiatry* 129, (August 1976): 120–24.

Schrenk, Martin. "Über Hysterie und Hysterie-Forscher." *Praxis der Psychotherapie* 19, no. 6 (1974): 250–62.

Schuller, Marianne. "'Weibliche Neurose' und Identität: Zur Diskussion der Hysterie um die Jahrhundertwende." In Dietmar Kamper and Christoph Wulf, eds. *Die Wiederkehr des Körpers*. Frankfurt am Main: Suhrkamp, 1982.

Sena, John F. "Belinda's Hysteria: The Medical Context of *The Rape of the Lock*." In Christopher Fox, ed., *Psychology and Literature in the Eighteenth Century*. New York: AMS Press, 1987.

Sentuc, Anne. "Myticisme hystérique ou hystérie mystique?" *Historama* 22, (1985): 83–85.

Shafter, Roberta. "Women and Madness: A Social Historical Perspective." *Issues in Ego Psychology* 12, no. 1 (1989): 77–82.

Sheehan, David V. "The Classification of Anxiety and Hysterical States. Part I: Historical Review and Empirical Delineation." *Journal of Clinical Psychopharmacology* 2, no. 4 (1982): 235–44.

Shorter, Edward. "Les désordres psychosomatiques: Sont-ils 'hystériques'? Notes pour une recherche historique." *Cahiers internationaux de sociologie* 76, special number (January–June 1984): 201–24.

———. *From Paralysis to Fatigue: A History of Psychosomatic Illness in the Modern Era*. New York: Free Press, 1992.

———. *From the Mind into the Body: The Cultural Origins of Psychosomatic Symptoms*. New York: Free Press, 1994.

———. "Mania, Hysteria and Gender in Lower Austria, 1891–1905." *History of Psychiatry* 1, no. 1 (March 1990): 3–31.

———. "Paralysis: The Rise and Fall of a 'Hysterical' Symptom." *Journal of Social History* 19, (Summer 1986): 549–82.

———. "Women and Jews in a Private Nervous Clinic in Vienna at the Turn of the Century." *Medical History* 33, no. 2 (April 1989): 149–83.

Showalter, Elaine. Chaps. 6 and 7 in *The Female Malady: Women, Madness, and English Culture, 1830–1980*. New York: Pantheon, 1985.

———. "Hysteria, Feminism, and Gender." In Gilman et al., *Hysteria Before Freud*.

———. "On Hysterical Narrative." *Narrative* 1 (January 1993): 24–35.

———. "Rivers and Sassoon: The Inscription of Male Gender Anxieties." in Margaret R. Higonnet et al., eds., *Behind the Lines: Gender and the Two World Wars*. New Haven: Yale University Press, 1987.

———. Chap. 6 in *Sexual Anarchy: Gender and Culture at the Fin de Siècle*. New York: Viking, 1990.

Signoret, Jean Louis. "Variété historique: Une leçon clinique à la Salpêtrière (1887) par André Brouillet." *Revue neurologique* 139, no. 12 (1983): 687–701.

Silverman, Debora Leah. *Art Nouveau in Fin-de-Siècle France: Politics, Psychology, and Style*. Los Angeles: University of California Press, 1989.

Simon, Bennett. "Hysteria—The Greek Disease." *Psychoanalytic Study of Society* 8 (1979): 175–215.

———. *Mind and Madness in Ancient Greece: The Classical Roots of Modern Psychiatry*. Ithaca, N.Y.: Cornell University Press, 1978.

Slavney, Phillip R. *Perspectives on "Hysteria."* Baltimore: Johns Hopkins University Press, 1990.

Small, S. Mouchly. "Concept of Hysteria: History and Reevaluation." *New York State Journal of Medicine* 69 (1969): 1866–72.

Smith-Rosenberg, Carroll. "The Hysterical Woman: Sex Roles and Role Conflict in 19th-century America." *Social Research* 39, no. 4 (Winter 1972): 652–78. Reprinted with minor changes in Smith-Rosenberg, *Disorderly Conduct: Visions of Gender in Victorian America*. New York: Knopf, 1985.

Sonolet, Jacqueline. *J.-M. Charcot et l'hystérie au XIXe siècle*. Exhibition catalogue, Chapelle de la Salpêtrière, June 2–18, 1982. Paris: Beba, 1982.

Spanos, Nicholas P., and Jack Gottlieb. "Demonic Possession, Mesmerism, and Hysteria: A Social Psychological Perspective on Their Historical Interrelations." *Journal of Abnormal Psychology* 88, no. 5 (October 1979): 527–46.

Stallybrass, Peter, and Allon White. Chap. 5 in *The Politics and Poetics of Transgression*. London: Methuen, 1986.

Steeves, Edna L. "Hysteria of the Heart: A Recurrent Theme in Novel Writing." Paper delivered at the Seventeenth Annual Meeting of the American Society of Eighteenth-Century Studies, Williamsburg, Virginia, March 13–16, 1986.

Stern, Judith. "Heretical Voices and Hysterical Tales: The Struggle for Narrative Authority in the Nineteenth-Century American Romance." Ph.D. diss., Columbia University, 1987.

Strachey, James, in collaboration with Anna Freud, Alix Strachey, and Alan Tyson. Editor's Introduction to *Studies on Hysteria*. Vol. 2 of *The Standard Edition of the Complete Psychological Works of Sigmund Freud*, 24 vols. London: Hogarth Press, 1953–75.

Strong, Beret E. "Foucault, Freud, and French Feminism: Theorizing Hysteria as Theorizing the Feminine." *Literature and Psychology* 35, no. 4 (Winter 1989): 10–17.

Strouse, Jean. *Alice James: A Biography*. London: Jonathan Cape, 1980.

Sulloway, Frank J. *Freud, Biologist of the Mind: Beyond the Psychoanalytic Legend*. New York: Basic Books, 1979.

"Sur l'hystérie." *Revue française de psychanalyse* 37, no. 3, special issue (May 1973).

Swain, Gladys. "L'âme, la femme, le sexe et le corps: Les métamorphoses de l'hystérie à la fin du XIXe siècle." *Le débat*, 24 (March 1983): 107–27.

Swales, Peter. "Freud, His Teacher, and the Birth of Psychoanalysis." In vol. 1 of

Paul Stepansky, ed., *Freud: Appraisals and Reappraisals*. Hillsdale, N.J.: Analytic Press, 1986.

———. "Freud, Katharina, and the First 'Wild Analysis.'" In vol. 3 of Paul Stepansky, ed., *Freud: Appraisals and Reappraisals*. Hillsdale, N.J.: Analytic Press, 1988.

Sydnor, Denise Newman. "Hysteria: A Historical Perspective." Ph.D. diss., Miami Institute of Psychology, 1991.

Szasz, Thomas S. "L'hystérie." *Cahiers confrontation* 9 (Fall 1983): 29–40.

———. Parts 2 and 3 of *The Myth of Mental Illness: Foundations of a Theory of Personal Conduct*. New York: Hoeber-Harper, 1961.

Taylor, Eugene. Lecture 3 in *William James on Exceptional Mental States: The 1896 Lowell Lectures*. Amherst: University of Massachusetts Press, 1984.

Telson, Howard W. "Une leçon du Docteur Charcot à la Salpêtrière." *Journal of the History of Medicine* 35 (1980): 58.

Thaler, Danielle. *La clinique de l'amour selon les frères Goncourt: Peuple, femmes, hystérie*. Sherbrooke, Canada: Naaman, 1986.

Thornton, Esther M. *Freud and Cocaine: The Freudian Fallacy*. London: Blond and Briggs, 1983.

———. *Hypnotism, Hysteria and Epilepsy: An Historical Synthesis*. London: William Heinemann, 1976.

Thuillier, Jean. *Monsieur Charcot de la Salpêtrière*. Paris: Laffont, 1993.

Trillat, Étienne. "Chorée de Sydenham, danse de Saint-Guy et chorée rythmée hystérique (essai de révision historique et critique)." *L'évolution psychiatrique* 53, no. 1 (January–March, 1988): 49–72.

———. *Histoire de l'hystérie*. Paris: Seghers, 1986.

———. "Hystérie et hypnose (une approche historique)." *Psychiatrie française* 19, special number (May 1988): 9–19.

———. "Promenade à travers l'histoire de l'hystérie." *Histoire, économie et société* 3, no. 4 (1984): 525–34.

———. "Regards sur l'hystérie." *L'évolution psychiatrique* 35, no. 2 (April 1970): 353–64.

———. "Sur la naissance de 'l'hystérie de Charcot.'" *Perspectives psychiatriques* 96, no. 2 (1984): 137–41.

———. "Le tableau, la copie et le faux: À propos de la nosographie de 'l'hystérie de Charcot.'" *Frénésie: Histoire. psychiatrie. psychoanalyse* 4 (Autumn 1987): 38–49.

———. "Trois itinéraires à travers l'histoire de l'hystérie." *Histoire des sciences médicales* 21, no. 1 (1987): 27–31.

Trombley, Stephen. *"All That Summer She Was Mad": Virginia Woolf and Her Doctors*. London: Junction Books, 1981.

Urban, Bernd. "Schnitzler and Freud as Doubles: Poetic Intuition and Early Research on Hysteria." *Psychoanalytic Review* 65, no.1 (Spring 1978): 131–65.

Van Deth, Ron and Walter Vandereycken. "Hysteria and Bulimia in the Nineteenth-Century." *Concept* (forthcoming issue).

Vaysse, Evelyne. "Contribution des études sur l'hystérie à la naissance de la psychanalyse." Ph.D. diss., University of Paris, Saint-Antoine, 1977.

Veith, Ilza. "Four Thousand Years of Hysteria." In Mardi J. Horowitz, ed., *Hysterical Personality*. New York: Jason Aronson, 1977.

———. "Hysteria." *Modern Medicine* 28, no. 4 (February 15, 1960): 178–83.

———. *Hysteria: The History of a Disease*. Chicago: University of Chicago Press, 1965.

———. "On Hysterical and Hypochondriacal Afflictions." *Bulletin of the History of Medicine* 30, no. 3 (May 1956): 233–40.

Villechenoux, Camille. "Le cadre de la folie hystérique de 1870 à 1918: Contribution à l'histoire de la psychiatrie, aspects de l'évolution des idées sur la frontière entre la névrose et la psychose." Ph.D. diss., University of Paris, 1968.

Vogel, L. Z. "The Case of Elise Gomperz." *American Journal of Psychoanalysis* 46, no. 3 (Fall 1986): 230–38.

Wajeman, Gérard. "The Hysteric's Discourse." In Helena Schulz-Keil, ed., *Hystoria: Lacan Study Notes*. New York: New York Lacan Study Group, 1988.

———. "L'hystérie de Morzine." *Ornicar?* 3 (May 1975): 37–59.

———. *Le maître et l'hystérique*. Paris: Navarin, 1982.

———. "Psyché de la femme: Note sur l'hystérique au XIXe siècle." *Romantisme: Revue du dix-neuvième siècle* 13–14 (1976): 57–66.

Weissman, Hope Phyllis. "Margery Kempe in Jerusalem: Hysteria Compassio in the Late Middle Ages." In M. J. Carruthers and E. D. Kirk, eds., *Acts of Interpretation: The Text in Its Context, 700–1600: Essays on Medieval and Renaissance Literature in Honor of E. Talbot Donaldson*. Norman, Okla.: Pilgrim Books, 1982.

Wesley, George Randolph. *A History of Hysteria*. Washington, D.C.: University Press of America, 1979.

Wettley, Annemarie. "Hysterie, ärztliche Einbildung oder Wirklichkeit." *Müncher Medizinische Wochenschrift* 101, no. 5 (January 30, 1959): 193–96.

Weyer, Johannes. *Witches, Devils, and Doctors in the Renaissance: Johannes Weyer's "De Praestigiis Daemonum," 1583*. Translated by John Shea. Edited, introduced, and annotated by George Mora, in collaboration with Benjamin Kohl, Erik Midelfort, and Helen Bacon. Binghamton, N.Y., Medieval and Renaissance Texts and Studies, University Center at Binghamton, 1991.

Wharton, Jean Ann. "Freud on Feminine Hysteria: A Re-Examination." Ph.D. diss., University of California, Santa Cruz, 1975.

White, Allon. *Carnival, Hysteria, and Writing: Collected Essays and Autobiography*. Oxford: Oxford University Press, 1993.

White, Deborah Elise. "*Studies in Hysteria*: Case Histoires and the Case against History." *MLN* 104 (December 1989): 1035–49.

Widlöcher, Daniel. "L'hystérie, cent ans après." *Revue neurologique* 138, no. 12 (1982): 1053–60.

———. "L'hystérie dépossédée." *Nouvelle revue de psychanalyse* 17, (Spring 1978): 73–87.

Williams, Katherine E. "Hysteria in Seventeenth-Century Case Records and Unpublished Manuscripts." *History of Psychiatry* 1, no. 4 (December 1990): 383–401.

Wood, Ann Douglas. "'The Fashionable Diseases': Women's Complaints and Their Treatment in Nineteenth-Century America." *Journal of Interdisciplinary History* 4, no. 1 (Summer 1973): 25–52.

Woolsey, Robert M. "Hysteria: 1875 to 1975." *Diseases of the Nervous System* 37, no. 7 (July 1976): 379–86.

Wright, John P. "Hysteria and Mechanical Man." *Journal of the History of Ideas* 41, no. 1 (January 1980): 233–47.

Wykert, John. "Anna O.—A Re-Evaluation." *Psychiatric News* 15 (May 2, 1980): 4–5, 22.

Zeldin, Theodore. Chap. 17 in *Intellect, Taste and Anxiety*. Vol. 2 of *France 1848–1945*. Oxford: Clarendon Press, 1977.

INDEX

Abraham, Karl, 28, 41
Abricossoff, Glafira, 34–35, 36, 37, 38, 66, 108; "L'hystérie aux XVIIe et XVIIIe siècles," 34
Ackerknecht, Erwin, 120–121
Addams, Jane, 72, 85
Addyman, Marie, 183–184, 249
Adler, Alfred, 125
Agassiz, Louis, 172
Ajuriaguerra, Julian, 54
Alam, Chris, 227
Alexander, Franz: *The History of Psychiatry* (with S. Selesnick), 125, 128
Althaus, Julius, 126
Amselle, Gaston, 35, 36, 37, 38, 46, 108, 150; *Conception de l'hystérie: Étude historique et critique,* 35
Andersson, Ola, 116
Annales de Notre-Dame de Lourdes, 269, 270, 271, 276
Anna O. (Bertha Pappenheim), 27, 59, 60–66, 80, 84, 85, 86, 117, 141, 142, 143, 144, 169; and the development of the "talking cure," 27, 142
anorexia nervosa, 65, 76, 85, 86, 290–291
Anstie, Francis, 127
antipsychiatry movement, 130, 181n.9
Apter, Emily, 196–197, 206
Aragon, Louis, 194
Arataeus of Cappadocia, 20
Archives de neurologie, 231
Arène, Paul, 218
Auclert, Hubertine, 212
Auden, W. H., 222
Augustine, Saint, 20
Aurevilly, Barbey d', 193, 194–195, 196, 281
Austen, Jane, 186
Auvray-Escalard, Bétrice, 117
Axenfeld, Alexandre, 193, 205, 228, 231; *Traité des nérvoses,* 193

Babinski, Joseph, 36, 39, 41, 110, 119, 144, 173, 174, 292; *Le semaine médicale,* 173

Bachelard, Gaston, 220
Baglivi, Giorgio, 21, 39; *De praxi medicina,* 21
Baillarger, J.-G.-F., 136
Balzac, Honoré de, 225
Bannour, Wanda, 195–196
Barnard, Christiaan, 140
Barrows, Susanna, 207, 210
Baruk, Henri, 173n.175
Bastian, Henry Charlton, 128
"battle fatigue," 162
Baudelaire, Charles Pierre, 190–191, 191n.47, 220, 240–241, 241n.53, 241n.54, 242–243, 243n.60, 243n.61, 244, 245, 250, 251, 251n.91, 255, 259, 280, 281
Beard, George, 99, 119, 120, 155, 159
Beauvoir, Simone de: *The Second Sex,* 67
Beizer, Janet, 193–194, 225, 237
Bernard, Claude, 137, 263
Bernhardt, Sarah, 198
Bernheim, Hippolyte, 26, 27, 35, 36, 37, 39, 54, 118, 119, 195, 204, 210, 218, 232, 264, 265, 266, 267, 268, 269, 271, 274
Bernheimer, Charles, 81, 215; *In Dora's Case* (with C. Kahane), 81, 83, 84
Berthelot, P.-E.-M., 263
Bertrand, Alexandre, 23
Bertrin, Georges, 267, 267n.137, 269, 270, 271, 272, 281; *Histoire critique des événements de Lourdes,* 267, 269; *Lourdes et les miracles,* 269; *Un miracle d'aujourd'hui,* 269
Bewell, Alan, 186, 250
Bicêtre Hospital, 228
Binet, Alfred, 95, 195, 199, 205
Blackmore, Richard, 122, 183
Bleuler, Eugen: *Dementia Praecox or the Group of the Schizophrenias,* 173
Blustein, Bonnie, 139
Boerhaave, Hermann, 35, 154
Boissarie, Gustave, 269–270, 271, 272, 274–275, 276, 277, 282–283; *Lourdes: Histoire médicale,* 269–270, 275

154, 155, 184, 221, 293; *Epistolary Dissertation*, 22; *Processus Integri*, 22
Symonds, John Addington, 162
Szasz, Thomas, 80, 182, 292–293

Taine, Hippolyte, 207, 208, 219, 220, 239, 253; *Les origines de la France contemporaine*, 207
Tarde, Gabriel, 209, 220
Tardieu, Ambroise, 230, 265–266
Temkin, Oswei: *The Falling Sickness*, 33, 38
Terrien, Firmin: *Hystérie et neurasthénie chez les paysans*, 189
Théanton, J. R., 210
Theresa, Saint, 275, 280–281
Thiec, Yves, 210
Thomas, D. M.: *The White Hotel*, 6, 7, 221, 224
Todd, Robert B., 126
Tolstoy, Lev Nikolaevich, 206
Tomes, Nancy, 134
Touroude, Abbé: *L'hystérie*, 273–274
Toynbee, Arnold, 162
transference, 56
Trélat, Ulysse, 136
Trillat, Étienne, 40–41, 45n.35, 46, 50, 53, 92–93, 97, 128, 134, 135, 138, 146, 169, 186; *Histoire de l'hystérie*, 40–41, 92–93

unconscious, theory of, 56, 81, 142, 256

Valéry, Paul, 245, 255
van Ginnekin, Jaap, 207, 210
"vapors," 3, 40, 121, 185, 186
Veith, Ilza, 38–40, 39n.14, 43, 44, 46, 48, 50, 66, 70, 89, 115, 128, 169, 199, 227, 228–229, 261–262, 285; *Hysteria*, 38–40, 43, 128, 261, 285
Verlaine, Paul, 245

Vesalius, Andreas, 35
Vigny, Alfred Victor de, 240, 244
Voisin, August, 263–264, 272
Voisin, Félix, 23, 136
Voltaire, François Marie Arouet, 267

Wagner, Wilhelm Richard, 206–207, 219
Wajeman, Gérard, 110, 145, 146, 285
Warren, J. C., 140
Wasserman, August, 172
Webb, Beatrice, 105
Weininger, Otto, 24
Wettley, Anne Marie, 66
Weyer, Johann, 21, 48, 53, 278–279n.189
Whytt, Robert, 22, 122, 183
Widlocher, Daniel, 54
Wilde, Oscar, 206, 282
Williams, Katherine, 112, 121, 124, 125, 155
Williams, Roger, 245
Williams, William Carlos, 222
Willis, Thomas, 3, 22, 23, 35, 36, 121, 122, 133, 138, 154, 184, 221, 293; *Affectionum quae dicuntur hystericae et hypocondriacae*, 22
Wittels, Fritz, 235
Wolfson, Susan, 187n.31, 250
Wood, Ann Douglas, 71–72, 74, 83
Woolf, Virginia, 116, 197
Wordsworth, William, 186, 241, 250; *Lyrical Ballads*, 250

Zeldin, Theodore, 202n.91, 271
Zilboorg, Gregory: *A History of Medical Psychology*, 125, 128, 261–262
Zola, Émile, 188–189, 192, 194, 198, 206, 207, 208, 218, 219, 222–223, 264–265, 270, 271–272, 275, 281, 282; *La débâcle*, 208; *Lourdes*, 264–265, 271–272, 275; *Nana*, 219; Rougon-Macquart series, 207, 264; *Les trois villes*, 264